D0842194

GEOCHEMISTRY
IN MINERAL
EXPLORATION

HARPER'S GEOSCIENCE SERIES

Carey Croneis, Editor

GEOCHEMISTRY IN MINERAL EXPLORATION

BY

H. E. HAWKES, *1912 –*

Herbert Edwin

PROFESSOR OF MINERAL EXPLORATION

UNIVERSITY OF CALIFORNIA, BERKELEY

AND

J. S. WEBB

PROFESSOR OF APPLIED GEOCHEMISTRY

IMPERIAL COLLEGE OF SCIENCE AND TECHNOLOGY

LONDON UNIVERSITY

HARPER & ROW, PUBLISHERS, NEW YORK AND EVANSTON

Library of Congress catalog card number: 62-8889

CONTENTS

EDITOR'S INTRODUCTION

Geochemistry in Mineral Exploration is a pioneering text and reference book dealing with the newer phases of an ancient and important subject that has intrigued man ever since the days he began to use metals rather than stones for his weapons and implements.

In times of war the search for minerals has always accelerated. With new uses resulting from technological advances common by the beginning of World War II, the 15-year period of 1938-1953 saw a fantastic worldwide "boom" in the exploration for mineral resources. In this search more and more sophisticated geochemical methods of prospecting began to be employed throughout much of the western world. The Soviet geologists, however, had developed a massive state-directed, Eurasian continent-spanning mineral search almost a decade earlier, using at least primitive variants of such methods.

In 1939 Hewlett Johnson, the so-called "Red Dean" of Canterbury, wrote his controversial "The Socialist Sixth of the World." In it he stated that the Soviet lands are "searched and scrutinized by geographers, geologists, mineralogists, chemists and engineers. Thousands of workers eagerly prospect for new sources of wealth, using all the resources of modern science, magnetometry, gravimetry, seismometry and radiometry. . . ." Although at the time a doubting audience in the main considered Johnson's writing essentially propagandistic, it turned out that, if anything, he had understated the situation. As early as 1932 Soviet geologists were engaging in some geochemical prospecting which they referred to as "metallometric" surveying. The growing volume of such surveying may be realized through a few statistics: the number of sites from which the Soviet geologists had collected samples totaled 31,656,000 by 1957. Since samples are now being collected at the rate of about 7 million a year, presently the Russian raw data units will total more than 50 million! Africa also is being sampled at the rate of about 1.5 million sites a year; North American geochemical samples may total 500,000 per annum.

The efforts of the United States Geological Survey in this field were unified in 1947 under the direction of Professor Hawkes; at the same time, Professor Webb was similarly involved in the British

Commonwealth geochemical prospecting program, which became formalized in 1954 through the creation of the Geochemical Prospecting Research Centre at the Imperial College of Science and Technology, London. The writers have thus been admirably equipped by background and experience to prepare the present book which, it is hoped, will fill a very apparent need—the need that has long existed for an authoritative compendium on a subject which has great scientific significance as well as practical importance.

The authors have presented the elements of *Geochemistry in Mineral Exploration* in eighteen chapters, an appendix (in which there are summarized the "Geochemical Characteristics of the Elements") and a bibliography. The latter is a particularly useful portion of the book. Not only is it unusually complete, as far as major contributions are concerned, but among the 421 references cited, 44, which are marked with an asterisk, provide the reader with a ready finding-key for those articles which represent significant case histories in geochemical prospecting. Some indication of the rate of acceleration of interest in "modern" mineral exploration may also be gained from the fact that less than 10 percent of the entire bibliography predates 1950.

In addition to the "Introduction," which contains a good synoptic history of the more recent developments in mineral exploration, there are chapters which outline the "Basic Principles" of the entire subject, and, in sequence, treat of the "Principles of Trace Analysis," "Primary Dispersion," "Weathering," "Soil Formation," "Secondary Dispersion," and "Dispersion Patterns."

There are also included four valuable chapters concerned with the problem of geochemical anomalies. These must be evaluated in dealing with geochemical data obtained from studies of residual overburden, the transported overburden, natural waters, and drainage sediments. In addition, Hawkes and Webb have prepared extensive sections on "Geochemical Soil Surveys," "Geochemical Drainage Surveys," and "Vegetation," as well as a general chapter on "Geochemical Methods in Mineral Exploration." The last two chapters are titled "Case Histories of Integrated Exploration Programs" and "Current Research and Future Trends."

The rich experience, in both laboratory and field, of the two authors is apparent in the scientific yet practical fashion in which the chapter materials have been presented. That experience may be briefly outlined as follows: Dr. H. E. Hawkes was educated at Dartmouth, Columbia, and the Massachusetts Institute of Technology. He was awarded his Ph.D. in Geology at the latter institution in 1940. From 1940 to 1953 Dr. Hawkes served with distinction as an economic geologist for the United States Geological Survey. He then was appointed Lecturer in the Department of Geology and Geophysics at M.I.T. In 1957, however, he was called to his present post as Professor of Mineral Exploration at the University of California. While Dr. Hawkes was with the U. S. G. S. he prepared several publications now generally recognized as "landmark" articles on the growing art and practice of geochemical prospecting. Chief among these are U. S. G. S. Bulletins 1000B (1954) and 1000F (1957), respectively titled, "Geochemical prospecting investigations in Nyeba lead-zinc district, Nigeria," and "Principles of geochemical prospecting."

Dr. J. S. Webb received his advanced professional training at London University where his thesis, "Origin of the tin lodes of Cornwall, England" (1947), was submitted in partial fulfillment of the requirements for the doctorate in Economic Geology. Like Dr. Hawkes, Dr. Webb has been one of the "western" pioneers in the development of geochemical prospecting. His work with J. S. Tooms and others has provided the foundation for much of the extensive commercial use of these methods in Africa and, more recently, has underlined their importance to mineral exploration in Southeast Asia, Australia, and the Pacific. Dr. Webb's "Review of American progress in geochemical prospecting" (1953) attracted considerable scientific attention, and his "Observations on geochemical exploration in tropical terrains" (1958) presented at the 20th Session of the International Geological Congress, helped focus worldwide interest on this general subject.

Geochemistry in Mineral Exploration should prove to be of great value, not only to economic geologists and geochemists, but to all others in the broadly expanded disciplines of the earth sciences. Moreover, the book is not without biological and physical overtones, as well as implications which should be of significance to economists and political scientists. Accordingly, the editor is happy to join with Harper & Brothers in presenting this important addition to the Geoscience Series.

CAREY CRONEIS

Rice University
January, 1962

PREFACE

The purpose of this book is to provide a comprehensive synthesis of the theory and applications of geochemistry in problems of mineral exploration. It is intended to be world-wide in scope, representing an integration of the two authors' personal experience in the northern, temperate, and arid climates of North America and in the tropical and desert climates of Africa and southeast Asia. It is offered as an introduction to the subject only, not as a handbook for the exploration geochemist. In it, an attempt is made to list references for the most significant literature and to glean from this literature the most significant conclusions in the form of maps, field observations, and generalization.

The book is addressed to four principal groups of readers: (1) to the student as an introductory textbook; (2) to research workers in allied fields such as general geochemistry and geophysics, who are looking for a summary of the findings and techniques of applied geochemistry; (3) to the nonspecialized practicing geologists or geophysicists who need a source of general information; and (4) to specialists in applied geochemistry as a source book and reference to the literature.

The ideas expressed in previously published summaries have been freely drawn upon. Particular mention should be made of Hawkes "Principles of Geochemical Prospecting," published by the U. S. Geological Survey as Bulletin 1000-F, and of the English translation of Ginzburg's "Geochemical Methods of Prospecting," summarizing the experience gained in twenty years of Russian work.

Many people have generously contributed their time, experience, and unpublished data to the preparation of this book. The authors are particularly grateful to Alexander Muir for reviewing and preparing substantial contributions to the discussion of weathering and soil formation; Robert Garrels, for reviewing the chapter on secondary dispersion; Helen Cannon for her help in preparing the chapter on vegetation; Ronald Stanton and Hubert Lakin for reviewing the chapter on analytical methods; and David Williams and John Tooms, for critical review of virtually the entire manuscript. The previously unpublished case history data appearing in Chapter 17 was contributed by Robert Searls and Alan Coope of the Newmont Exploration Company, by William Callahan and E. A. Goranson of the New Jersey Zinc Exploration Co. (Canada) Ltd., and by Fred Cornwall of Chartered Explorations Ltd. The general discussion contains detailed reference to other unpublished material that was generously made available by Claude Beaumont (Bureau de Recherches Géologiques et Minières, Paris), Arnold Grimbert (Commissariat de l'Energie Atomique, Paris), Jacques Jedwab (Université Libre, Brussels), L. K. Kauranne (Geological Survey, Otaniemi, Finland), Aslak Kvalheim (Statens Råstoffslaboratorium, Trondheim, Norway), and L. Van Wambeke (Euratom, Brussels). Assistance with typing and drafting was provided by Jean Webb and Ann and Wayne Cavender. Clifford James kindly undertook the considerable task of reading and checking the proofs.

Acknowledgment of a very special and personal kind is due the senior members of the profession who encouraged and inspired the authors during the early years before the actuality and scope of geochemical prospecting was generally appreciated. Walter Newhouse and Wilmot H. Bradley provided the faith and support that started Hawkes with this research program in the Geochemical Prospecting Unit of the U. S. Geological Survey. Similarly, Webb's program at the Geochemical Prospecting Research Center of the Royal School of Mines never would have materialized without the personal encouragement and support received from David Williams, H. H. Read, and Frank Dixey. It is a pleasure to record that this program was made possible only by the generous assistance given by the U. K. Department of Scientific and Industrial Research, the Directorate of Overseas Geological Surveys, and many sections of the mining industry.

In conclusion, the authors are deeply conscious of the debt owed to their colleagues and students who, by their efforts, have contributed so much to the data and experience incorporated in this book.

H. E. HAWKES
J. S. WEBB

GEOCHEMISTRY
IN MINERAL
EXPLORATION

CHAPTER I

INTRODUCTION

The period from 1940 to 1957 witnessed an unprecedented scale of activity in prospecting. It marked the growing awareness of the mining industry to the fact that it could not depend indefinitely on discoveries brought to its attention by relatively untrained prospectors. Most mining companies developed a more consciously organized approach to exploration and prospecting, and annual exploration budgets of several millions of dollars were not unusual with some of the larger mining groups.

Part of the effort was directed to a repeated re-examination of areas of rock outcrop for ore exposures. This work in general was not very rewarding, as very few exposed ore bodies had escaped discovery by the earlier generation of independent prospectors. A larger part of the new industrial effort in prospecting was devoted to outcrop examination in search of geologic guides to buried ore. In addition to these activities, however, an increasingly significant fraction of the effort was directed toward the development and application of new techniques of mapping geologic structures and of detecting ore concealed beneath a mantle of organic debris, soil, or barren rock. Included here are the recently developed photogeological, geophysical, and geochemical techniques.

1-1. Geochemistry in Mineral Exploration

Geochemical prospecting for minerals, as defined by common usage, includes any method of mineral exploration based on systematic measurement of one or more chemical properties of a naturally occurring material. The chemical property measured is most commonly the trace content of some element or group of elements; the naturally occurring material may be rock, soil, gossan, glacial debris, vegetation, stream sediment, or water. The purpose of the measurements is the discovery of abnormal chemical patterns, or *geochemical anomalies*, related to mineralization.

Geochemical methods of exploration should be viewed as integral

1

components of the arsenal of weapons available to the modern prospector. They are distinguished from other methods of gathering geological data only because they call for certain specialized techniques.
The goal of every exploration method is, of course, the same—to find
clues that will help in locating hidden ore.

1–2. History

The principles of geochemical prospecting are as old as man's first
use of metals. The earliest prospector soon learned that the environment of many mineral deposits was marked by certain conspicuous
and diagnostic features. Fragments of fresh or weathered ore might be
scattered about the surface of the ground near its source in the bedrock. Smaller fragments of similar material could be seen in the sediments deposited by streams draining the mineralized area. The
prospector found that by searching for such material and then
following the trail of increasing concentrations, he was often led to the
bedrock source of the metals. Here he was guided only by what he
could see with the unaided eye. However, basically, he was following
dispersion patterns that are strictly analogous to those used in modern
geochemical methods.

Trace-element analysis as a supplement to visual observations
began to find its place in exploration technology in the middle 1930s.
Inspired by the classical researches of Goldschmidt, Fersman, and
Vernadsky in the field of fundamental geochemistry, research workers
in Scandinavia and the Soviet Union independently carried out
successful experiments using spectrographic trace analysis of soils and
plants as a prospecting method. In the 1940s, with continually improving methods of wet chemical analysis as well as spectrography, geochemists in Japan, the United States, and Canada continued with the
development of progressively more economical and effective methods
of geochemical prospecting. In 1950 the growth of active research
spread to Great Britain and thence to other countries in western
Europe, accompanied by a concomitant activity in their overseas
territories, notably in Africa and the Far East. In addition, experimental work was initiated in Australia, India, and many other parts
of the world until today there are relatively few mineral fields in
which no geochemical studies of any sort have been made.

The evolution of the various techniques is by no means complete,
and not all are in the same stage of development. Geochemical soil
and vegetation surveys are undoubtedly the most advanced and were
first applied on a commercial scale in the 1930s. Geochemical drainage
surveys on a routine basis did not come into their own until the middle

1950s, but are now expanding rapidly both in scope and application. In contrast, exploration based on systematic sampling and analysis of unweathered ore and rock is still in the early experimental stage.

Soil Surveys. The first chemical analysis of systematically collected samples of soil and weathered rock as a prospecting method was undertaken in 1932 by Soviet geologists (Fersman, 1939; Sergeyev, 1941). In the Russian literature this technique is referred to as "metallometric" surveying. By 1935 the geological staff of the Central Geological and Prospecting Institute in Moscow had perfected spectrographic analytical equipment and sampling procedures suitable for routine geochemical soil surveys. Three field projects were undertaken in 1935, eight in 1936, six in 1937, and three in 1938. Seven of these depended upon semiquantitative spectrographic analyses of soil and stream sediment for tin, or "stannometric surveying." The remainder of the Russian projects during this prewar period were orientation and prospecting surveys for Cu, Pb, Zn, Ni, Cr, W, Mo, and B.

In Western countries, the first experimental work on geochemical soil surveying was carried out in 1947 by the U. S. Geological Survey (Hawkes and Lakin, 1949). This was followed by an active program of field investigation in virtually all climatic areas of the United States. The U. S. Geological Survey maintained a parallel program of research and development of rapid and simple techniques of colorimetric analysis, in contrast with the spectrographic techniques of the Russian program. By the early 1950s routine geochemical soil surveys had been applied by several of the large mining companies to their exploration problems, particularly in the southern Appalachians and in the Pacific Northwest, with favorable results. Descriptions of some of this early work have been published (Fulton, 1950; Gilbert, 1951, 1953, Kingman, 1951; Fulton et al., 1958). In Canada, field experiments with these methods were being carried out concurrently with the American work. Because of complexities introduced by glaciation, the results of the Canadian work have not been uniformly encouraging. Even so, routine geochemical soil prospecting there has been applied on a substantial scale (Riddell, 1960).

In the British Commonwealth, after preliminary work in the United Kingdom and Africa, an intensive program of research and development, based initially on the American system, was undertaken in 1953 (Webb, 1953, 1958a; David Williams, 1956). The greater part of this work has been carried out, mostly in Africa and the Far East, by the Geochemical Prospecting Research Center at the Imperial College of Science and Technology, London. These studies have been concerned with methods for Cu, Pb, Zn, Co, Ni, Cr, Sn, W,

Mo, Be, As, and Sb under a wide range of conditions. Probably the most striking outcome to date has been the increasing large-scale application of geochemical methods to mineral reconnaissance in the Rhodesias. Here, guided by geology and photogeology, systematic sampling and chemical analysis of soil and stream sediment for copper and other metals has proved to be the most effective combination of methods for exploration in poorly exposed, deeply weathered terrain.

Vegetation Surveys. Visual observation of the distribution and morphology of plants as related to ore has probably helped the traditional prospector almost as much as his observations of rock exposures and soils. The most famous indicator plant of early times was the "calamine violet," which grows only on Zn-rich soils in the zinc districts of central and western Europe. Within the past generation, several other specific plant indicators of ore have been found and used successfully in prospecting (Nesvetaylova, 1955b; Cannon, 1957, 1960b; Horizon, 1959).

Biogeochemical prospecting, or chemical analysis of plants as a method of prospecting, started in 1936 with the experiments of Palmqvist and Brundin of the Swedish Prospecting Company. Trial geochemical plant surveys in Cornwall and Wales indicated abnormally high contents of Sn and W in Cornwall and of Pb and Zn in Wales in the leaves of trees and shrubs growing over soils containing correspondingly large proportions of those metals (Swedish Prospecting Co., 1939). On the basis of these experiments, a patent (Brundin, 1939) was obtained to cover systematic sampling of plant material followed by spectrographic analysis of the plant ash as a method of prospecting. For several years the Swedish Prospecting Co. conducted geochemical surveys in conjunction with its regular geophysical service to the mining industry, and many areas were systematically prospected by plant analysis. Very few of the results of this work have been published.

In 1945, H. V. Warren and his co-workers at the University of British Columbia undertook a research program on the metal content of vegetation, and a few years later they began applying systematic plant analysis to practical prospecting problems. During the uranium boom from 1948 to 1956, a substantial volume of biogeochemical survey work was carried out in the western United States by the U. S. Geological Survey. Although biogeochemical methods have been used successfully in many areas, a more widespread application has been limited by the fact that essentially the same geochemical patterns can usually be obtained by using the simpler and more straightforward geochemical soil survey methods.

Drainage Surveys. Geochemical drainage surveys stem from the time-honored practice of tracing resistant heavy minerals by panning stream gravels. The presence of alluvial gold and cassiterite in panned concentrates has led to the discovery of virtually every one of the world's great hardrock gold and tin camps. At the present time, one of the principal methods of mineral reconnaissance in the Soviet Union, the "shlikh" method, consists of systematically mapping the heavy minerals in stream sediments.

The possible application of chemical tests of stream water to prospecting was conceived at an early date. Indeed, Vannoccio Biringuccio in his "Pirotechnia," first published in 1540, says, "There are some who praise highly as a good sign certain residues that waters make where they are still, and after having stood for several days, frequently warmed by the rays of the sun, they show in some parts of their residues various tinctures of metallic substances. There are others who usually take this water and cause it to evaporate or dry up entirely by boiling it in a vessel of earthenware, glass, or some other material, and they test the gross earthy substance that remains at the bottom by testing, by the ordinary fire assay, or in some other way that pleases them. In this way (although they do not have an exact proof) they approach some sort of knowledge of the thing."

Chemical analysis of stream sediment was apparently first attempted in the early 1930s by Soviet scientists. They used spectrographic techniques to determine the Sn content of the fine fraction of stream sediments as a method of finding bedrock deposits of cassiterite. This method has now been integrated with mineralogical examination of the samples in mineral reconnaissance.

The first extensive, routine exploration program based on geochemical drainage surveying was apparently the Russian use of the uranium content of water as a primary method of prospecting for uranium-rich areas (Vinogradov, 1956b). In the West, the first large drainage survey was undertaken in 1954 in eastern Canada. This survey was based on determining the readily soluble heavy-metal content of samples of stream sediments collected over an area of 27,000 square miles (Hawkes *et al.*, 1956). Subsequently, several extensive surveys have been carried out in Africa and the Far East using stream sediment analysis for Cu, Pb, Zn, and Ni.

Rock Surveys. Experimental field work is uncovering an increasing number of examples of bedrock features, detectable only by chemical analysis, that are associated in one way or another with ore. Although several elaborate geochemical rock surveys have been and are being conducted on an experimental basis, no actual prospecting surveys

6

based on the systematic sampling of fresh bedrock have yet been undertaken.

1-3. Present Status

Geochemical methods of prospecting have been credited in the literature with a number of mineral discoveries. Almost invariably, geochemical methods were used in conjunction with other geological or geophysical exploration methods, so that an assignment of "credit" to a single method is hardly realistic. Inasmuch as very few detailed case histories are available, it is difficult to assess the contribution made by the geochemical data toward the sum total of information that in each case led to the discovery of a deposit. Therefore, a tabulation of discoveries is perhaps not as good an index of the status of the methods as is the spectacular growth of activity in the field over the past decade. Growth and scale of operations may be interpreted as an indication of the over-all opinion of the exploration profession, based on practical experience under many conditions and in many parts of the world.

The Soviet Union unquestionably has the largest volume of research activity devoted to the principles and methodology of geochemical

TABLE I-I. Russian Organizations Conducting Research and Development of Geochemical Prospecting Methods

Academy of Sciences, U. S. S. R. (AN SSSR)

Chukhrov Institute of Geology of Ore Deposits, Petrography, Mineralogy and Geochemistry, Moscow (IGEM)

Institute of Mineralogy, Geochemistry and Crystal Chemistry of Rare Elements, Moscow (IMGRE)

Vernadsky Institute of Geochemistry and Analytical Chemistry, Moscow (GEOKHI)

Ministry of Geology and Conservation of Resources (MGiON)

All-Union Aerogeological Trust, Moscow (VAGT)

All-Union Geological-Scientific Research Institute, Leningrad (VSEGEI)

All-Union Scientific Research Institute of Exploration Geophysics (VIRG)

All-Union Scientific Research Institute of Hydrogeology and Engineering Geology, Moscow (VSEGINGEO)

All-Union Scientific Research Institute of Methods and Procedures of Exploration, Leningrad (VITR)

All-Union Scientific Research Institute of Mineral Raw Materials, Moscow (VIMS)

Main Geophysical Organization (Glavgeofizika): includes regional geophysical trusts for carrying out routine survey work.

Universities

Leningrad Technological Institute
Leningrad State University
Moscow State University
Tomsk Polytechnical Institute

Union Republic Academies of Sciences

Armenian Academy of Sciences, Yerevan
Kazakh Academy of Sciences, Alma-Ata

TABLE 1-2. Principal Western Organizations Conducting Research and Development of
Geochemical Prospecting Methods in 1960

Country	Organization	Address
Canada	Geological Survey of Canada	Ottawa, Ont.
	Geology Department, University of British Columbia	Vancouver, B.C.
Finland	Geological Survey of Finland	Otaniemi
France	Bureau de Recherches Géologiques et Minières (B.R.G.M.)	74 Rue de la Fédération, Paris XV
	Commissariat à l'Énergie Atomique	Fontenay-aux-Roses, Paris
Norway	Råstoffslaboratorium	Trondheim
United Kingdom	Geochemical Prospecting Research Center	Imperial College of Science and Technology, London, S.W. 7
United States	U. S. Geological Survey	Federal Center, Denver 25, Col.
	Department of Mineral Technology, University of California	Berkeley 4, Calif.

exploration. This work is being carried out by many state organizations, as summarized in Table 1-1. In Western countries, organized research programs of substantial size are mostly confined to relatively few government and university departments, of which the principal ones are listed in Table 1-2. In addition, however, there is a growing volume of individual research in certain university and industrial laboratories, which amounts in the aggregate to an appreciable contribution.

A useful measure of the scale of industrial operations is given by the number of geochemical samples collected during the course of prospecting surveys. In using these figures, it must be borne in mind that the relationship between sampling numbers and prospecting effort can vary widely according to local conditions and the geochemical method employed. Furthermore, the available sampling statistics are by no means complete, and the estimated figures presented here are open to serious error.

In the Soviet Union, production geochemical prospecting work at least until 1956 was concentrated on metallometric surveying based on analysis of systematically collected samples of soil and weathered rock. Other geochemical methods were being applied only on an experimental basis, although sometimes on a fairly large scale. In 1955, by order of the Ministry of Geology and Conservation, the use of metallometric surveying was made compulsory in all geological organizations for exploration work on any scale (Solovov, 1959, p. 10). Table 1-3 shows the growth of metallometric surveying in the

U. S. S. R. from 1948 to 1957. Most of this work is concentrated in the desert terrain of Central Asia (Kazakhstan and neighboring territories), where the metallometric methods seem to be especially applicable.

TABLE 1-3. Volume of Metallometric Surveying in the Ministry of
Geology and Conservation

Year	No. of Sample Sites
1948	67,000
1949	238,000
1950	778,000
1951	2,325,000
1952	2,673,000
1953	3,063,000
1954	4,680,000
1955	4,955,000
1956	6,155,000
1957	6,722,000
Total	31,656,000

Source: Solovov (1959), p. 12.

Africa ranks second only to Central Asia for scale of operations. In 1959, an unofficial estimate of the total effort in all territories put the rate at nearly 1.5 million samples per year, of which at least 1 million were collected in Central Africa.

For the same year (1959), Canadian and American operations combined probably accounted for about 500,000 samples. The scale of activity in the remaining parts of the world probably totaled no more than 100,000 to 250,000 samples.

The cost of geochemical sampling and analysis varies too widely to permit any conclusions concerning expenditures on geochemical methods. In this connection, however, it is interesting to note that in 1958 one of the largest exploration companies operating in Canada allocated 6 percent of its annual budget to geochemical work, as compared with 18 percent to geophysical methods, 35 percent to field geology and 41 percent to exploration drilling (Solow, 1959). In the same year, a canvass of Canadian exploration companies showed that more than half were using soil and drainage surveys on a routine basis (Riddell, 1960).

1-4. Literature

The principal summaries of geochemistry as applied in mineral exploration are by Ginzburg (1960) and Hawkes (1957). Collections of articles and individual papers have been published as Bulletin 1000 of the U. S. Geological Survey; the Technical Communications and

Theses of the Geochemical Prospecting Research Center, Imperial College; Transactions of the All-Union Conference on Geochemical Methods of Prospecting for Ore Deposits, Moscow, 1956, edited by Krasnikov (1957); the contributions, mostly from Western countries, contained in the reports of the Symposia on Applied Geochemistry at the XX and XXI Sessions of International Geological Congress in Mexico City and Copenhagen respectively; and papers on geochemical methods of exploration for U contained in the Proceedings of the First and Second International Conferences on the Peaceful Uses of Atomic Energy. All these contain abundant references to earlier literature. The principal book on geochemical prospecting for petroleum is by Kartsev *et al.* (1959).

The technical journals most likely to carry current literature on geochemical prospecting include Economic Geology, Mining Engineering, Transactions of the Institution of Mining and Metallurgy (London), Razvedka i Okhrana Nedr, and Geokhimiya. The remainder of the literature is scattered throughout a wide variety of scientific and trade journals in geology, chemistry, and mining engineering. Publications prior to 1954 are listed in Bulletins 1000-A and 1000-G of the U. S. Geological Survey. Reference to virtually all the more recent contributions may be found by following Section 8 of Chemical Abstracts for the Western literature, and the Mineral Exploration section of Referativny Zhurnal-Geologiya for the Soviet Union and the Chinese People's Republic.

CHAPTER 2

BASIC PRINCIPLES

Geochemistry, as originally defined by Goldschmidt and summarized by Mason (1958, p. 2), is concerned with (1) the determination of the relative and absolute abundance of the elements . . . in the earth, and (2) the study of the distribution and migration of the individual elements in the various parts of the earth . . . with the object of discovering principles governing this distribution and migration.

A twofold aspect of the field of geochemistry is implicit in Goldschmidt's definition—part of the subject being devoted to descriptive studies of the distribution of elements in earth materials and part to exploring the basic principles governing this distribution.

Geochemistry as applied in mineral exploration is of course primarily descriptive, inasmuch as it is concerned with the preparation and interpretation of geochemical maps rather than the investigation of basic principles. Even so, the full scope of geochemical prospecting can be realized only through a thorough understanding of the principles that govern the distribution of elements in the earth.

2–1. The Geochemical Environment

Pressure, temperature, and the availability of the most abundant chemical components are the parameters of the geochemical environment that determine which mineral phases are stable at any given point. On the basis of these variables, it is possible to classify all the natural environments of the earth into two major groups—primary and secondary.

The primary environment extends downward from the lower levels of circulating meteoric water to the deepest level at which normal rocks can be formed. It is an environment of high temperature and pressure, restricted circulation of fluids, and relatively low free-oxygen content.

The secondary environment is the environment of weathering, erosion, and sedimentation at the surface of the earth. It is characterized by low temperatures, nearly constant low pressure, free movement of solutions, and abundant free oxygen, water, and CO_2.

The movement of earth materials from one environment to another can be conveniently visualized in terms of a closed cycle, as illustrated in Figure 2-1. Starting on the right-hand side of the diagram

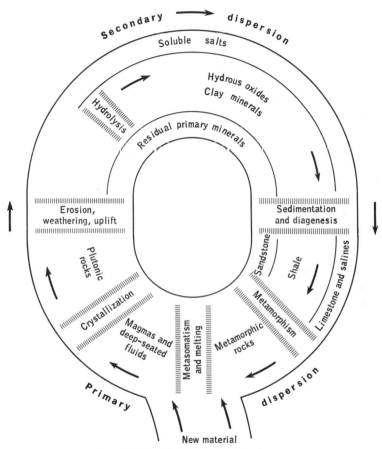

Fig. 2-1. The geochemical cycle.

and moving clockwise, sedimentary rocks are progressively metamorphosed as they are subjected to increasing temperature, pressure, and increments of new materials from outside the system. They may eventually attain a state of fluidity such that on recrystallization they can differentiate into various kinds of igneous rocks and hydrothermal extracts. When erosion brings the resulting suite of rocks into the surficial environment again, the component elements are redistributed by weathering agencies primarily in accordance with their relative solubility in water. A new series of sedimentary rocks is then deposited, and the cycle is closed. The diagram presented as Figure 2-1 is, of course, highly simplified, as in reality large parts of the cycle may be missing in any given case. It is quite normal, for example, for sedimentary sandstone and shale to be exposed to weathering and erosion without remelting or even significant metamorphism. Furthermore, this major cycle incorporates several important minor cycles, such as the circulation of carbon from the air into living plants, animals, organic deposits, and back into the air again.

The major geochemical cycle embraces both the primary deepseated processes of metamorphism and igneous differentiation and the secondary, surficial processes of weathering, erosion, transportation, and sedimentation. The horizontal division in Figure 2-1 indicates the boundary between these two sectors of the geochemical cycle.

2–2. Geochemical Dispersion

Dispersion is the result of the interaction of processes that may be broadly classified into two groups—mechanical and chemical. Dispersion may be the effect of exclusively mechanical agencies as, for example, the injection or extrusion of magma and the movement of

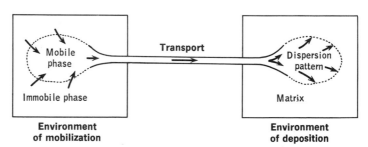

Fig 2-2 The dispersion process.

surficial material by glacial action. Apart from the alluvial sorting of clays and sands, purely mechanical dispersion of this kind results in little or no differentiation of the dispersed material. The contribution of chemical and biochemical processes, on the other hand, is primarily a sorting of material into fractions of differing mobility, where the more mobile phase tends to leave the source area if adequate channelways and a chemical or physical potential gradient are at hand. When the mobile phase eventually enters a new environment where conditions favor precipitation, a part of the introduced material may be deposited (Figure 2-2).

Dispersion may be either primary or secondary, according to the geochemical environment in which it takes place. The same principles underlying the dispersion process apply, however, in both the primary environment of high pressure and high temperature and in the secondary, low P-T environment. In primary dispersion, the channel-ways and sites of redeposition are generally the fissures and intergranular openings of deep-seated rocks. Secondary dispersion on the other hand, takes place at or near the surface of the earth, where patterns are formed in the fissures and joints of near-surface rocks, in the pore spaces of the overburden or even in the open air.

2–3. Geochemical Mobility

Fundamentally, the response of an element to dispersion processes is governed by its mobility, i.e., the ease with which it may be moved in any given environment. To a certain extent, mobility depends on the mechanical properties of the mobile phase, on factors such as the viscosity of magmas and solutions and the size, shape, and density of clastic grains in flowing stream water. The relationship between mobility and chemical differentiation, on the other hand, is rather more involved. Here the prime factors are the changes in the relative stability of the various coexisting fluid (mobile) and crystalline (immobile) phases that result from changes in the environmental conditions.

Mineral Stability. The disturbance of equilibrium consequent on passing from one part of the geochemical cycle to another is usually manifested by the appearance of new mineral species that are stable in the new environment. The growth of any new minerals at the expense of previously existing phases always has an effect that tends to oppose and neutralize the new conditions. Thus, with increasing pressure, high-density minerals form at the expense of minerals of lower density, and with increasing temperature the formation of new mineral phases is normally a reaction that absorbs heat. Similarly, an increase in the concentration of one of the chemical constituents will promote the growth of mineral phases which tend to reduce the concentration of that constituent in the fluid phase.

At least two phases must be present wherever new minerals are being formed—a mobile, generally fluid phase and one or more immobile, crystalline phases. In the crystallization of an igneous rock, the mobile phase is the magma. In metamorphism, it is an intercrystalline fluid fed in part by introduced material and in part by the decomposition products of locally occurring minerals that are unstable under the prevailing conditions of temperature and pressure. In the surficial environment, the mobile phase is the aqueous solution in which the soluble products of weathering of primary minerals are dissolved and carried away.

Where stable, and hence immobile, minerals are growing at the expense of the mobile phase, certain chemical elements that can be accommodated in the crystal lattices of the growing minerals are withdrawn from the fluid phase and immobilized. Elements that cannot be accommodated remain in the mobile phase and are free to move out of the system if the opportunity is provided. A knowledge of which minerals are stable under any set of conditions is thus the key to understanding the mobility of the elements contained in those minerals.

Most minerals are stable only in a system where the concentration of the component elements is relatively high. Under deep-seated conditions, only the ten commonest elements that comprise over 98 percent of the mass of the earth's crust normally occur in concentrations high enough to meet this specification. These elements are, in order of decreasing abundance, O, Si, Al, Fe, Ca, Na, K, Mg, Ti, and H. The overwhelming bulk of all common igneous and metamorphic rocks is made up of minerals containing only these elements as principal constituents. If carbon is added to the list, the same may be said with regard to the minerals of sedimentary rocks. A few other elements, such as Zr, F, P, S, and the lanthanides (rare earths), may occur as principal components of accessory minerals.

Trace Elements in Stable Minerals.   Most of the less common elements can be incorporated into one or more of the common rockforming minerals by occupying a position in the crystal lattice that is ordinarily filled by one of the principal constituents. The interchangeability of cations in a crystal structure is related to their contribution to the bond energy of the crystal. This may be expressed as an "index of ionic replacement" computed from the valence, ionic radius, coordination number, and electronic configuration of the

TABLE 2-1.   Index of Ionic Replacement of Common Cations

Tl^+	.03	Cu^{++}	.14	Be^{++}	.24
K^+	.03	Co^{++}	.14	Nb^{4+}	.28
Ag^+	.04	Ni^{++}	.14	W^{4+}	.28
Na^+	.06	Mg^{++}	.14	Mo^{4+}	.28
Cu^+	.06	Th^{4+}	.16	Ti^{4+}	.28
Ba^{++}	.07	U^{4+}	.19	Al^{3+}	.35
Pb^{++}	.08	Zr^{4+}	.20	Ge^{4+}	.46
Ca^{++}	.09	Sc^{3+}	.20	Si^{4+}	.48
Mn^{++}	.13	Fe^{3+}	.22	As^{5+}	.60
Zn^{++}	.14	Cr^{3+}	.22	P^{5+}	.62
Fe^{++}	.14				

Source: Green (1959).

cation (Green, 1959, p. 1155). Cations possessing comparable ionic indices show the strongest tendency to be mutually replaceable (Table 2-1). Thus, Mn, Zn, Cu, Co, and Ni tend to occur in the ferromagnesian minerals, and U and Th tend to be preferentially enriched in zircon.

It is reasonable to assume that the content of the minor constituents of minerals is a function of their concentration in the mobile phase from which the minerals were formed. Where other factors such as temperature are constant, therefore, a Sn-rich mica in a pegmatite implies a Sn-rich pegmatitic fluid, and a Cu-rich limonite in a seepage area implies a high content of Cu in the ground water from which it was precipitated.

Mobility Under High P-T Conditions (Hypogene Mobility). In the crystallization of magmas, the constituents that cannot be accommodated in the lattice structures of stable rock-forming minerals are concentrated in the mobile residual fluid. As the rock cools, a very small part of this mobile phase may be mechanically trapped either as occlusions within the lattice, as bubbles, or as minute films between the crystal interfaces. The bulk of it, however, is free to go out of the system provided an outlet is at hand. Water, which cannot be entirely accommodated in the minerals of igneous rocks, is progressively enriched in the residual fluids. With decreasing temperature the water-rich residual fluids begin to assume the familiar properties of aqueous solutions. Hydrothermal vein deposits may be precipitated at this stage in the primary geochemical cycle. Eventually the residual fluids reach the surface of the earth where they may either blend with the ground water or come to the surface as springs.

In metamorphism the same general trends may be traced. At high temperatures and pressures the hydrous minerals of sedimentary rocks become unstable, and the water is released to become the principal constituent of the mobile phase. Any other constituents of the original rocks that cannot be accommodated in the new suite of minerals also join the water-rich mobile phase. These constituents may include substantial quantities of minor elements, including many of the ore metals. The presently available quantitative data on the stability fields of minerals under conditions of high temperature and pressure are not adequate to permit a forecast of mobility of minor elements based on purely theoretical considerations. The stability of minerals, and hence the relative immobility of the elements that are contained in them, therefore must be surmised from empirical observations.

Empirical information on the hypogene mobility of minor elements may be gained from observing their progressive impoverishment or enrichment in a specific mineral species formed at different stages of a deep-seated differentiation cycle. Thus the higher Sn, Sr, and Li content of micas in late pegmatite differentiates as compared with the same species of mica in the parent igneous mass suggests that these elements are relatively mobile under the prevailing conditions. The occurrence of an element as a characteristic constituent of deposits formed from fluids of various kinds, either vapors, supercritical solutions, or normal aqueous solutions, may also be an indication of their hypogene mobility. In this group are the elements of complex pegmatites, hydrothermal vein deposits, juvenile water, and gaseous emanations.

Mobility Under Low P-T Conditions (Supergene Mobility). The relation between the stability fields of minerals and the mobility of the constituent elements is essentially the same under low P-T conditions as for deep-seated conditions. Where the identity of the stable mineral species and of the soluble ionic phases is known, and where at the same time the thermodynamic constants for these species have been determined, it is possible to compute the relative solubility and hence the mobility of minor elements in natural surface waters (Garrels, 1960). Unfortunately, the equilibria are normally disturbed by a variety of factors that as yet cannot be quantitatively appraised. The most important of these are the effects of coprecipitation of minor elements with certain common mineral species that have a strong scavenging action (principally the hydrous Fe and Mn oxides) and the effect of organic reactions and of the life processes of organisms in contact with natural solutions at the earth's surface. The qualitative effect of these factors is discussed in Chapter 7.

Although a quantitative estimate of relative mobility under surficial conditions is difficult, an empirical estimate can be obtained by comparing the minor-element composition of coexisting mobile and immobile phases. Complete equilibrium between two such phases is rarely, if ever, attained in the dynamic surface environment. However, an approximation may be sought by comparing the composition of natural drainage water and the soil with which it is in contact. Equivalent information may also be obtained by comparing the composition of either the water or the soil with the composition of the unweathered rock that has served as the parent material for the weathering products.

Smyth (1913) and Polynov (1937) have pointed out the significance of these relationships as a measure of the mobility of the elements in the zone of weathering. Smyth's assessment of the relative mobility of the major elements is based on two simplifying assumptions: (1) that the composition of parent rocks could be approximated by the composition of average crustal rocks and (2) that the composition of the drainage water resulting from weathering could be approximated by the composition of average fresh water. Polynov, using a similar approach to the problem, compared the average composition of igneous rocks with the composition of the mineral residue of rivers whose catchment basins are mostly in areas of massive igneous rocks. The reported order of decreasing mobility shown by both of these computations was $Ca > Na > Mg > K > Si > Al = Fe$.

More recently, Anderson and Hawkes (1958) made chemical analyses of stream waters and rocks from three local drainage basins in glaciated areas of northern New England. The relative mobility of each major element was expressed as the ratio of its content in the mineral residue of the stream water to its content in the rock drained by the stream. The order of mobility in each of the three cases was $Mg > Ca > Na > K > Si > Al = Fe$.

In a similar way, the relative mobility of the minor elements as well as the major ones might be obtained by comparing the composition of stream water with the composition of rocks. Unfortunately, data of adequate reliability to make such calculations are not yet available. A qualitative assessment for a few elements, based on practical experience in geochemical prospecting work, is given in Table 2-2. It must be borne in mind that the groupings indicated in

TABLE 2-2. Supergene Mobility of Elements in Siliceous Sulfide-Free Environment[a]

Relative Mobility	Major Elements	Minor Elements
Very mobile	S, Cl	Br, I, Mo, B, Se
Moderately mobile	Ca, Na, Mg, K	Zn, Ba, U
Moderately immobile	Si, Mn	Ni, Co, Cu, As, Sb, Pb
Very immobile	Fe, Al, Ti	Cr, Rare Earths

[a]The relative mobility of several of these elements is liable to vary considerably under special conditions, particularly in the presence of Fe, $CaCO_3$, and organic matter.

the table are subject to modification by many local factors of the environment. Thus, the mobility of Mo is suppressed in an Fe-rich environment, and Mn becomes very mobile in the reducing environment at the base of a peat bog.

In geochemical prospecting, attention is often focused on the dispersion of metals resulting from the decomposition of ore bodies. In the vicinity of an oxidizing sulfide deposit, for example, the chemical reactions dominating the mobility of elements may be quite different from those characteristic of normal environments. Large quantities of both sulfate and metals go into solution in the ground water, and extreme conditions of acidity are created by the oxidation of pyrite and marcasite.

Empirical observations have been made by different workers on the mobility of the ore metals in acid mine waters rich in sulfate. Emmons (1917, pp. 68–70) concluded that in the zone of secondary enrichment, Ag in the absence of chloride is more mobile than Pb or Au, Cu is relatively mobile under oxidizing conditions, and Zn is mobile in an acid environment. In his study of the Breckenridge mining district, Colorado, Lovering (1934) concluded that Zn is leached out of the surface material, whereas Pb tends to be enriched, although some Pb apparently moves short distances as soluble compounds formed by reaction with organic matter derived from the forest humus. In later work on the metal content of efflorescences in underground workings of the mines of the Tintic district, Utah, Lovering (1952) reported that where the country rocks consist of shale and quartzite, the ore metals could be arranged in order of increasing mobility as follows: Pb, Au, Cu, Zn, and Ag. In fractures traversing carbonate rocks rather than shale and quartzite, Ag is relatively immobile. His conclusions were based on the maximum distance from the nearest known ore that each of these metals had traveled in the solutions circulating through capillary rock fissures. Work by the U. S. Geological Survey at the Union Copper Mine, Gold Hill district, North Carolina, showed that the Pb:Zn ratio in the C horizon of residual soil derived from the weathering of sulfide

TABLE 2-3.   Mobility of Elements from Weathering of
Sulfide Deposits

Relative Mobility	Siliceous Environment	Calcareous Environment
Mobile	S, Mo, Zn, Ag	
Intermediate	Cu, Co, Ni, Mo[a], As	S, Mo, Zn, Ag
Immobile	Fe, Pb, As[a]	Fe, Cu, Pb

[a]Iron-rich environment.

mineralization is thirty times higher than the ratio of the same elements in the unweathered ore; the decrease in the absolute content of Zn during weathering is from 4 to 0.04 percent, a factor of 100 (Hawkes, 1957, p. 265). Data from the Northern Rhodesian Copperbelt indicate that at Baluba the Cu:Co ratio suffers little change during weathering, thus suggesting that the relative mobility of these two elements is equivalent under those conditions (Tooms and Webb, 1961).

The relative mobility of metals derived from the weathering of sulfide deposits has been summarized in Table 2-3.

2–4. Association of Elements

Certain elements tend to occur together under a given set of conditions. This tendency may be thought of simply as a manifestation of similar relative mobility. Since the mobility of an element can vary in response to changes in the environment, the resulting geochemical associations are correspondingly susceptible to environment.

Some elements retain characteristic associations throughout a wide range of different geological conditions. Some others that commonly

TABLE 2-4.   Some Common Geochemical Associations of Elements

Group	Association
Generally associated elements	**K**-Rb **Ca**-Sr **Al**-Ga **Si**-Ge **Zr**-Hf **Nb-Ta** Rare Earths **Pt**-Ru-Rh-Pd-Os-Ir
Plutonic rocks General association (lithophile elements)	**Si-Al-Fe-Mg-Ca-Na-K**-Ti-Mn Zr-Hf-Th-U-B-Be-Li-Sr-Ba-P-V- Cr-Sn-Ga-Nb-Ta-W-the halogens- and the rare earth elements
Specific associations	
Felsic igneous rocks	**Si-K-Na**
Alkaline igneous rocks	**Al-Na**-Zr-Ti-Nb-Ta-F-P-rare earths
Mafic igneous rocks	**Fe-Mg-Ti**
Ultramafic rocks	**Mg-Fe**-Cr-Ni-Co
Some pegmatitic differentiates	Li-Be-B
Some contact metamorphic deposits	Mo-W-Sn
Potash feldspars	**K**-Ba-Pb
Many other potash minerals	**K-Na**-Rb-Cs-Tl
Ferromagnesian minerals	**Fe-Mg**-Mn-Cu-Zn-Co-Ni
Sulfide ores General association (chalcophile elements)	**S-Cu-Zn-Pb**-Fe-Ag-Au-Hg-Cd-In- Se-Te-As-Sb-Bi-Ni-Co-Mo-Platinum metals
Specific associations	
Limestone replacement	**Zn-Pb**-Ba-F-Sr
Complex base metal	**Fe-Zn-Pb**-Ag-Cu-Se-Sb-Bi
Simple precious metal	**Ag-Au**-As
Complex precious metal	**Ag-Au**-As-Sb-Zn-Cu-Pb-Hg
Ores associated with mafic igneous rocks	**Fe-Ni**-Co-Pt
Porphyry copper	**Fe-Cu**-Mo-Re
Fumarolic deposits	**Hg-Sb**-As-Se
Sedimentary rocks	
Iron oxides	**Fe**-As-Co-Ni-Se
Manganese oxides	**Mn**-As-Ba-Co-Mo-Ni-V-Zn
Phosphorite	**P**-Ag-Mo-Pb-F-U
Black shales	**Al**-Ag-As-Au-Bi-Cd-Mo-Ni-Pb-Sb-V-Zn

Source: Goldschmidt (1954) and Krauskopf (1955).

travel together during metamorphism and igneous activity may part company in the cycle of weathering and sedimentation. Still others are characteristic of very specific plutonic rocks and associated oxide ores, of sulfide ores, or of certain kinds of sedimentary deposits. Some of the more important geochemical associations of elements are listed in Table 2-4. The presence of one member of an association will suggest the probable presence of the other members that for one reason or another may be difficult to detect.

TABLE 2-5.   Pathfinders

Pathfinder Element	Material Sampled	Ore Type
As	Wall-rock, residual soil, stream sediment	Vein-type Au ore
Hg	Wall-rock and soil	Complex Pb-Zn-Ag ores
Se	Gossan, residual soil	Epigenetic sulfides
Ag	Residual soil	Ag-bearing Au ore
Mo	Water, stream sediment, soil	Porphyry Cu deposits
SO_4	Water	Sulfide deposits

In mineral exploration, geochemical associations have led to the concept of *pathfinder* elements, that can be used as guides in searching for buried ore deposits where the principal ore metals cannot be easily traced (Warren and Delavault, 1956). Pathfinders have application in all phases of geochemical prospecting. They may be major

TABLE 2-6.   Example of As Content of Soil
as a Pathfinder for Au Ore

Position on Traverse	As Content of Soil (ppm)	Au Content of Soil (ppm)
300 N	40	0.1
50 N	100	0.1
10 N	480	1.0
0	1000	3.0
15 S	560	1.0
50 S	190	0.5
300 S	80	1.0
400 S	10	0.25

Source: James (1957a).

as well as minor constituents and may occur in gangue mineral as well as ore minerals. Thus S, Se, and Sb occurring in both commercial sulfide minerals and accompanying pyrite may be pathfinders for base-metal ores. The one essential criterion is that they should have a characteristic distribution with respect to mineralization. The most widely used pathfinders are listed in Table 2-5. Table 2-6 gives an example of the use of the As content of soils as a guide to Au ore.

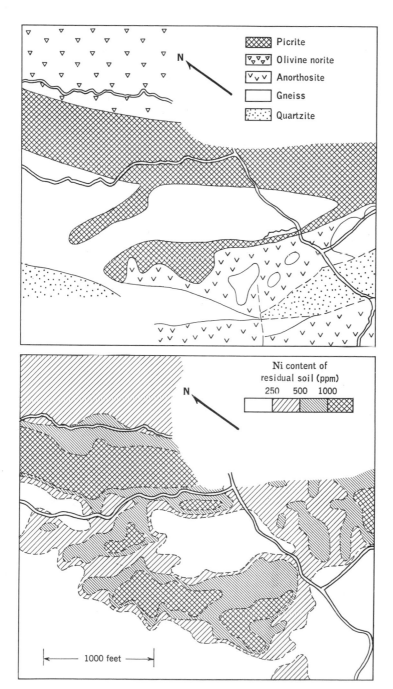

Fig. 2-3. Relationship between geology and the pattern of nickel in residual soil, Nguge region, Tanganyika. (Colluvial and alluvial overburden occur flanking the main rivers.) After Coope (1958).

2–5. The Pattern of Geochemical Distribution

In any given area, the net effect of all the dynamic forces concerned in the movement of earth materials will be reflected in the over-all pattern of distribution of the elements, This pattern has been referred to as the *geochemical landscape*, wherein the *geochemical relief* is determined by geographical variations in the levels of concentration of the elements. Geochemical relief is defined not only by the contrast between high and low values but also by the homogeneity of their distribution.

According to local conditions, the distribution of each geological unit will be more or less apparent from the patterns composing the geochemical landscape (Figure 2-3). Recognition of those patterns characteristically related to ore deposits is, of course, the aim and function of geochemical exploration. In order to do this effectively, it is necessary first to determine the background related to the unmineralized rocks.

TABLE 2-7.   Abundance of Elements in Average Igneous Rocks

Element	Content (ppm)	Element	Content (ppm)
Aluminum	81,000	Molybdenum	1.7
Antimony	0.3	Nickel	100
Arsenic	2	Niobium	20
Barium	640	Osmium	0.0001
Beryllium	4.2	Oxygen	473,000
Bismuth	0.1	Palladium	0.02
Boron	13	Phosphorus	900
Bromine	1.8	Platinum	0.005
Cadmium	0.13	Potassium	25,000
Calcium	33,000	Rhenium	0.001
Carbon	230	Rhodium	0.001
Cerium	40	Rubidium	280
Cesium	10	Ruthenium	0.0001
Chlorine	230	Scandium	13
Chromium	117	Selenium	0.01
Cobalt	18	Silicon	291,000
Copper	70	Silver	0.2
Fluorine	660	Sodium	25,000
Gallium	26	Strontium	350
Germanium	2	Sulfur	900
Gold	0.001	Tantalum	2.7
Hafnium	3	Tellurium	0.001
Indium	0.1	Thallium	1.7
Iodine	0.4	Thorium	13
Iridium	0.001	Tin	32
Iron	46,500	Titanium	4,400
Lead	16	Tungsten	2
Lithium	50	Uranium	2.6
Magnesium	17,000	Vanadium	90
Manganese	1,000	Zinc	80
Mercury	0.06	Zirconium	170

Source: Green (1959).

Normal Background Values. The normal abundance of an element in barren earth material is commonly referred to as *background*. For any particular element, the background value is naturally likely to vary considerably according to the nature of the earth material in which it occurs. Furthermore, the distribution of an element in any particular class of material is rarely uniform. Thus it is usually more realistic to view background as a range rather than as an absolute value. This is true even in a relatively uniform environment. The nature of the environment itself, however, can also have marked influence on distribution, in that under certain conditions some elements may be enriched and others impoverished. Consequently, whatever earth material is involved, the ever-present need to determine the background range in a new area can hardly be overstressed.

As a guide to the general order of magnitude of background values that may be expected in rocks, it is helpful to refer to data that have

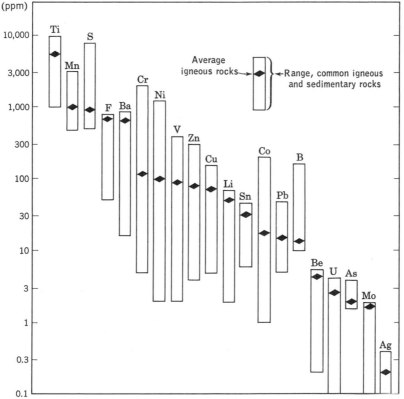

Fig. 2-4. Average and range of the content of the principal ore elements in normal rocks. Data from Green (1959) and Vinogradov (1956a).

been compiled on the composition of average igneous rocks (Table 2-7; Figure 2-4). The composition of many types of rock, however, differs substantially from the average, both as regards the minor elements as well as the major constituents. For example, ultramafic rocks are characterized by an unusually high content of Cr, Ni, and Co, and some granitic rocks contain higher than average amounts of Li and Rb. Figure 2-4 also shows the range for selected minor elements covered by the average compositions of five principal rock types (ultramafic, mafic, intermediate, felsic, and sedimentary), as well as the data for average igneous rocks.

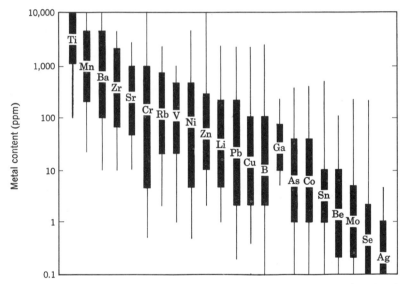

Fig. 2-5. Range of the content of selected minor elements in normal mineral soil. Thin lines indicate more unusual values. From Mitchell (1955).

For many elements the composition of residual soil and glacial till does not differ greatly from that of the rocks from which they were derived. Thus, the data on rocks can be used as a first approximation to the background composition of the overburden. However, background in soils is also subject to appreciable variation, according to soil type and soil horizon, particularly in well-differentiated profiles characterized by marked enrichment of some constituent such as iron oxide or organic matter. The range of values actually observed in normal soils is given in Figure 2-5.

Present data concerning the normal minor-element content in different mineral species, water, and vegetation are either inadequate or show too wide a variation to be usefully summarized in table form. Some data are given in the Appendix, but for more detailed information the reader is referred to references cited by Rankama and Sahama (1950), Fleischer (1954), Goldschmidt (1954), and Green (1959).

Statistical Distribution of Background Values. Following a provocative paper by Ahrens (1954), the geochemical literature has carried a lively controversy concerning the statistical distribution of elements in rocks (Chayes, 1954; Miller and Goldberg, 1955; Aubrey, 1956; Vistelius, 1960). Ahrens argued that most geochemical distributions in felsic and mafic rocks appear to be more nearly lognormal than normal, i.e., the logarithms of the metal content tend to be distributed symmetrically about the geometric mean as distinct from a symmetrical distribution of the natural values about the arith-

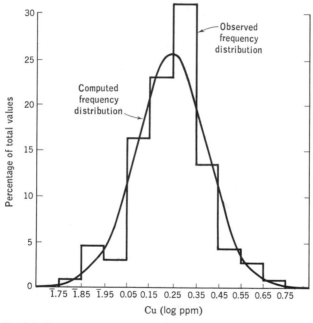

Fig. 2-6. Frequency distribution of readily soluble copper in 216 samples of background stream sediment from Northern Rhodesia.

metic mean. Objections have been raised concerning the validity of the data, and while accepting that some distributions approach lognormality, examples of essentially normal distributions have been advanced together with many that show no evidence of being either normal or lognormal. The telling point has been raised in this controversy that any given natural distribution is not necessarily either normal or lognormal, but may conform to a completely independent pattern of its own.

Whether or not Ahrens' hypothesis of lognormal distribution lacks generality, it is certainly true that data collected during the course of geochemical surveys often *appear* to be distributed lognormally. For example, apparently lognormal distributions of background values have been recorded for combined Zn-Cu-Pb in rocks and soils (Tennant and White, 1959), for Cu in soil and stream sediments (Figure 2-6) and for the $U:HCO_3$ ratio in water. Coulomb (1958) found normal and lognormal distributions for U in soils derived respectively from barren granite and from granites associated with uranium deposits. Each of these distributions includes the effect of laboratory and field sampling errors. Inasmuch as these errors may be of considerable magnitude, geological interpretation of the data, without allowing for these errors is open to question.

Dispersion Patterns. The classification of dispersion patterns as primary or secondary according to the sector of the geochemical cycle in which they were formed has already been discussed (Figure 2-1). They may be further subdivided into *syngenetic patterns* formed at the same time as the matrix in which they occur, or as *epigenetic patterns* formed by the subsequent introduction of metal from an outside source. Examples of syngenetic patterns include those developed (1) in igneous rocks during their crystallization, (2) in residual soil, gossan, or leached rock as a residual product of weathering, and (3) in glacial till, as clastic material mechanically transported and deposited by glacial action. Epigenetic primary patterns are most commonly the effect of precipitation from hydrothermal solutions or other fluids in the fissures and pore spaces of the rocks through which they were flowing. Epigenetic secondary patterns are formed by precipitation of material introduced either by circulating ground water or by plant activity. The different types of primary and secondary patterns and the processes by which they are formed will be considered in detail in later chapters.

The Geochemical Anomaly. By definition, an anomaly is a deviation from the norm. A geochemical anomaly, more specifically, is a departure from the geochemical patterns that are normal for a given area or geochemical landscape. Strictly speaking, an ore deposit, being a relatively rare or abnormal phenomenon, is itself a geochemical anomaly. Similarly, the geochemical patterns that are related either to the genesis or to the erosion of an ore deposit are anomalies.

Anomalies that are related to ore and that can be used as guides in exploration are termed *significant* anomalies. Anomalies that are superficially similar to significant anomalies but that are unrelated to ore are known as *nonsignificant* anomalies. For all practical purposes, significant anomalies are characterized only by abnormally high concentrations of indicator elements; "negative" anomalies, or patterns of abnormally low values, rarely have any application in exploration.

In order to define what constitutes an anomaly, it becomes necessary to establish the *threshold* or upper limit of normal background

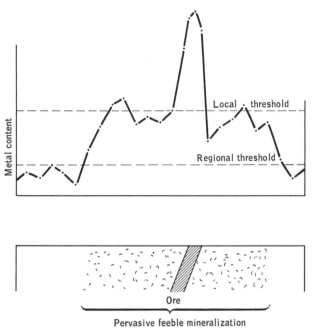

Fig. 2-7. Diagram illustrating local and regional threshold values.

fluctuation. The magnitude of anomalies may then be expressed in terms of the contrast between the peak values and threshold. Sometimes it is found that the anomalies themselves are set in a broad area of higher-than-normal threshold values, presenting a geochemical relief composed of (1) a low-lying plain of regional threshold surrounding, (2) a plateau of higher local threshold from which rise, (3) the anomalies as separate peaks (Figure 2-7). In these circumstances anomaly contrast is based on the local threshold value. Recognition of regional and local thresholds can be extremely important in prospecting, as it may then be possible to limit the search for peak anomalies to the plateaus of high local threshold delimited by a preliminary reconnaissance survey.

2–6. Principles of Interpretation

Developing an effective system of interpretation of geochemical data involves a consideration of multiple populations of data. Ore or potential ore is only one of a host of genetic factors that may play a part in the development of the over-all geochemical pattern or geochemical landscape. These include a variety of common, or normal, factors that contribute to minor irregularities in background areas, together with the more unusual factors that give rise to patterns that because of their relative scarcity are considered anomalous. Each one of these factors leaves its trade-mark on the over-all pattern.

The Ni content of residual soil provides an instructive example of multiple populations. In soils over homogeneous granite or shale the Ni content will be low and uniform; over mafic igneous rocks it will probably be somewhat higher and uniform; over serpentine it may be very high and somewhat erratic; and over Ni sulfide deposits it may be very high and very erratic. The Ni content of soils within an area underlain by a single one of these rocks will show a characteristic mean and standard deviation. An area underlain by more than one of the rock types mentioned, where each population corresponds to one of the contrasting parent rocks, will contain a multiple population of Ni values. Because of the striking differences in the means and standard deviations of the Ni content of soils over these rocks, the associated areal patterns in many cases will be immediately recognizable by simple inspection of the geochemical map.

This example, of course, is an unusually simple one. More commonly, sorting out multiple populations is hampered by extreme difficulty, first in recognizing the existence of more than one source of metal and then in determining the threshold value by which the members of each population are defined.

A fully dependable value for threshold can come only from an orientation survey in an area of known geology and mineralization, conducted and interpreted by a geologist experienced in geochemical interpretations. There is as yet no real substitute for a competent, visual estimate based on a comparison of the geochemical patterns given by a series of tentative threshold values, correlated with the known distribution of metal in the bedrock.

Unfortunately, for many exploration problems, areas suitable for orientation studies are either lacking or not fully suitable. Here the threshold levels chosen on the basis of simple, qualitative analysis of the data may need further confirmation before interpretation is made. For problems of this kind, semiquantitative and quantitative statistical approaches are attracting increasing attention and show promise of having a considerable field of application in the interpretation of geochemical data. It should be stressed, however, that statistical methods should be used solely as a disciplinary guide and never as a replacement for qualitative appraisal. Inasmuch as the statistical approach is based on the same principles as are used in subjective appraisal, it perhaps deserves some explanation.

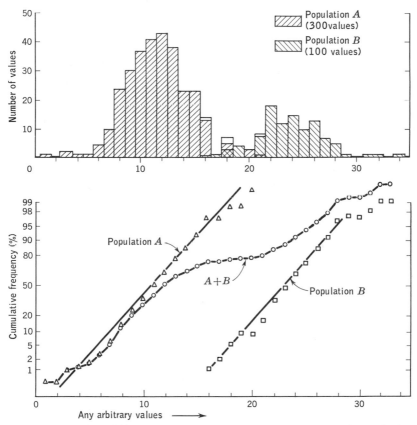

Fig. 2-8. Histogram and corresponding cumulative-frequency plots for multiple populations, modified after Tennant and White (1959).

The statistical distribution of an element in a particular sample type may be presented as a simple histogram or bar diagram on which the frequency of values is plotted against concentration on normal graph paper. If the data are from a single population and distributed normally, the plot shows the familiar "bell-shaped" symmetry. Lognormal distributions give a positive skew when plotted in this way, but will be symmetrical if plotted on logarithmic paper.

Frequency distributions may also be examined by using special graph paper, known as probability paper, which is so designed that the cumulative percentage of frequency plotted against concentration gives a straight line if the frequency distribution is normal (Figure 2-8). Lognormal distributions will plot on straight lines in the same way when the concentrations are scaled logarithmically. Deviations from normal and lognormal distribution respectively will show as curves in the plotted line.

Where the data are made up of two or more contrasting populations, each normally or lognormally distributed, the resulting cumulative frequency plot will not ordinarily be straight, but will show breaks or inflections as illustrated by curve A + B in Figure 2-8.

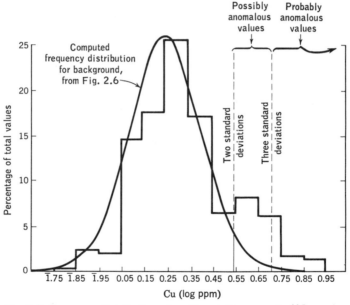

Fig. 2-9. Frequency distribution of readily soluble copper in 825 samples of stream sediment from both background and anomalous areas, Northern Rhodesia. Data from same field problem as Fig. 2-6.

For a single population of values that are distributed symmetrically (either normally or lognormally), the threshold for that material may be conventionally taken as the mean plus twice the standard deviation. This is equivalent to saying that only 1 in 40 background samples is likely to exceed the threshold content, whereas only 1 in 667 background samples is likely to exceed the mean plus three times the standard deviation. This treatment is illustrated in Figure 2-9, wherein the mean and standard deviation are derived from the data for background given in Figure 2-6.

With small bodies of single-population background data, or where the statistical distribution is irregular, probably the best approximation is to take the median value as background and to estimate threshold as that value which is exceeded by no more than $2\frac{1}{2}$ percent of the

TABLE 2-8.   Illustration of a Method of Estimating a Provisional Value for Threshold from Limited Background Data

Metal Content (ppm)	Number of Observations	
10	14	
20	2	
30	56	
40	77	Median value
50	24	i.e., mean background = 40 ppm
60	4	
70	18	
80	4	
90	2	Threshold value (exceeded by
100	2	$2\frac{1}{2}$ percent of total observations)
150	1	= 80 ppm
Total	204	
300	1	Erratic high values omitted from
500	2	estimation of threshold

total number of observations, excluding markedly high erratic values, as illustrated by the treatment of the data in Table 2-8.

Clearly much more work remains to be done in the investigation of statistical methods of treating geochemical data before their ultimate scope and usefulness can be determined. In particular, it is important that the effect of sampling and analytical errors should be fully taken into account. It should be emphasized that although statistics may help in presenting and analyzing geochemical data, it cannot provide the interpretation. A reliable interpretation of anomalies in terms of ore requires a combination of complex human experience and a capacity to recognize significant geometrical correlations. Pure mathematical analysis, therefore, is not likely to replace the subjective interpretive talents of the exploration geologist for some time to come.

CHAPTER 3

PRINCIPLES OF TRACE ANALYSIS

The practical effectiveness of any geochemical method of exploration depends in large part on the availability of an analytical procedure that is properly suited to the problem at hand. The procedure must be sensitive enough to detect elements present in very small concentrations. It must be reliable enough that the chances of missing an important anomaly are negligible. And it must be economical enough that very large numbers of samples can be processed in the course of a routine survey. Added desirable features are simplicity of techniques, so that the analysis can be entrusted to relatively untrained personnel, and portability of equipment, so that the analytical laboratory can, if desirable, be set up near field operations.

Four steps are involved in almost every trace analysis procedure. First, the sample must be treated to prepare it for transport, storage, and subsequent steps in the analytical procedure. Then the sample must be partially or completely decomposed, so that the element to be determined is released in a form that can be easily manipulated. The third step is the separation of the element from other constituents that might interfere with later measurements. And finally, the quantity of the element present must be estimated. In some trace-analysis systems, as in X-ray spectrography, one or two of the intermediate steps may be omitted. Also, in some systems, such as cold-extraction colorimetry and emission spectrography, several of the steps may be carried out essentially simultaneously as a single process.

In the following discussion, each of the principal methods of preparation and decomposition of the sample and of separation and estimation of trace constituents will be briefly mentioned. These methods are tabulated in Table 3-1. The manner in which the various methods of preparation, decomposition, separation, and estimation are most commonly combined into the analytical procedures used in geochemical prospecting are summarized in Figure 3-1. For a more comprehensive review of trace analysis techniques, the reader should consult the references listed at the end of the chapter.

TABLE 3-1.   Components of Analytical Procedures Used in Trace Analysis

Step I Preparation of Sample	Step II Decomposition of Sample	Step III Separation of Element	Step IV Estimation of Element

1. Removal of water
by
  a. Drying of or-
   ganic and clastic
   samples
  b. Evaporation of
   water samples
 	
2. Pulverization
 	
3. Sizing
 	
4. Mineral separations
  according to
  differences in
  a. Density
  b. Magnetic
   susceptibility
  c. Electrical
   properties
	1. Volatilization
	
	2. Fusion with
	  a. Acid flux
	  b. Alkali flux
	  c. Oxidizing flux
	
	3. Vigorous acid
	  attack with
	  a. Oxidizing acid
	  b. Dehydrating acid
	  c. Hydrofluoric
	   acid
	
	4. Weak attack by
	  a. Dilute acids
	  b. Solutions of
	   complexing
	   agents
	  c. Pure water
	
	5. Simple oxidation
	  by
	  a. Ignition
	  b. Wet oxidation
		1. Separation in
		  vapor phase by
		  a. Distillation
		  b. Sublimation
		
		2. Separation in
		  liquid phase by
		  a. Solvent extrac-
		   tion
		  b. Complex
		   formation
		
		3. Separation in
		  solid phase by
		  a. Ion exchange
		  b. Precipitation
			1. Gravimetry
			
			2. Optical measure-
			  ments
			  a. Colorimetry
			  b. Turbidimetry
			   and nephelo-
			   metry
			  c. Spot tests
			  d. Paper chro-
			   matography
			  e. Visible
			   fluorescence
			
			3. Radiation
			  measurements
			  a. Flame
			   spectrometry
			  b. Emission
			   spectrometry
			  c. X-ray
			   spectrometry
			  d. Radiometry
			
			4. Electrical
			  measurements

3–1.   Preparation of Sample

Samples of any kind of naturally occurring material almost always require some kind of preparatory treatment before they are ready for chemical analysis. The purpose of such treatment may be (1) to put the sample into a form that can be readily transported and stored, (2) to homogenize the sample so that erratic variations are eliminated, or (3) to effect a preliminary separation of the elemental constituents according to their occurrences in the different kinds of clastic particles.

Water is normally removed from samples before shipment to the laboratory. Water not only is an unnecessary component of clastic or organic samples, but it can also actively interfere with subsequent processing in a variety of ways. Wet samples tend to cause decay of paper containers or corrosion of metal containers. Wet clastic material cannot be readily pulverized or sieved. Furthermore, analytical results are normally desired on a dry-weight basis, so that the sample must be dried before weighing. Soil or plant samples are most commonly dried either in the sun or in drying ovens set up at the field

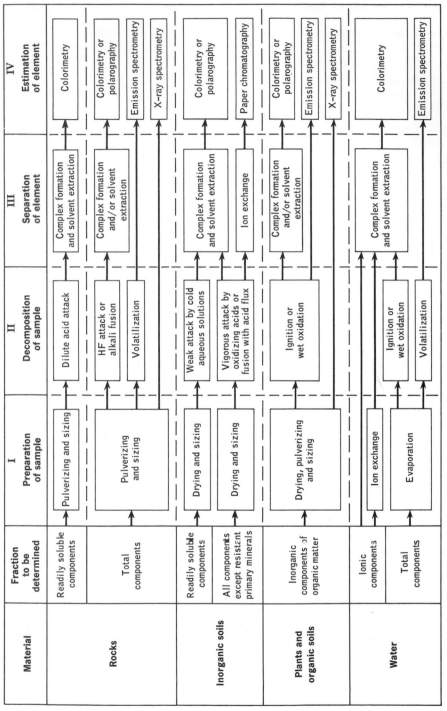

Fig. 3-1. Combinations of components of analytical procedures most commonly used in geochemical prospecting.

camp. The inorganic constituents of water samples are usually concentrated preparatory to analysis, either by evaporation in the laboratory or by ion exchange in the field.

Pulverization of samples of rock or vegetation by crushing, grinding, or chopping serves in part to increase the surface area of the sample that is exposed for subsequent chemical attack and in part to homogenize the sample.

Sizing of samples may have two functions. One is to remove larger fragments of the sample for recycling through the pulverization step and thus to render the sample more homogeneous. Another important function, particularly with soils, is to separate and discard the coarse grains of quartz or other mineral diluents so that only the metal-rich fine-grained material is retained for analysis.

Mineral separations of various other kinds may be made on clastic samples prior to chemical analysis. These separations take advantage of the principal physical properties of the minerals, particularly the density, magnetic susceptibility or electrical properties.

3–2. Decomposition of Sample

The mode of extraction of a trace element from a sample of rock, soil, or plant material will depend on how the element is bound within the sample. This is a fundamental problem that will come up for discussion many times in the course of this book. It involves the destruction of a solid-phase system and the release of the element in some reactive form. Following are the most commonly used methods of sample decomposition.

Volatilization. The sample may be partly or wholly decomposed by volatilization in the extreme heat of an electric discharge (emission spectrography), in the more moderate heat of a flame (flame spectrometry), or in an electric distillation furnace (distillation of Hg).

Fusion. An effective method of attack is to fuse the sample with an inorganic salt that melts at a reasonably low temperature but that at the same time is capable of a vigorous chemical attack on the sample. The nature of the chemical action of a flux may be acid, alkaline, or oxidizing; examples of these are $KHSO_4$, Na_2CO_3, and Na_2O_2 respectively.

Vigorous Acid Attack. Concentrated mineral acids, especially when heated, will destroy many minerals, including some of the common silicates such as the clay minerals and the micas. Mineral acids may react purely by virtue of their high hydrogen-ion concentration (HCl), or they may have additional corrosive chemical properties, such as an oxidizing (HNO_3) or dehydrating (concentrated H_2SO_4) action. Hydrofluoric acid is unique among aqueous acids in that it destroys the silicate lattice of the majority of rock-forming minerals.

Attack by Weak Aqueous Extractants. The fraction of the trace-element content of a sample that is loosely bonded by exchange forces or that occurs in other readily soluble forms may be differentially extracted by suitable weak aqueous reagents. These include dilute acids (HCl, H_2SO_4), solutions of complexing agents (citrate, tartrate), or simple pure water.

Oxidation. The inorganic constituents of vegetation or organic soils can be liberated for subsequent determination only by destruction of the organic matter, either by ignition or by wet oxidation with one of the strong chemical oxidizing agents (HNO_3,$HClO_4$, H_2O_2).

3–3. Separation

Once the trace element under study has been released from the sample, it is usually necessary to separate it from interfering elements liberated from the sample at the same time. The process of separation often results in concentrating the element in a separate phase, thus increasing the effective sensitivity of the over-all method. Where the desired element is present in extremely low concentrations, as is often the case in natural waters, enrichment of the element is often essential for its determination.

Separation in Vapor Phase. Vapor-phase separations can be made extremely quantitative, and are for that reason especially useful for some purposes. Separation may be by distillation and condensation of a liquid phase, as with native Hg; sublimation of a solid phase, as exemplified by the sublimation of SnI_4; or the ionization of atoms into an evacuated space from a strongly charged electrode, as in the mass spectrometer.

Separation in Liquid Phase. Many separations in trace analysis involve liquid-liquid solvent extraction permitting the transfer of dissolved material between two immiscible liquid phases. Solvent extraction requires vigorous mechanical shaking of the system to emulsify the two component phases and thus increase the effective surface area across which the transfer of dissolved components takes place. Separation may be facilitated by the use of appropriate complexing agents that modify the solubilities of the trace element in the two phases. Solvent extraction is the basis of many of the colorimetric tests extensively employed in geochemical prospecting.

Separation in Solid Phase. A solid phase containing the desired elements may be separated from a liquid phase by ion exchange or by precipitation. These methods may be applied to samples of natural water or to aqueous solutions obtained by some of the sample extraction procedures mentioned earlier.

3–4. Estimation

Table 3-2 lists the principal methods of estimation and the elements for which they are especially well suited. Some of the advantages and disadvantages of these methods in geochemical prospecting work are mentioned in the following summary.

Gravimetry. Gravimetric methods of estimation involve weighing the separated constituent. Ordinary laboratory balances cannot easily handle masses much less than 100 micrograms. Inasmuch as almost every problem in geochemical prospecting requires measurements several orders of magnitude below this level, gravimetric methods have not been found generally applicable. An exception is the extremely sensitive fire-assay method for Au, Ag, and the Pt metals.

Colorimetry. A trace element may be made to form a compound that, when dissolved or suspended in a suitable liquid medium, will absorb or scatter light of certain characteristic wavelengths. Where this absorption or scattering is quantitatively related to the amount of metal present, the effect may be used as a method of quantitative analysis. Separation of elements by solvent extraction and estimation by colorimetry can often be combined by using organic solvents in which a compound of the desired element forms a strongly colored solution in one of the two solvents. The advantages of colorimetric techniques in geochemical prospecting are the simplicity and portability of the equipment and the ease of training unskilled personnel in their operation. The disadvantages are that generally only one element or a small group of elements can be determined at one time.

Turbidimetry and Nephelometry. Turbidimetric and nephelometric methods involve respectively the unselective absorption and the scattering of light of all wavelengths by suspended particles of a precipitate containing the element to be determined. The most common application of these methods is in the turbidimetric determination of sulfate after precipitation as $BaSO_4$.

Spot Tests. Some trace elements may also be made to form strongly colored compounds that can be collected and observed as colored spots on a solid surface, usually paper. Observation of the color then can serve as a qualitative identification of the element present. With suitable precautions, the procedure can be made

TABLE 3-2. Methods of Estimation and Minor Elements for Which They Are Commonly Used

Element	Gravimetry	Colorimetry	Spot Tests	Paper Chromatography	Flame Spectrometry[a]	Emission Spectrometry	Radiometry	Polarography
Antimony		X						
Arsenic			X					
Barium		X			X	X		
Beryllium		X				X	X	
Bismuth		X						X
Boron							X	
Cadmium		X				X		X
Chromium		X				X		
Cobalt		X	X	X		X		
Copper		X	X	X	X	X		X
Fluorine		X						
Gold	X		X					
Iron		X						
Lead		X				X		X
Lithium					X	X		
Manganese		X			X	X		
Mercury		X						
Molybdenum		X				X		
Nickel		X		X		X		
Niobium[b]		X		X				
Platinum	X	X				X		
Rare earths					X	X		
Rubidium					X			
Selenium		X						
Silver	X	X	X			X		
Strontium					X	X		
Sulfur		X						
Tantalum		X		X				
Thorium							X	
Tin		X				X		
Titanium		X				X		
Tungsten		X						
Uranium					X		X	
Vanadium		X				X		
Zinc		X						X

[a]Specially applicable for analyzing waters or cold aqueous extracts of soils.
[b]A commonly used method is X-ray spectrometry.
[c]Most commonly used method is visible fluorescence.

semi-quantitative. The advantages of the method are the same as for colorimetric methods, except that the precision of the determinations is somewhat lower.

Paper Chromatography. Ions may be separated by their differential rates of movement in a solvent as it flows by capillarity along a strip of filter paper; under suitably controlled conditions, the ions will arrange themselves on the strip in a sequence of bands according to the strength of the bonds they form with the cellulose of the paper. After drying, the paper can be developed much like a photographic film, by applying a reagent solution that forms colored compounds with the ions. The identity of the element is determined by the hue of the colored compound or by its relative position on the chromatogram. The quantity present is then indicated by the depth of color and the width of the band. An outstanding feature of paper chromatography is that it can separate the desired element from elements that would normally interfere with the determination. Thus U can be separated from Fe and Nb from Ta prior to determination. A more general advantage of paper chromatography over colorimetric methods and spot tests is that in some cases it is possible to separate and determine two or more elements simultaneously, although not always with the desired sensitivity. A serious disadvantage is that the techniques require relatively constant conditions of temperature and humidity that are difficult to maintain except in certain climates or in suitably equipped laboratories.

Visible Fluorescence. Samples containing U, when fused with a suitable flux and cooled, emit a visible luminescence under ultraviolet activation. Under properly controlled conditions, the luminescence is quantitatively proportional to the amount of U present down to extremely low concentrations. This effect may be measured either visually by comparison with standards, or instrumentally with photoelectric devices. It is one of the most precise, and at the same time the simplest, methods of determining traces of U.

Flame Spectrometry. Many elements may be vaporized and ionized in the heat of a flame. In this state, some elements emit characteristic radiation in the visible or near-ultraviolet part of the spectrum. The identity of the ions and hence of the elements may be qualitatively determined by the wavelength of the spectral lines, and their quantity estimated by the intensity of the lines. The advantage of flame spectrometry is that it gives highly precise determinations for several elements, particularly the alkalis and alkaline earths, that are more difficult to determine by other methods. Unfortunately, only a very few of the trace elements are amenable to the method, and even with these some preconcentration may be necessary in order to determine concentrations in the normal background range.

Emission Spectrometry.   Almost all the elements, when vaporized and ionized in the intense heat of an electric discharge, emit radiation of characteristic wavelengths in the ultraviolet range. As with flame spectrometry, the element is identified by the wavelength, and the quantity present is determined by the intensity of the line. Measurement of lines may be done photographically or directly by electronic photometers. The advantages of emission spectrometry are the large number of elements that can be determined simultaneously, the permanent record of the analysis in the form of a photographic plate or film and the very low unit cost for large scale operations. The disadvantages are the high cost of capital equipment and hence the unsuitability for small programs, together with the need for a highly trained operator.

X-Ray Spectrometry.   The inner orbital electrons of atoms may be activated by X rays in such a way that they re-emit X rays of a wavelength that is characteristic of the activated element. Although the equipment is different, the basic principles of X-ray spectrometry are analogous to emission spectrometry. Advantages and disadvantages of X-ray spectrometry are the same as for emission spectrometry plus the added favorable feature that the samples are not destroyed. Also, X-ray spectrometry is effective for a number of elements that cannot be analyzed by emission methods, as it is equally satisfactory for virtually all elements above titanium in the periodic table.

Radiometric Methods.   Uranium, thorium, and potassium are naturally radioactive. Nonradioactive elements may be made radioactive by exposure to neutrons generated in an atomic reactor. Both natural and artificial radioactive elements give off gamma radiation of characteristic energy. As with other spectrometric methods of analysis, the identity of the element is determined by the energy of the gamma ray, and the amount present may be measured by the intensity of the gamma-ray flux at that particular energy level. The advantages of gamma-ray spectrometry are the extremely low detection limits that may be achieved with certain elements, many orders of magnitude below the nearest competing analytical method. The disadvantages are the high cost of analysis, the general unavailability of a neutron source for activation, and the need for a well-equipped laboratory and a highly trained technician. Certain radiometric methods, however, depend on specific nuclear reactions that do not require heavy equipment. Beryllium, for example, may be made radioactive by bombardment with gamma rays or alpha particles, either of which may be obtained from a relatively portable source. The radioactive product of the bombardment then decays with the evolution of neutrons which may be counted as a measure of the Be content of the sample. Boron has an extremely high neutron-absorption cross section. This property makes it possible to detect B-rich rocks by neutron logging of bore holes.

Electrical Measurement—Polarography. A number of analytical methods depend on instrumental determination of the electrical properties of solutions as a measure of the species and concentration of ions dissolved in the solution. Examples are the instrumental techniques for measuring pH, Eh, and the end points of titrations. The only one of these methods that has been applied extensively in geochemical prospecting work is the polarographic method. Polarography involves the application of a gradually increasing potential across a pair of electrodes which are immersed in the solution under analysis; as a result of reduction of ions at a polarizable electrode, a small current is produced which is related to the concentration of the ion species present in the solution. The potential at which the reduction occurs is indicative of these reducible ions, the second electrode serving as reference. The advantages of polarography are the high precision and the production of a permanent record. Square-wave and radio-frequency polarography give also extremely good sensitivity, which is a considerable advantage in the trace analysis of natural water. Disadvantages are the high capital cost of equipment, the need for a well-equipped laboratory and a skilled technician, and particularly the difficulty in maintaining standard conditions with many of the instruments and procedures now in use.

3–5. Analytical Procedures

Selecting an analytical system that combines the most suitable procedures for the preparation and decomposition of the sample and for the separation and estimation of the desired constituents must be based on an appraisal of a number of factors. The principal of these are (1) the mode of occurrence of the element in the material sampled, (2) the number and nature of the elements to be determined, (3) the sensitivity and precision required, and (4) the economics and logistics of the operation.

The mode of occurrence of the element in the material sampled determines the method of decomposition that must be used, and this in turn determines how the sample should be prepared prior to decomposition. Where the element is tightly bound in the lattice structure of resistant primary silicate minerals such as feldspars or hornblende, a strong attack involving more or less complete destruction of the sample by volatilization, fusion, or HF attack is necessary. Where the element is associated with minerals that are more readily destroyed, such as magnetite or clay minerals, a weaker attack with a common mineral acid may be just as effective as the more time-consuming fusions or HF treatment. Where the element is held in a relatively soluble form, such as limonite or ions adsorbed to the surface of clay minerals or organic matter, the most suitable method of decomposition may be a weak attack by a cold dilute aqueous solution, a process that is comparatively rapid and simple.

Mention has already been made that some of the methods of estimation such as emission or X-ray spectrometry can be readily adapted for simultaneous determination of a list of elements; other methods such as colorimetry are suitable only for single elements or an undifferentiated group of elements. The elements that can be detected and measured by each of the principal methods of estimation are shown in Table 3-2.

The method of separation of the element depends almost entirely on the method of estimation that has been selected. Thus, colorimetric methods normally require that the element to be measured occurs as a simple ionic component of an aqueous solution, and that other elements present in the solution be inhibited in some way from entering the reaction. This separation is commonly effected by tying up the unwanted elements as complex ions so that they cannot take part in the reaction. X-ray spectrometry, for precise determinations, may require a low content of Fe in the sample; here a prior removal of Fe by solvent extraction may be necessary. A method of estimation that is otherwise suitable may not have a sufficiently low limit of detection for the desired element; here a pre-enrichment of the sample by solvent extraction, sublimation or ion exchange may solve the problem.

Precision of estimation is different for different methods. Thus for Cu, Co, and Ni, spot tests and paper chromatographic methods have fair precision; colorimetric methods have moderately good precision, whereas X-ray spectrometry when properly controlled has the highest precision of the methods commonly used. It is more difficult to generalize on the relative sensitivity of the various methods of estimation. Thus, whereas emission spectrometry has a high sensitivity for Ag it has a very low sensitivity for Sb and W.

The economics of an operation makes itself felt where the capital investment of a large sum of money for an expensive instrument is

TABLE 3-3.   References to Literature Describing Principal
Analytical Procedures Used in Geochemical Prospecting

Element	Material	References
Ag	Soil and rocks	Almond et al. (1953)
As	Soil	Almond (1953b)
B	Rocks	Ivanova and Khristianov (1956)
Be	Soil	Brownell (1959)
		Bowie et al. (1960)
		Hunt et al. (1960)
Co	Soil	Almond (1953a)
		G.P.R.C. (1961a)
Cr	Soil	Stanton and McDonald (1961b)
Cu	Soil and rocks	Almond (1955)
	Soil (cxCu)[a]	Holman (1956a)
	Plants	Warren and Delavault (1949)
	Water	Huff (1948)
Hg	Soil	Ward and Bailey (1960)
HM[b]	Soil (cxHM)[a]	Bloom (1955)
	Water	Huff (1948)
Mo	Soil and rocks	Ward (1951a)
		North (1956)
		G.P.R.C. (1961b)
	Plants	Reichen and Ward (1951)
Nb	Rocks	Ward and Marranzino (1955)
	Soil	Hunt et al. (1955)
Ni	Soil and rocks	Stanton and Coope (1958)
Pb	Soil and rocks	Lakin et al. (1952)
		G.P.R.C. (1961c)
	Water	Huff (1948)
Sb	Soil and rocks	Ward and Lakin (1954)
		Stanton and McDonald (1961b)
Sn	Soil	Stanton and McDonald (1961a)
U	Soil and rocks	Grimaldi et al. (1954)
		Thompson and Lakin (1957)
		Grimbert (1956)
		Vaughn et al. (1959)
	Water	Ward and Marranzino (1957)
V	Rocks	U. S. Geological Survey (1953)
W	Soil	Ward (1951b)
		North (1956)
Zn	Soil	Lakin et al. (1949)
	Plants	Reichen and Lakin (1949)
	Water	Huff (1948)

[a]cx = cold-extractable.
[b]Heavy metals (Zn + Cu + Pb).

required. For very large projects, many of the instrumental methods of estimation are far cheaper per unit than the methods that do not require any substantial investment. Thus, if hundreds of samples per day are to be processed continuously over a long period of time, an X-ray spectrometer or a radiometric instrument could easily be amortized by the savings in cost per sample.

The logistics of the operation are involved where the problem of prompt reporting of analytical data and hence the desirability of a field analytical laboratory arises. Many of the expensive instruments that offer a real economy in cost per unit determination are too heavy or delicate to transport to the field. The need for a high-capacity power supply for many of the instrumental methods may also limit their applicability.

The analytical procedures that have found the widest acceptance in geochemical prospecting are listed in Table 3-3. In general terms, however, each geochemical survey presents its own analytical requirements. It cannot be emphasized too strongly that the optimum procedure in each case can only be devised in close collaboration between the geologist and the analyst, each with a full appreciation of the other's problems.

SELECTED REFERENCES ON TECHNIQUES OF CHEMICAL ANALYSIS

General	Yoe and Koch (1957)
Colorimetric techniques (with specific procedures for geological and biological problems)	Sandell (1959)
Spot tests	Feigl (1958)
Instrumental techniques	Smales and Wager (1960)
Analysis of water	Rainwater and Thatcher (1960)
Analysis of soils and plant material	Piper (1950)
Analysis of rocks	Shapiro and Brannock (1956)

CHAPTER 4

PRIMARY DISPERSION

The environment of primary geochemical dispersion is characterized by deep-seated conditions of relatively high pressure and
temperature. This definition distinguishes it from the low P-T conditions prevailing at the surface of the earth where secondary-dis-
persion processes are operative. The products of primary dispersion
are the geochemical patterns that are preserved in rocks of igneous,
metamorphic, or hydrothermal origin that are now exposed for study
at the surface.

The characteristics of the principal kinds of primary dispersion
patterns are summarized in Figure 4-1. Syngenetic patterns are
defined as dispersion patterns formed at the same time as the enclosing rock, whereas epigenetic patterns are those formed by material
introduced in some way into a pre-existing matrix. Syngenetic
patterns formed in sedimentary rocks are for convenience included
in Figure 4-1, even though by origin they might just as well be thought
of as "fossil secondary patterns."

Epigenetic patterns may be further classified according to whether
they are the effect primarily of the introduction and precipitation of
new material, as hydrothermal dispersion patterns, or of recrystallization or fractionation of the original constituents in response to
changed conditions of pressure and temperature.

Gaseous dispersion patterns are somewhat similar to hydrothermal
dispersion patterns in that they are both epigenetic and not directly
related to processes of weathering. They are therefore included in
this discussion of primary dispersion even though they are most
commonly formed at relatively low pressure and temperature.

4–1. Syngenetic Patterns

The association of certain kinds of ore deposits with certain kinds
of plutonic rocks has been known and used by exploration geologists
for many decades. Familiar examples include the association of cassiterite with potassic granites, ilmenite with anorthosites, chromite

Genetic classification		Origin	Emplacement	Matrix	Form of dispersion pattern
Syngenetic patterns	Geochemical provinces	Compositional variations affecting large segments of the earth's crust	Igneous intrusion, granitization, or sedimentation	Rocks of diverse types and ages occurring over wide area	Varied
Syngenetic patterns	Local syngenetic patterns	Local processes of petrogenesis, differentiation, metamorphism, or sedimentation	Igneous intrusion, granitization, or sedimentation	Local plutonic bodies or sedimentary rocks	Varied
Epigenetic patterns — Hydrothermal dispersion patterns	Wall-rock anomalies	Precipitation from solutions related to ore-forming fluids	Movement of solutions; diffusion of solutes	Rocks adjoining ore deposits	Aureoles
Epigenetic patterns — Hydrothermal dispersion patterns	Leakage anomalies	Precipitation from spent ore-forming fluids	Movement of solutions	Rocks in and adjoining solution channelways leading upward from ore	Halos
Epigenetic patterns — Hydrothermal dispersion patterns	Compositional zoning	Differential depletion of certain constituents of ore fluids with distance from source	Movement of solutions	Minerals deposited from hydrothermal solutions	Systematic variation with distance from source
Epigenetic patterns — Pressure temperature effects in epigenetic minerals	Mineral reconstitution	Pressure-temperature control of stability of mineral species	Bulk of reacting components already present	Alteration halos	Generally concentric isotherms indicating higher temperatures toward ore channels
Epigenetic patterns — Pressure temperature effects in epigenetic minerals	Chemical geothermometers	Pressure-temperature control of fractionation of elements between coexisting mineral species	Bulk of reacting components already present	Mineralized rock	Generally concentric isotherms indicating higher temperatures toward ore channels
Epigenetic patterns — Pressure temperature effects in epigenetic minerals	Isotopic geothermometers	Pressure-temperature control of fractionation of stable isotopes between minerals and hydrothermal fluids	Bulk of reacting components already present	Mineralized rock	Generally concentric isotherms indicating higher temperatures toward ore channels

Fig. 4-I. Classification and general characteristics of the principal types of primary dispersion patterns.

with ultramafic rocks, and nickeliferous sulfides with both mafic and ultramafic rocks. The identity of the significant rock types is readily apparent from the mineralogical composition, and as a rule, their distribution can be determined during the normal course of geologic mapping, supplemented perhaps by geophysical surveys or soil studies in poorly exposed terrain.

Variations in the minor-element composition of igneous rocks, particularly in elements that do not constitute principal components of any of the rock-forming minerals, may be equally closely related to the occurrence of ore. In this case, however, systematic sampling and chemical analysis may be the only practical way of detecting some of these more subtle manifestations of the association between ore and rock type.

In sedimentary rocks, ore of various kinds may occur as syngenetic deposits formed at the same time as the enclosing beds. Sedimentary Fe ores, phosphorite beds, and gypsum deposits are well-established examples of syngenetic mineral deposits. Less widely accepted examples of syngenetic ores are the Cu ores of the Rhodesian Copperbelt and the White Pine district of Michigan, and the Witwatersrand Au-bearing conglomerates. Just as with syngenetic patterns in plutonic rocks, the distribution of traces of the ore metals in sedimentary rocks may be useful as a guide to economic concentrations of the same metals.

The size of the dispersion patterns of minor elements in rocks of both deep-seated and sedimentary origin ranges from hundreds of miles down to the scale of individual mines or groups of mines. The larger patterns are commonly known as geochemical provinces, whereas the more local associations of ore with minor element patterns are referred to simply as local syngenetic patterns.

Geochemical Provinces.   A geochemical province may be defined as a relatively large segment of the earth's crust in which the chemical composition is significantly different from the average. Geochemical provinces are most commonly manifested by suites of igneous rocks, all members of which are relatively rich or relatively impoverished in certain chemical elements. These rocks may not necessarily be of the same age. In fact, one of the criteria of a bona fide geochemical province is that the characteristic chemical peculiarities should be recognizable in rocks representing a considerable period of geologic time.

Large areas of the earth's surface may also be characterized by an unusual abundance of ores of a particular metal or of a particular type. Areas of this kind, known as *metallogenic provinces*, have long been the object of speculation by geologists (Turneaure, 1955). Examples are cited of the Cu-producing areas of Peru and Chile, the Sn fields of northwestern Europe, and the uranium fields of the Canadian Shield. Figure 4-2 shows the location of the great Cu mines that define the Cu province of the southwestern United States. These

Fig. 4-2. Copper province of the southwestern United States.
After Schmitt (1959).

classic examples of metallogenic provinces are defined on the basis of known mines and their mineral production statistics.

Metallogenic provinces may be the effect of any combination of a number of different factors. They may coincide with areas that are characterized by similar processes of ore concentration, similar conditions of tectonism or similar host rocks. The abundance of ore deposits may, however, be at least in part the effect of an unusual abundance of the ore metals throughout a large segment of the earth's crust. In this event, a metallogenic province is simply one manifestation of a geochemical province. Where the metallogenic province is in fact coextensive with a geochemical province, simple studies of the trace-element composition of igneous rocks may help to define geographical areas within which the chances of mineral discovery are relatively good. Particularly in inaccessible or poorly explored terrain, geochemical provinces may provide an extremely useful guide in reconnaissance exploration.

A geochemical province defined by an over-all difference in composition may easily be confused with variations in the composition of igneous or metamorphic rocks due to other causes. Normal processes of petrogenesis starting with materials of average composition may produce large volumes of rocks that differ substantially from average igneous rocks. Accidents of erosion may cause nonrepresentative differentiation products to be exposed at the surface more commonly than other members of the same igneous suite. Similarly, the tectonic history of an area may have resulted in the introduction of large volumes of normal but nonrepresentative igneous rocks such as basalt or peridotite, to give an apparent composition that differs from the average for the earth's crust. The results of these processes, while they produce a surficial distribution of rocks that departs materially from the average, do not reflect absolute differences in composition and hence are not geochemical provinces in the strict sense of the word.

A geochemical province may be indicated by rocks of widespread distribution that, within a well-defined area, display a characteristic variation in minor-element content. Scattered intrusive bodies of diabase, for example, may be distributed on a continental scale. Conceivably, a restricted area within the large pattern may be found where all diabase intrusions contain four times as much Ti, for example, as similar intrusions outside the area. An occurrence of Ti-rich diabase of this kind would then be an indication of a Ti-rich province, at least as far as the composition of diabase is concerned.

The origin of geochemical provinces is beyond the scope of this discussion. Some geochemical provinces undoubtedly reflect variations in the primeval composition of the earth. Other provinces may be the effect of chemical differentiation of very large areas as a result of sedimentary processes, followed by later reconstitution of the sediments into plutonic rocks.

The characteristics, or for that matter even the existence, of geochemical provinces are not well enough established to warrant any very extensive generalization as to the mode of occurrence of the metal, size of the anomalous area or correlation with economic mineralization. Rather than generalize, it is safer to describe the characteristics of geochemical provinces by means of case histories taken from the literature.

Tin provinces have received the most widespread attention, undoubtedly because of the very striking concentration of Sn deposits in the extensive yet well-defined tin fields of the world. Goldschmidt (1954, p. 393) states, "A region of great frequency of granites with associated cassiterite deposits is southeast Asia. . . . Another type of tin deposit characterized mainly by stannite and cassiterite veins associated with quartz diorites and granodiorites is confined to the Andean regions of Bolivia. . . . The absence of workable tin deposits in large regions of the earth, which are also characterized by the scarcity of even small amounts of tin minerals, seems to be followed by a scarcity of tin as a trace element as indicated by spectroscopic observations on magmatic rocks." Goloubinoff (1937) has reported from 100 to 2500 ppm Sn in late igneous differentiates from the tin fields of southeast Asia as compared with 40 ppm for average igneous rocks. Ahrens and Liebenberg (1950) report that mica from pegmatite dikes near Sn veins in South-West Africa contains from ten to one hundred times as much Sn as mica from similar dikes in areas where no Sn mineralization is known.

Uranium provinces were the subject of intensive study during the period of most active uranium prospecting after World War II (Davidson, 1951; Klepper and Wyant, 1957). Three large areas characterized by both uranium deposits and U-rich rocks are cited by Klepper and Wyant (1956, p. 219), as follows.

1. In the Colorado Front Range, late Cretaceous or early Tertiary pitchblende veins are intimately associated and probably genetically related to uraniferous quartz bostonites; some pitchblende veins of this same age also occur in the vicinity of uraniferous Precambrian pegmatites.

2. In the Erzgebirge and Riesengebirge of Saxony, Silesia and Czechoslovakia, uraniferous granite, uraniferous pegmatite and pitchblende veins are closely associated.

3. In the Precambrian shield of Canada, uraninite-bearing pegmatites and pitchblende veins are in close association, though they may not be of the same age, in the Goldfields region and at Stack Lake on the east arm of Great Slave Lake.

Many other observations bearing on the possible correlation of geochemical provinces with mineralization are scattered throughout the literature. These include discussion of combined geochemical-metallogenic provinces in boron (Smith, 1960), Li-Be-Ta-Nb (Chumakov and Ginzburg, 1957), Ta-Nb (Montgomery, 1950), and Au (Goloubinoff, 1937; Bolgarsky, 1950). Unfortunately, the evidence in many of these accounts, although extremely suggestive, cannot always be uniquely interpreted in terms of geochemical provinces. Experimental regional surveys are currently being undertaken by rock sampling in Canada (R. H. C. Holman, personal communication) and by stream-sediment sampling in Northern Rhodesia. Preliminary experiments conducted in the latter territory since 1957 have shown promising regional variations in the over-all trace-element content of stream sediments between known Cu-Co, Cu-Zn, and Nb districts and otherwise comparable barren areas.

Local Syngenetic Patterns. Where the scale of the geochemical pattern is measured in miles rather than hundreds of miles, it is unrealistic to ascribe the origin of the pattern to primeval differences in the composition of the earth's crust. The genesis here is much more likely to be related to local processes of petrogenesis, differentiation, and metamorphism.

For example, a systematic increase in both the radioactivity and in the silica content of a granite stock over a distance of 5 miles in the direction of an important area of Au mineralization was reported by Gross (1952), as shown in Figure 4-3. He attributes the variation

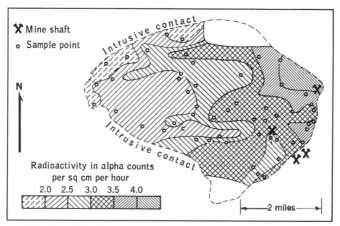

Fig. 4-3. Map showing radioactivity of granite in Dome Stock, Red Lake, Ontario, as related to gold deposits. After Gross (1952).

in radioactive elements and silica to the same genetic processes that resulted in the emplacement of the ore.

According to Warren and Delavault (1960), the presence of Cu and Zn deposits in certain parts of British Columbia is reflected to a degree in the content of readily extractable Cu and Zn in fresh samples of the plutonic rocks associated with the ore deposits (Table 4-1); it is not known, however, whether the metal is truly syngenetic or whether it was introduced by mineralizing solutions after the host rock was formed. Slawson and Nackowski (1959) report that

TABLE 4-1.   Copper and Zinc Extractable by Hot Aqua Regia from Plutonic Rocks in Mineralized and Unmineralized Areas of British Columbia

	No. of Samples	No. of Areas	Cu (ppm) Range	Cu (ppm) Mean	Zn (ppm) Range	Zn (ppm) Mean
Unmineralized areas	33	14	0.5–13	3	16–136	49
Areas of copper deposits	28	4	3–120	29	3–124	50
Areas of zinc deposits	27	4	1–24	12	35–200	105

Source: Warren and Delavault (1960).

the Pb content of the potash feldspars from quartz monzonites in areas of Pb mining is higher than in other areas (Table 4-2).

Jedwab (personal communication) reports that a granite containing commercial pegmatitic vein deposits can be distinguished from an associated, barren granite by the trace-element content of the

TABLE 4-2.   Lead Content of Potash Feldspars from Plutonic Rocks Associated with Lead Deposits in the Western United States

District	Lead Production	No. of Samples	Pb (ppm) Range	Mean
Bingham, Utah	Major	22	11–126	61
Park City, Little Cottonwood, Utah	Major	21	10–85	47
Tintic, Utah	Major	10	10–44	29
Robinson, Nevada	Minor	25	9–37	14
Iron Springs, Utah	None	3	12–18	15
Background Pb content of K-feldspar[a]				25

Source: Slawson and Nackowski (1959).
[a]Wedepohl (1956).

biotite. He found that the biotite from the productive granite contained on the average 10 ppm Ni, 455 ppm Sn, and 3450 ppm Li as compared with 30 ppm Ni, 200 ppm Sn, and 380 ppm Li in the biotite from the barren granite.

Care must be taken when applying this type of criterion in the field, as variations in trace-element distribution may arise solely as a result of progressive differentiation of the host rock. For example, successive phases of the granite constituting the Carnmenellis intrusion in the heart of the Cornish tin field have widely differing trace-metal characteristics (Table 4-3) despite the geographical proximity of all phases to mineralization.

TABLE 4-3.   Trace Element Variations in a Single Polyphase Granite Intrusion Associated with Tin Mineralization, Cornwall, England

| Element | Content in Fresh Rock (ppm) | | |
	Phase I Granite	Phase II Granite	Phase III Granite
Co	8	4	<2
Ni	10	4	2
Sn	25	5	30
Li	700	1500	3000

Source: Webb (1947).

4–2.   Hydrothermal Dispersion Patterns

An epigenetic mineral deposit is only one manifestation of the extremely complex processes that are covered by the general term "hydrothermal activity." Other effects include wall-rock alteration in all its ramifications and the introduction of ore minerals in sub-economic quantities either before, during, or after the ore-forming stage.

The nature and origin of the fluids responsible for the emplacement of epigenetic ore deposits have been the subject of debate since the beginning of the science of economic geology. Few geologists, however, will argue against the premise that these fluids contain water and that they are hot. The term "hydrothermal" is therefore probably as good as any, as in its broad sense it can apply to fluids introduced at temperatures above the critical point as well as the more familiar aqueous solutions.

The emplacement of metal in hydrothermal dispersion patterns is most commonly the effect of mass movement of the hydrothermal solution itself. Movement by diffusion through a static matrix is generally regarded as a minor factor except in special cases.

The direction of movement of the metal-bearing hydrothermal fluids has also been a subject of debate among economic geologists. Movement of solutions upward from a source at depth has been the most popular theory. At the same time, some investigators see evidence for movement either laterally into the vein system from the wall rock or for movement downward from above.

Regardless of the mechanism or the direction of the movement of ore solutions, the imprint left by hydrothermal solutions on the channel-ways through which they pass can be an extremely useful ore guide. It may be feasible to find and identify these channel-ways by chemical analysis for certain diagnostic trace elements precipitated from the solutions. In this way it may be possible to restrict the number of directions in which to go in search of ore.

Wall-Rock Anomalies. Ore-stage metasomatism is commonly characterized by enrichment of the ore metals in the country rock adjoining the deposit. Where the diagnostic minerals that define the pattern are sufficiently coarse grained, the aureoles may be readily determined by mineralogical studies. For example, aureoles of such *indicator* minerals have been observed around some of the ore shoots of the Coeur d'Alene district of Idaho (Mitcham, 1952), and certain types of tourmalinization and chloritization are characteristically associated with some classes of Sn veins in Cornwall. On the other hand, however, visible criteria of ore-stage metasomatism may be lacking on account of inconspicuous alteration, ultra-fine grain size of the indicator minerals, or the occurrence of the indicator metals as a variable minor constituent of some widely distributed mineral species. In such cases, wall-rock aureoles can best be sought and mapped by chemical analysis of systematically collected rock samples.

The most common patterns of local enrichment of ore metals in the country rock are consistent with an outward movement of the components of the mineralizing solutions. The metal content of aureoles developed in massive rocks, for instance, commonly decays logarithmically with distance from the ore contact (Figures 4-4 to 4-6). This logarithmic pattern is what would be expected if the

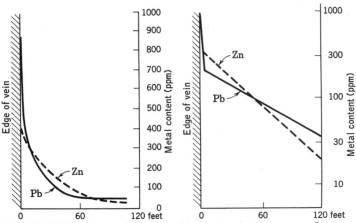

Fig. 4-4. Wall-rock aureole as defined by lead and zinc content of quartz monzonite, Tintic district, Utah. After Morris (1952).

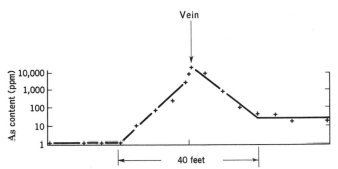

Fig. 4-5. Wall-rock aureole as defined by arsenic content of sandstone adjoining gold vein, Bell Mine, Southern Rhodesia. After James (1957a).

mechanism for the transfer of material was diffusion through a static medium. Fracturing, even on the micro-scale, however, permits a certain amount of flow of mineralizing solutions and results in a more irregular and possibly more extensive distribution of metal in the aureole than where diffusion is the only process (Table 4-4).

The width of the aureole varies also with the chemical reactivity of the rock. In highly reactive rock such as limestone or dolomite, the

TABLE 4-4.   Primary Pb and Zn Aureoles in Massive and Fractured Wall Rocks
Alongside Galena-Sphalerite Veins in Derbyshire, England

Distance from Vein (ft)	Metal Content of Limestone Wall Rock (ppm)			
	Massive Wall Rock		Fractured Wall Rock	
	Pb	Zn	Pb	Zn
0	1600	1900	600	34,000
5	600	850	1700	500
10	230	180	1600	800
15	220	220	1400	900
20	120	260	1300	900
25	60	80	3500	1700
30			1200	400
40			1250	850
50			130	60
60			440	170
70			1400	600
80			750	1250
90			250	70
150	30	140	1200	1000

Source: Webb (1958b).

aureole is commonly restricted to a zone 5 to 20 feet wide immediately adjoining the ore. In fact, in the limestone country rock of the Gilman deposit in Colorado, very careful sampling failed to reveal any evidence whatever for a wall-rock aureole (Engel and Engel, 1956). In less reactive rocks, such as igneous or metamorphic silicate rocks, the aureole may extend hundreds or even thousands of feet from the ore contact (Morris, 1952; Lovering, 1952; Hawkes, 1959).

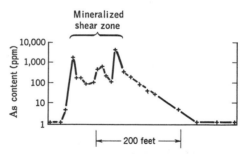

Fig. 4-6. Wall-rock aureole as defined by arsenic content of greenstone adjoining shear zone, Motapa Gold Mine, Southern Rhodesia. After James (1957a).

Secondary dispersion patterns resulting from supergene leaching and redistribution of the ore metals may sometimes be confused with aureoles formed at the time of ore deposition. Confusion of this kind is particularly easy with Zn, inasmuch as Zn is relatively mobile in the weathering cycle and hence readily dissolved and reprecipitated in the environment of an oxidizing sulfide deposit. Residual soil patterns defined by immobile elements such as Pb and As may, however, provide a reasonably dependable indication of primary patterns in the parent rock.

Following are some representative examples of mineralized aureoles as described in the published literature.

In the Tintic district of Utah, Morris (1952) describes a wall-rock aureole where the Cu, Pb, and Zn content of the limestone country rock decays logarithmically from a maximum value next to the ore to background within a distance of 3 to 15 feet. Where the ore occurs in quartz monzonite—a less reactive rock—the aureoles extend up to 80 to 100 feet (Figure 4-4).

At Santa Rita, New Mexico, Graf and Kerr (1950) found wall-rock aureoles of Pb and Zn in fractured limestone adjoining Pb-Zn deposits, with the maximum Zn content close to the ore and the maximum Pb content farther away. They conclude that the metal was introduced through systems of small fractures, inasmuch as they found only negligible dispersion into unfractured wall rock.

At the Darwin Mine, California, Austin and Nackowski (1958) describe a similar pattern of Pb in silicated limestone country rock extending from 8 to 20 feet from the contact of Pb-Zn-Ag ore.

In the Freiberg district of Germany, Starke and Rentzsch (1959) report aureoles of Pb, Ag, Zn, Cu, Sn, As, Co, and Ni extending into the gneiss adjoining the base-metal veins for distances up to 15 feet. The secondary mica of the gneiss showed a more highly contrasting pattern than the undifferentiated gneiss.

In Southern Rhodesia, James (1957a) studied the distribution of As in the wall rock of shear zones containing Au and As veins. The As content of unweathered rock collected from underground workings showed very marked logarithmic decay curves extending into the wall rock from the shear zones, as shown in Figures 4-5 and 4-6. At the Bell Mine, where the country rock is sandstone, the aureole is only 25 feet wide, whereas at Motapa, with a greenstone country rock, the aureole is almost 200 feet wide. Probably this difference is related in some way to either the chemical reactivity or the permeability of the two rock types, together with the duration of the period of hydrothermal activity.

Stoll (1945) found increased concentrations of Be in the wall rocks of New England pegmatites. He postulates that the Be was added to the wall rock by solutions emanating laterally from the main channels through which the pegmatitic liquids were flowing.

Very extensive mineralized aureoles have been reported from some districts. In places they may be large enough to include a group of deposits or even an entire mineralized district. These very large aureoles frequently appear in the course of geochemical soil surveys as areas of high local background.

The regionally mineralized aureole is exemplified by the Black-bird cobalt district of central Idaho (Hawkes, 1959). Analysis of soil samples collected at 100-foot intervals along traverses covering a total area of about 8 square miles outlined a well-defined area of some 3 square miles within which the average Co content is 100 ppm as compared to a threshold Co content of approximately 30 ppm, as shown in Figure 4-7. Inasmuch as none of the soil represented in

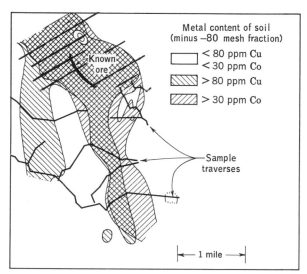

Fig. 4-7. Regional aureole as defined by the copper and cobalt content of residual soil, Blackbird cobalt district, Idaho. After Hawkes (1959). Reprinted with permission from P. H. Abelson, *Researches in Geochemistry*, copyright 1959, John Wiley & Sons, Inc.

this pattern has been transported for any great distance, the 30-ppm Co contour almost certainly reflects a geochemical feature of the unweathered bedrock, in which a large volume of rock has been pervasively mineralized with Co. Within the anomalous area, the principal Co mineral in all the known sulfide deposits is cobaltite ($CoAsS$), whereas outside the area the Co mineral in all but two deposits is cobaltiferous arsenopyrite, which is of no commercial value. Any prospecting for cobaltite deposits thus might profitably be limited to the area enclosed by the 30-ppm Co contour.

A regionally mineralized aureole of even greater dimensions has been observed in Northern Rhodesia, where the Cu and Zn content of soils is considerably higher than background over an area of more than 50 square miles. A number of strong local anomalies, one of which is known to reflect low-grade sulfide mineralization in the bedrock, occur within the areal anomaly (Figure 4-8).

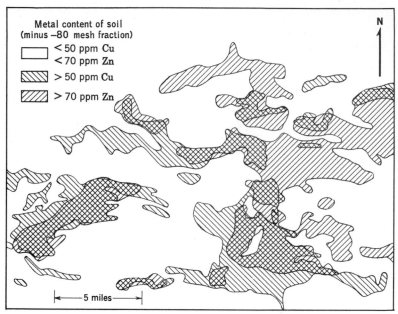

Metal content of soil
(minus −80 mesh fraction)

☐ < 50 ppm Cu
  < 70 ppm Zn

▨ > 50 ppm Cu

▨ > 70 ppm Zn

N

5 miles

Fig. 4-8. Areal geochemical anomaly, Kasempa district, Northern Rhodesia. Near-surface soil sampled at 200-foot intervals on north-south lines 2000 feet apart. Data supplied by Chartered Exploration Ltd.

Leakage Anomalies. Ore-stage material, either in the form of visible minerals or of trace elements that must be determined chemically, may be dispersed in the massive rocks and in fracture zones over blind ore deposits. In the literature of economic geology, dispersion of this kind has been called *leakage*, following the concept that some of the metal has leaked upward from the ore deposit. In some instances, leakage anomalies may represent precipitates from nearly spent mineralizing fluids moving upward after the major part of their metallic load has been left behind. In others, the mineralizing solutions may have been on their way to deposit an orebody that has since been eroded. Leakage anomalies entirely similar to those related to ore, however, may mark the passage of nonproductive hydrothermal solutions that lacked either the opportunity or the potential to deposit large concentrations of metal.

An example of a leakage anomaly is seen in the increase in the Mg:Ca ratio in calcareous rocks over blind ore, as demonstrated by Agnew (1955) in the Gutenberg limestone in the southwestern Wisconsin Pb-Zn district. Fe and S introduced with ore-stage solutions may be precipitated as pyrite in halos overlying ore deposits. Oxidized pyrite gives rise to the bright red color of rocks exposed in the vicinity of many of the porphyry copper deposits.

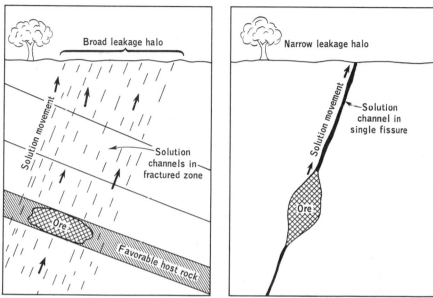

Fig. 4-9. Diagram illustrating relation of ore-solution channels to width of leakage halo.

A halo of pyrite occurs in the flat-lying sedimentary rocks overlying zinc ore in the Shullsburg district of southwestern Wisconsin (Kennedy, 1956). Pb and Zn also occur in the pyritized cap rock, but in such small quantities that their distribution is more easily determined by chemical analysis.

The position of a leakage anomaly with respect to the underlying blind ore deposit will depend on local structural conditions. If the ore structure is vertical, the anomaly may be expected to lie directly above the deposit. On the other hand, an inclined structure is likely to result in an anomaly displaced laterally from the vertical projection of the ore at depth. The shape of leakage patterns also depends on local structural conditions, and ranges from more or less homogeneous impregnations in permeable rocks overlying a deposit to narrower patterns closely related to well-defined fissures (Figure 4-9).

The following examples taken from the literature illustrate some characteristic relations of leakage anomalies to the underlying mineral deposits.

In the Tintic district of Utah, complex Pb-Zn-Ag ore occurs in limestone of Paleozoic age overlain by barren rhyolite that predates the mineralization (Lovering *et al.*, 1948). Surface studies of the rhyolite over known ore have disclosed extensive areas of argillic and pyritic alteration. The alteration halos are so extensive, however, that they are of limited use in guiding diamond-drill exploration. Sampling and chemical analysis of the altered rhyolite disclosed a well-defined heavy-metal anomaly that coincides closely with the up-rake projections of one of the principal ore shoots. Lovering, Sokoloff, and Morris suggest that this anomaly corresponds to the surface trace of the channels through which the nearly spent mineralizing solutions escaped. Even though the rhyolite was not a favorable host for ore deposition, enough metal was deposited along the solution channels to be detectable by trace analysis.

At the Amulet deposit near Noranda, Quebec, Riddell (1950) analyzed rock samples for heavy metal that could be extracted in cold acid. The results outlined a broad area of high metal content in the rock directly overlying two flat-dipping ore bodies. The threshold value was 9 ppm of extractable metal, compared with a background of about 2 ppm. A mineralized alteration halo is also associated with the ore but is not related in any simple way to the geochemical anomaly and is thought to be earlier than the ore.

At Johnson Camp near Willcox, Arizona, Cooper and Huff (1951) have described a broad leakage halo in the fractured rock 400 feet above the concealed Moore ore body. The ore is localized in one bed of a moderately dipping sequence of partly silicated calcareous rocks. Chip samples of rock collected at close intervals across outcrop surfaces were composited in sections of 50 feet or more. The heavy-metal content of samples collected in this manner along a series of traverses showed an anomalous area similar in shape to the horizontal projection of the ore deposit, but displaced about 200 feet to one side (Figure 4-10).

At the Gregory mine, Derbyshire, a Pb and Zn anomaly in shallow residual soil occurs over a vertical fissure vein in limestones situated beneath 700 feet of shales and sandstones, as illustrated in Figure 4-11. The anomaly is absent where the fracturing of the overlying cap rock was not sufficiently extensive to allow the upward migration of the ore solutions.

Leakage patterns may also occur in "barren" veins and fissure zones, where they may indicate the presence of ore shoots at greater depth. For example, in the Parral district of Mexico, Schmitt (1939)

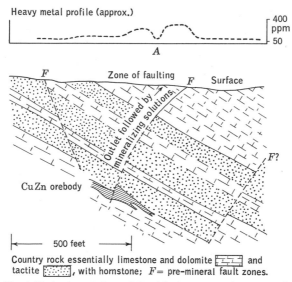

Country rock essentially limestone and dolomite ▦ and tactite ▦, with hornstone; F = pre-mineral fault zones.

Fig. 4-10. Leakage halo as defined by heavy-metal content of rocks exposed at surface, Johnson Camp, Arizona. Based on Figs. 2, 3, and 5 of Cooper and Huff (1951).

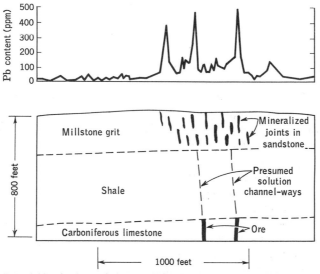

Fig. 4-11. Leakage halo as defined by the lead content of residual soil overlying base-metal deposit at depth of 700 feet, Gregory Mine, Derbyshire. Data on minus-80-mesh fraction. After Webb (1958b).

reports that the distribution of Ag in noncommercial veins can be used as an indication of an ore shoot down the dip of the vein. In the Santa Rita district of New Mexico, Graf and Kerr (1950) found Pb anomalies in Tertiary fault zones that could be correlated with ore bodies in the underlying pre-Tertiary rocks. In the complex sulfide deposits of Kazakhstan, Mukanov (1957) reports high Pb values in "barren" fissures connecting contiguous ore bodies. In the

TABLE 4-5.   Content of Minor Elements in Jasperoid, East Tintic Mountains, Utah

| Element | Content in Jasperoid (ppm) | | |
	Ore Grade (Av. of 11 Samples)	Associated with Ore (Av. of 12 Samples)	Not Related to Ore (Av. of 21 Samples)
Ag	115.3	46.3	1.6
Bi	200	93	40
Ca	2,800	4,100	6,810
Cu	800	730	270
Mn	550	392	1,302
Na	13,700	2,100	1,428
Pb	72,700	4,185	202
Sb	100	55	45
Tl	90	20	—
Zn	103,000	2,300	1,266

Source: Bush and Cook (1960).

East Tintic District, the work of Bush and Cook (1960) has shown that the minor-element content of "productive" jasperoid in the rocks overlying and adjoining ore deposits serves as a simple method of distinguishing it from jasperoid of similar appearance occurring in unmineralized areas (Table 4-5).

Compositional Zoning of Ore.   Mineral zoning as shown by variations in the relative proportions of the principal ore minerals is an ore guide of long standing (Park, 1955, 1957). Variation in the minor-element content of ores, however, is usually less obvious and can be detected only by systematic sampling and chemical analysis. As far as practical application in exploration is concerned, chemical zoning of minor elements is identical with mineral zoning; the only difference lies in the method of gathering the data.

In the Michigan Cu deposits, a regional zoning in the As content of the ore across a horizontal distance of 9 miles was demonstrated by Broderick (1929), as shown in Figure 4-12. In the deposits of massive magnetite of the New Jersey Highlands, James (1954) found that the Cr content of magnetite varies directly with distance from the principal center of mineralization, whereas the V content varies inversely. In the Colorado Plateau uranium fields, the U:V ratio in the ores shows a trend that parallels the known trend of mineralized ground (Miesch, 1954). Brown (1935), working in the Austinville zinc mine in Virginia, reports that the Zn:Pb ratio of the ore increases at faults, on the footwall of the ore, and with depth in the mine.

Compositional zoning of ores on a scale of thousands of feet or a few miles in most cases appears to be largely the effect of differential depletion of certain constituents of the ore-forming fluids with

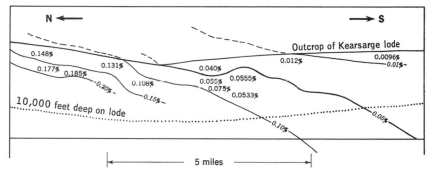

Fig. 4-12. Chemical zoning in native-copper deposits of the Kearsarge Lode, Michigan, as brought out by lines of equal As:Cu ratio. From Broderick (1929).

increasing distance from the source. These variations, where they can be correlated with the direction of flow of the ore solutions, can be useful as guides to the focus of mineralizing activity.

Regional zoning of minor elements in epigenetic sulfide minerals has been described by Burnham (1959). Specimens of carefully cleaned sphalerite and chalcopyrite from 172 deposits of all ages and all types throughout the western United States and northern Mexico were analyzed spectrographically for minor elements. The Sn, Ag, and the combined Co-In-Ni-Ag-Sn content of chalcopyrite and sphalerite apparently defined three broad zones that parallel both regional tectonic features and previously defined metallogenic provinces. Here the author attributes the zonal pattern to regional differences in the chemical composition of deep-seated source materials rather than to variations in the temperature of formation of the ores.

4–3. Pressure-Temperature Effects in Epigenetic Minerals

The epigenetic dispersion patterns discussed in the preceding section are dominated primarily by the composition of the hydro-thermal fluids from which they were precipitated. The effect of temperature and pressure on the character of the material comprising the patterns is secondary, or at most indirect.

Pressure-temperature conditions at the time of deposition may be reflected by the species of mineral and by certain chemical and isotopic relationships that may be observed in coexisting phases. A gradient of temperature or pressure is then indicated by a zonal pattern in the mineralogical, chemical, or isotopic features of the epigenetic minerals. Inasmuch as the influence of pressure is generally very small compared with that of the temperature, it has been commonly assumed that the effects measured are the result of temperature variations alone. For this reason, the mineralogical, compositional, and isotopic indices have come to be called *geothermometers*.

Mineral Reconstitution. Alteration patterns, where the effect of the hydrothermal solution is a reconstitution of the components of the original mineral assemblage in response to a change primarily in pressure, temperature, and the availability of water, have been studied as ore guides in many districts (Sales and Meyer, 1950; Schwartz, 1955). Alteration studies are based on identifying and mapping the distribution of diagnostic secondary minerals, either in hand specimen, under the microscope or by X-ray analysis.

Where the secondary minerals of alteration patterns have been deposited contemporaneously with the ore and at no other time, their distribution may be a direct guide in locating deposits of blind ore. Much of the reconstitution, however, commonly either precedes or follows the deposition of the ore. Furthermore, the solutions responsible for catalyzing the mineral changes may follow a pattern of channel-ways that differs more or less from that followed by the ore-forming solutions themselves. Alteration patterns, therefore, may indicate only general areas of hydrothermal activity and not the exact channel-ways through which ore-stage solutions passed.

Secondary minerals may represent a simple reconstitution of indigenous materials, together with a removal of some of the more mobile elements such as Ca and Na, but with the addition of very little material other than water. Many secondary minerals resulting from the reconstitution of indigenous material are stable only within restricted fields of temperature and pressure. If these temperatures and pressures are also those at which the ore minerals are stable, then the occurrence of certain diagnostic secondary minerals may be helpful in exploration. Thus, in porphyry Cu deposits, the type of alteration where K-feldspar tends to form at the expense of sericite appears to show a strong positive correlation with the higher grades of primary ore.

Chemical Geothermometers. It has been pointed out that the partition of trace elements between any two mineral phases in mutual equilibrium is a function of pressure and temperature at the time of precipitation (Bethke and Barton, 1959). This concept has led to the application of the *sphalerite geothermometer* where the

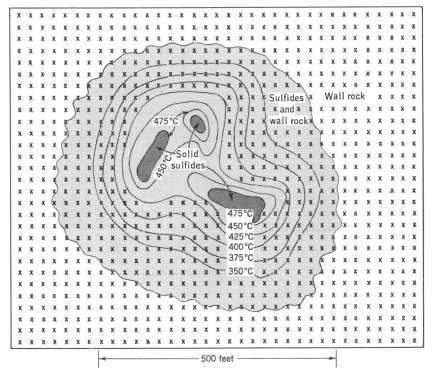

Fig. 4-13. Schematic plan view of the 1500-foot level of the Balmat No. 2 Mine, New York, showing isotherms based on the iron content of sphalerites. From Doe (1956) as reported by Kullerud (1959). Reprinted with permission from P. H. Abelson, *Researches in Geochemistry*, copyright 1959, John Wiley & Sons, Inc.

Fe content of sphalerite formed in equilibrium with pyrrhotite is related to the temperature at which the minerals were formed. Paleotemperatures based on Fe in sphalerite have been determined on specimens from the Balmat Mine in New York State. The results show a systematic variation in temperature outward from a hot center that coincides with ore-grade mineralization, as shown in Figure 4-13.

A similar situation was found in the base-metal deposits of Cornwall and Devon, where Shazly *et al.* (1957) showed that the content of In, Mn, and Sn in sphalerite and of the Bi, Sn, and Ag in galena tended to be higher in the veins that lie nearest to the contacts of granite masses. No attempt was made here to establish a quantitative correlation of trace-element content with temperature.

Isotopic Geothermometer. The site of ore deposition and the channel-ways through which the mineralizing solutions move are commonly hotter than the surrounding rocks. The ratio of the two principal oxygen isotopes, $O^{18}:O^{16}$, in some minerals, varies inversely with the temperature of the solutions from which the minerals were precipitated. Studies of oxygen-isotope ratios in the medium and coarse-grained dolomite of dolomitized Leadville limestone near the Zn deposits at Gilman, Colorado, suggest systematically decreasing temperatures with distance from the ore (Figure 4-14). In cases of this kind, ore should be sought in the direction of decreasing $O^{18}:O^{16}$ ratios in the dolomite.

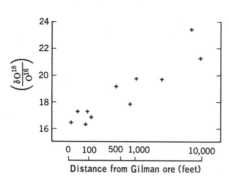

Fig. 4-14. Relationship between oxygen isotope ratios in medium- and coarse-grained hydrothermal dolomite, and distance from ore in the Gilman area, Colorado. $\delta O^{18} = \dfrac{R}{R_{std}} \times 1000$, where $R = O^{18}/O^{16}$ in sample, and $R_{std} = O^{18}/O^{16}$ in standard. After Engel *et al.* (1958).

4–4. Characterization of Primary Ore

Not all mineral deposits are ore bodies. One of the most difficult problems facing the exploration geologist is the decision as to whether a discovery of mineralized rock does or does not have a reasonable likelihood of developing into a commercially profitable ore body. Traditionally, the geologist looks for certain structural and mineralogical criteria that will help him in this decision. For example, "glassy" quartz has been considered an ill omen for gold ore in the Canadian Shield. Quartz monzonite showing a very special kind of "crackling" has been found by experience to be a favorable guide to porphyry Cu ore. In each of these examples, the problem is to determine from the study of a small specimen or from a limited area of outcrop whether the chances are good for the occurrence of a large deposit of ore-grade material.

A few geochemical criteria for characterizing ore have been reported in the literature. In each the evidence suggests that chemical properties of the ore that can be determined by study of a small specimen are diagnostic of the economic potentialities of the occurrence. For example, the concentration of U, Y, Na, Fe, Zr, Mn, Ca, and Ni in sandstone-type U deposits in the Morrison Formation of the Colorado Plateau apparently shows a well-defined statistical correlation with the size of the deposit (Miesch *et al.*, 1960).

Clues to the previous history of elements now occurring in an ore deposit may be preserved in the isotope ratios of those elements. For example, the S in sedimentary sulfide minerals that have been formed by the reduction of sulfates shows a characteristic isotope ratio. The S in sulfide deposits that are the result of mobilization and redeposition of sedimentary sulfides would presumably show the same ratio (Jensen, 1959). The isotope ratios of Pb in sulfide deposits may indicate the relative contributions from radiogenic Pb from the decay of U and Th, as distinguished from normal "rock" Pb. A study in the southeast Missouri Pb district indicates that the Pb of ore deposits is more radiogenic near the central ore channels than at a distance (Eckelmann and Kulp, 1959). No practical applications of these isotopic relationships to exploration have yet been attempted.

4–5. Geochemical Rock-Sampling Surveys

The application of primary geochemical dispersion patterns to mineral exploration is still strictly in the experimental stage, although the results of field surveys in a substantial number of areas have shown that the methods are potentially very powerful.

The study of geochemical provinces shows promise as a method of defining the limits of mineralized districts and in the appraisal of large territories, particularly those that have been little explored or where the geology is poorly exposed. The methods should be especially applicable in the case of deposits that are most likely to be overlooked in reconnaissance by conventional methods, including oxidized Zn ores, Be minerals, and low-grade or finely disseminated deposits of many kinds.

The dimensions of other types of primary dispersion patterns range from several miles down to a few feet. For each one, the field of applicability will depend on the scale at which exploration is being conducted. Local syngenetic patterns, alteration patterns, compositional zoning of ores, isotope patterns and the larger aureoles will be most useful in surveys of mineralized districts to locate small areas that may offer exceptional promise for intensive exploration. Leakage anomalies may assist in determining the pattern of mineralized channel-ways in the vicinity of known ore and in choosing areas for deep drilling for possible blind ore. In the East Tintic District of Utah, for example, experimental studies of leakage patterns, carried out in conjunction with other exploration methods, have contributed materially to the discovery of Pb-Zn-Ag ore. Wall-rock aureoles will probably be most useful in underground mapping and in the appraisal of drill core. Morris (1952) in fact describes an example of a cross-cut ending in limestone where the metal content was well above background. Later extension of the crosscut broke through into a new ore body within 10 feet.

Carefully planned orientation experiments in the vicinity of known ore are virtually mandatory in geochemical rock sampling surveys. Not only the ore but also all the various kinds of primary geochemical patterns that occur in association with the ore of a mining district are subject to the same variables of temperature and pressure at the time of formation, composition of the mineralizing solution, and control by geologic structures or lithology. Therefore, it is virtually impossible to forecast from one mineralized district to another what form the anomalies will take or what sampling and analytical technique will be the most effective. What can be done, however, is to outline in some detail the experimental steps in following through an orientation survey that may assist in establishing an effective technique, if such is possible.

Orientation for reconnaissance rock surveys should include consideration of both syngenetic patterns and broad epigenetic anomalies. In the case of syngenetic patterns, first attention will be given to taking representative spot samples of commonly distributed rocks and minerals which may have a parental relationship with the ore mineralization. Suites of samples, each strictly comparable as regards rock type, weathering, and alteration, are collected from selected mineralized and background areas. In the laboratory, analysis should be carried out on the separated minerals, as well as the bulk rocks. It is advisable to collect, if possible, samples from several areas of known mineralization in order to test the consistency of any apparent relationships that may be disclosed.

Ideally, epigenetic halos and leakage dispersions are investigated by collecting composite chip samples of the cap rock above a known deposit. All rock types are sampled separately and particular note taken of fracturing and major structures. Traverses should extend for a substantial distance on either side of the deposit in order to disclose the full width of the anomaly.

Orientation for leakage dispersion in rocks should also include the systematic collection of rock and fault material at the surface above blind ore bodies and from fracture planes exposed in underground workings. When sampling fault planes, it is advisable to include samples of the adjoining wall rock as well as the gouge or breccia within the fault itself. A water sample should also be collected if there is any active flow.

As in all orientation surveys, comparable samples must be collected in barren areas far removed from mineralization in order to establish the background value for each type of material sampled.

It is essential that the results of orientation for leakage dispersion should be interpreted in terms of the geology in three dimensions and care taken to discriminate wherever possible between primary dispersion and secondary redistribution of metal by percolating meteoric waters. In the latter connection it is very helpful to determine the primary ratio of metals possessing markedly different mobilities in the zone of weathering. Thus, in supergene redistribution patterns, the ratio of Zn (mobile) to Pb (immobile) would be expected to show a marked increase compared to the Zn:Pb ratio in the primary ore.

For wall-rock aureoles, the usual procedure is to take a continuous series of channel or composited chip samples extending away from the deposit into the unweathered country rock. Again, it is extremely important to avoid including more than one rock type in the same sample. Fault or vein material should also be sampled separately. Needless to say, it is essential that the geology of the sample traverse should be logged in complete lithological and structural detail. Samples may conveniently be collected along crosscuts or taken from drill core. The former gives the more complete section, but removal of surficial contamination may be troublesome. Drill core is more convenient for sampling but suffers from the disadvantage that core recovery is rarely 100 percent complete and that structures are more difficult to interpret. The analytical examination should be supplemented by macroscopic and microscopic studies, with particular reference to mineralogical wall-rock alteration.

In many areas, poor exposures will militate against systematic rock sampling at the surface. The primary pattern, whatever its nature, may be reflected in the soil, however, particularly if the overburden is residual.

It is common practice, therefore, to compare the anomalies obtained by rock and soil sampling during the course of orientation. The procedure for examining metal distribution in the soil and the factors that need to be taken into account are similar to those outlined later in connection with detailed soil surveys.

4–6. Gaseous Dispersion Patterns

A few of the components of the earth's crust move at low temperatures as gases through the open pore spaces of rocks and soils, from
which they escape directly into the atmosphere. Free movement
of this kind can occur only above the water table in a pervious
matrix through which the gas can move without hindrance. Near
the surface the flow of gas may be modified by changes in baro-
metric pressure, causing alternating inward and outward movement
or "breathing."

Certain gases may also move in dissolved form in ground or pore
water. Dissolved gas may move either by movement of the free-
flowing ground water itself, or by diffusion through static water
held in the pore spaces of impermeable rocks such as shales.

Gaseous dispersion patterns may be detected by analysis either of
soil air, of gas dissolved in underground water or of gas condensed
in the rocks and soil.

Hydrocarbon Anomalies.   It is claimed that volatile hydrocarbons
may escape from oil reservoirs through the overlying rocks and
pass by way of the soil into the air. This possibility is the basis
for many of the geochemical methods of exploration for petroleum,
where soil or soil air is systematically sampled and analyzed for
traces of certain diagnostic hydrocarbon compounds. Hydrocarbon
anomalies may be thought of as very weak oil or gas seeps, so weak
that the deposition of material at the surface cannot be recognized
without chemical analysis.

Although geochemical methods of locating petroleum are the
subject of a very extensive literature, their general effectiveness is
a matter of considerable difference of opinion among petroleum
geologists. A full discussion of these problems is beyond the scope
of this book. Technical aspects of the subject have been covered in
detail by Kartsev *et al.* (1959).

Radiogenic Gas Anomalies.   The nuclear decay of certain radioactive elements results in the generation of gases. Rn^{222} and He are
produced from the disintegration of U, and Rn^{220} and He from Th.
Similarly, Ar is produced by the radioactive decay of the K^{40} isotope. The natural fission of U yields very small quantities of the
noble gases Kr^{85} and Xe^{133}.

All the gases formed by natural nuclear reactions are members of
the noble-gas group. Being chemically inert, they are not immobilized
by precipitation in the channels through which they travel. Below
the water table, the ground water is under enough hydrostatic
pressure to keep the dissolved gases in solution. At the water table,

the noble-gas content of ground water may enter the vapor phase and become a part of the air in the pore spaces of the rock or soil. Either by movement of the air in the pore spaces or by diffusion through the air, the radiogenic gases may reach the surface where their presence may be detected. Ground water coming to the surface as springs may also contain radiogenic gases brought from depth.

Radon-222 has received more study than any of the other radiogenic gases. This isotope is a member of the U decay series and is derived directly from the disintegration of Ra. Its short half-life of only about four days does not allow enough time for very extensive travel. The presence of Rn in ground water or soil air, therefore, indicates the occurrence of Ra and probably also U in the immediate vicinity. Radon systematically measured in the natural gas fields of the Texas Panhandle led to the discovery of asphaltite containing up to 1.6 percent U (Faul et al., 1954; Pierce et al., 1956).

An intensive investigation was made of the Rn content of spring and stream water in the Wasatch Mountains of Utah (Rogers, 1958). It was found that the Rn content of streams indicated primarily the points of inflow of Rn-bearing ground water. The Rn in the ground water could be accounted for by the decay of background quantities of Ra in the rocks but not by the presence of Ra in solution. In streams the Rn is rapidly lost to the atmosphere through turbulence. In quiet streams half the Rn content of the water was normally lost within a distance of 1000 feet, whereas in turbulent streams the same fraction was lost to the air in a distance of only 100 feet. As a result of this rapid rate of loss to the atmosphere, Rogers concluded that Rn in stream water appears to have greater applications as a means of locating points of ground-water inflow than it has as an ore guide in uranium exploration.

The detection and measurement of Rn requires relatively elaborate equipment that must be set up either in a truck or in a permanent laboratory. Technical difficulties in measuring Rn, together with the limited range of its dispersion seriously restrict the applicability of Rn as an aid in exploration.

Radon-220, the noble-gas member of the Th series, has a half-life of 54 seconds and hence is of little value in exploration. The $He^3:He^4$ ratio in He extracted from rocks, waters, and soils has been suggested as a method of distinguishing radiogenic He containing no He^3 from atmospheric He. The distribution of Kr^{85} and Xe^{133} also has not yet been applied as a guide to U ore (Amiel and Winsberg, 1956).

Radon-220 and Rn-222 both decay to Pb through a series of radioactive products including isotopes of Po, Pb, and Bi. Conceivably, dispersion patterns formed by some of the daughter products of the radioactive noble gases could be detected and used in exploring for U and Th.

Mercury Anomalies. Of the nonradiogenic elements, Hg is the only one whose gaseous dispersion patterns have been given any serious thought as an aid in prospecting.

Liquid Hg has a finite vapor pressure. Native Hg in liquid form occurs as a primary constituent of some hydrothermal ores and as a

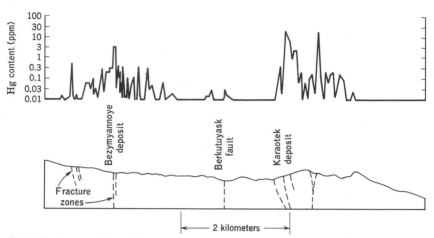

Fig. 4-15. Gas aureole as defined by the mercury content of shallow residual soil near base-metal deposits of the Fergansk Karatau district, U. S. S. R. After Ozerova (1959).

product of oxidation of sulfides, particularly cinnabar and low-temperature, Hg-rich sphalerite and galena. An equilibrium is maintained in the pore spaces of rocks and soils between Hg vapor and liquid Hg condensed on the walls of the pore spaces. In a porous medium that is not saturated with water, Hg vapor will move as a constituent of the air for relatively great distances from the source. The shape of the resulting Hg anomalies depends on the geometry of the fractures and pore spaces that control the movement of the air. Hg vapor, of course, cannot move through impermeable rocks or through permeable material that is saturated with water.

Hg anomalies have most commonly been detected by analysis of bedrock rather than soil. The analytical method used in Soviet work is a special spectrographic technique with a detection limit well below 1 ppm Hg (Sergeyev, 1957).

The only published case histories of the use of Hg anomalies as ore guides are from the Russian literature. At the Khpek mercury mine, Saukov (1946) describes a zone of Hg-rich shale and sandstone 2000 meters wide embracing all the known occurrences of Hg in the local mineralized district. At the Achisai Pb-Zn deposit, Fursov (1958) describes an Hg anomaly derived from the oxidation of Hg-rich sphalerite and galena. High Hg concentrations extend into the fracture zones around and about the ore for distances of as much as 300 meters. The Hg threshold is 0.3 ppm, and anomalous values range up to 27 ppm Hg in samples of rock material taken from fracture zones.

In the Fergansk Karatau district in the mountains of Turkestan, Ozerova (1959) found Hg aureoles 1 to 2 kilometers wide embracing Pb-Zn deposits occurring in zones less than 100 meters wide. The Hg patterns across two deposits in this district are shown in Figure 4-15. Here the Hg content of a composite of 75 ore samples from the Karaotek deposit was 36 ppm and of 226 samples from the Bezymyannoye deposit was 200 ppm. The Hg content of the anomalies is in the order of 0.05 to 0.5 ppm as compared with a background of 0.01 ppm.

Hg aureoles appear to hold very considerable promise as guides to ore. The method might be especially applicable to the location of areas of base- and precious-metal mineralization in poorly exposed desert areas because of deep weathering and low water table.

CHAPTER 5

WEATHERING

The preceding chapter was concerned with geochemical dispersion patterns formed at depth by igneous or metamorphic processes. By uplift and erosion, however, the rocks and minerals typical of the deep zone may be brought into the vastly different environment prevailing near the surface of the lithosphere. This environment is characterized by low temperature and pressure and high concentrations of water, free oxygen, and carbon dioxide. Most of the minerals that are formed under deep-seated conditions are not stable at low pressures and temperatures. When rocks of igneous or metamorphic origin are exposed at the surface, therefore, the original materials tend to be reconstituted to new forms that are stable under the new conditions. The term *weathering* includes all the processes of reconstitution that take place in the near-surface zone.

5–1. Nature of Weathering

As defined by Reiche (1950), weathering is "the response of materials which were in equilibrium within the lithosphere to conditions at or near its contact with the atmosphere, the hydrosphere, and perhaps more importantly, the biosphere." Taking a simpler and more descriptive view, Polynov (1937) considers weathering as "the change of rocks from the massive to the clastic state."

In the most restricted sense of its definition, weathering is only the first phase in the secondary geochemical cycle illustrated in Figure 2-1. It is the phase dominated by the initial physical and chemical changes arising in response to the demand for equilibrium in the surface environment. The process begins with a progressive disintegration and decomposition of rock material *in situ*. The product of this decay is a mixture of resistant primary minerals with a suite of new mineral constituents that are stable in the new environment. Together these form the mantle of unconsolidated material overlying the solid rock known as the *regolith*. At and near the surface, special processes related to the activity of living organisms may bring about differentiation into a sequence of layers, or *horizons*, comprising the soil profile. In this context, soil formation is essentially an integral part of weathering.

At any stage during these processes, the products of weathering and soil formation may be eroded, transported, and redeposited elsewhere. The nature of subsequent physical and chemical changes en route to the site of sedimentation are influenced to a very considerable degree by various transporting or "processing" agents. Thus the dispersion patterns of the products of weathering are conditioned primarily by the flow of water, as it moves through soil, down drainage courses and through the metabolic systems of plants. Depending on their individual properties, the various primary constituents of the parent rocks are liable to part company and be deposited in areas far removed from each other and from their point of origin. Some constituents, indeed, may remain in solution in the waters of the oceans.

The processes of weathering, soil formation, erosion, transportation, and sedimentation together comprise the secondary geochemical cycle. Although these processes are often intimately associated both in their operation and their effect, clarity of presentation requires that they be considered separately. Following their sequence in the geochemical cycle, weathering and soil formation are reviewed first, followed by erosion, transport, and deposition. No attempt is made here to give more than an outline of the basic principles, a general understanding of which is essential for the efficient planning and interpretation of geochemical surveys. Soil formation is treated in rather more detail in a separate chapter, because geologists are generally less familiar with this aspect of the secondary cycle which is of so much importance in geochemical exploration. For further information on weathering and related topics, the reader should consult the selected references given at the end of this and the following two chapters.

5–2. Weathering Processes

Three main types of weathering may be distinguished: physical, chemical, and biological. Physical processes include all those that cause rock disintegration without appreciable chemical or mineralogical changes. Progressive comminution increases the reactive surface area and thus facilitates the decomposition of rocks by reaction with the abundant water, oxygen, and carbon dioxide of the surface environment. Biologic activity contributes either directly or indirectly to both physical and chemical weathering. All these processes may take place side by side, as indeed they usually do, though their relative importance varies according to environment. Thus, in the extremes of arid deserts and arctic conditions and in many areas of mountainous relief, physical disintegration is usually the dominant mechanism of rock decay. Under most other climates, chemical attack is by far the dominant factor in controlling the nature of the weathering products at all depths within the zone of weathering. By contrast, the principal domain of biologic activity is restricted to the near-surface zone of soil formation.

Physical Weathering. The first step in the physical disintegration of massive rock consequent on uplift and erosion is the development of a lacework of cracks and joints. These cracks increase in abundance as the surface is approached.

Simple unloading apparently results in rupture of the rock principally along crystal interfaces. This effect arises from the fact that on release of stress, crystals expand at different rates in different crystal directions so that local concentrations of shear stress build up at the grain boundaries. Expansion and contraction resulting from climatic variations in temperature (insolation) have long been held to have an important effect on the physical disintegration of rocks and minerals at the surface. Quantitative studies show, however, that at least for granite the stresses that develop in this way are appreciably less than the elastic strength of the rock (Griggs, 1936). In consequence, insolation is no longer considered to be as destructive as was formerly supposed. Exposure to the extreme heat of forest fires, however, can bring about appreciable rock disintegration (Blackwelder, 1927); thermal expansion and contraction of this type must be particularly effective in those regions such as are found in many parts of Africa where extensive burning of the vegetation is a periodic, even annual, occurrence.

Once the first cracks are formed in a rock, a number of forces may work together to increase the width of the cracks and thus cause further rupture of the rock. In cold or temperate climates with abundant precipitation, the expansion of water freezing in cracks may have a strong disruptive effect. Of more importance may be the action of frost on some permeable rocks in a manner analogous to the "heaving" of clay and soil (Reiche, 1950). Heaving depends on the growth of large ice crystals where they are fed by a continuous supply of moisture from the underlying unfrozen ground. Under appropriate conditions, the growth of salt crystals from saline solutions occupying cracks and interstices in rocks may also aid disintegration. In this instance, the driving force is believed to be osmosis, which ensures a continuous supply of saline material to the growing crystals (Taber, 1930).

Chemical Weathering. By comparison with physical processes, the chemical agents of weathering are capable of much more powerful attack on rocks and their constituent minerals. In extreme cases the resulting changes in composition, properties, and texture may be such as to obliterate almost completely the original nature of the parent material. Thus, under appropriate conditions, coarsely crystalline silicate rocks can be reduced to an ultra-fine complex of clay minerals; limestones and dolomites may be completely leached

TABLE 5-1. Composition of Some Natural Waters

Constituent	Content in Rain Water (ppm) (1)	Content in Ground Water (ppm)				Content in Thermal Water (ppm) (6)
		(2)	(3)	(4)	(5)	
Ca^{++}	0.1–10	30	40	12	19	4
Mg^{++}	⩾0.1	31	22	6.6	5.1	2
Na^+	⩾0.4 ⎫	279	0.4	7.2	4.4	48
K^+	⩾0.03 ⎭		1.2	3.1	3.2	30
SiO_2	—	13	8.4	38	13	303
HCO_3^-	⩽1.0	445	213	85	39	
SO_4^{--}	2.0	303	4.9	4.4	30	1100
Cl^-	0.5	80	2.0	1.2	5.8	5
Others	0.7	18	6.5	0.7	16	348
Salinity		973	190	115	116	1850

(1) After Hutchinson (1957, p. 551), except HCO_3^- after Gorham (1955).
(2) Well in shale-sandstone formation, New Mexico (Hem, 1959, p. 88).
(3) Spring from dolomite, Tennessee (Hem, 1959, p. 83).
(4) Well in basalt, Washington (Hem, 1959, p. 55).
(5) Well in gneiss, Connecticut (Hem, 1959, p. 114).
(6) Spring, Yellowstone National Park, Wyoming (White and Brannock, 1950).

except for a fractional residuum of insoluble material; and considerable thicknesses of hydrated iron and aluminum oxides (laterite and bauxite) or calcium carbonate (calcrete or caliche) may be developed at the expense of a variety of different rocks.

At all levels and in all environments, chemical weathering depends on the presence of water and the solids and gases dissolved therein. All minerals are more or less soluble even in pure water. The presence of dissolved oxygen, carbon dioxide, and humic complexes greatly increases the corroding power of natural solutions. Rain water contains small but significant quantities of dissolved oxygen and carbon dioxide, together with chlorides and sulfates derived from the ocean and man's domestic and industrial activities. Percolation through the soil adds humic compounds, further carbon dioxide, and many other products of organic origin. Ground waters can acquire diverse new constituents liberated from the rocks undergoing decomposition or by mixing with thermal waters rising from the depths (Table 5-1).

The chemical processes which take place during weathering are many and complex. The principal types of reaction include hydration and hydrolysis, oxidation, the action of acids, dissolution, colloid formation, and exchange reactions. These processes rarely work separately. As a rule, two or more complement one another, reacting simultaneously in a variable combination.

Hydration (absorption of water) and *hydrolysis* (absorption of OH^- and H^+ ions) are commonly regarded as the most important chemical reactions involved in rock decomposition. Apart from figuring prominently in the decomposition of many rock-forming silicates, these reactions also promote ionization and colloid formation, thereby opening the way for other reactions and further changes in composition. Hydration implies the incorporation of water molecules into the crystal lattice of the mineral. A simple illustrative example is the transformation of anhydrite, $CaSO_4$, to gypsum, $CaSO_4 \cdot 2H_2O$. Of greater importance in rock weathering is the absorption of water by primary silicates preparatory to their hydrolysis. Hydrolysis of silicates results in the production of complex silicic and aluminosilicic colloids. Cations released by this reaction may be removed in solution or may be adsorbed on the colloid phase. The adsorbed ions are then available for subsequent reaction and exchange with the constituents of passing solutions. Although hydrolytic decomposition can take place in pure water, the reaction is intensified in the presence of natural acids, of which the most common is carbonic acid. Hydrolysis is an exothermic reaction and is attended by an increase in volume. The stress that results is one of the principal factors in the disintegration of rocks, and its effect may extend to appreciable depths from surface, far below the effective range of most of the purely physical agents of disintegration.

Exchange reactions almost invariably accompany and succeed hydration and hydrolysis, cooperating with them in the progressive chemical breakdown of minerals. These reactions arise from the selective adsorption on solid-particle surfaces of ions present in the surrounding aqueous phase. As a result, ions are exchanged and removed from the outer layers of crystalline material and, even more importantly, from the colloidal products of hydrolysis. The nature of the exchange is dependent on a number of factors, notably the kind of cations or anions present and their concentrations, the mineral or colloid concerned, and the pH of the solutions.

The *hydrogen-ion concentration* exerts a particularly powerful effect on the course of weathering. Hydrogen ions readily replace other cations, thereby affecting the products of the exchange reactions which lead to the formation of clay minerals. One of the most important sources of hydrogen ions in natural waters is carbonic acid, which dissociates more readily than water. In this way, the common presence of dissolved CO_2 greatly stimulates mineral decomposition through its control on pH. Other acids exert a similar effect, as for example the sulfuric acid released by the oxidation of sulfide minerals. Of more general importance are acid clays, common in humid regions, in which a high proportion of the exchange positions are occupied by H ions. Hydrogen-clays are highly reactive, and in many systems behave much like simple dissolved acids. Graham (1941) has demonstrated that many of the common rock-forming silicates can be attacked directly by colloidal clay acids.

Oxidation reactions are characteristic of the aerated environment of the weathering zone. The presence of water is probably essential for active oxidation by gaseous oxygen. Optimum conditions naturally occur in the moist ground above the zone of permanent saturation. In places, however, descending oxygenated waters can extend oxidation to depths far below the water table. The common hypogene minerals most affected by oxidation are those which contain Fe^{++} or Mn^{++}, where decomposition in the presence of oxygen and water result in the formation of the higher-valency oxides or hydroxides.

Biologic Agents in Weathering. Strictly speaking, all biologic weathering is, in effect, only a phase of physical and chemical weathering. Separate consideration of biologic agents is merited, however, in order to emphasize their importance in rock decomposition and soil formation.

Plants contribute to the physical weathering of rocks by widening the cracks into which they insinuate their roots. A vast amount of near-surface material may be mixed and sorted by worms, termites, and rodents. The resulting disaggregation and increased permeability facilitate the entry of air and water, thereby promoting more intense chemical weathering.

The chemical activity of biologic agents is far more important than their contribution to physical weathering. The local conditions of extreme acidity generated at the root tips of plants can act as a powerful corrosive force in the chemical breakdown of rocks. Computations based on the silica content of tropical vegetation show that the rate at which plants remove silica from silicate minerals is adequate to account for a large part of the observed high mobility of silica in tropical weathering (Lovering, 1959). Plant respiration is a major factor in the biochemical cycle of oxygen and carbon dioxide, which are two of the most important reagents in chemical weathering. Plant tissue is the basic raw material of a series of organic compounds which contribute directly to many chemical reactions. Bacteria and fungi are primarily responsible for the complex organic oxidation reactions which result in the progressive breakdown of plant debris to soluble humic compounds and ultimately to carbon dioxide and water. The activity of soil bacteria also produces organic acids, nitric acid, ammonia, hydrogen, oxygen and other compounds which take part in chemical weathering processes.

Biologic activity is essentially confined to the soil, but through solution and colloidal dispersion, the products of decomposition can contribute materially to reactions in the deeper zones of weathering.

5–3. Factors Affecting Weathering Processes

The processes just outlined operate over the entire land surface and throughout a wide variety of environments. Although the processes are basically the same everywhere, local environmental conditions can have a considerable influence on the rate and type of weathering and the nature of the end products. The principal factors that condition the processes of weathering are: (1) the resistance to weathering of the primary rock-forming minerals, (2) climate, with particular reference to temperature and rainfall, and (3) topographic relief and drainage.

Increasing stability		
Olivine	Calcic plagioclase
Augite	Calc–alkalic plagioclase
Hornblende	Alkali–calcic plagioclase
Biotite	Alkalic plagioclase
Potash feldspar	
Muscovite	
Quartz	

Fig. 5-1. Relative stability of common rock-forming silicates in chemical weathering. After Goldich (1938).

Resistance of Minerals in Weathering. Mineral species differ widely in their resistance to weathering processes. Goldich (1938) has summarized the relative resistance to weathering of the common rock-forming silicates (Figure 5-1). His arrangement is essentially the same as Bowen's reaction series, which sets out the order of progressive reaction during the course of magmatic crystallization (Bowen, 1922). Goldich's series indicates that the minerals that crystallized at the highest temperatures, under the most anhydrous conditions, are more readily weathered than those that crystallized last from the lower-temperature, more aqueous magmas. As a general rule, the closer the conditions of crystallization approximate those now prevailing at the earth's surface, the more resistant is the mineral in the weathering environment. The Goldich stability series also applies to the same minerals when they are of metamorphic origin.

Fieldes and Swindale (1954) have presented a scheme to show how primary minerals change to successive secondary minerals with increasing weathering. In Figure 5-2, the primary minerals are listed in order of increasing resistance to weathering as in Goldich's

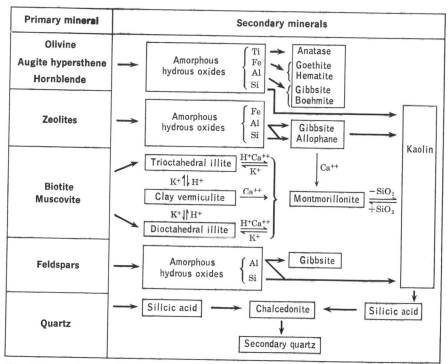

Fig. 5-2. Weathering of primary rock-forming minerals. After Fieldes and Swindale (1954).

weathering sequence, but the secondary minerals have been arranged to indicate their relation to the minerals from which they originate.

It is important to appreciate that the relative durability of hypogene minerals in the weathering cycle depends not only on their chemical susceptibility, as listed above, but also on their grain size. This arises from the fact that the weathering process is dominated by surface reactions and that the specific surface (surface per unit volume) of mineral grains is inversely proportional to the diameter. Thus, a relatively more resistant but fine-grained mineral may decompose more rapidly in weathering than a less resistant coarse-grained mineral. An example of this effect is seen in glacial clay made up of rock flour in which the potash feldspars are commonly altered to clay minerals, whereas in moraine of the same age the coarse-grained ferromagnesian minerals may still be relatively fresh.

The weathering of sedimentary rocks poses additional problems, for the bulk of many such rocks may be composed of secondary material generated during earlier cycles of weathering. During the course of simple diagenesis these products of previous weathering cycles may have suffered relatively little metamorphism and re-constitution. The chemical response of such material on returning

TABLE 5-2. Weathering Sequence for Clay-Size Minerals in Soils and Sedimentary Deposits

	Weathering Stage	Clay-Size Minerals Characteristic of Different Stages in the Weathering Sequence
Increasing Stability	1	Gypsum (halite, etc.)
	2	Calcite (dolomite, aragonite, etc.)
	3	Olivine-hornblende (diopside, etc.)
	4	Biotite (glauconite, chlorite, etc.)
	5	Albite (anorthite, microcline, etc.)
	6	Quartz
	7	Illite (muscovite, sericite, etc.)
	8	Intermediate hydrous micas
	9	Montmorillonite
	10	Kaolinite (halloysite)
	11	Gibbsite (boehmite, etc.)
	12	Hematite (goethite, limonite, etc.)
	13	Anatase (rutile, ilmenite, etc.)

Source: Jackson et al. (1948). Reproduced with permission of the American Chemical Society.

to the zone of weathering may be very slight compared with that of the minerals of more highly metamorphosed rocks. The principal mineral constituents of sedimentary rocks are the clay minerals, hydromicas, chlorites, quartz, and calcium-magnesium carbonates. Kaolin, montmorillonites, chloritic material, and hydromicas are usually ultra-fine-grained and readily susceptible to such rehydra-tion, hydrolysis, and leaching of cations as may be necessary to restore them to equilibrium with the new environment. The resulting chemical changes may well be small, however. Carbonates are prone to solution under practically all conditions in the zone of weathering. Quartz, providing it is coarse grained, remains relatively resistant. Table 5-2 gives the weathering sequence for clay-size minerals in soils and sedimentary deposits as worked out by Jackson et al. (1948, 1952).

The relative resistance to weathering of the constituent minerals of ore deposits is naturally a matter of prime importance in the development of geochemical anomalies. Generally speaking, the order of increasing susceptibility to decomposition by weathering appears to be oxides < silicates < carbonates and sulfides. Sulfide minerals are particularly vulnerable to oxidation and solution. The oxidation of pyrite and marcasite results in the formation of free sulfuric acid and ferric sulfate. In the resulting strongly acid environment, the gangue minerals and silicates of the wall rocks are attacked at a rate far in excess of that in a nonsulfide environment. The presence of abundant carbonate or other alkaline constituents in the gangue or wall rock naturally results in more rapid neutralization of the acid than is the case in a dominantly silicic environment.

An important factor in the oxidation of sulfides is the electrochemical reaction which develops in aggregates consisting of more than one electrically conducting sulfide (Gottschalk and Buehler, 1912). In these circumstances the oxidation of one mineral is favored over that of others. Thus, in a deposit consisting of chalcopyrite and pyrite, the chalcopyrite is oxidized preferentially to the pyrite. Some sulfides, notably pyrite, can show considerable variations in stability, apparently related to structural and compositional disorders in their crystal lattices. Other primary sulfides, galena for example, may be transformed on weathering to insoluble secondary minerals which coat the primary sulfides and thereby impede further alteration. A compact stable gangue can also provide a measure of protection for unstable minerals imbedded within it.

In both normal rocks and ore deposits the intensity of weathering is affected considerably by the texture and permeability of the mineral assemblage. Coarsely granular rocks are often more susceptible to decomposition than fine-grained compact material. In general, the effects of oxidation and leaching of disseminated sulfides are more pervasive in grits than in shales. Weathering often extends to greater depths within an epigenetic mineral deposit than in the enclosing rock, in part because vein structures commonly provide preferential channel-ways for circulating waters and in part because of the effect of the acid generated by the oxidation of sulfide minerals. Fracturing on both the macro- and micro-scale usually results in a marked increase in the intensity and depth of chemical decomposition. Moreover, the selective removal of soluble carbonates and sulfides provides further access for weathering solutions. Primary wall-rock alteration alongside mineral deposits is frequently attended by an increase in porosity, though silicification usually renders a rock more resistant to weathering.

Climate. The principal climatic elements that bear on weathering are rainfall and temperature. Rainfall controls the amount of water

84   GEOCHEMISTRY IN MINERAL EXPLORATION

available for chemical weathering, while temperature influences the rate of chemical reactions and, in particular, the rate of decomposition of organic matter. Temperature affects the availability of water by increasing evaporation at high temperatures or by freezing at low temperatures. Climate also controls the amount and type of vegetation which in turn provides the raw material for organic reagents. Chemical weathering is generally most intense in tropical areas of high rainfall and uniformly high temperature. The intensity of weathering is somewhat less in temperate climates of moderate rainfall and seasonal variations in temperature. An example of the contrast between the products of chemical weathering of dolerite in tropical and in temperate climates is given in Table 5-3. Under

TABLE 5-3.   Changes in Chemical Weathering in Temperate and Tropical Zones

| Constituent | Dolerite Staffordshire, England | | Dolerite Bombay, India | |
	Content in Fresh Rock (%)	Content in Overlying Clay (%)	Content in Fresh Rock (%)	Content in Overlying Laterite (%)
SiO_2	49.3	47.0	50.4	0.7
Al_2O_3	17.4	18.5	22.2	50.5
Fe_2O_3	2.7	14.6	9.9	23.4
FeO	8.3		3.6	
MgO	4.7	5.2	1.5	
CaO	8.7	1.5	8.4	
Na_2O	4.0	0.3	0.9	
K_2O	1.8	2.5	1.8	
H_2O	2.9	7.2	0.9	25.0
TiO_2	0.4	1.8	0.9	0.4
P_2O_5	0.2	0.7		
Total	100.4	99.3	100.5	100.0

Source: Warth (1905).

arid and arctic conditions, chemical weathering is at a minimum, and physical processes are dominant. As a result of the extremes of aridity in some desert climates, corrosion by wind-borne sand may be an important factor in physical weathering.

Relief and Drainage.   In very mountainous terrain, physical erosion may cause the rock debris to be removed faster than it can be decomposed chemically. Chemical weathering here is confined largely to decomposition of eroded fragments as they are carried away first by soil creep and subsequently by stream waters. Moderate to strong relief is commonly associated with extreme variability in the depth to the water table. In these areas, chemical decomposition is most active beneath the crests of ridges, where the water table tends to lie at maximum depth below the surface. A shallow water table and near-surface zones of permanent saturation are usually limited to the immediate vicinity of springs and drainage channels. The circulation of ground-water solutions is most vigorous in the areas between the ridge crests and the drainage channels.

Flat-lying terrain, by contrast, is characterized by less active erosion and by relatively sluggish ground-water movement. Swamp conditions are common where the precipitation is sufficient to maintain a high water table. Under such conditions, the low rate of erosion inevitably leads to the slowing down of rock decomposition until eventually equilibrium is approached and the weathering process comes to a virtual standstill.

5–4. Products of Weathering

The secondary geochemical anomalies on which most geochemical prospecting is based are composed of the weathering products of ores, superimposed upon the weathering products of the normal unmineralized rocks in which the ore occurs. The products of weathering of both rocks and ores take three forms: residual primary minerals, secondary minerals stable in the weathering environment, and soluble material that can be removed by circulating waters.

Residual Primary Minerals. In the zone of weathering where pressure and temperature are low and where water, carbon dioxide, and free oxygen are abundant, the only rock-forming minerals that are commonly stable are certain clay minerals, hydromicas, quartz, and possibly some chlorites. Most common igneous and metamorphic minerals are unstable and survive only because of their slow rate of inversion to stable forms. In practice, the weathering process rarely achieves equilibrium, as witnessed by the fact that rock-forming minerals in all stages of decomposition occur as common components of residual products of weathering. The more resistant mineral species naturally persist longest, with the result that the most common primary constituents of residual soils are muscovite and the heavy accessory minerals, such as magnetite, ilmenite, and rutile.

Of the ore minerals, gold, platinum, cassiterite, columbite-tantalite, chromite, and beryl are the most common representatives of the residual primary category. Minerals that are reasonably resistant chemically may yet be too friable or soft to withstand physical abrasion. Thus wolframite, scheelite, and barite tend to persist in the regolith as residual products of weathering but are quickly destroyed by abrasion during erosion and transport.

Secondary Minerals. Primary rock-forming silicate minerals on weathering tend to undergo both leaching and hydrolysis to form a characteristic suite of secondary minerals. This suite includes primarily the clay minerals and hydrous oxides of Fe and Al. In addition to products developed strictly *in situ*, new substances may be formed by the coagulation of colloids and by precipitation from solutions of local origin, such as some near-surface accumulations of hydrous iron oxide, amorphous silica, and calcium carbonate. Almost all the secondary products are extremely fine grained, the characteristic particle size being less than 0.02 millimeter.

Clay minerals are essentially hydrous silicates of Al, Fe, and Mg. They are classified on the basis of their physical properties and lattice structure into three main groups, namely kaolinites, montmorillonites, and illites or hydrous micas; other clays of less general importance are halloysite (a member of the kaolinite group), chlorite and vermiculite, palygorskite and allophane. Some of the properties of clay minerals, particularly their base-exchange capacity, are of great importance in the development of geochemical dispersion patterns.

Kaolinites are composed of hydrated aluminum silicate with a silica-alumina ratio of 2:1, the formula being expressed as $(OH)_8$-$Al_4Si_4O_{10}$. Their formation is favored by an acid environment, with free drainage, leading to the thorough leaching of bases. They develop most readily, therefore, in relatively humid climates where rainfall exceeds evaporation and where downward percolation and lateral movement of underground water is active. Kaolinite is the commonest clay mineral in the zone of weathering.

In montmorillonite, theoretically $(OH)_4Si_8Al_4O_{20}nH_2O$, Mg and Fe partly replace Al, and the silica-alumina ratio is 4 : 1. In contrast to kaolinite, the development of montmorillonite is favored by neutral to alkaline conditions and by the incomplete leaching of bases. The bases may be retained within the system as the result of either impeded drainage or excessive evaporation. Montmorillonites are, therefore, typical end products of weathering in waterlogged ground or in semiarid climates. Characteristically, all members of this group have the property of expanding considerably on wetting and thereby assist in maintaining a poorly drained environment. A high concentration of available Fe and Mg is naturally a strong predisposing factor in the formation of montmorillonite. Even in freely drained ground, montmorillonite may be a transient intermediate product in the course of the decay of the ferromagnesian constituents of mafic rocks to kaolinite. When drainage conditions change and leaching becomes effective, montmorillonite may alter to kaolinite.

The illites, also known as hydrous micas, contain potassium as an essential constituent in addition to magnesium, iron, alumina, and silica, the structural formula being $(OH)_4K_y(Al_4 \cdot Fe_4 \cdot Mg_4 \cdot Mg_6)(Si_{8-y} \cdot Al_y)O_{20}$. Illite, although typically developed in deep sea sediments, also forms on land under appropriate conditions. The environment of its formation is probably much the same as that described for montmorillonite, providing there is, in addition, an adequate supply of potash. Where leaching is incomplete, illite can be expected among the products of weathering derived from feldspar-rich igneous and metamorphic rocks. It may also occur as a residual mineral derived from the decomposition of argillaceous and calcareous sediments. Under conditions of free drainage and humid environment illite is subject to degradation by leaching.

Halloysite and metahalloysite are chemically similar to kaolinite but possess a very different form. Although they are characteristic of certain tropical soils, they are not otherwise common among the products of weathering. Vermiculite and chlorite share a degree of structural and chemical similarity with montmorillonite. Magnesia enters more into their composition, however, and in consequence these minerals commonly occur in the weathering products of mafic rocks. Allophane is the name given to poorly crystalline or amorphous clay-mineral material regardless of its composition. Such material has been noted in soils, but nothing is known concerning its mode of origin.

The hydrous oxides of iron and aluminum are widely distributed among the products of weathering. The most important representatives of this group are limonite ($Fe_2O_3 \cdot nH_2O$), turgite ($2Fe_2O_3 \cdot H_2O$), goethite ($Fe_2O_3 \cdot H_2O$), diaspore ($Al_2O_3 \cdot H_2O$), and gibbsite ($Al_2O_3 \cdot 3H_2O$). Most limonite is probably a mixture of goethite and hematite (Fe_2O_3). Iron not required for clay formation is precipitated as a hydrated ferric oxide, particularly in an oxidizing environment. Under reducing conditions, however, ferrous iron is liable to be removed in solution. Aluminum hydroxide may develop directly from mafic and intermediate rocks. Both hydrous Fe and Al oxides attain their maximum development under humid tropical climates. Here, given adequate drainage and leaching, they can be the ultimate solid end products of weathering. Their accumulation may give rise to deposits of massive laterite and, under appropriate conditions, bauxite. The widespread occurrence of hydrous oxides, including those of Mn as well as Fe and Al, is important in connection with the geochemical dispersion of the many elements which are absorbed or coprecipitated by them.

Ores on weathering yield a characteristic suite of secondary minerals, including not only hydrous iron oxides but a host of secondary metalliferous minerals. Unlike clay minerals, many of

these are visibly crystalline and are not so readily dispersed. Different
secondary minerals of the same metal may be formed under a variety
of chemical conditions, thereby leading to a great diversity of mineral
species. Thus, under certain conditions of Eh, pH, CO_2 pressure,
Cu concentration, etc., malachite is the principal product of weathering, whereas under other conditions, chrysocolla, cuprite, antlerite,
atacamite, or tenorite is dominant.

Residual hydrous Fe oxide derived from the oxidation of Fe-
bearing sulfides and carbonates has long been of significance in
mineral exploration. In the massive form, accumulations of hydrous
Fe oxide are known as gossan. Gossans are formed most commonly
from the weathering of pyrite, marcasite, pyrrhotite, copper-iron
sulfides, arsenopyrite, siderite, and ankerite. The mineralogy of
gossans derived from a dominantly sulfide ore is limited to species
that are stable in contact with acid sulfate solutions. Later, as active
oxidation recedes from the surface, percolating waters of more
normal composition in which bicarbonate is usually the predominant
anion may bring about further changes in composition. In all gossans,
regardless of whether they were derived from sulfide or carbonate
ores, the predominant minerals are limonite, quartz, and secondary
silica. Depending on the parent material and the maturity of the
gossan, other minerals may occur as accessory constituents, including a wide variety of sulfates, arsenates, carbonates, silicates,
and many other secondary metalliferous salts; clays derived from
vein silicates or incorporated country rock may also be present.

Not all of the metallic constituents of the ore that are dissolved
in the course of weathering necessarily escape in ground and surface
waters. Appreciable amounts may be absorbed or coprecipitated
with the ubiquitous hydrous Fe oxides. Examples have been reported
where the limonitic material of gossans contains up to several percent
of Zn derived in this manner from sphalerite associated with the
primary ore. The metal content of gossans and their significance
in prospecting are considered more fully in a later chapter.

Soluble Products.   The soluble products of weathering consist of
those constituents that are released by the decomposition of primary
minerals and that are not required in the formation of insoluble
secondary minerals. Analyses of ground and surface waters show
that much of this material is removed in solution from the site of
weathering (Table 5-1). In the general case, the soluble constituents
reflect the composition of the parent rocks. Ca^{++}, Mg^{++} and CO_3^{--}
are naturally the principal soluble products derived from the weathering of calcareous rocks. In contrast, siliceous rocks yield alkalis,
alkaline earths, and excess colloidal silica resulting from hydrolysis

of the primary silicates. The proportions of these constituents vary according to the felsic or mafic nature of the parent material. For example, Ca and Mg predominate in the case of mafic rocks, while granites, felsic schists and argillaceous sediments yield higher proportions of K and Na. In general, Ca is more liable to be removed than is Mg, which may be strongly adsorbed by clays or incorporated in the structure of montmorillonite or chlorites. Potassium may be retained to a certain extent in illites, whereas Na tends to remain almost entirely in solution. Iron and Mn are appreciably soluble only under reducing conditions, although ferric hydroxide may in part be removed in stabilized colloidal solution.

Insofar as the solid products of weathering are controlled by climate and relief, so these factors will also modify the nature of the soluble products. Thus, in arid climates, soluble salts may be precipitated by evaporation; under humid tropical conditions silica is rendered relatively mobile, and ultimately all but the hydrous oxides tend to be removed in solution. Relief, through its relationship with drainage, influences the solubility and removal of many metals. For example, under conditions of impeded drainage such as occur where ground water comes to the surface in topographically low situations, montmorillonite may form, thereby retarding the solution of Fe and Mg and favoring the retention of other cations by adsorption on the clay mineral.

Ores on weathering similarly yield soluble products that can escape from the immediate environment of the source if they are not trapped during the precipitation of secondary minerals. The relations here are more complex than in the case of the weathering products of silicate rocks because of the more diverse mineralogy and the more complex stability fields of the secondary minerals that make up the soluble end products. Many of the latter minerals are stable only in the presence of relatively concentrated solutions of the component elements. Consequently, if ground-water circulation is at all active, a substantial proportion of the metals will leave the site of oxidation in soluble form (Table 5-4). The many physical and chemical factors affecting the solubility of trace elements in the zone of weathering are considered in following chapters.

Residual Structures and Textures.   Most igneous and siliceous sedimentary and metamorphic rocks do not usually appear to change greatly in volume as a result of weathering. Traces of bedding, foliation, and vein structures in the bedrock can often be traced well up into the residuum even after the most intense weathering. The texture of the original rock itself may also be preserved, despite the fact that alteration of the unstable primary minerals is essentially complete and the entire rock rendered loose and friable. Ruxton (1958), however, has demonstrated that under certain conditions appreciable compaction may take place as a result of subsurface erosion. The removal of carbonates from calcareous rocks results in a very substantial reduction in volume, and the resultant slumping causes partial or total obliteration of the original rock structures.

TABLE 5-4.   Composition of Ground Water
Draining Sulfide Ore Deposits

Element	Content in Water (ppm)	
	(1)	(2)
Ca	68	260
Mg	41	49
Na	23	13
K	20	3.2
SiO$_2$	56	23
Al	433	12
Fe	2178	143
Cu	312	
Zn	200	345
SO$_4$	6600	1650
Cl	0.1	3.7
Salinity	9990	2500

(1) Burra-Barra Mine, Ducktown, Tennessee.
(2) Victor Mine, Joplin district, Missouri (data from Emmons, 1917).

In extreme cases, pure limestone and saline deposits may be completely removed by solution. In the upper layers of residual overburden, relic structures have been almost invariably destroyed by physical disturbance accompanying soil creep, frost heaving, and biologic activity. Compaction following eluviation of clays in soil formation is another common contributory factor in the eradication of relic structures.

The weathering of ore deposits composed predominantly of carbonate or sulfide minerals may be accompanied by cavitation and slumping. In contrast, a resistant quartz gangue favors the preservation of vein structures. Relic textures inherited from both of these types of primary ore material, however, are commonly preserved in limonite inherited from weathering sulfide and carbonate minerals. These cellular "box-work" pseudomorphs, as they are called, have received special study as a means of identifying the specific parent minerals originally present in the primary ore (McKinstry, 1948, pp. 268–276).

SELECTED REFERENCES ON WEATHERING

General reviews	Polynov (1937)
	Reiche (1950)
	Keller (1957)
Clay mineralogy	Grim (1953)

CHAPTER 6

SOIL FORMATION

In the simplest terms, soil is the upper, layered part of the regolith. To the pedologist soil is "a natural body of mineral and organic constituents, differentiated into horizons, of variable depth, which differs from the material below in morphology, physical make-up, chemical properties and composition, and biological characteristics" (Joffe, 1949, p. 41). As emphasized by Jenny (1941), the unique characteristic of soil lies in the organization of its constituents and properties into layers that are related to the present-day surface and that change vertically with depth. This is in direct contrast to the character of the parent material from which the soil is formed. Biologic activity figures prominently in soil-forming processes, and most soils are more or less fertile in that they can support plant growth to an extent far greater than the parent material. During weathering, rock decomposition and soil formation merge indistinguishably into one another. As a rule, they proceed simultaneously, the former paving the way for the latter. From this point of view, soil formation can be considered as an advanced stage of weathering.

It is perhaps surprising that geologists in general have little understanding of the soils which mantle so much of the land surface, since any information that can be gained from soils concerning the bedrock geology must be of value. Furthermore, the secondary dispersion of metals can be profoundly influenced by soil-forming processes. Consequently, an appreciation of soils and their formation is even more necessary in geochemical prospecting. In this book it is possible only to consider briefly the more important soils and soil-forming processes relevant to mineral exploration technique. For further information the reader should consult the selected references listed at the end of the chapter.

6–1. Soil Profile Development

As previously stated, soils are characteristically organized into layers differing from each other and from the underlying parent

material in their properties and composition (Figure 6-1). Apart
from differences in color and texture which aid recognition in the
field, the properties of greatest significance that affect geochemical
dispersion of the elements are pH, organic-matter content, clay-
mineral type and assemblage, and the amount of sesquioxides.
The individual layers are referred to as soil horizons and may range
from a few inches to several feet in thickness. Taken together, these

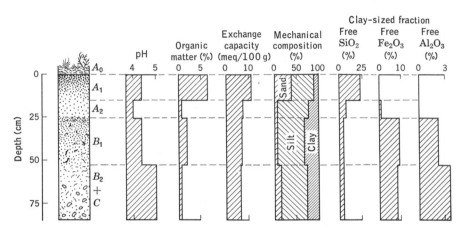

Fig. 6-1. Some variations in the physical and chemical properties of the different horizons
comprising a soil profile. Based on data for a tropical podzol by Hardon (1936).

horizons comprise the soil profile. In general terms, profile development is synonymous with soil formation. It is primarily the result
of vertical (upward and downward) movement of material in solution
and suspension, accompanied by a complex series of chemical
reactions, many of which are organic in origin. Water is the essential
medium in which this transfer and reconstitution takes place.

Soil profiles vary in make-up within wide limits according to
their genetic and geographic environment. Most profiles, however,
comprise three principal horizons. From the surface downward
these are identified by the letters A, B, and C. The A and B horizons
together constitute the solum, or "true soil," while the C horizon
is the parent material from which the solum has been derived by
soil-forming processes. A hypothetical soil profile is shown diagrammatically in Figure 6-2.

The entire sequence need not always be represented. For instance,
immature soils frequently lack a B horizon, or erosion may lead to
truncated profiles sometimes to the extent of exposing the C horizon.
When studied in detail, each of the principal horizons may be
further subdivided. These subdivisions are identified by subscript

numbers thus: A_1, A_2, B_1, B_2, B_3, and so on. Recognition of these subdivisions, apart from the A_1 and A_2 horizons, is usually unnecessary in geochemical prospecting. The distribution of metals may vary markedly with major changes down the profile, however, and it is therefore important to distinguish the master horizons and to recognize immature and truncated profiles when these are encountered.

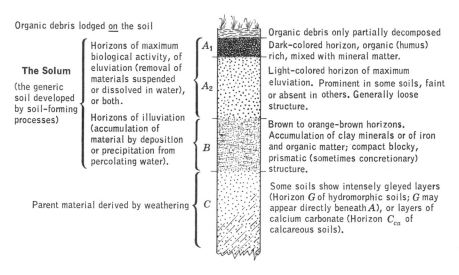

Fig. 6-2. Hypothetical soil profile showing the principal horizons.

The A horizon develops primarily as the result of partial losses in original material by leaching and mechanical removal, or *eluviation*, resulting from the percolation of rain water downward through the soil. The principal constituents likely to be removed are soluble bases, clays and colloidal sesquioxides and/or silica. Resistant primary minerals, rock material undergoing decomposition and flocculated colloids tend to remain. The A horizon is also characterized by intense biological activity. The accumulation and bacteriological decay of plant debris are responsible for the two main subdivisions of the A horizon into a dark upper layer containing humus, the A_1 horizon, and an underlying light-colored horizon of maximum eluviation, designated A_2. The relative thicknesses of these two horizons vary considerably according to the supply of organic debris, the rate at which it is decomposed, the effectiveness of leaching and eluviation, and the age of the profile. Both A_1 and A_2 can generally be discerned in mature profiles developed under moist climates, although the A_2 may be absent in dry regions or in young soils.

Under moist conditions and free drainage, the more soluble constituents leached from the A horizon will descend to the water table and eventually pass into the surface drainage. Some suspended matter may follow the same course. More usually, however, colloidal sesquioxides and clays eluviated from the A horizon are soon redeposited in the zone of accumulation, or *illuviation*, constituting the B horizon. As a result, the B horizon characteristically tends to be enriched in clay relative to the A horizon and to assume a red- or yellow-brown color in those profiles where illuviation also involves iron sesquioxide. Under appropriate conditions, the B horizon may also gain organic matter at the expense of the A horizon. In many soils, however, organic matter is likely to be completely broken down in the A horizon to carbon dioxide and water. In some profiles, the B horizon may also gain material by precipitation of soluble matter derived from underlying horizons by ground-water circulation.

The C horizon consists of more or less weathered rock and serves as the parent material of the overlying A and B horizons. It is important to appreciate that the parent material may be rock *in situ*, transported alluvial or glacial overburden, or even soil of a past pedological cycle. As a rule, inorganic decomposition extends deeper than soil formation, and the C horizon can often be subdivided into zones of weathering that decrease in intensity with depth. Organic matter is at a minimum in the C horizon, which usually contains less clay and is lighter in color than the B horizon. Relic rock structures and textures are also more commonly preserved than in the overlying horizons.

The development of a soil profile can be viewed as taking place in two stages, first by preparation of the parent material and, secondly, by differentiation into horizons. Usually the two processes proceed simultaneously. The onset of soil formation is generally marked by the appearance of a faint A horizon, which grows at the expense of the C horizon. Often a B horizon cannot be distinguished until the A horizon is distinct, although both may form together. In general, therefore, immature soils may be recognized by an ill-defined profile in which the B horizon is weak or absent. Truncated profiles may be more difficult to detect, particularly where a new, youthful profile is in the process of developing at the expense of an exposed deep horizon of the old profile.

The importance of the soil profile in geochemical prospecting will be readily appreciated from the foregoing paragraphs. Metals indigenous to the parent material vary in their response during the development of the soil horizons. Soluble metals and those incorporated or adsorbed on clays and colloids are liable to be removed from the A horizon, whereas those contained in resistant primary minerals are liable to be enriched in that horizon. Metals taken up by deep-rooted plants will be returned to the surface in the organic debris, and their subsequent fate will depend on the stability of their organic compounds in the A_1 horizon. Some of the metals which are removed from the A horizon may tend to accumulate along with hydrous Fe and Mn oxides or clays in the B horizon. A striking example of metal distribution in a latosol profile developed over granite bedrock is shown in Figure 6-3.

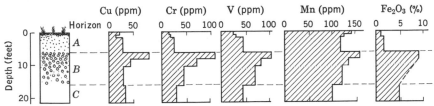

Fig. 6-3. Variation in metal content with soil horizon, latosol profile, Northern Rhodesia. Alkalis increase with depth; cobalt and nickel show little change. Data on minus-80-mesh fraction. Sampling by J. S. Tooms; analyses by J. D. Kerbyson, Geochemical Prospecting Research Centre.

6–2. Factors Affecting Soil Formation

In nature, soil profiles may differ widely from the necessarily idealized picture conveyed in the preceding paragraphs. Their diversity arises from the fact that the direction and rate of horizon differentiation are governed by no less than five major factors, namely, parent material, relief, climate, biological activity, and time.

Parent Material. The parent rock contributes the raw material of the soil and might therefore be expected to be a dominant factor in controlling the nature of the resultant soil. Owing to the interplay of the other factors, however, this supposition lacks generality. Comparisons made on a continental basis show poor correlation between soil type and geology. The composition and properties of the parent rock can, however, have a general influence on the rate at which weathering and soil formation take place. Thus, soils are developed more rapidly from permeable or readily decomposed rocks than from those which are relatively impermeable or resistant to decay. In certain circumstances, the influence of the parent rock may be more positively discerned. The first is where the change from parent material to soil has not been profound, a condition that is found in desert and arctic regions, or in young residual soils such as those which occur in mountainous terrain. The second is where the soils have been degraded to a greater or less extent by erosion. Geologic features may also be reflected in residual soil in regions of relatively uniform climate and constancy of other soil-forming factors. On the grand scale, however, climate appears to be more potent than geology in determining soil type. Fortunately, even under conditions of the deepest weathering and diversity of soil type, it is often possible to detect variations in the underlying rocks,

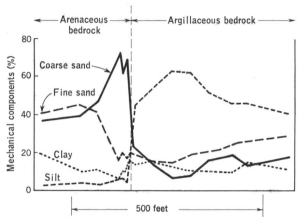

Fig. 6-4. Influence of bedrock on mechanical composition of the A-horizon soil, Mutupa, Northern Rhodesia. After Govett (1958).

providing the overburden is residual. Thus, characteristic assemblages of resistant minerals and the mechanical composition of the soil may be diagnostic of certain parental rock types (Figure 6-4). The original concentration of bases may influence the clay mineral assemblage. Furthermore, the relative concentrations of trace elements in the soil may also provide a clue as to the bedrock geology (Figure 6-5). This latter approach is, of course, the basis of geochemical soil surveys.

Climate. The significance of temperature and rainfall in rock decomposition has already been mentioned. These two climatic elements are also of the utmost importance in soil formation. It has long been recognized that vastly different soils may develop from similar parent materials according to the climatic environment. In general terms, the soils of humid regions tend to be the more thoroughly leached and to possess iron-rich B horizons. Arid climates, on the other hand, militate against the formation of well-eluviated A horizons, while calcareous soils are characteristic of semiarid, warm regions.

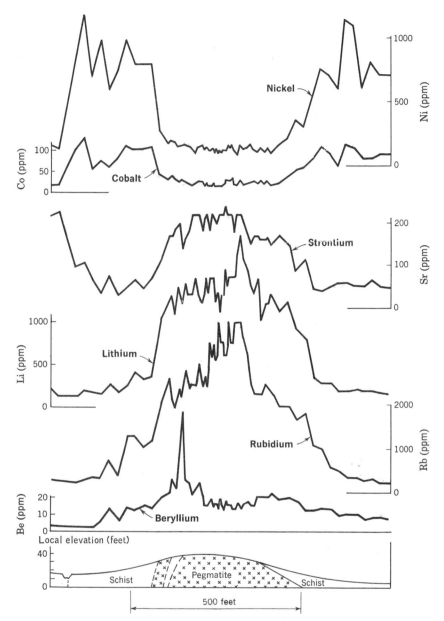

Fig. 6-5. Relationship between minor elements in residual soil and bedrock geology, Bepe pegmatite vein, Southern Rhodesia. Data on minus-80-mesh fraction. Spectrographic analysis by J. D. Kerbyson, Geochemical Prospecting Research Center.

The interrelations between rainfall and temperature govern the precipitation-evaporation ratio. This not only affects the amount of water and the depth to which it may percolate through the soil but also the direction of movement. A high ratio of precipitation to evaporation favors downward percolation, whereas a low ratio favors rise of soil moisture from the underlying water table. Where the rainfall is markedly seasonal, the direction of soil-water movement may reverse periodically during the course of the year. Upward movement of water above the capillary fringe has been shown to be possible (Marshall, 1959). Precipitation of alkali and other soluble salts by evaporation thus may be a feature of soil formation under the influence of relatively dry climates. Less soluble colloid materials may likewise rise toward the surface and coagulate to form a concretionary horizon near the upper level reached by the

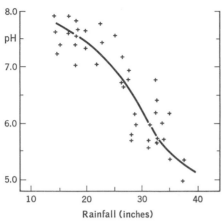

Fig. 6-6. Effect of rainfall on soil pH. After Jenny (1941). By permission from *Factors of Soil Formation* by Hans Jenny. Copyright 1941. McGraw-Hill Book Company, Inc.

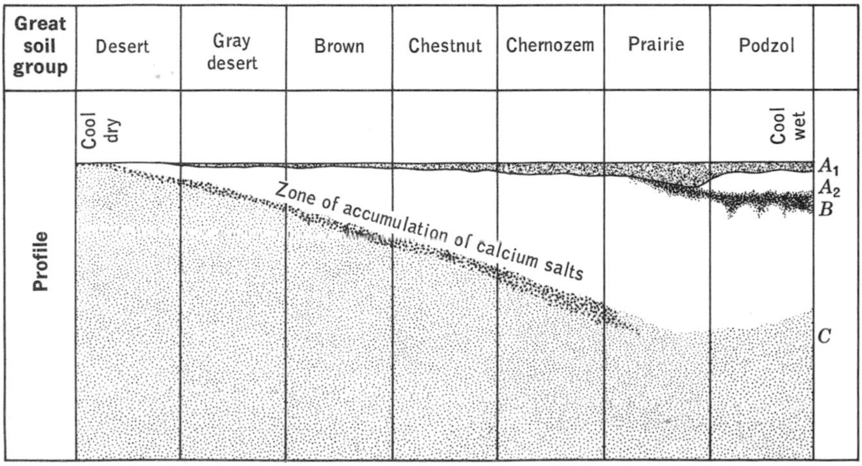

Great soil group	Desert	Gray desert	Brown	Chestnut	Chernozem	Prairie	Podzol	
Profile	Cool dry						Cool wet	A_1 A_2 B
		Zone of accumulation of calcium salts						C

Fig. 6-7. Influence of climate on concentration of organic material and carbonate in soil profiles. Reprinted with permission from C. E. Millar, L. M. Turk, and H. D. Foth, *Fundamentals of Soil Science*, copyright 1958, John Wiley & Sons, Inc.

water table. Colloidal silica and the sesquioxides are the outstanding materials to accumulate in this way. As a result of incomplete leaching, the soils of arid and semiarid areas tend to be alkaline, and thus favor the formation of high base-exchange clays. Neutral or acid soils with low base-exchange clays are more typical of humid regions.

In addition to their other properties, the soil types characteristic of different climates may differ widely in pH, clay-mineral assemblage and content of lime, iron, and organic matter, all of which affect metal dispersion (Figures 6-6 and 6-7). Indirectly, therefore, climate has a bearing on the choice of the optimum geochemical techniques in different parts of the world.

Biologic Activity. The biologic factor in soil formation is largely a function of vegetation, although microorganisms play an important part in decomposing plant debris and in determining the fate of organic matter in the soil. The amount and kind of vegetation, its

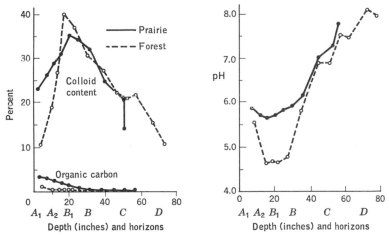

Fig. 6-8. Effect of vegetation on soil properties. After Jenny (1941). By permission from *Factors of Soil Formation* by Hans Jenny. Copyright 1941. McGraw-Hill Book Company, Inc.

decay products, and microorganisms are in turn related to climate. In general terms, the drier the climate the less vegetation there is available to produce soil organic matter, and the higher the temperature the more rapidly and more completely is organic matter decomposed. In desert regions, sparse organic matter is quickly oxidized at the surface, and little or none ever descends into the body of the soil. In cool, humid climates, abundant plant debris may provide much humus and active organic acids. In hot moist conditions, on the other hand, organic matter will tend to decompose rapidly to carbon dioxide and water, although under dense vegetation a high content of organic matter may be maintained in the upper horizons. Different types of vegetation yield different organic decay products which, in turn, affect profile development and soil properties (Figure 6-8). Deep-rooted plants offset leaching to some extent by taking up elements which are returned to the surface soil when the plant dies or sheds its leaves. Plants also affect the all-important moisture regime in the soil by transpiration and by decreasing evaporation. Moreover, vegetation tends to protect soils from erosion and to limit disturbance by soil creep, thereby favoring the development of soil horizons. On the other hand, horizon differentiation may be retarded when the soil is mixed by root and animal activity.

Saline soils developed behind levee
River flanked by levees
Temporary wet-season water table

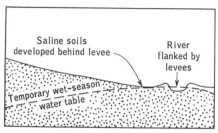

Fig. 6-9. Development of saline soils under the influence of ground water in an arid climate. After Jenny (1950). Reprinted with permission from P. D. Trask, *Applied Sedimentation*, copyright 1950, John Wiley & Sons, Inc.

Relief. Topographic relief influences soil formation through its relationships with groundwater levels, drainage, and erosion. Even in regions of high rainfall, well-developed A and B horizons can form only where there is free drainage and effective leaching. Such profiles develop most readily, therefore, on the interfluves in

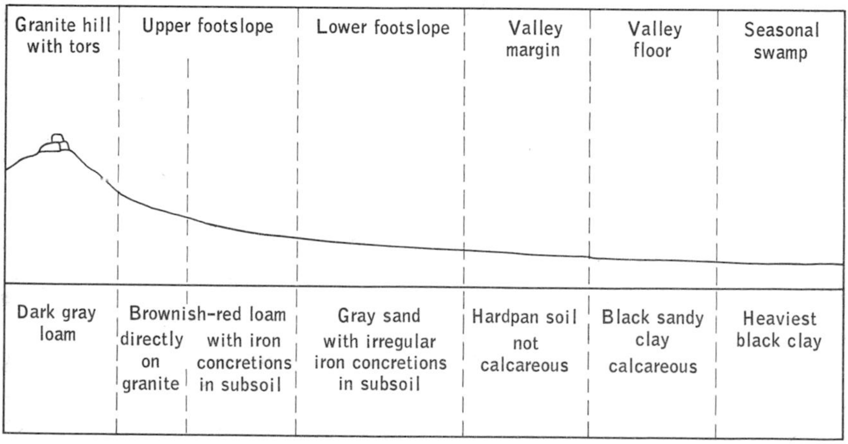

Granite hill with tors
Upper footslope
Lower footslope
Valley margin
Valley floor
Seasonal swamp
Dark gray loam
Brownish-red loam
directly on granite
with iron concretions in subsoil
Gray sand with irregular iron concretions in subsoil
Hardpan soil not calcareous
Black sandy clay calcareous
Heaviest black clay

Fig. 6-10. A soil catena or repetitive sequence of soil types dependent on slope and drainage. After Milne (1936) as quoted by Clarke (1938).

undulating country. In low-lying areas, the terrain may be saturated with water, almost to the surface. In such circumstances, a very different profile may develop, often consisting of an organic-rich surface layer, overlying a pallid or mottled subsoil, in which reducing conditions prevail and leaching is at a minimum. If water stands at the surface, peat may form. In semiarid regions, a temporary water table may exist alongside rivers in the wet season and induce the formation of saline profiles behind the levee where the water table lies near the surface (Figure 6-9).

Changes from one drainage condition to another are usually transitional and give rise to a related sequence of profile types which constitute a *soil catena* (Figure 6-10).

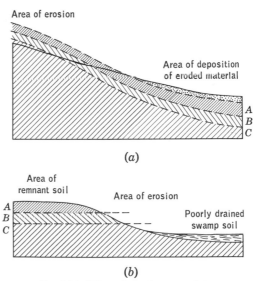

(a)

(b)

Fig. 6-11. Effect of erosion on soil type.

The angle of slope affects drainage and erosion. In general, there is more rapid erosion, a greater volume of surface runoff and less percolation on steep slopes than on gentle ones. Consequently, soils on steep slopes tend to be shallower and show less distinct horizon development and a higher content of stony material than those on gentler slopes. In some areas, an increased rate of erosion may result in truncated profiles on the upper slopes, accompanied by burial of the original profile at lower topographic levels (Figure 6-11a). In other areas, truncated profiles may occur on the lower slopes (Figure 6-11b). In areas of very high relief, the elevation determines the local climate, with the result that soil types characteristic of the different climates occur in topographically controlled patterns (Figure 6-12).

Time. Generally speaking, the accumulation of parent material by weathering takes longer than its differentiation into soil horizons. Given a moderate humidity and free drainage, faint A horizons may become apparent in weathering parent material after some decades. The development of a distinct B horizon normally needs a much greater length of time, often measured in centuries or even tens of

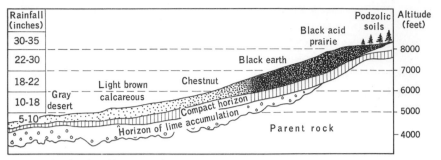

N.B. Scale of soil profiles is greatly exaggerated

Fig. 6-12. Gradation of soil types from desert to humid mountain top, west slope of Big Horns, Wyoming. After Thorp (1931).

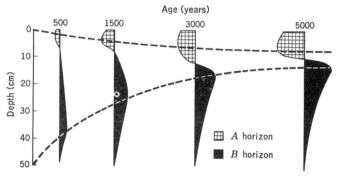

Fig. 6-13. Formation of A and B horizons of a podzol profile as a function of age. Jenny (1941). By permission from *Factors of Soil Formation* by Hans Jenny. Copyright 1941. McGraw-Hill Book Company, Inc.

thousands of years (Figure 6-13). Soils are sometimes classified as juvenile or mature according to their state of development with respect to the present-day surface. Where erosion is active, soils will necessarily remain in a juvenile condition irrespective of time. If the time factor is adequate, and erosion proceeds no faster than soil formation, a mature profile will eventually result.

6–3. Principal Soil Groups and Their Geographic Distribution

The great diversity of possible soil environments is reflected in the range of different soil types that may be encountered. For present purposes it is only necessary to consider the more important groups of similar soil type which, by virtue of their characteristic geneses

TABLE 6-1.   A Classification of Soils into Orders, Suborders, and Great Soil Groups

Order	Suborder	Great Soil Groups
Zonal soils	1. Soils of the cold zone	Tundra
	2. Light-colored podzolized soils of timbered regions	Podzol soils Brown podzolic soils Gray-brown podzolic soils Red-yellow podzolic soils Gray podzolic or gray wooded soils
	3. Soils of forested warm-temperate and tropical regions	A variety of latosols are recognized. They await detailed classification
	4. Soils of the forest-grassland transition	Degraded chernozem soils Noncalcic brown or Shantung brown soils
	5. Dark-colored soils of semiarid, subhumid, and humid grasslands	Prairie soils (semipodzolic) Reddish prairie soils Chernozem soils Chestnut soils Reddish chestnut soils
	6. Light-colored soils of arid regions	Brown soils Reddish-brown soils Sierozem soils Desert soils Red desert soils
Intrazonal soils	1. Hydromorphic soils of marshes, swamps, flats, and seepage areas	Humic-gley soils (includes wiesenboden) Alpine meadow soils Bog soils Half bog soils Low humic-gley soils Planosols Ground-water podzols Ground-water latosols
	2. Halomorphic (saline and alkali) soils of imperfectly drained arid regions; littoral deposits	Solonchak (or saline soils) Solonetz soils (alkali soils) Soloth soils
	3. Calcimorphic soils	Brown forest soils (Braunerde) Rendzina soils
Azonal soils	(No suborders)	Lithosols Regosols (includes dry sands) Alluvial

Source: Lyons et al. (1952).

and properties, may have a considerable bearing on secondary metal dispersion.

Soils have been classified under three main headings as zonal, intrazonal, and azonal. In *zonal soils*, which comprise the great soil groups of the world, climate and vegetation are the dominant factors controlling soil type. *Intrazonal soils*, on the other hand, are those that reflect the dominating influence of some local factor other than climate. Under conditions of impeded drainage, for example, soils from different climatic belts may possess many features in common

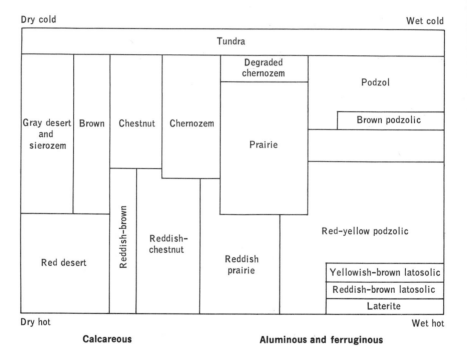

Fig. 6-14. Classification of soils in relation to climate. Reprinted with permission from C. E. Millar, L. M. Turk, and H. D. Foth, *Fundamentals of Soil Science*, copyright 1958, John Wiley & Sons, Inc.

and resemble each other more closely than the great soil group characteristic of the zone in which they occur. The third class, *azonal soils*, are characterized by little or no differentiation of the parent material because of their youthfulness. Mountain soils and soils developing on recent alluvium are typical examples of this class.

The principal soil groups and the relationship between zonal soils and climate are given in Table 6-1 and Figure 6-14 respectively. Figure 6-15 depicts their global distribution in greatly simplified

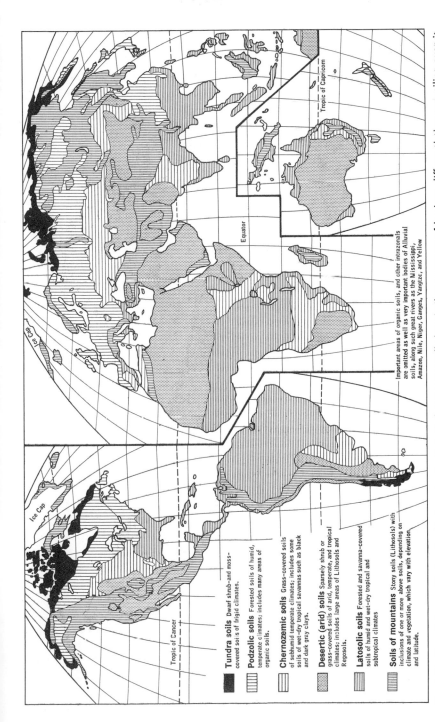

Tundra soils Dwarf shrub- and moss-covered soils of frigid climates.

Podzolic soils Forested soils of humid, temperate climates; includes many areas of organic soils.

Chernozemic soils Grass-covered soils of subhumid temperate climates; includes some soils of wet–dry tropical savannas such as black and dark grey clays.

Desertic (arid) soils Sparsely shrub or grass-covered soils of arid, temperate, and tropical climates; includes large areas of Lithosols and Regosols.

Latosolic soils Forested and savanna-covered soils of humid and wet–dry tropical and subtropical climates

Soils of mountains Stony soils (Lithosols) with inclusions of one or more above soils, depending on climate and vegetation, which vary with elevation, and latitude.

Important areas of organic soils, and other intrazonals are omitted as well as very important bodies of Alluvial soils, along such great rivers as the Mississippi, Amazon, Nile, Niger, Ganges, Yangtze, and Yellow

Fig. 6-15. Map of the world, showing six broad soil zones. Each zone generally has similar processes of horizon differentiation prevailing over it. From Simonson (1957).

form. In each of the broad belts other groups are usually present to complicate the pattern. Figure 6-16 shows idealized profiles of some of these soil groups.

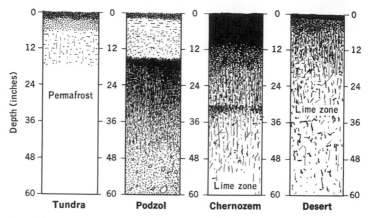

Fig. 6-16. Idealized profiles of four zonal soils. From Winters and Simonson (1951).

6–4. Soils of Humid Regions

The humid zone is characterized by an annual rainfall greater than about 25 inches. Vegetation ranges from forest and grasses in temperate and tropical regions to low order plants and shrubs in the colder belts. Mature soils are generally characterized by an accumulation of sesquioxides in some part of the profile and the absence of calcareous horizons.

Tundra Soils. The cold climate restricts biological activity, and in parts of the tundra region the subsoil may remain permanently frozen (permafrost). Where the ground is well drained, thin indistinct profiles similar to those of podzols may develop. Frozen subsoil conditions are usually accompanied by poor drainage. Where this prevails for much of the year, the soil is then characterized by an accumulation of peaty matter at the surface, overlying a bluish-gray compact subsoil. Soils of this type are extensively developed, often on parent material of glacial origin, in latitudes north of 60° N.

Podzols and Podzolic Soils. The authors are indebted to Alexander Muir for the following brief description of these soils. The two groups occur in humid temperate regions under free drainage. They are associated with forest cover, the podzol with coniferous trees and the podzolic soils with mixed or broadleaved forest. Both derive their name from the Russian (Old Russian *pod* = soil and *zola* = ashes) on account of the presence of a subsurface gray A_2 horizon, which may be almost white in the podzol. The inherent distinction between the two groups is based on the nature of this horizon and the presence or absence of an A_1 horizon.

In both groups the first stage in development is presumably loss of bases with concomitant or subsequent translocation of clay and free sesquioxides to enrich and give stronger color to the succeeding B horizon. In the podzolic soils this movement is effected without any appreciable decomposition of the clay minerals, the bleached appearance of the A_2 horizon being due solely to the relative increase in quartz. There is also invariably present a clearly defined darker A_1 horizon. In podzols, on the other hand, active decomposition of clay takes place in the A_2 horizon with the result that there is a marked difference in the clay composition of the A_2 and B horizons. An A_1 horizon is absent in a well-developed podzol. It is possible that the difference between the two groups is in part due to the nature of the organic matter from the two types of forest and its relative *base* status since the podzolic soils under mixed or broadleaved forest commonly have a higher pH in the A horizon than podzols under conifers or heathland.

By virtue of the intense leaching in the A horizon, metal dispersion patterns are commonly sought in the underlying B horizon. As a rule, this horizon is encountered within 12 to 24 inches of surface and is, therefore, conveniently situated for most prospecting purposes. It is possible that the distribution of some metals during soil formation may vary according to whether the profile is that of a podzol or of a podzolic soil. Lead is a case in point where marked surface enrichment has been noted under deciduous cover but not where the vegetation is coniferous (Webb, 1958b).

Latosolic Soils. These soils are characteristic of moist tropical and subtropical regions. Forest or savannah vegetation, a high temperature, and seasonal rainfall provide the most favorable conditions for their development. Free drainage in the upper part of the soil is essential. Although varying considerably in detail, latosols are typified by deep weathering, extremely thorough leaching and, commonly, a marked accumulation of sesquioxides. The iron oxide is responsible for the prevalent red-brown and yellow colors of these soils. Kaolinite or halloysite or both are the typical clay minerals, and many latosols are well described as "ferruginous kaolins" (A. Muir, personal communication). In general, the A_1 horizon is not strongly developed, and some profiles may be a uniform reddish brown with no distinct textural variation. Other profiles show a well-defined, yellow or brown A_2 horizon overlying a compact red B horizon, enriched in sesquioxides, which commonly exhibits a concretionary texture. The top of the B horizon is often marked by an accumulation of rounded to subangular quartz pebbles, constituting a "stone line." Below the B horizon the transition to a lighter-colored C horizon is marked by fewer concretions and a red mottling which decreases with depth. The parent material is often strongly bleached in the lower part. In mature latosols the individual horizons may attain thicknesses of several feet, and profiles exceeding 10 feet in depth are common.

In many respects there is a considerable measure of similarity between latosols on the one hand and podzols on the other. They are both strongly leached and show accumulation of sesquioxides somewhere in the profile. The basic differences appear to lie mainly in the intensity of weathering rather than any difference in the processes involved. Under tropical temperatures, decomposition of aluminosilicates proceeds faster, and there is a higher turnover of organic matter than is the case in more temperate climates. Under such conditions the surface soil may contain considerable amounts of aluminosilicate clays, but silica is removed fast enough, particularly from the subsoil, for accumulations of sesquioxides readily to be built up. Particular attention has been given to these accumulations in latosolic soils to which the name "laterite" has been given. This name arose from the time-honored use of this material for building construction in tropical countries (Latin, *later* = brick). Some laterites have also been used as low-grade iron ore. At the other extreme, similar accumulations rich in the alumina component of laterites constitute the important bauxitic ores of aluminum.

The origin of laterite and bauxite is controversial, and there is a voluminous literature on the subject (Prescott and Pendleton, 1952, and bibliographies listed at the end of the chapter). Most students are agreed that ground-water movement usually plays an essential part. There seems little doubt that active laterization takes place near the upper level attained by the seasonally fluctuating water table. Some of the sesquioxides may be leached from the A_2 horizon if it is present (see above). The common presence of a bleached pallid zone near the lowest point reached by the water table supports the contention that iron is leached in depth and precipitated on oxidation in the capillary fringe immediately above the water table proper. For this reason, the maximum accumulation of iron in the B horizon occurs near the highest level reached by the ground waters. Mottling in the zone of water-table fluctuation reflects the periodic oxidation to which this zone is subjected during the course of the year. Appreciable thicknesses of laterite may be built up if the general water-table level slowly falls over an appreciable period of time. For this reason, peneplains provide an ideal topographic condition under which laterites may attain their maximum development. When fresh, laterite is relatively soft, but on exposure to air it dehydrates and generally becomes hard and compact. The indurated material is strongly resistant to erosion, and in this respect contrasts sharply with the A horizon, which is usually loose and unconsolidated. Most of the extensive exposures of hard, lateritic "duricrust" in parts of Africa, India, and elsewhere probably represent the truncated remnants of an earlier profile that developed when the water table was at a shallower depth than at present.

Not all laterites are formed as a result of horizon differentiation. It is important also to recognize those that are formed by deposition from ground-water seepages, sometimes involving the cementation of fragmented primary laterites. Latosols of this origin more commonly occur on slopes and lower topographic levels than the primary or "high-level" laterite.

Intrazonal Hydromorphic Soils. In the present context the most important intrazonal modifications are those resulting from impeded drainage. Lack of aeration is mainly responsible for the characteristic profile developed in waterlogged soils. Although they naturally occur more frequently in humid regions, they may also develop under comparatively dry climates. Their common distinguishing features are: a grayish to black surface horizon grading sharply into a pale, bluish-gray subsoil often with rusty streaks, mottling, or concretions. The necessary waterlogged condition may arise in the presence of a shallow water table or impeded drainage due to an impervious subsurface layer. For this reason, ground-water or hydromorphic soils, as they are called, are often developed in depressions and areas of ground-water seepage. Here the entire profile is commonly subjected to alternate oxidation and reduction as the shallow water table rises and falls according to the season of the year. Plant growth is restricted to shallow-rooted species, commonly grasses, appropriate to the local climate. Breakdown of humus is retarded when the ground is waterlogged, and consequently organic matter tends to accumulate in the surface horizon, even under tropical climates. In cooler regions these soils pass into peat soils with increasing accumulation of organic debris. Predominantly reducing conditions are reflected in the pallid, bluish-gray colors of the subsoil where iron tends to remain in the ferrous state; such horizons are known as *gley* horizons. Rusty mottling and iron concretions testify to some oxidation in the zone of ground-water fluctuation near the surface. In drier climates calcareous nodules may be deposited in the subsoil. As a rule, leaching is restricted by a sluggish flow of water which is dominantly in a lateral direction. Under these conditions clay minerals of the montmorillonite type tend to develop. Where organic acids are developed in quantity, however, kaolinitic clays will predominate. Mohr has drawn attention to the rapidity with which parent material may be kaolinized beneath some tropical swamps where the pH may be as low as 3.0.

If water stands at the surface for much of the year, thick deposits of partially decayed organic matter may accumulate. Peat soils of this type are more common in temperate and cool climates and cover extensive areas in northern Europe and America. Peats can also occur in the tropics, as for example in mangrove swamps.

As already mentioned, impeded drainage in the surface soil may result from the presence of an impervious horizon. Thus, hydromorphic soils can develop at times over basic rock, such as norite, the weathering of which may produce an abundance of clay. Or, the parent material itself may be clay-rich and impermeable, and for this reason waterlogged soils are common on glacial overburden in northern latitudes. An impervious layer may also be developed by the extreme accumulation of clay in the B horizon of an originally well-drained profile. Profiles containing a thoroughly eluviated A horizon overlying a compact, poorly permeable B horizon are called *planosols*.

It should perhaps be mentioned that although tundra soils are essentially hydromorphic in that they owe their characteristic features, in part at least, to impeded drainage arising from a frozen subsoil, they are usually regarded as zonal soils since their distribution is dependent on a regional climatic control.

6–5. Soils of Subhumid and Arid Regions

The zonal aridic soils form in areas with an annual rainfall that is generally less than about 30 inches. A thin forest cover may be present in the wetter parts, but more commonly the vegetation, if any, includes certain shrubs, grasses, and desert plants appropriate to local conditions. In the absence of a plentiful supply of water, chemical weathering and leaching are restricted. Most profiles are characterized by the development of calcareous horizons. In others there may be little or no horizon differentiation or, indeed, any breakdown of the primary rock-forming minerals.

Chernozems and Black Tropical Clay Soils. Chernozems and analogous soils are developed in temperate and tropical regions under a rainfall ranging from approximately 15 to 30 inches. Typically, the profile consists of a dark A horizon overlying lighter-colored parent material. The B horizon is usually indistinct. Concretions and earthy accumulations of calcium carbonate are commonly present below the A horizon. In temperate zones the A_1 horizon is high in organic matter but is less so in the tropics.

By virtue of the low rainfall, leaching and eluviation of clay is not so marked as in the soils of humid regions. Nevertheless, some material is dissolved in the A horizon and may be reprecipitated, mostly as carbonate, in the lower horizons. The typical accumulations of calcium carbonate are mostly formed in this way. The depth to the upper limit of the calcareous horizon increases with annual rainfall (Figure 6-17). The lower limit of this horizon usually indicates the maximum depth to which rain water percolates before being dissipated by evaporation or by transpiration by plants.

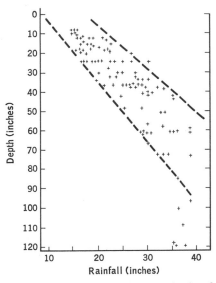

Fig. 6-17. Relationship between depth of lime accumulation and rainfall. From Jenny (1941). By permission from *Factors of Soil Formation* by Hans Jenny. Copyright 1941. McGraw-Hill Book Company, Inc.

In contrast to the foregoing, carbonates may also accumulate in the soil by evaporation of ground-water solutions in the capillary fringe immediately above the water table. Given a slowly falling ground-water level, the calcareous horizon may then attain a very considerable thickness. Accumulations of indurated calcium carbonate are often known as *caliche* or *calcrete*.

Other things being equal, calcareous horizons can form only on terraces and interfluves providing the underlying rock is lime-bearing. Under the influence of a shallow water table, however, the soil of semiarid regions may contain calcium carbonate irrespective of the nature of the immediate underlying parent material.

Chernozems are usually neutral or slightly alkaline in reaction, whereas the tropical analogues are more strongly alkaline and tend to be richer in montmorillonitic clays. The high pH and high base-exchange capacity of the soil are not conducive as a rule to the ready dispersion of soluble ore metals.

Desert Soils. Every gradation exists between the chernozemic soils of semiarid regions and the soils of truly arid deserts. Extreme shortage of moisture greatly restricts weathering, leaching, and plant growth. As a result, desert soils usually possess indistinct shallow profiles. Organic matter is invariably low, and the predominant soil color is gray or reddish. There may be some loss of carbonate from the A horizon and a slight accumulation of clay in the B horizon. Generally speaking, however, there is a high proportion of relatively fresh undifferentiated parent material throughout the profile. Under such circumstances, the most effective agent of secondary metal dispersion is likely to be through plant species whose deeper roots are capable of penetrating to ground-water level.

Intrazonal Saline and Alkali Soils. These soils occur most commonly under arid conditions, but they may also be found in semiarid and subhumid regions. They represent modified desert and chernozemic soils and are characterized by the accumulation of soluble salts of magnesium or sodium. In some instances, potassium salts may be present in appreciable amounts. There are two principal profile types, known as saline, white alkali, or *solonchak* soils, and alkali, black alkali, or *solonetz* soils. Both varieties are usually found in depressions where they originate by evaporation under shallow ground-water conditions. They are, therefore, the counterpart of hydromorphic soils in more humid climates. The salt content of these soils may represent the soluble products of hydrolysis of silicates or the vestiges of former seas or salt lakes.

The typical salts of solonchak are sulfates and chlorides of sodium, calcium and magnesium. These often appear as a white efflorescence at the surface which is liable to be dissolved and temporarily washed downward when it rains. Solonetz, on the other hand, is characterized by sodium carbonate as the predominant salt and a dark-colored B horizon which is strongly alkaline in reaction. A rather bleached A_2 horizon is commonly present. By comparison, solonchak is only moderately alkaline.

All gradations exist between these two soil types which are believed to be closely related. Thus, solonetz is assumed to be a development from solonchak as a result of the soil clay becoming dominated by exchangeable Na, so that when drainage is improved both clay and organic matter move downward to give the dark compact B horizon.

6–6. Mountain Soils

Some of the principal features of mountain soils have been mentioned earlier when considering relief as a factor in soil formation. In general terms, relief and altitude combine to impart specific modifications on the zonal soil type most nearly characteristic of the local climatic conditions. Where erosion is active, the soil tends to be maintained in a juvenile state of development with thin, indistinct horizons containing a high proportion of partially weathered rock debris. Such skeletal soils are known as lithosols and rightly belong to the azonal group. Where erosion is retarded, horizon differentiation takes place and bears the stamp of the local climate and vegetation. The resulting profile possesses in greater or less degree the characteristics of the appropriate zonal soil type.

Zakharov (quoted by Joffe, 1949, p. 620) considers the influence of the different grades of mountainous topography on soil development as follows:

1. The soils of low mountains, hills and plateaus resemble in a large measure well-developed soils.
2. The soils of the medium height mountains are characterized by (a) the skeletal nature in the upper portions of the slope and the fine texture at the bottom; (b) an increase in soil depth in the same direction; (c) the frequent absence of a genetic relation between the soils on the lower portion of the slope and the underlying parent rock; (d) the frequent occurrence of veins of deluvial material in the soil profile, and the occurrence of buried soils in the deeper layers.
3. The soils of the high mountains are characterized by (a) highly developed skeletal features; (b) shallowness; (c) weakly expressed horizon differentiation; (d) strongly eroded soil cover.
4. The soils in the valleys and glens are characterized by: (a) a marked change in mechanical composition and (b) by a poor differentiation into horizons or layers.

In geochemical prospecting the most important features of many mountain soils include (1) active movement of material by soil creep; (2) relatively little leaching in some environments or accelerated oxidation in others, according to the relative rates of chemical weathering and erosion; (3) the accumulation of transported eroded material (colluvium) at the base of slopes.

SELECTED REFERENCES ON SOIL FORMATION

Short summaries	Jenny (1950)
	Simonson (1957)
General texts	Jenny (1941)
	Robinson (1949)
	Joffe (1949)
Tropical soils	Prescott and Pendleton (1952)
	Mohr and Van Baren (1954)
Trace elements in soils	Vinogradov (1959)

CHAPTER 7

SECONDARY DISPERSION

As rocks weather, so their substance is made available for erosion and dispersion away from the place of origin. During the course of transportation, selective deposition or sedimentation can result in a far-reaching redistribution of the dispersed products of weathering. Redistribution is governed by the chemical and physical properties of the various dispersed constituents and of the media within which they move. Some understanding of the chemical and mechanical factors controlling dispersion is clearly essential for effective geochemical prospecting.

No more than a brief descriptive outline of these factors is possible in these pages. For further details the reader is referred to the selected literature cited at the end of the chapter.

7-1. Chemical and Biochemical Factors

The products of weathering at the earth's surface are partitioned between the relatively immobile solid phase that constitutes the regolith and the mobile, fluid phase made up of free-flowing underground and surface waters. The solid phase is composed of the insoluble products of weathering, which are dispersed by relatively slow mechanical movement of clastic fragments. Weathering products that are either water soluble or that occur in forms that can be readily suspended and swept along by flowing water are dispersed more rapidly.

The mobility of the chemical elements in the secondary dispersion cycle is therefore largely controlled by their solubility in water. Some elements, such as the Si of detrital quartz grains, characteristically occur as components of insoluble minerals. Others, such as Na or Cl, are almost always found in the water-soluble phase. Most elements, however, fall somewhere between these extremes—under some conditions they are soluble, and under other conditions they join the solid products of weathering. Empirical observations on the mobility of elements in the sedimentary cycle are reviewed in Chapter 2 and in the Appendix. The following paragraphs will summarize some of the factors of the chemical and biochemical environment that have an effect on the partition of elements between the more mobile aqueous phase and the less mobile solid phases.

Bulk Composition. The normal content of major and minor elements in natural fresh water is given in Tables 5-1 and 7-1 respectively. The total salinity depends on both climate and rock type.

TABLE 7-1.   Range of Minor Element Content of Natural Fresh Waters[a]

Element	Range (ppb) Low	Range (ppb) High	Element	Range (ppb) Low	Range (ppb) High
Ag	0.01	0.7	Hg	0.01	0.1
As	1	30	Li	0.3	3
Au	0.0001	0.0073	Mn	0.3	300
B	1	10,000	Mo	0.05	3
Ba	4	35	Ni	0.02	10
Co	0.03	10	Pb	0.3	3
Cr	0.5	40	Ti	0.2	30
Cu	0.2	30	U	0.05	1
F	50	1000	Zn	1	200
Fe	40	1500			

[a]For source of data, see Appendix.

It ranges from a minimum of perhaps 10 ppm in areas of cold climate and high rainfall to several percent in warm, desert environments. The presence of calcareous or other readily soluble rocks naturally tends to raise the total salinity in all environments. The bulk of the solids dissolved in water normally consist of dissociated ions, principally Na^+, K^+, Mg^{++}, Ca^{++}, Cl^-, SO_4^{--} and HCO_3^-. To these should be added soluble but undissociated H_4SiO_4 and the stable colloidal suspensions of hydrous Fe oxide. The relative proportions of the major constituents depend to a large extent on the rocks through which the water percolates. High relative and absolute amounts of Ca^{++}, Mg^{++} and CO_3^{--} with associated high pH values occur in waters derived from the chemical weathering of calcareous rocks. High SO_4^{--} concentration ranging up to thousands of ppm may occur in areas of oxidizing sulfide minerals. Extremely high contents of Ca^{++}, SO_4^{--} and sometimes Na^+, K^+, and Cl^- may result from the leaching of saline deposits.

Variations in the major constituents affect the dispersion of the minor elements in fresh water primarily by providing reactants, either for the precipitation of insoluble minerals or for the formation of soluble complex ions with the minor elements. These effects are considered separately in the following sections.

Hydrogen-Ion Concentration. The relative acidity or alkalinity of an aqueous solution may be expressed in terms of pH units, numerically equal to the negative logarithm of the hydrogen-ion concentration. A strongly acid solution has a pH in the range <1.0 to 3.0 and a strongly alkaline solution in the range 11.0 to 15.0. A neutral solution has a pH value of 7.0. The pH of a soil is defined as the pH of the slurry prepared by adding distilled water or a neutral solution to the soil.

Normally the pH of surface waters lies between 4.5 and 8.5, and of soils between 4.0 and 9.0. Under exceptional circumstances, these limits may be exceeded. Extremely acid waters, of pH less than 2.0, are not uncommon in the vicinity of oxidizing sulfides, while highly alkaline conditions exist in some desert soils.

The solubility of most elements and the stability of their compounds are extremely sensitive to the pH of the aqueous environment. Only the alkali metals, such as K^+ and Na^+, and to a lesser extent the alkaline earths, such as Ca^{++}, are soluble as dissociated cations throughout the normal geologic range of pH values. Most metallic elements are soluble as cations in acid solutions, but tend to be precipitated as hydroxides or basic salts with increasing pH. Thus with progressive neutralization of an acid solution, Cu commonly begins to go out of solution at a pH between 5.0 and 5.5, whereas Zn does not begin to precipitate until the pH exceeds 7.0. At still higher pH values, certain elements showing amphoteric properties may again become soluble as complex oxide anions, such as the aluminate and chromate radicals. So many competing factors, however, can affect the limiting pH at which the constituents of an aqueous solution are stable that it is not realistic to quote fixed values for the pH of hydrolysis of the minor elements.

Both acid and alkaline solutions tend toward neutrality as they become diluted. Acid solutions are also particularly prone to neutralization by chemical reaction with the rocks with which they are in contact. Of great importance in geochemical dispersion is the neutralization of the strong acid evolved by the oxidation of sulfides. As the pH of these acid solutions is progressively reduced by dilution and chemical reaction, the metals derived from primary sulfide deposits tend to be withdrawn from solution and concentrated in newly precipitated secondary minerals.

Apart from its effect on solubility, pH has an important bearing on the absorption of cations by clays and organic matter, by virtue of the preferential bonding of hydrogen ions in exchange reactions. The formation and stability of colloids are also affected by pH.

Redox Potential. The oxidizing power of a system may be quantitatively expressed by a factor known as the redox potential, usually
designated as Eh and expressed in volts. The Eh of a solution may be
experimentally determined by measuring the electric potential between a platinum electrode and a standard hydrogen electrode, both
immersed in the same solution. A high Eh value indicates a highly

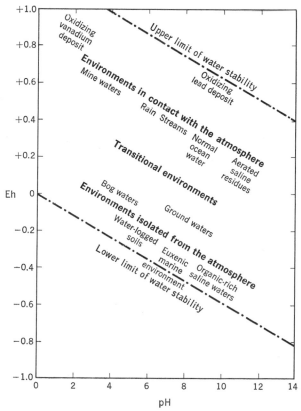

Fig. 7-1. Approximate position of some natural environments
as characterized by Eh and pH. From Garrels (1960).

oxidizing system. Oxidation as thus defined is any reaction whereby
the positive valence state of an ion increases, or the negative valence
decreases. Reduction is the reverse process.

Oxidizing conditions are favored by the presence of free oxygen
and free drainage. As the amount of free oxygen decreases and drainage conditions deteriorate, the environment becomes progressively
less oxidizing and more reducing. The strongest reducing conditions

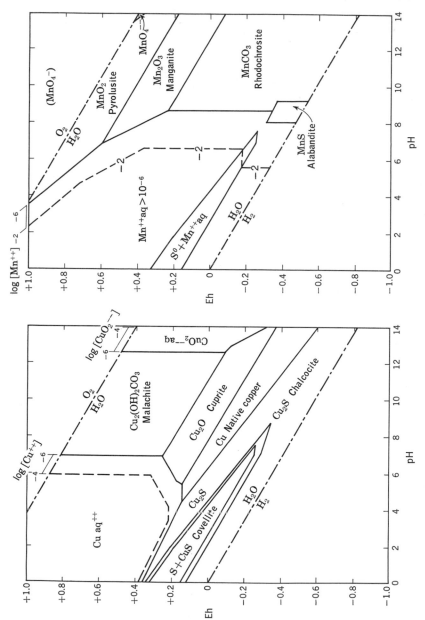

Fig. 7-2. Fields of stability of some copper and manganese minerals. From Garrels (1960).

are found where free oxygen has been consumed by organic activity and where carbonaceous matter has accumulated.

Most redox reactions involve either hydrogen or hydroxide ions. The redox potential at which a given equilibrium may be maintained therefore is commonly a function of pH. In such reactions, increasing the pH in the presence of an oxidizing agent decreases the Eh at which an oxidizing reaction can occur. Thus, making a solution more alkaline can, under proper conditions, cause the oxidation of many ion species.

The change in valence resulting from a redox reaction completely changes the chemical behavior of an element. Under a given set of conditions, an ion of one oxidation state may be readily

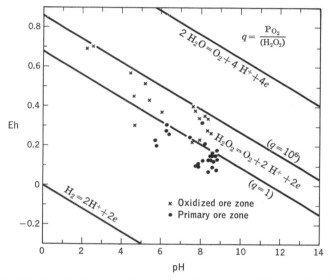

Fig. 7-3. Eh and pH values of mine waters. From Sato and Mooney (1960).

soluble, whereas in another it may form extremely insoluble compounds. Thus solubilization and precipitation of many elements in the sedimentary cycle may be largely controlled by the combined influence of Eh and pH.

Figure 7-1 illustrates the normal range of Eh and pH in some natural surface environments. The upper and lower lines are the boundaries of the field in which water is stable; above this field water decomposes with evolution of oxygen, and below it decomposes with evolution of hydrogen.

Figure 7-2 illustrates the relations between Eh, pH and the stability of some of the common oxides and sulfides of Cu and Mn. Simple diagrams such as these do not take into account modifications in the boundaries of the stability fields that would result if reactants other than the ones mentioned in the captions were added to the systems. Figure 7-3 shows some Eh-pH relations actually observed in underground waters in Cu mines in the western United States.

Mode of Occurrence of Solutes. Inorganic material dissolved in water may occur in a variety of forms, including simple ions (Na^+, Zn^{++}, Cl^-), complex ions with hydrogen and oxygen (HCO_3^-, $ZnOH^+$, MoO_4^{--}), complex ions with other elements ($CuCl^+$, $AgCl_2^-$), and undissociated molecules ($CuCO_3$, H_4SiO_4). Most metals in strongly acid solutions occur as simple cations. The amphoteric elements also occur as complex oxide anions in strongly alkaline solutions. In general, the stability of a given solute phase is controlled by the pH, Eh, and the concentration of its components. Thus a high chloride concentration favors the stability of a complex chloride ion. Although until recently the mode of occurrence of minor elements dissolved in natural waters has been understood only very imperfectly, modern methods of investigating dilute aqueous solutions are beginning to resolve some of the many problems (Silman, 1958; Garrels, 1960).

Stability of Secondary Minerals. The solubility of an element in an aqueous system is limited by the stability of the minerals it forms by reaction with the other components of the system. Many secondary minerals containing the ore metals as principal constituents are stable in extremely dilute solutions of the metal ions. A selected list showing experimentally determined or computed compositions of

TABLE 7-2. Solubility of Salts Occurring in Nature as Secondary Minerals

Salt	Equivalent Mineral	Component	Content of Component in Saturated Aqueous Solution (ppm)[a]	Median Content in Natural Fresh Water (ppm)
AgCl	Cerargyrite	Ag^+	1.46[b]	3×10^{-6}
$BaSO_4$	Barite	Ba^{++}	1.3[b]	0.16
CaF_2	Fluorite	F^-	8[c]	0.25
$CaSO_4 \cdot 2H_2O$	Gypsum	SO_4^{--}	1140[c]	5.5
$CuCO_3 \cdot Cu(OH)_2$	Malachite	Cu^{++}	12[d]	0.002
$2CuCO_3 \cdot Cu(OH)_2$	Azurite	Cu^{++}	7[e]	0.002
$PbCO_3$	Cerussite	Pb^{++}	1.3[c]	0.002
$PbSO_4$	Anglesite	Pb^{++}	27[c]	0.002
$Pb_5Cl(PO_4)_3$	Pyromorphite	Pb^{++}	0.03[f]	0.002
$ZnCO_3$	Smithsonite	Zn^{++}	107[c]	0.01

[a]Unless otherwise specified, figures are for pure neutral water taken from data assembled by Seidell (1940).
[b]Determined at 25° C.
[c]Determined at 18° C.
[d]In presence of 0.29 gram CO_2 per liter, at 20° C.
[e]In presence of 0.34 gram CO_2 per liter, at 20° C.
[f]Computed from solubility product value of $10^{-79.115}$ at 37.5° C determined by Jowett and Price (1932). At pH 5.0, solubility of pyromorphite is 0.6 ppm.

TABLE 7-3. Concentrations of Some Minor Elements in Iron Oxide and
Manganese Oxide Sediments

Element	Content in Average Igneous Rocks (ppm)	Content in Fe Oxide Sediments (ppm)	Content in Mn Oxide Sediments (ppm)
As	2	10–700	70
Ba	640	90–370	1000–7000
Cu	70	180	2000–20,000
Mo	1.7	—	300–3000
Ni	100	20–2000	1600–2200
Se	0.01	0.5–5.0	

Source: Krauskopf (1955) and Green (1959).

saturated solutions of some common secondary ore minerals is given
in Table 7-2. Included in the table are figures for the average concentration of the ore metals in natural fresh water. Comparison of
these figures with those for the concentration of the same metals in
saturated solutions of their common
secondary minerals suggests that, if
other factors are the same, all the
minerals listed in Table 7-2 will dissolve readily on contact with normal
fresh water. The same minerals will
normally be stable, however, in the
vicinity of a weathering mineral
deposit or in areas where the component ions are enriched by evaporation.

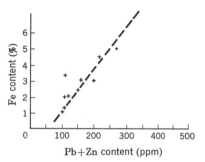

Fig. 7-4. Relation of lead and zinc to iron
in modern stream sediments of the
Colden River, Isle of Man. Data on
minus-80-mesh fraction. From de Grys
(1959).

Another limitation on the dispersion of a minor element is the degree
to which it may be scavenged from
the solution by coprecipitation as a
minor constituent of the precip-
itated minerals. The principal secondary minerals that contain relatively large concentrations of minor elements are the hydrous Fe and
Mn oxides. The mechanism by which the minor elements are fixed in
secondary oxide minerals is not well understood. Suggested mechanisms include incorporation within the crystal lattice, occlusion of
foreign ions or microcrystals, and either surface or interlayer
sorption.

Table 7-3 shows the relative enrichment of certain minor elements
in Fe and Mn oxide marine sediments. In a parallel manner the limonite of gossans and hydrous oxide precipitates in surface drainage
channels tend to become preferentially enriched in many minor
elements. Figure 7-4 shows the relation of Pb and Zn to Fe in the

active sediments of the Colden River, Isle of Man. No known sulfide mineralization occurs in this drainage basin, so that the Pb and Zn now occurring with the Fe almost certainly represent enrichment from normal background concentrations. The same association of many minor elements with Fe and Mn is observed in soils. Figure 7-5

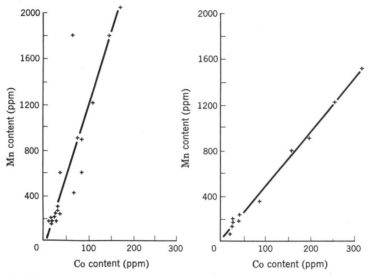

Fig. 7-5. Relationship between manganese and cobalt in soils from Northern Rhodesia. Data on minus-80-mesh fraction. After Jay (1959).

shows the correlation of Co with Mn in soils over unmineralized rocks in Northern Rhodesia.

Sorptive Capacity of Solids. Ions in solution may be attracted and held by unsatisfied electrical charges existing at the surface of solid particles. Ions adsorbed in this way are in active equilibrium with the solutions in which they are immersed. A change in the composition of the passing solutions will be reflected in the content of the ions adsorbed on the solid surfaces exposed to the solutions. This is illustrated by the results of experiments on the amount of Cu adsorbed on finely ground quartz (Figure 7-6) and on clay minerals (Figure 7-7) as related to pH and the Cu concentration of the solution. The exchange capacity or ability to adsorb ions varies widely according to grain size and the nature of the particles concerned. Adsorption on an important scale is usually restricted to clay-size fractions. Clay minerals, organic material, and colloids of hydrous Fe and Mn oxides are the materials primarily responsible for the adsorption of cations in natural surface environments.

Clay minerals adsorb cations by virtue of the unsatisfied electric charges both at the edges of crystal layers and within the layers. Inasmuch as different clay minerals have different crystal properties,

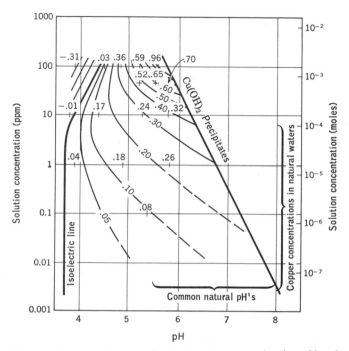

Fig. 7-6. Amount of copper adsorbed on quartz as related to pH and copper content of solution. From Richardson and Hawkes (1958). Reprinted with permission from *Geochimica et Cosmochimica Acta*, copyright 1958, Pergamon Press Incorporated.

they have correspondingly different exchange reactions (Table 7-4). Montmorillonite shows the highest exchange capacity of all the common clay minerals.

The organic matter normally present in soils and modern stream sediments contributes a very considerable proportion of the total exchange capacity of these materials. Here the mechanism by which the cations are held is most commonly the carboxylic acid radicals attached to extremely large insoluble organic molecules. Although this mechanism is different from that causing ion exchange in clay minerals, the net effect is virtually identical. Very close correlations have been observed between the organic content and the ratio of readily extractable to total metal in soils and sediments (Figure 7-8).

The strength of the bond holding an ion to the surface of a particle varies with the different ion species, its concentration in the solution,

TABLE 7-4.　Exchange Capacity of Some Clay
Minerals and Common Soils

Minerals and Soils	Cation Exchange Capacity (meq/100 g)[a]
Kaolinite	3–15
Halloysite	5–50
Montmorillonite	80–150
Illite	10–40
Chlorite	10–40
Vermiculite	100–150
Organic fraction of soils	150–500
Podzolic soils (U.S.A.)	5–25
Chernozem (U.S.S.R.)	30–60
Black cotton soil (India)	50–80
Latosol (N. Rhodesia)	2–10
Gley soil (N. Rhodesia)	15–25

Source: Joffe (1949), Grim (1953), Mohr and Van Baren (1954),
Tooms (1955), Govett (1958).
[a]Milliequivalents per 100 grams.

other ions present, pH and temperature. A commonly observed
sequence of increasing replacing power of the common simple cations
is as follows:

$$Li^+ < Na^+ < K^+ < Rb^+ < Cs^+ < Mg^{++} < Ca^{++} < Ba^{++} < H^+$$

In general terms, polyvalent ions are more strongly adsorbed than
univalent ions. Hydrogen is the outstanding exception, being normally the most strongly bonded of all the common cations.

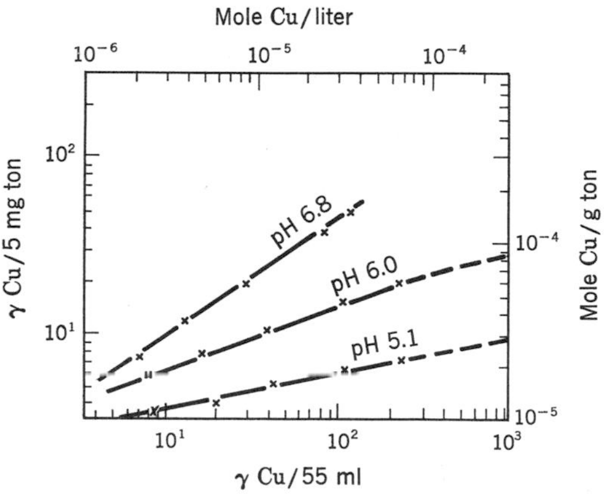

Under certain conditions, ions can become enclosed or even incorporated within the lattice structure of the host mineral. Such ions are more firmly held and are said to be *ab*sorbed rather than *ad*sorbed. This distinction between absorption and adsorption is essentially one of degree.

Relatively little is known about the mechanism and geochemical significance of anion sorption. There are indications that the ability of soil clays to hold anions may be correlated with the presence of

Fig. 7-7. Adsorption of copper on kaolinite as a function of pH and Cu concentration of the solution. From Heydemann (1959). Reprinted with permission from *Geochimica et Cosmochimica Acta*, copyright 1959, Pergamon Press Incorporated.

Fe and Al. It is also probable that clay minerals can absorb anions by replacement of OH groups.

Metallo-Organic Compounds. Metals may also combine with naturally occurring organic compounds to form metallo-organic complexes such as porphyrins and salts of various organic acids. Some metallo-organic compounds are soluble in water, whereas others are insoluble. Even when they are soluble, many of these compounds do not dissociate into their component ions, so that the sequestered metal is not available for chemical reaction. Organic acids have been shown to be capable of solubilizing otherwise insoluble constituents of soils, or of preventing the reaction of dissolved components with other constituents of the solution (Mandl

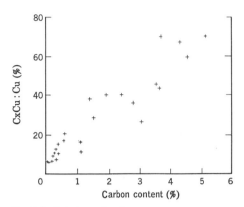

Fig. 7-8. Relation of carbon content to extractability of copper in soils from Northern Rhodesia. Data on minus-80-mesh fraction. After Govett (1960).

et al., 1953; Hem, 1960). The formation of metallo-organic compounds is considered responsible for the mobilization of Pb in the zone of secondary enrichment in the Breckenridge District, Colorado (Lovering, 1934). In contrast, some of the Cu, Zn, and Pb which at times accumulate in organic-rich soil may be held as insoluble organic complexes. Organic complexes containing U are thought to be instrumental both in the precipitation of U in organic soils and in the solubilization of nonorganic U by natural solutions containing humic acids (Manskaya et al., 1956). Beyond a number of empirical observations of this kind, however, the nature of the compounds actually formed under natural conditions is largely conjectural. There can be no doubt, however, that organic compounds containing metals as part of their molecular structure play a significant role in the dispersion of metals in the surficial environment.

Stability of Colloidal Dispersions. Substantial amounts of nonionic silica, alumina, and hydrous Mn and Fe oxides can be stabilized in natural solutions. Some of this material occurs as undissociated molecules, such as H_4SiO_4. Another large fraction occurs as colloidal dispersions of very large hydrated molecules. These molecules carry an electric charge that under most conditions effectively prevents them from coagulating and settling out. In addition to the metal oxides, very finely divided crystalline material, such as the clay minerals, may be held in colloidal suspensions and so become amenable to transport by circulating waters.

The sign of the electric charge on the colloidal particles depends on the nature of the colloid and, in certain cases, on the reactions by which they are formed. In natural solutions, colloidal silica, hydrous Mn oxide, and humic colloids are negatively charged. Colloidal alumina is positively charged, while ferric hydroxide may be either negative or positive. According to their positive or negative charge, these colloids can adsorb anions or cations present in the dispersion medium.

If the electric charges are neutralized, colloidal particles tend to flocculate and settle out. Flocculation may therefore be brought about by a change in the concentration of electrolytes in the dispersion medium or by the presence of an oppositely charged colloid. Colloidal solutions may, however, be protected from flocculation by the preferential absorption of certain ions, molecules, or other colloidal particles. In this connection, the protective action of humic substances in stabilizing colloidal ferric hydroxide is an important example.

The Effect of Vegetation.   Living vegetation has a profound effect on the dispersion of weathering products. The uptake of a given element by the root system of a plant is a function of the relative solubility of the element in the soil solution, as modified by the extremely corrosive environment created by the plant in the vicinity of its root tips. The biogenic processes whereby elements may be solubilized from relatively stable mineral phases and ingested into the plant's circulatory system vary with different species of plants. These extremely complex processes are discussed at greater length in Chapter 15 in connection with plant nutrition.

The net effect of these combined inorganic and organic factors is an uptake of substantial quantities of inorganic matter which is then distributed in greater or less amount through the body of the plant. As the leaves and other plant organs fall to the ground and decay, rain water leaches out the more soluble constituents. The bulk of the soluble products of plant decay are normally removed in ground and surface water. A part, however, may again be taken up by living plants or reprecipitated with Fe, Mn, and Al in the B horizon of many soils. The less soluble constituents released by plant decay tend to remain in the humus layer, wherein ions may also be retained by adsorption on organic matter. This effect, as originally pointed out by Goldschmidt (1937), is cumulative, and over the years very appreciable enrichment may take place. The entire sequence of processes is referred to as the biogeochemical cycle (Figure 7-9).

Process		Soil horizon
Metals rising in nutrient uptake to be incorporated in plant tissue Metals returned to surface as leaves, etc. wither and fall	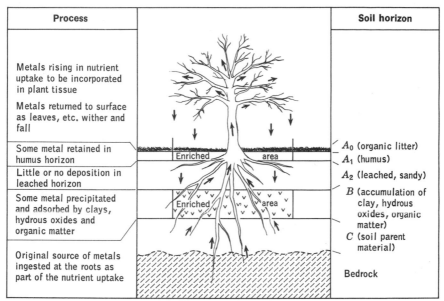	
Some metal retained in humus horizon	Enriched area	A_0 (organic litter) A_1 (humus)
Little or no deposition in leached horizon		A_2 (leached, sandy)
Some metal precipitated and adsorbed by clays, hydrous oxides and organic matter	Enriched area	B (accumulation of clay, hydrous oxides, organic matter) C (soil parent material)
Original source of metals ingested at the roots as part of the nutrient uptake		Bedrock

Fig. 7-9. The biogeochemical cycle.

The Effect of Microorganisms. Bacteria, algae, fungi, and other microorganisms exert a powerful influence on metal dispersion in the soil and in surface drainage systems. Apart from their vital role in the production of humus, microorganisms are intimately associated with other important redox reactions. Bacterially induced oxidation may lead to the precipitation of Mn and Fe oxides and also the production of soluble sulfates from sulfur and certain sulfides (Rudolfs and Helbronner, 1922). Experiments have shown that under certain conditions microorganisms can precipitate native Cu and Cu sulfide by reduction of Cu-bearing solutions (Lovering, 1927; Arkhangel'sky and Soloviev, 1938). It is important to realize that the effect of bacteria on these reactions is primarily catalytic. Reactions that are possible and the compounds that can be formed are restricted to those consistent with the pH and Eh of the environment.

There is also evidence that microorganisms are capable of assimilating and concentrating certain metals. In many cases it is not clear, however, whether the metal is in fact assimilated within the living organism or whether it is absorbed on the external mucilage or fixed in metabolic products. Riley (1939) has shown that much of the total Cu in lake waters in Connecticut is tied up by organisms in the plankton. *Spirogyra*, a fresh-water alga, growing in mine drainage water carrying 16 ppm total heavy metals, has been shown to contain

2900 ppm Zn, 6600 ppm Pb, and 920 ppm Cu in the dried algal material (Cannon, 1955). Under some conditions, soil microorganisms may be responsible for reducing the availability of metals for plant nutrition. An example of Zn deficiency caused either by assimilation or fixation in metabolic products is described by Hoagland *et al.* (1937).

7–2. Mechanical Factors

Dispersion by movement of clastic fragments is largely restricted to the surface of the regolith where erosion is in active progress. The principal force responsible for mechanical dispersion is gravity, acting either directly on soil and loose debris or through the media of flowing water and ice. Wind action and animals are contributory agents and locally may even assume a dominant role. Mechanical dispersion by volcanism has no general significance in prospecting and is not considered here.

Simple Gravity Movement.   Under the influence of gravity, solid components of the overburden tend to move downhill either by slow lateral creep or by more rapid landsliding. A classification of these phenomena, based on the kind and rate of movement, is presented in Figure 7-10.

Even on moderate to gentle slopes, there is a continual, imperceptible flow of rock debris and soil in the downslope direction. In general terms, the rate of lateral movement within the regolith progressively increases from bedrock to surface. As a result, vestigial rock structures in the moving overburden tend to bend over in the direction of movement, as illustrated diagrammatically in Figure 7-11. The distribution of residual weathering products related to an underlying metalliferous deposit may be similarly affected, as illustrated by the data of Figure 7-12.

The presence of vegetation tends to stabilize the overburden and so reduce the rate of creep. In those areas where the vegetation is dense and shallow rooted, maximum movement may in fact take place immediately below the surface layer of matted roots.

In temperate and humid climates creep is facilitated by the lubricating effect of soil moisture. Alternate freezing and thawing of interstitial water, or alternate wetting and drying of the soil, tend to facilitate the down-slope movement of clastic material.

Accelerated flow due to abundant interstitial water is known as *solifluction*. With increasing mobilization, a slurry of unconsolidated material mixed with water may develop, which can take the form of a rapidly moving mud flow. In northern climates, the high water

content necessary for solifluction and mud flowage may be provided
by the melting of frost crystals formed from upward-moving capil-

Movement		Chiefly ice	Earth or rock plus ice	Earth or rock, dry or with minor amounts of ice or water	Earth or rock plus water	Chiefly water
Kind	Rate	Ice		Earth or rock	Water	

			Chiefly ice	Earth or rock plus ice	Earth or rock, dry or with minor amounts of ice or water	Earth or rock plus water	Chiefly water	
With free side	Flow	Usually imperceptible	Glacial transportation		Rock creep			Fluvial transportation
				Rock-glacier creep	Talus creep		
				Solifluction	Soil creep	Solifluction	
		Slow to rapid				Earth flow	
	Perceptible			Debris avalanche		Mud flow Semi arid, alpine, volcanic	
		Rapid				Debris avalanche	
	Slip (landslide)	Slow to rapid			Slump		
		Perceptible			Debris slide		
					Debris fall		
		Very rapid			Rockslide		
					Rockfall		
No free side	Slip or flow	Fast or slow			Subsidence		

Fig. 7-10. Classification of mechanical factors in the dispersion of weathering products. From Sharpe (1938).

lary soil moisture. In spring thaws, vast amounts of overburden may
thus be mobilized on slopes as gentle as 1 to 3 degrees.

Whenever the load exceeds the
internal strength of the soil or
rock resting on a sloping surface,
differential flow gives way to catastrophic displacement or landsliding of very large segments of
unconsolidated cover. When movement of this kind takes place,
geochemical soil anomalies may be
completely disrupted, displaced, or
buried, as illustrated in Figure
7-13. Thus, landsliding can have a most important bearing on geochemical interpretation, particularly in mountainous terrain.

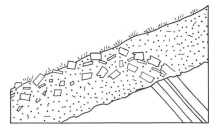

Fig. 7-11. Dispersion of resistant rock fragments by soil creep.

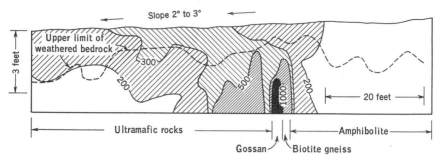

Fig. 7-12. Section showing predominantly mechanical dispersion of copper in soil near Cu-rich gossan, Magogophate, Bechuanaland. Data on minus-80-mesh fraction. After Coope (1958).

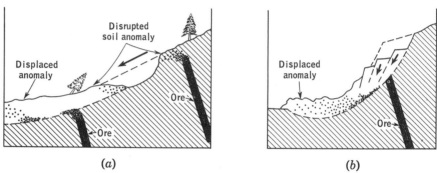

(a) *(b)*

Fig. 7-13. Disruption and displacement of geochemical soil anomalies by (*a*) landsliding and (*b*) slumping.

Fragmental material that has moved down a mountainside by creep and landsliding will tend to accumulate at the foot of the slope. Very considerable thicknesses of transported material, or *colluvium*, may be built up in this way. The accumulation of colluvium is important in geochemical prospecting in that (1) the colluvium represents to some extent a composite sample of the overburden covering the slopes above, and (2) residual soil anomalies in the base of slope zone may be effectively concealed (Figure 7-14). In deeply dissected areas undergoing vigorous erosion, material moving down the valley slopes may feed directly into stream courses, to be channeled away through the surface drainage system.

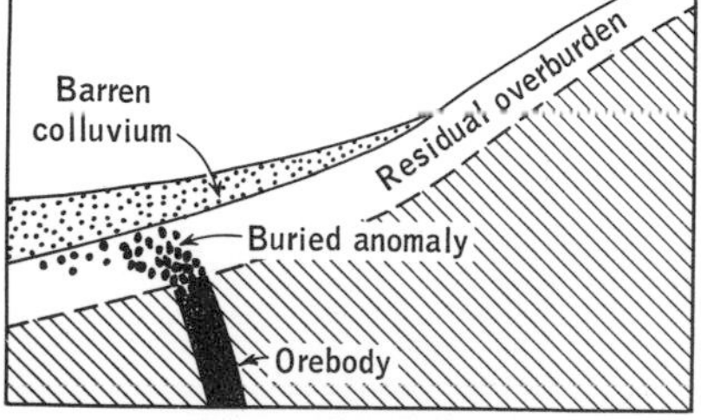

Fig. 7-14. Burial of anomaly in residual overburden beneath footslope colluvium.

Dispersion in Ground Water. The bulk of the water that falls to the ground as rain moves relatively rapidly either as ground water in the fractures or pore spaces of rocks and soils, or as surface runoff. This free-flowing water provides the principal vehicle for the dispersion of weathering products at and near the earth's surface.

The movement of subsurface water under the influence of gravity or of a hydrostatic head is a fairly simple matter of flow from a higher to a lower level, or from an area of higher to an area of lower pressure. Rain water soaks into the soil and replaces the air in the pore spaces of the surficial material or rocks. The upper unsaturated section is known as the zone of aeration, and the water contained

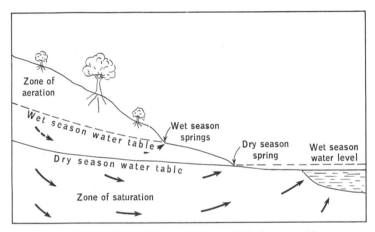

Fig. 7-15. Effects of seasonal rise and fall of water table.

in it as vadose water. If the pore spaces extend to sufficient depth and precipitation exceeds evaporation, the rain water eventually reaches the water table, which is defined as the surface below which the air in the pore spaces has been completely replaced by water. The ground water, or water below the water table, then tends to move downward and laterally in the direction of the easiest means of escape. It may emerge at the surface as springs and as seepages along the banks or in the beds of streams. The pattern of ground-water flow beneath the water table is such that a certain proportion of the water coming to the surface as seeps and springs may have come from substantial depth, as indicated by the arrows in Figure 7-15. Under ordinary circumstances, a swamp, spring, or stream is in effect an "outcrop" of the water table. In climates with sufficient rainfall, the water table slopes in essentially the same direction as the surface of the ground, and its contours are more or less parallel with topographic contours. This simple pattern of lateral ground-water flow may be complicated by the upward movement of water under artesian pressure.

The gravity movement of ground water is impeded by the material through which it flows. Consequently, during a period of heavy rainfall, fresh rain water entering the underground reservoir of the ground-water system cannot escape as fast as it is added and tends to pile up. The effect of this piling up is to raise the water table so that higher escape channels are available, and new springs and seepages become active, as illustrated in Figure 7-15. Conversely, during a period of light rainfall, the water table will be lowered, and springs will progressively dry up.

In areas of crystalline or metamorphic rocks which have negligible pore space, a true water table may not exist unless the cover of surficial material is deep enough. Here, rain water that has soaked into the soil tends to flow along channels on the surface of bedrock. When a channel of this kind crosses a permeable zone of fracturing or shearing, the water may enter the fractures to emerge again at the surface of bedrock at a lower elevation.

Water and the salts dissolved in it can move upward from the water table against the force of gravity as a result of capillary forces. The experimental upper limits of capillary rise range from a few inches in coarse sand to 30 feet or so in clays. The rate of movement varies markedly in an inverse relationship to particle size, and more than a year may be required to attain the full height in fine-grained material. The rate of capillary rise is further diminished as the content of dissolved salts is increased, although the magnitude of the effect is dependent on the composition of the solutes. Recent experiments have shown, however, that water and dissolved salts can readily move upward for substantial distances through unsaturated soils above the capillary fringe (Marshall, 1959). The mechanism, at least in part, appears to involve migration of water and dissolved ions on the surface of minerals. These effects are most conspicuous in the zone of aeration between the water table and the land surface. The net result of movement of this kind against the force of gravity is commonly a dispersion of the dissolved constituents both upward and laterally in the direction of decreasing concentration.

Under an appropriate seasonal climate, upward dispersion of this kind may be assisted by the movement of material associated with a periodically rising and falling water table. Above the water table, moisture moves downward as rain water soaks in from above, while at the same time the ground-water level is rising; in dry periods, on the other hand, these directions of movement are reversed as moisture rises from the falling water table in order to replenish the water removed nearer the surface by evaporation and transpiration (Figure 7-16). The pattern of movement is naturally modified in those areas

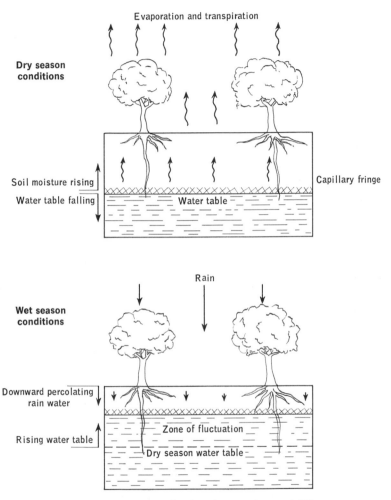

Fig. 7-16. Seasonal movements of soil moisture where rainfall penetrates to water table.

where the rainfall is insufficient to saturate the ground right down to the water table. Here, although there is a seasonal reversal in the direction of flow of soil moisture in the surface horizons, the movement of water at the water table is always upward (Figure 7-17). The over-all effect of this rather complex "pumping" action is to assist in spreading soluble constituents upward from their source in the bed-

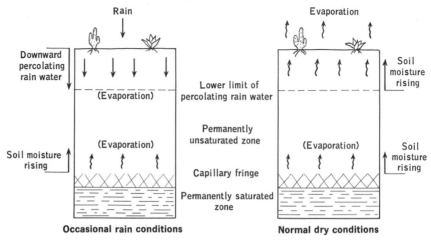

Fig. 7-17. Movements of soil moisture where rainfall is insufficient to penetrate to water table.

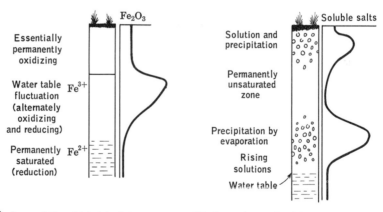

(a) Accumulation of lateritic B horizon under a warm, humid seasonal climate and shallow water table (see Fig. 7.16 for moisture regime)

(b) Accumulation of soluble salts under a semiarid climate and deep water table (see Fig. 7.17 for moisture regime)

Fig. 7-18. Some relationships between the subsurface water regime and the redistribution of soluble constituents.

rock for distances depending on the local environment. In addition to dispersions formed by adsorption of the solute ions in the matrix through which the solutions move, accumulations of salts may develop by precipitation in zones where evaporation or oxidation is active (Figure 7-18).

Special conditions influence the flow of subsurface water in the immediate vicinity of drainage channels which are underlain by permeable material. Here a substantial proportion of the water contained in a stream or river system will move as *underflow* through the permeable stream bed. The partition of water between channel flow and underflow varies greatly depending on the gradient of the stream and the width, depth and permeability of the bottom material at any given point.

Mechanics of Dispersion in Surface Water.   The dispersion of solid weathering products by surface water takes place in three main environments: on the land surface by runoff or sheetwash, in stream channels, and in the relatively quiet environment of swamps and bodies of standing water.

The same general principles of erosion, transport, and deposition apply in all three environments. The amount of material that can be picked up is governed primarily by particle size, the rate of flow, and turbulence. Erosion is only effective so long as the water remains underloaded. As soon as the load capacity is reached, no further net erosion is possible. If the rate of flow or turbulence decreases in a fully loaded water, then material will be deposited until the load capacity at the new energy level is attained. It is important to appreciate that each of the foregoing relationships refers only to a specific particle size. Thus, a moving body of water may be fully loaded with respect to one particle size while at the same time being capable of picking up and carrying more particles of another size.

Material may be transported in suspension, or by jumping and rolling along the bottom (*saltation*). Large fragments may also glide along over smaller rounded particles, which act as ball bearings. Transport, whether by suspension or saltation, is greatly enhanced by turbulence, which is itself a function of volume and velocity of the water and the roughness or irregularity of the surface over which it is flowing. The distance that material may travel before being deposited depends on the turbulence, the load, the ratio of settling velocity to the velocity of flow, and the depth of water. The settling velocity is a function of the size of the particles and their relative densities. It is also influenced by shape of the particles, inasmuch as flat particles tend to settle more slowly than rounded grains of equivalent size. Provided velocity and turbulence remain reasonably uniform, the particles deposited will tend to be well graded in size. The energy relationships between velocity and turbulence are such that sediments deposited from slowly moving water tend to be more poorly sorted than those deposited from fast-moving water.

Dispersion by Surface Runoff.   The eroding and transporting power of surface runoff depends on a number of factors, notably the slope of the land, the nature of the overburden, the amount and intensity of the rainfall, and the proportion that soaks into the soil. The last is greatly influenced by the presence of vegetation, rubble, or other obstacles to effective sheet flow, as well as by the permeability of the overburden. Under favorable conditions, very considerable masses of material may be eroded and transported by simple surface runoff, accompanied by the development of extensive alluvial fans down-slope from the outcrop areas. Channeling of runoff may result in catastrophic erosion by gulleying. Under most conditions, however, the effect of sheet wash is limited to the selective erosion and transport of the finest products of weathering, namely clays and finely divided sesquioxides.

Dispersion in Stream Water.   Streams acquire their load by erosion of the banks, scouring of the stream bed and by direct contributions from sheet wash and soil creep. Catastrophic floods occurring at relatively infrequent intervals probably account for a very large part of the total mass of material moved by streams. During such flood periods, very large boulders may be moved several miles in a matter of hours. Flood deposits may subsequently be sorted out and the components redistributed in an orderly manner during quieter periods of stable runoff conditions. Then the clay minerals and other fine products of weathering will move predominantly in suspension at the same speed as the water, while the coarser material moves by saltation and gliding in the bed of the stream at a somewhat slower speed.

Resistant primary minerals, notably quartz and the heavy accessory minerals, together with partially weathered rock fragments, are the dominant constituents of the sediment in fast-flowing streams. Micaceous minerals also occur, but because of their flat habit are more readily carried in suspension. Some of the stable secondary minerals are also coarse grained and may travel with the stream-bed material. Chief among these is secondary Fe oxide, which is particularly common in areas of concretionary laterite. Manganese oxides and a variety of secondary ore minerals also may be dispersed in the sand and silt fraction.

During the course of transport along the stream bed, the particle size is liable to be progressively reduced by chemical and physical disintegration. Minerals and rocks differ in their physical resistance to abrasion. According to experiments carried out by Friese (1931), mafic rocks are more readily worn away by running water than felsic rocks, and metamorphic rocks resist abrasion better than do igneous rocks of similar mineralogical composition. Friese also determined the relative rate of disintegration of primary minerals under the abrasive action of flowing water. He found that minerals could be arranged in the following order of increasing transportation resistance: galena, quartz, zircon, ilmenite, sphalerite, cassiterite, magnetite, wolframite, rutile, chromite, pyrite, and tourmaline. This sequence does not necessarily represent the relative distance the minerals will travel from their source, as no account was taken of the relative rate of chemical decomposition of the minerals or the effect of shape of the mineral grains and the resulting differences in the buoyant effect of running water. Recent experiments by Kuenen (1959), however, indicate that purely mechanical abrasion of sand-size grains of quartz, limestone, and feldspar is entirely negligible in river transport. A combination of chemical attack and mechanical disintegration is probably needed to effect any appreciable reduction in the particle size of the finer alluvial fractions. If this is generally true, then effective comminution during fluviatile transport depends primarily on the stability of the mineral species involved.

Erosion and transportation naturally predominate over deposition in the upper reaches of a stream. As turbulence decreases in the quieter and flatter reaches, suspended material begins to settle out, and movement by saltation diminishes. Downstream, deposition continues on an increasing scale as the load capacity progressively falls. Considerable thicknesses of sediment may build up in the lower reaches, where the stream often flows in a channel carved through its own alluvium. As the water at this stage is usually fully loaded, erosion of the banks is balanced by deposition in the channel. At times of flood, erosion is enhanced and material previously deposited is liable to be picked up, eventually to settle down again further downstream. If the stream should overspill its banks, the sudden loss of velocity causes suspended material to be deposited on the flood plain flanking the main stream channel. Natural levees of the coarser sediment tend to build up nearest the channel, while the material laid down at greater distances is mostly finer grained.

Except where the flow is strong and uniform, river and flood-plain sediments will be poorly sorted. Changes in velocity and direction may result in gross variations in grain size, both laterally and in depth. The characteristic distribution of coarse and fine material around bends in the channel is a well-known feature related to velocity of flow. As a result of seasonal changes in the flow, the sediment is liable to be re-sorted and redistributed, sometimes resulting in stratification and cross-bedding. During the course of repeated erosion and redeposition, gravity sorting may result in the concentration of heavy minerals at critical points along the stream bed.

Introduction of material from a second source can be an important factor in locally modifying the over-all tendency toward a progressive decrease in average grain size downstream. Part, at least, of the load carried by tributary streams is usually dumped at the confluence as velocity is lost on entering the main stream.

Ore elements undergoing dispersion in the solid products of weathering may travel preferentially either in the coarse or in the fine fraction, depending on the individual characteristics of the elements in question. The factors controlling grain-size distribution of minor elements during successive stages of erosion, transport, and deposition can have a marked bearing on technique and interpretation of geochemical drainage surveys. Furthermore, stream sediment may be reworked and redistributed consequent on rejuvenation of the drainage system by uplift. Drainage sediments dating from an earlier erosional cycle may be preserved as high-level terraces, or in abandoned channels remaining after river capture or even past glaciation. It is important, therefore, to recognize any aspects of the local geomorphological history which may have influenced the course of sedimentation in the past.

Deposition in Quiet Environments.   Swamps are characterized by extremely sluggish flow and a dense mat of vegetation. Surface waters entering such an environment tend to lose practically all their load by a combination of deposition and filtration. Most of the dispersion processes in a swamp environment are chemical, involving either solubilization or precipitation of elements that react with organic matter. At the outlet of a swamp, mechanical erosion may once again become effective as flow increases in the vicinity of the outlet stream.

Lakes and marine basins provide a similarly quiet environment within which deposition predominates. Erosion is limited to the action of waves and currents, resulting in abrasion along the shore or bottom in shallow water, and in the scouring of unconsolidated sediment. Although turbulence may be negligible, fine-grained suspended material may still be carried substantial distances by mass movement of lake or marine water before it settles out. In general, stream waters deposit the bulk of their load as deltaic deposits at the point of discharge into the quiet water. Deltas shelve gently away from the point where the stream enters, but steepen sharply at the advancing front of active deposition before flattening again at greater distances from the shore.

Glacial Dispersion.   Scandinavia and Canada together with adjoining areas of Europe and North America have been periodically covered by ice during the last million years of geologic time. As a result, the processes of weathering and the development of dispersion patterns in these glaciated areas are materially different from those in areas of residual weathering.

The distances over which glacially eroded material has been moved by the ice can be very great. Fragments of native copper derived from the Keweenaw Peninsula of northern Michigan have been found 600 miles distant in southern Illinois, and a boulder of a distinctive norite gneiss from near the city of Quebec has been picked up in southern Ohio some 700 miles away (Flint, 1957). The bulk of the material in glacial tills, however, is of relatively local origin. Chamberlin (1883) estimated that 90 percent of the material in the moraines of southern Wisconsin traveled less than 1 mile, and studies of the glacial boulders in northern New Brunswick show that the most abundant rock type is a fairly reliable indication of the lithology of the bedrock directly beneath. Thus, although a few glacial erratics have traveled a very great distance from the source, the overwhelming majority of pebbles and boulders contained in glacial till are of local origin. It is possible that the bulk of the rock load of the continental ice mass was contained in a lower layer that moved relatively little and was overridden by a layer of cleaner ice carrying fewer boulders but for far greater distances.

The direction of movement of continental ice during a single glacial epoch is generally outward from a central area in the heart of the ice mass. At any one locality, however, the direction may fluctuate somewhat around a mean value, with the result that glacial erratics are commonly distributed in the form of a fan spreading from the source in the direction of ice movement, rather than as a linear pattern. The prerequisite for the formation of a simple fan-shaped pattern of glacial dispersion is the existence of a relatively small outcrop of a unique, mechanically resistant and readily identified rock type. In New England alone, well-defined glacial fans have been mapped in association with fourteen occurrences of distinctive rock types, some of which are shown in Figure 7-19

The source material of glacial deposits is in part the preglacial regolith and in part fresh rock that has been plucked directly from the bedrock by the action of the ice. The preglacial regolith, at least before the last glacial stage, consisted predominantly of deeply weathered glacial deposits left over from the preceding period of glacial activity, together with some alluvial material and newly weathered bedrock. Mineralogically, this material probably consisted predominantly of quartz and clay minerals.

Glacial deposits are of several types, depending on whether the ice-borne material has been sorted in the course of deposition, and if so, how much. Till, or the completely unsorted material left by the simple melting of the ice, occurs as ground and terminal moraines. Till contains all the material, including the fine-grained clay minerals derived from the erosion of the preglacial regolith. Any peculiar chemical properties of that regolith will be reflected in the chemical properties of the till. Where the ice melts into a body of flowing water, the clay fraction is washed out, leaving only the coarser material. The result is a partially sorted *subaqueous till*, consisting only of the sand fraction and coarser. Melt water, when it sweeps up the material released by the melting of the ice, causes a sorting action similar to that in any fluvial environment. *Glaciofluvial* deposits formed in this way consist of gravels and sands with only a trivial content of clay-sized material. Because of the complex history of glaciofluvial deposits, deciphering the provenance of the material contained in them is a much more complex problem than determining the source of fragments in till. Where muddy water from the melting of glacial ice enters the quiet environment of lakes, thick deposits of clay commonly form. Deposits of glacial lake clay cover very large areas of the Precambrian shield in Canada and pose one of the principal exploration problems for that area.

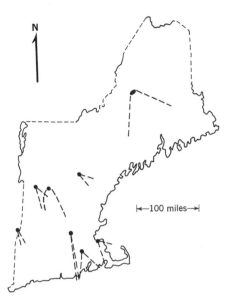

Fig. 7-19. Fan-shaped trains of glacial boulders in New England. From Flint (1957). Reprinted with permission from R. F. Flint, *Glacial and Pleistocene Geology*, copyright 1957, John Wiley & Sons, Inc.

Dispersion by Wind Action. Erosion and transport by wind action is naturally most effective in arid or semiarid regions, where there is little or no vegetation to protect the surface. Under favorable conditions, vast tracts of land have been covered by wind-blown desert sand and by loess, which is generally considered to be mainly wind-sorted material of glacial origin.

In addition to obvious wind-blown accumulations, there is a certain proportion of aeolian material in all superficial deposits. As a rule the amount is relatively small and is not an important factor in geochemical prospecting. However, detectable aeolian dispersions of material derived from weathering ore deposits have been reported on rare occasions. Locally too, wind-blown dust and fumes from mine dumps and smelter stacks can interfere in geochemical surveys.

Dispersion by Animal Activity. Burrowing species, particularly worms and termites, are responsible for bringing vast amounts of weathered material to the surface. For example, in the Rhodesian Copperbelt individual termitaries of up to 300 tons are distributed at a density of one termitary per acre, representing a depth of 3 to 6 inches of soil over the land surface as a whole. As a result of this animal activity the metal content of surface horizons may be enriched, permeability of the overburden increased, and a loose aggregate prepared, facilitating lateral dispersion by gravity, water, and wind.

7–3. The Influence of Environment on Dispersion

From the foregoing it will readily be appreciated that environment necessarily exercises a very strong influence on metal dispersion. As with weathering and soil formation, the principal environmental factors are those relating to climate, relief, geology, life processes, and time. The close interaction between these fundamental factors has been stressed earlier and need not be repeated here.

Climate. Climate affects dispersion mainly through its control of the moisture regime, vegetation, and soil type. In arid regions, paucity of water and vegetation are reflected in the subordinate role of chemical as compared to mechanical dispersion. Ground water usually lies far below the surface, but some metals, particularly those which form soluble anion complexes such as Mo and W, may be brought up by certain deep-rooted plant species. Although chemical dispersion assumes greater importance as the rainfall increases, calcareous soils characteristic of semiarid and subhumid climates provide a poor environment for the dispersion of soluble elements on account of high pH and the presence of abundant lime. Humid tropical or temperate climates, on the other hand, provide optimum conditions for chemical dispersion. The relative importance of mechanical dispersion is largely determined by the vegetation and relief. In the colder regions chemical reactions are slowed down by the low temperature and low organic activity. Ultimately, in areas of permanently frozen ground, mechanical dispersion becomes the dominant factor.

Relief. Through its bearing on erosion and ground-water movement, relief exerts a most powerful effect on the dispersion of weathering products. In flat-lying terrain, the rate of mechanical dispersion is restricted, and although chemical weathering may extend to great depths, dispersion of the soluble products can be accomplished only slowly by the sluggish flow of surface and ground waters. With increasing topographic relief, more vigorous flow results in ready dispersion of soluble material. At the same time, however, the effectiveness of mechanical erosion is also increasing, and in mountainous terrain surface material may be removed faster than potentially soluble material can be released by weathering. Thus, while moderate relief undoubtedly promotes extensive chemical dispersion, the balance may swing in favor of mechanical dispersion in areas of strong topographic relief. By virtue of its relationship with ground-water level, the relief also influences the dispersion of soluble metals which may be precipitated in seepage areas at points where the water table crops out at the surface.

Geology.   The prime importance of the geologic environment lies in its influence on the composition and the freedom of movement of ground-water solutions both through the rock and through the overburden. Dispersion of many semimobile elements such as Cu and Zn is more restricted in an alkaline, calcareous environment than it is in the more acid conditions commonly associated with relatively unreactive siliceous rocks. The high content of Ca^{++} and HCO_3^- characteristic of ground waters in calcareous terrain can also effectively restrict the dispersion of Mo by precipitation of $CaMoO_4$. Elements such as As and Mo that tend to be precipitated in the presence of Fe will be preferentially retained in the iron-rich soils derived from mafic rock. Permeability and the degree of fracturing of the bedrock may impede or facilitate flow of ground-water solutions. The permeability of the overburden, largely related to clay content, is primarily dependent on the nature of the parent material. This relationship is witnessed by the clay-rich residual soils derived from limestones, argillaceous and mafic rocks, as contrasted with the more permeable residua associated with arenaceous and felsic rocks. Equally variable is the permeability of transported overburden ranging from fine-grained glacial boulder clay and lake or flood-plain clay sediments to more permeable coarse-grained alluvial deposits.

Life Processes.   The distribution and activities of plants, animals, and microorganisms are largely controlled by climate, topography, and drainage. Although the modifying influence of organisms is evident in metal distribution in most environments, the influence of biological processes attains predominant geochemical significance only under certain rather specialized conditions. Thus, plants may play the leading role in bringing metal to the surface in areas of transported overburden and in "living" desert regions. The extremely widespread dispersions of metal in soil in parts of the Central African peneplain are considered to be due in part to metal taken up by the vegetation from moving ground-water solutions (Tooms and Webb, 1961). The most significant accumulations of metals by micro-organisms take place as a rule in swamps and lakes wherein the Eh and pH are in part controlled by the microbial population, which in turn reflects the anaerobic conditions and temperature in these relatively stagnant environments.

Time. Where the environment predisposes a slow rate of weathering and erosion, or a slow rate of transport, appreciable time is clearly essential for widespread dispersion to take place. In residual overburden the maturity of metal dispersion patterns probably parallels that of the soil profile. Other things being equal, immature dispersion patterns tend to be narrower and more intense than do the mature patterns. The time required for soluble metals to move up into transported overburden must clearly depend on a number of factors, such as the rate of oxidation, the rise and fall of ground water, and the rate at which metal can be transferred to the surface soil by the local vegetation. From a few empirical observations it appears that appreciable dispersion in transported overburden can take place, under some conditions at least, in a few hundred years.

By comparison with the soil environment, the rate of change of conditions is much greater where weathering products are being transported in the subsurface and surface drainage system. Very little is known about the rate at which reactions involved in chemical dispersion tend to come into equilibrium. Answers to this problem could have a material bearing on metal dispersion in sediments and waters, particularly where there are seasonal variations in the nature and amount of eroded material and in the metal content of the transfluent solutions.

SELECTED REFERENCES ON SECONDARY GEOCHEMICAL DISPERSION

General	Krauskopf (1955)
	Pettijohn (1957)
	Garrels (1960)
pH	Britton (1956)
Redox potential	Latimer (1952)
Ion exchange	Carroll (1959)
Hydrology	Meinzer (1923)
	Hem (1959)
Glaciology	Flint (1957)
	Zeuner (1959)
Geobotany	Cannon (1960b)

CHAPTER 8

SECONDARY DISPERSION PATTERNS

The characteristics of secondary dispersion patterns are a natural consequence of the dynamic processes of dispersion discussed in the previous chapter. These processes and the wide range of environments in which they operate are complex in the extreme, and the resultant patterns of redistributed material show a corresponding diversity in origin, mode of occurrence of their constituents, and physical form.

The present chapter reviews the more important general features of secondary dispersion patterns. Later chapters present more detailed discussions of the various kinds of anomalous patterns, with special emphasis on their significance in mineral exploration.

8–1. Classification of Secondary Dispersion Patterns

Genetically, secondary dispersion patterns may be classified according to (1) time of formation, relative to the host matrix, and (2) mode of formation. This system of classification is employed because correct recognition of the time and mode of formation of a geochemical pattern provides the only sure foundation for its interpretation in terms of bedrock geology.

On the foregoing basis, therefore, patterns introduced or deposited at the same time as the host matrix are classified as *syngenetic*, while those which were introduced into the matrix after its formation are distinguished as *epigenetic*. Patterns may be further classified as (1) *clastic*, where the dispersion is mainly by movement of solid particles; (2) *hydromorphic*, where the dynamic agents are aqueous solutions; and (3) *biogenic*, where the patterns are the result of biological activity. The principal characteristics of the various kinds of secondary dispersion patterns are summarized in Figure 8-1.

Because of the fact that secondary patterns are often the net result of a combination of processes, a genetic system of classification such as the one proposed cannot be applied too rigidly. Careful studies of the chemical and physical characteristics of a dispersion

Genetic classification		Dispersion process	Principal transporting agent	Matrix	Mode of occurrence of dispersed elements	Form of dispersion pattern
Syngenetic patterns	Clastic	Weathering *in situ*		Weathered rock / Residual overburden / Gossan	Resistant primary and secondary minerals; minor constituents of clay minerals and secondary hydrous oxides	Superjacent patterns
		Movement of solid particles by:	Gravity	Residual overburden / Gossan / Colluvium		Fans and asymmetrical superjacent patterns
			Ice	Moraine		Fans
				Glaciofluvial deposits		Trains and irregular patterns
			Water	Sheetwash deposits		Fans
				Stream sediment		Trains
				Lake sediment		Delta fans
			Wind	Aeolian deposits		Fans
	Hydro-morphic	Movement of solutions	Ground water	Ground-water solution	Soluble salt complexes and sols	Fans
			Surface water	Surface-water solution		Trains
				Precipitates and evaporite deposits	Precipitated salts	Lateral patterns
	Biogenic	Plant metabolism	Uptake by living plants	Living-plant tissue / Organic debris	Metallo-organic compounds	Superjacent and lateral patterns
Epigenetic patterns	Hydro-morphic	Movement of solutions followed by precipitation	Ground water	Any clastic overburden	Ions sorbed on clay minerals; hydrous oxides and organic matter; ions coprecipitated and occluded in hydrous oxides; metallo-organic compounds; precipitated salts	Superjacent patterns; fans
				Soils of seepage areas		Lateral patterns
			Surface water	Stream sediments		Trains
	Biogenic	Plant metabolism followed by redistribution of organic decomposition products	Nutrient solutions; soil moisture	Any clastic overburden		Superjacent and lateral patterns

Fig. 8-I. Classification and general characteristics of the principal types of secondary dispersion patterns.

pattern may, however, lead to a fairly reliable prognosis as to its source, even where its genetic history has been relatively complicated.

8–2. Syngenetic Patterns

Syngenetic patterns may be either clastic, hydromorphic, or biogenic. For the most part, these patterns are relatively simple to interpret, inasmuch as the history of the matrix provides a direct link between the pattern of dispersed metal and its primary source in the bedrock.

Clastic Patterns. Residual soil, colluvium, alluvial sediments, and glacial till are the common media for virtually all clastic patterns. In residual soil, they reflect the distribution of the elements in the underlying bedrock surface; the bedrock patterns of distribution of the immobile elements are usually more faithfully preserved than those defined by the more mobile constituents, which are subject to leaching and redistribution in the weathered residuum. Syngenetic patterns in colluvium and glacial moraine also point to a metal source at the bedrock surface, although here the relationship between the dispersion pattern and the bedrock source may be complicated by substantial lateral movement and by the vagaries of glacial transport and redeposition.

Clastic patterns in stream sediment result from the erosion and alluvial transport of metal-rich overburden. Here the relationship between the anomaly and the bedrock source may be complicated by the previous dispersion history of the metal in the overburden. If the sediment anomaly is derived directly from the erosion of a residual soil anomaly, the bedrock source of metal will occur in the immediate vicinity of the soil anomaly. If the sediment anomaly comes from the erosion of a seepage soil anomaly, however, the bedrock source must be sought up the slope of the water table from the seepage anomaly.

Hydromorphic Patterns. The soluble load of ground and surface water is another kind of syngenetic dispersion pattern. Here the matrix is water rather than soil or some other solid-phase material. As with syngenetic soil anomalies, determining the source of the metal-rich matrix, in this case water, goes a long way toward determining the bedrock source of the anomalous constituents. For this reason, it seems more realistic to think of dispersion patterns in water as syngenetic, rather than epigenetic as proposed by Ginzburg (1960, p. 155).

Massive chemical precipitates and evaporite deposits would be properly classified as syngenetic patterns of hydromorphic origin. Where the precipitates are not massive but are disseminated in the interstices of a clastic matrix (e.g., soil or stream sediment), the pattern would be regarded more appropriately as epigenetic. An important example of syngenetic patterns of this kind would be those formed in and contemporaneously with extensive deposits of bog iron and manganese ores.

Biogenic Patterns. An anomalous concentration of readily available metals in the soil will normally be reflected by an anomalous metal pattern in the plants growing on the soil. Plant anomalies are syngenetic in that they were formed contemporaneously with the growth of the plant itself. Similarly, dispersion patterns in organic debris derived solely from the accumulation of partially decomposed plant material are syngenetic. Biogenic patterns of syngenetic origin reflect in part the composition of local bedrock or overburden and in part the composition of circulating ground-water solutions.

8–3. Epigenetic Patterns

Epigenetic patterns of dispersed materials introduced subsequent to the matrix are necessarily the result of either hydromorphic or biogenic processes. For this reason, they are most commonly defined by the semimobile elements, such as Zn and Cu, that can be both readily dissolved and readily precipitated with local changes in the environment.

Hydromorphic Patterns. Natural aqueous solutions normally leave a pattern of precipitates of one kind or another in the matrix through which they flow. The resulting epigenetic dispersion patterns are superimposed on indigenous (syngenetic) patterns originally present in the matrix, whether rock or soil of either residual or transported origin. Hydromorphic anomalies of this type are always particularly well developed wherever the local environment is especially favorable to precipitation. Such conditions are common in spring or seepage areas and in organic swamps. The source of hydromorphic anomalies naturally lies upstream, updrainage, or in depth, according to the route followed by the metal-bearing solutions.

Biogenic Patterns. With the decay of the living or dead organic matter serving as the host for a plant anomaly, a major part of the mineral content may be leached away. A certain fraction of the mineral matter released by the decay may, however, be retained in the soil where it forms an epigenetic anomaly of biological origin. Biogenic patterns of this kind can develop in either residual or transported overburden. Their relationship to the bedrock source is naturally the same as that of the particular syngenetic vegetation patterns from which they are immediately derived.

8–4. Partition of Dispersed Constituents Between Liquid and Solid Media

The behavior of the individual chemical elements in the cycle of secondary dispersion is conditioned throughout by their relative mobility. Immobile elements tend to lag behind with the clastic products of weathering, while the mobile elements tend to travel away from the site of weathering as part of the soluble load of ground and surface water. It is important to realize, however, that during the course of dispersion there is usually interchange to a greater or less extent between solutions and the solid phase with which they are in contact. This interchange is illustrated schematically in Figure 8-2.

Liquid Media. A dispersed constituent will be relatively mobile when it is carried in natural waters as a component of stable solutes or suspensoids. Where the constituent is carried in the water in a form that is less stable and hence more prone to reaction with the matrix in contact with it, the chances of forming a precipitate are higher, and the effective mobility is lower. The partition of an element between any two competing phases such as natural waters and the surrounding clastic matrix depends not only on its relative stability in the two phases but also on the speed of the reaction that leads from the less stable to the more stable form. The reactivity of the minor constituents of natural waters thus depends on their mode of occurrence—whether they are carried with highly reactive components of the water or with components that are either stable or that do not react rapidly.

The ionic constituents of water are generally by far the most reactive. Ions are free to react very rapidly either to form precipitates or to enter into ion-exchange reactions on the surface of charged solid particles. It is the ionic constituents of water, therefore, that most commonly take part in the formation of hydromorphic dispersion patterns in soils and stream sediments. The other components of natural water, including dissolved gases, undissociated soluble organic and inorganic matter, and dispersed material of colloidal dimensions, are by comparison far less reactive.

Solid Media. Except where the metals occur in distinctive, coarse-grained minerals, it is not always easy to tell what mineral or nonmineral phases of the matrix are serving as hosts for the trace elements. Nevertheless, indirect evidence that may be useful as a guide to the probable partition of metals in residual or transported overburden and in stream sediments can often be obtained by (1) considering the general geochemical behavior of the elements in the

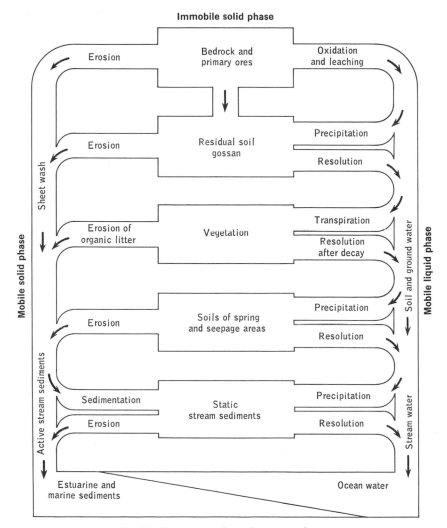

Fig. 8-2. Dispersion of weathering products.

zone of weathering, as reviewed in the Appendix, and (2) determining the relative proportions of metal released by different chemical extractants, as indicated below.

Resistant primary minerals include some ore and gangue minerals as well as resistant rock-forming minerals. The relative stability of the primary constituents and the degree of weathering are the controlling factors. The chemical and physical properties characteristic of the mineral species involved determine the methods by which they may be detected. If chemical analysis is required, it is usually necessary to resort to a vigorous attack by strong, hot acids or fluxes, in order to break down the primary minerals.

Secondary ore minerals include a variety of oxides and oxy salts. Oxides and carbonates are mostly soluble in cold, weak acids; sulfates range from water-soluble to those which, in company with secondary silicates, normally require strong or hot acids for solution. Phosphates are likely to be relatively insoluble, so that very strong, hot acids or fluxes may be necessary to release the metals.

Clay minerals make up the bulk of the solid breakdown products of the rock-forming silicates. Metals may be incorporated within the clay-mineral lattice or adsorbed in exchange positions on the particle surface. Complete extraction of lattice-held metal, which is commonly of residual origin, requires destruction of the mineral, which can be accomplished by treatment with strong, hot acids or by fusion. Metal adsorbed on clay minerals is indicative of the ions dissolved in the solutions with which they are in contact. Adsorbed ions are loosely held and can normally be released by leaching with cold aqueous extractants. With time, adsorbed metal may become incorporated within the lattice and will then be less readily extracted.

Secondary hydrous oxides of Fe and Mn may be derived from the weathering of rock-forming minerals as well as from primary ore minerals. Important amounts of many soluble ore metals may be coprecipitated, occluded, or adsorbed with the hydrous oxides. Metal held in this way may be either residual or acquired from soil moisture or ground-water solutions. The readiness with which the metal may be extracted varies greatly according to the nature of the bonding and the condition of the oxide host. Freshly precipitated or adsorbed metals may be readily extracted by cold reagents. The proportion of readily extractable metal tends to decrease with time and with progressive dehydration and crystallization of the host, and can then be released only by hot acids or fluxes.

Organic matter may contain appreciable amounts of many metals. The greater part of this metal has usually been introduced by ground water, stream water, or decaying vegetation. The bonding is extremely variable and complex, ranging from simple adsorbed ions to metallo-organic compounds and metal incorporated in the structure of living organisms. The adsorbed fraction, as might be expected, is readily extracted by cold aqueous solutions, though often less readily than from clays. Complete release of the more firmly bonded metal generally requires complete destruction of the organic matter. This is usually accomplished by ashing or wet oxidation.

8–5. Extractability of Metal from Clastic Samples

It will readily be appreciated from the foregoing that the syngenetic or epigenetic character of a dispersion pattern may be recognized by the partition of the metal between the various solid phases,
and that the mode of occurrence of the metal may in fact be suggested by the relative extractability of the metal in different reagents.
Broadly speaking, the epigenetic components of a sample tend to be
more readily extractable in weak aqueous reagents than syngenetic
components.

By convention, the content of a metal that can be extracted from
weathered rock, overburden, or stream sediment, by weak chemical
reagents (e.g., cold HCl or citrate solutions) is referred to in the
literature of geochemical prospecting as *readily extractable* or *cold-
extractable* metal. These terms are conveniently abbreviated "cxMe"
or, in the case of a specific metal such as Cu or Zn, "cxCu" or "cxZn."
In this terminology, "cxMe:Me" refers to the fraction of the total
metal content of a sample that is soluble in weak chemical extractants, and is usually expressed as a percentage.

Conclusive evidence of syngenetic clastic origin is, of course, the
presence of residual or detrital grains of primary ore minerals. However, with unstable ore minerals, most of the metal of clastic patterns, including anomalous metal, is contained in secondary minerals,
principally in the clay minerals and hydrous oxides. Insofar as these
minerals have resisted the chemical attack of natural solutions during
weathering and possibly also a cycle of erosion and transport, they
usually tend to be relatively resistant to attack and solution by
laboratory extractants. As a result, the cxMe:Me ratio in syngenetic
clastic anomalies tends to be low. Exceptions to this rule occur, particularly where weathering is incomplete, where soluble secondary
minerals are present, and in poorly drained material where leaching
may not have been effective.

In epigenetic patterns where the introduced metal is of hydromorphic origin and formed by the relatively recent precipitation of
soluble material from ground or surface waters, the content of readily
extractable metal is maintained by active exchange with the metal
in solution. In consequence the cxMe:Me ratio tends to be high. The
original metal content of the matrix occurs in the same forms as in
purely syngenetic patterns and is usually strongly bonded.

A more complex situation exists in biogenic patterns. Here, part of the
introduced metal is held in the same manner as in hydromorphic
patterns while part is more firmly bonded in residual organic compounds that differ widely in their solubility in standard extractants.

The cxMe:Me ratio varies accordingly but is typically higher than for syngenetic patterns and is usually less than for hydromorphic patterns in the same general environment.

8–6. Contrast

The contrast in metal content between secondary geochemical anomalies and normal background is dependent on a number of factors. These include (1) the primary contrast between ore and

TABLE 8-1. Average Contrast Between the Metal Content of Marginal Ore and Unmineralized Rock

Principal Metals	(A) Content in Igneous Rocks (ppm)[a]	(B) Content in Workable Ore (ppm)[b]	Contrast (Ratio B:A)
Chromium	2,000[c]	250,000	125
Cobalt	18	5,000	250
Copper	70	10,000	140
Gold	0.001	10	10,000
Iron	46,500	300,000	6
Lead	16	50,000	3,000
Manganese	1,000	250,000	250
Molybdenum	2	5,000	2,500
Nickel	160[d]	15,000	95
Silver	0.2	500	2,500
Tin	30	10,000	300
Tungsten	2	5,000	2,500
Vanadium	90	25,000	300
Zinc	80	80,000	1,000

[a]Green (1959) except as noted.
[b]Figures for Cr, Cu, Au, Fe, Pb, Mn, Ni, Ag, Sn, Zn from Fleischer (1954).
[c]Average ultramafic rock (Vinogradov, 1956a).
[d]Average gabbro (Vinogradov, 1956a).

country rock, (2) the relative mobility of elements in the dispersion environment, and (3) dilution with barren material. Primary contrast varies widely for the different metals and classes of mineral deposits (Table 8-1). In clastic anomalies, primary contrast is preserved to a greater extent by immobile elements such as Sn and Be than by more mobile elements such as Zn and Cu, which are more susceptible to leaching. Even with the most mobile elements the degree of leaching is, of course, determined by the intensity of weathering, the rate of flow of water, the pH, and the many other factors that play a part in the formation of dispersion patterns. These same factors influence the contrast shown by hydromorphic anomalies. In waters, contrast is also a function of mobility in that, other things being equal, the highest contrast is shown by elements possessing the greatest mobility. Mobile elements that are susceptible to precipitation with moderate yet critical changes in the chemical and biological environment tend to give the best contrast in hydro-morphic soil and sediment anomalies.

Contrast in plant anomalies is dependent to a degree on the contrast in the metal available in the soil of the root zone. The availability of an element to plants is often an approximate reflection of its mobility in the more general sense. In biogenic soil anomalies, on the other hand, contrast is governed by the metal content of the present vegetation, subject only to modification to a greater or less extent by accumulation or leaching of the biogenic metal during the course of soil formation.

Dilution consequent on mixing with barren material is essentially a local problem, although the effect is liable to be more pronounced in some environments than in others. Generally speaking, rapid dilution of an anomaly with distance from the source is more serious with a vigorous dispersion mechanism and with an abundant supply of barren material at the point of origin of the dispersion pattern. Thus, dilution and a resulting reduction in contrast is characteristic of glacial and fluvial dispersion and is less severe with residual soils in flat terrain or on ridge crests.

Ideally the aim of a geochemical exploration survey is to detect only those patterns of metal derived from mineral deposits. If it is possible to exclude that part of the total metal content that is not related to the mineralization, then anomaly contrast will be greatly enhanced. *Fractional analysis* is most likely to be successful in mapping epigenetic patterns, both hydromorphic and biogenic, where the introduced metal is often more readily extractable than the original component. Even in syngenetic anomalies, however, the metal derived from ore minerals may occur in a different form to that from the country rock, though for many metals the partition is usually less marked or is not so readily detectable by fractional analysis.

8–7. Form of Secondary Patterns

Classification of secondary patterns according to their geometrical shape and location with respect to the bedrock source is helpful not only in laying out sampling programs but also in interpreting the data in terms of the probable cause of anomalies. The various characteristic forms that result from the different modes of formation of dispersion patterns are illustrated in Figures 8-3 to 8-8.

The terminology used is purely descriptive. Patterns developed more or less directly over the bedrock source are said to be *super-jacent*, as distinct from *lateral* patterns that are displaced to one side and entirely underlain by barren bedrock. Superjacent patterns more or less symmetrically disposed about the source are termed *halos*. Directional movement during dispersion results in asymmetry, the pattern then taking the form of a *fan* spreading outward from the source, or a *train* if dispersion takes place along a restricted channelway.

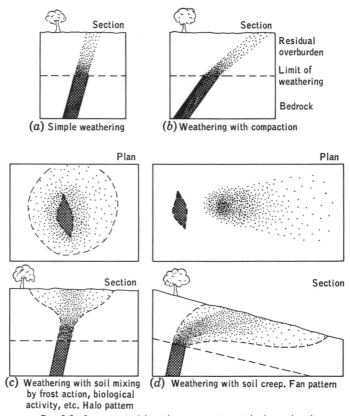

Fig. 8-3. Syngenetic (clastic) patterns in residual overburden.

For complete description it is necessary also to take into account the distribution of anomalous metal values within a pattern. Anomalies are said to be *intense* if values rise sharply to well-defined peaks, or *diffuse* if the pattern is more subdued and does not show any pronounced focal point. The *homogeneity* of an anomaly is also determined by the regularity with which values are distributed within the pattern.

Clastic Patterns. The form of clastic anomalies of syngenetic origin depends very much on the dispersion medium. Superjacent patterns are typical of residual overburden. Lateral patterns may result from

compaction during weathering, though as a rule the amount of displacement is small. Gravity creep causes distortion, leading in extreme
cases to well-developed fans extending downslope from the deposit.
Fans are also characteristic of syngenetic patterns in glacial till and
aeolian deposits, the apex of the fan lying near the deposit and spread-

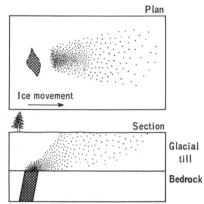

Fig. 8-4. Syngenetic (clastic) patterns in trans-   (*a*) Fan pattern by glacial action
ported overburden.

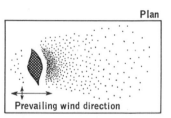

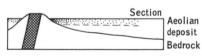

(*b*) Fan pattern by wind action

ing out in the direction of ice or wind movement. In deposits of alluvium laid down by sheet wash flowing across unrestricted pediment
areas, the anomalies again take the form of fans, spreading out from
the bedrock deposit or from the point where the surface water leaves
a restricted channel. Where the drainage channel is well defined
throughout its course, the alluvial anomaly is a linear train. At the
point of entry into a lake, fans may again develop in deltaic sediments.

Hydromorphic Patterns. The form of hydromorphic patterns depends first on the local flow pattern of the solutions. Linear dispersion trains result where the flow is strongly channeled, as in surface

Plan

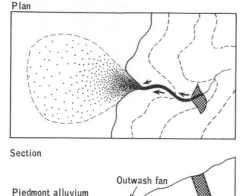

Fig. 8-5. Syngenetic (clastic) pattern in outwash fan and piedmont sheet-wash alluvium.

Section

Piedmont alluvium

Outwash fan

Hydromorphic patterns

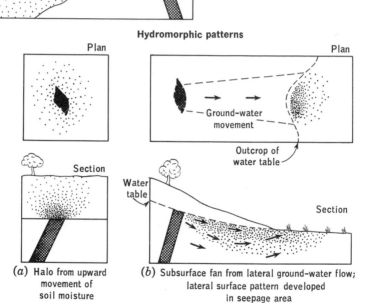

Plan

Plan

Ground-water movement

Outcrop of water table

Section

Water table

Section

(a) Halo from upward movement of soil moisture

(b) Subsurface fan from lateral ground-water flow; lateral surface pattern developed in seepage area

Biogenic pattern

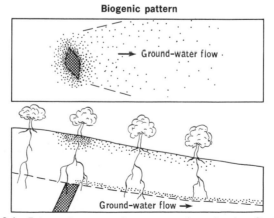

Ground-water flow

Ground-water flow →

Fig. 8-6. Epigenetic patterns in transported overburden. Similar dispersion may also contribute to patterns in residual overburden.

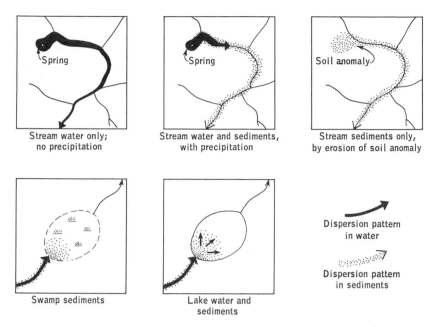

Fig. 8-7. Principal types of dispersion patterns in surface drainage.

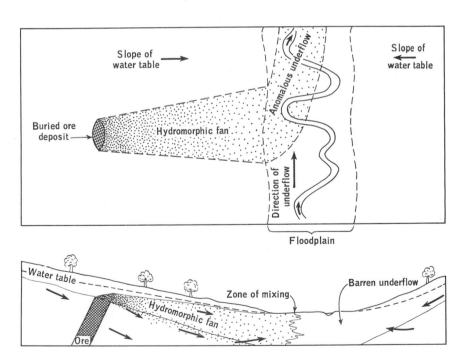

Fig. 8-8. Relation of ground-water anomalies on valley slopes to anomalous underflow.

drainage patterns. Ground-water patterns, on the other hand, tend to be more nearly fan-shaped with local modifications resulting from preferential flow along bedrock channel-ways or permeable horizons in the overburden. Superjacent hydromorphic patterns, sometimes precipitated from ground-water solutions in the overburden above a concealed deposit, range in form from halos to fans, according to the amount of lateral flow. The form of hydromorphic patterns may be further complicated by the uneven distribution of local environments that favor precipitation. This effect is particularly noticeable in the lateral patterns developed in seepage zones, where the solutions may be canalized by the bedrock topography and precipitation is governed by the local distribution of appropriate Eh-pH conditions, organic matter, and clay minerals.

Biogenic Patterns.   The form of biogenic anomalies in plants and in the soil beneath the plants is determined by the pattern of available metal in the root zone. Biogenic anomalies may range, therefore, from superjacent to lateral, from halos to fans, and even to trains, where metal-bearing ground water is canalized along a subsurface drainage system. In view of the complexity of the biogeochemical cycle, however, biogenic anomalies are often less well defined than the parent syngenetic or hydromorphic patterns in the root zone. Strong halos may form, however, when the plants are rooted directly in an underlying mineral deposit.

8–8. Anomalies Not Related to Mineral Deposits

Most geochemical surveys disclose a bewildering array of anomalies, or departures from the geochemical patterns that are considered normal for the survey area. One of the most critical and often one of the most difficult tasks is that of discriminating between anomalies that should be followed up and anomalies that are of no economic significance. Nonsignificant anomalous patterns usually fall into one of three main types.

1. Patterns related to certain rocks that are characterized by a relatively high background metal content.
2. Anomalies due to contamination as a result of man's activities.
3. Apparent anomalies resulting from sampling or analytical errors.

These misleading patterns will be discussed in more detail in later chapters; suffice here to review briefly some of their general characteristics, for comparison with those of patterns related to mineral deposits.

High-Background Source Rocks.   Many kinds of rocks are characterized by relatively high concentrations of many of the same elements that occur in ore deposits, but that have no genetic relation to the ore. Secondary dispersion patterns developed from the weathering of these high-background rocks may show many of the features of patterns that are derived from ores. Discriminating between nonsignificant anomalies resulting from high-background rocks and significant anomalies resulting from ore deposits can be an extremely difficult problem. Fortunately, many metals in high-background rocks occur in a different form and are accompanied by different associated elements or primary minerals than the same metals in ores. Where this contrast in primary mineralogy and associations is carried over into the secondary patterns, it may be possible to develop criteria for screening out anomalies due only to high-background rock.

The family of ultramafic rocks, including peridotite, serpentine, and kimberlite, is probably the most spectacular example of a high-background source rock. These rocks are typically very much enriched in Cr, Ni, Co, and Mg. The weathering product of ultramafic rocks commonly contains a high concentration of montmorillonite, and thus has a high exchange capacity and possibly also a high content of readily extractable cations. The association of the four elements, Cr, Ni, Co, and Mg, normally carries through into the secondary dispersion patterns and serves as a key to the source. The stunted nature of vegetation growing on "serpentine soils" also is a guide to ultramafic rocks.

The family of mafic rocks, including gabbro, basalt, and diabase or dolerite, is characterized by a relatively high content of Fe, Ti, and Cu. The high pH associated with weathering calcareous rocks may restrict dispersion of their metal content to the extent that apparently anomalous patterns occur in the residuum. Acid from the oxidation of pyrite-rich rocks such as pyritic shale may have the reverse effect and cause the accelerated leaching of metals from rocks of normal composition and the resulting development of anomalous hydromorphic patterns unrelated to ore.

Less common high-background rocks that should be kept in mind in sorting out anomalies are black shale (see Appendix), phosphorite (P, V, U, Mo, Zn), saline deposits (SO_4), and carbonatite (Zr, Nb, rare earths).

Contamination. Probable sources of metal contamination arising from human activity are many and varied. The most common are mine dumps, old mine workings, smelting operations, metal-rich agricultural chemicals, road metalling, industrial and domestic fumes, effluent and waste of many kinds.

Dispersion is normally by gravity movement of solid particles, wind-blown material or in aqueous solutions, while plants may ingest contaminating metal at any stage of its dispersion. Contamination patterns may thus form in any type of clastic, hydromorphic, or biogenic environment.

In clastic patterns, the modes of occurrence of exotic contaminating metal are usually very different from those of the natural metal, although the distinction may not be so readily made when the contaminating source derives from the spoil of ancient mining activity. In most hydromorphic and biogenic dispersion patterns, however, it is extremely difficult to tell whether the metal came from a natural or an artificial source.

Initially the form of contamination patterns is conditioned by the geometrical shape of the source area. On dispersion away from the source of contamination, fans and trains may be developed which, in the case of wind-blown material, stream sediment, and aqueous solutions, may be very extensive. The outstanding feature of contamination, however, is the fact that it almost invariably originates at the surface of the ground. As a result, soil patterns are most strongly developed in, and in many cases confined to, the surface horizon, in contrast to natural superjacent soil patterns of clastic and hydromorphic origin. Apart from this, however, the surface origin of contamination need not lead to any dissimilarities with hydromorphic and biogenic patterns, either in the overburden or in the drainage system.

Nevertheless, despite the limitations and difficulties sometimes imposed by contamination, it has rarely, to the authors' knowledge, presented an insuperable problem in geochemical surveys, even in well-populated or intensively prospected areas.

Sampling Errors. Spurious anomalies related to sampling errors may be more difficult both to detect and to guard against, particularly in a routine survey where sampling is usually carried out by relatively untrained labor. For the most part, they arise from the collection of samples which, though superficially similar to the main body of samples, are enriched in metal by some natural process unrelated to ore. Natural processes of weathering, erosion, and secondary dispersion not uncommonly result in patterns of enrichment of ore metals in areas of background composition that can readily be confused with significant anomalies related to ore deposits. Natural enrichments of background metal commonly occur in the organic matter of humus horizons, in the limonitic B horizon of podzols, and in clastic material that for one reason or another has a high exchange capacity. Enrichments are characteristic of seepage areas and any other points along the drainage pattern where conditions favor the preferential accumulation of metal. Enrichment of metals in plants also may take place for a variety of reasons, all unrelated to the amount of metal in the supporting soil. As a rule, apparent anomalies arising from the inadvertent collection of naturally enriched material may tend to be related to some recognizable geomorphological feature of the environment, such as the topography, in which case they are readily recognized for what they are. The need to collect material that is strictly comparable in all respects and to note all changes in the sample environment that may possibly affect the dispersion of both background and anomalous metal cannot be overemphasized.

Analytical Errors. Anomalous patterns of no significance whatever may appear in geochemical data as the result of errors in analytical technique. Such patterns, if suspected, can be eliminated simply by a repeat analysis of the samples in question. Isolated erratic values are immediately suspect and should be rechecked. Apparent patterns arising from analytical bias may be recognized by their association with groups or batches of samples or with individual analysts. A commonly used method of protection against analytical bias is a system of routine repeat analysis of samples selected at random from previous batches.

8–9. Suppression of Significant Anomalies

Some of the same factors responsible for anomalies unrelated to mineral deposits may also operate in the reverse direction, with the result that significant anomalies in the vicinity of a metal-rich bedrock source may be missed. Thus during soil formation, for example, the A horizon may be leached so effectively that no anomalous values may be detectable in this horizon, whereas the underlying horizons may show strong anomalies. Samples intended to represent material from hydromorphic soils may have mistakenly been taken from freely drained ground, and hence miss a seepage anomaly. Not uncommonly, anomalies are overlooked because of gross failures in recognizing the nature of the matrix. Transported loess, alluvium, or moraine may be mistaken for residual soil. The absence of anomalous patterns in material that is assumed to be residual can be misinterpreted as an indication of the absence of an underlying metal-rich source.

CHAPTER 9

ANOMALIES IN RESIDUAL OVERBURDEN

The nature of the parent material from which a residual soil has been formed is not always apparent from a cursory inspection of the color or texture of the soil. As a result, many ore deposits have undoubtedly escaped detection because there is no conspicuous diagnostic pattern in the residual overburden. Even where the bedrock is exposed, weathering and leaching may still obscure evidence of the primary metal content.

Vestigial traces of the chemical and mineralogical characteristics of the original parent material, however, will normally be retained more or less *in situ* in the residuum even where the more obvious criteria are lacking. Vestigial features resulting from simple weathering in place of a metal-rich parent material provide an extremely direct and straightforward geochemical guide to buried ore. For this reason, geochemical anomalies in weathered rock and residual soil have become the most widely used and successful of all the geochemical prospecting methods.

The simple residual pattern is often complicated, however, by hydromorphic patterns of metal superimposed on the residual material by precipitation from metal-rich ground waters draining the mineralized ground. These patterns may be formed at a considerable lateral distance from the deposit. The picture may be further complicated by anomalous concentrations of metal that bear no relation at all to the occurrence of ore.

9–1. Anomalies in Leached Ore Outcrops and Gossans

Residual limonite derived from the oxidation of Fe-bearing sulfides and carbonates has been one of the most reliable of the traditional prospecting guides in areas of residual cover and deep weathering. According to the degree of leaching and the massive or disseminated nature of the primary mineralization, the resulting product of weathering may range all the way from a leached rock often containing cavities only partially filled with limonitic material to the massive accumulations of limonite known as gossans.

The principal problem in using leached outcrops and gossans as ore guides is the difficulty in determining the tenor of the primary mineralization. Many criteria for distinguishing productive from barren gossans have been used by geologists and prospectors with varying degrees of success. The color of limonites is used widely as an indication of primary grade; quantitative studies suggest that, in general, this is not a reliable guide (Kelly, 1958). Texture has also

TABLE 9-1. Analyses of Limonites Showing Contrasting Ore-Metal Contents in Gossans and "Pseudogossans"

Metal Content of Gossan and Pseudogossan, Borneo[a]			
Sample	Cu (ppm)	Co (ppm)	Ni (ppm)
Sulfide gossan	11,000	500	50
Pseudogossan derived from ultramafic rock	110	200	2,000
Gossan of unknown derivation but probably related to sulfides	3,200	25	130

Metal Content of Gossan Derived from Mineralized and Unmineralized Sulfide Veins, Sierra Leone[b]			
Sample	Pb (ppm)	Mo (ppm)	Au (ppm)	Ag (ppm)
Quartzose gossan (mineralized)	900	600	20	6.6
Gossan stringers (mineralized)	400	400	0.3	13
Massive gossan (mineralized?)	300	10	Nil	
Gossan with muscovite (unmineralized)	50	10	Tr.	

[a]Samples supplied by Geological Survey of Borneo, analyses by Geochemical Prospecting Research Centre, Imperial College, London.
[b]Data supplied by Geological Survey of Sierra Leone.

been used in distinguishing limonite derived from ore minerals from that derived from barren iron sulfides or carbonates of no economic significance (McKinstry, 1948, p. 268-276). Diagnostic textures are not always clearly developed, however, and even an accurate qualitative interpretation of their significance is often difficult.

Chemical composition as a basis for appraising secondary limonitic material, however, can be put on a nonsubjective, quantitative basis much more easily than studies of color or texture. Leached cappings and gossans formed from the weathering of ores of Cu, Co, Ni, Mo, and other metals that are commonly coprecipitated with Fe hydroxide can often be recognized by their high ore-metal content as compared with lateritic limonites, bog iron ores, and the weathering products of barren syngenetic sulfides and Fe-bearing carbonates (Table 9-1). According to Sindeyeva (1955), gossans derived from epigenetic sulfide are also characterized by a high content of Se. A hint even as to the relative proportions of metals in the primary ore may be provided by the ratios of ore metals in the gossan. In the

Nyeba district of Nigeria, for example, blocks of gossan collected over a known Pb-Zn deposit contained in the order of 4000 ppm Pb and 500 ppm Zn. Similar material from an undeveloped prospect, where a geochemical soil survey showed the presence of Zn but no Pb, contained about 50 ppm Pb and 8000 ppm Zn (Hawkes, 1954, p. 76).

So-called *transported* gossans have an origin somewhat different from the residual gossans discussed above. Some transported gossans are simply colluvial accumulations of fragments of normal gossan that have moved down the slope from the site of weathering. Another variety of transported gossan of an entirely different origin is effectively a fossil spring or seepage deposit, where at one time Fe-rich ground water resulting from the leaching of Fe minerals has precipitated massive limonite at or near the daylight surface. The composition of lateral hydromorphic gossans of this type will also tend to reflect the metal content of the parent mineral deposit, although differences in the relative mobilities of the ore metals will show up more strongly than with residual gossans, where transport in ground-water solutions is not an important factor.

Leached outcrops are more difficult to appraise by geochemical methods than gossans because of the impoverishment not only of the ore metals but also of the limonite. The residual metal content, however, can still be used as an ore guide even where extreme leaching of disseminated sulfide ores has left only traces of residual limonite. In practical survey work, the metal content of the limonite can be approximated by using a chemical extractant that is selective for limonite, followed by a determination of the ratio of metal to Fe in the extract.

9-2. Syngenetic Anomalies in Residual Soil

Geochemical patterns of distribution of major and minor elements in residual soils are first of all a reflection of the distribution of the elements in the parent rocks. This primary distribution pattern is the key to buried ore and is the ultimate goal of the geochemical soil survey.

Superimposed on this relatively simple primary pattern, however, are the effects of agents that tend to make the soil more homogeneous and hence suppress the primary patterns (frost, plants, animals, gravity, local solution and redeposition), and the forces that tend to differentiate the soil and hence impose new chemical patterns unrelated to the parent material (soil formation). This dynamic system is further complicated by factors tending to remove elements from the soil (leaching by rain water, uptake of mineral matter by plants), balanced against the factors that tend to bring in new material from outside (deposition from ground-water solutions, addition of metal from decaying vegetation).

These genetic factors that go into the formation of residual soil anomalies will perhaps be easier to understand after a consideration of their individual physical and chemical characteristics. The most important of these characteristics are (1) the mode of occurrence of the metal, (2) form and magnitude of the anomaly, (3) homogeneity of the pattern, and (4) depth variation.

Mode of Occurrence. Elements derived from the weathering of both ores and normal, unmineralized rock are partitioned between the various components of residual soils in a manner that is characteristic of the elements and of their occurrence in the parent material. A few metals, such as W and Sn, are normally retained in the soil as components of resistant primary minerals. By far the major proportion of most metals released by the breakdown of primary ore and rock-forming minerals occurs in the soil either as secondary ore minerals or as firmly bonded components of clay minerals and hydrous oxides. A relatively small part of the total amount of metal derived from the weathering of the parent rock or ore may be held as readily extractable components of organic matter or as ions adsorbed on clay particles.

The ore minerals that are relatively resistant to chemical breakdown in the environment of weathering include cassiterite, wolframite, scheelite, columbite-tantalite, pyrochlore, diamond, gold, platinum, beryl, chromite, ilmenite, corundum, and cinnabar. Common resistant gangue minerals are quartz, tourmaline, garnet, magnetite, barite, and fluorite. Less resistant minerals may also persist where mechanical weathering predominates over chemical weathering, as is often the case in arid or very cold climates and on steep slopes undergoing active erosion. The grain size will depend on the original particle size and the degree to which this may have been reduced by solution or abrasion during weathering. Commonly an appreciable proportion of the metal held in resistant minerals occurs in the intermediate to coarse fraction, as suggested by the data for immobile metals in Table 9-2.

Primary ore minerals that are not resistant to chemical attack will tend to be decomposed and the constituents made available for incorporation in secondary ore minerals. Many of these secondary minerals, however, are present in important amounts in the soil only under certain special conditions. For example, readily soluble secondary copper carbonates have been noted in the soil at the Bushman

TABLE 9-2. Distribution of Mobile and Immobile Metals in Different Size Fractions of Anomalous Residual Soil[a]

Size Fraction	Mesh (BSS)	Micron Size	Immobile Metals (ppm) Remaining in Resistant Primary Minerals				Residual Portion of Mobile Metals (ppm) Remaining in Secondary Soil Minerals				
			Cr (S. Rhod.)	Sn (Malaya)	Be (S. Rhod.)	Nb (N. Rhod.)	Zn (U.K.)	Cu (N. Rhod.)	Co (N. Rhod.)	Ni (Tangan.)	Mo (Sierra Leone)
Coarse sand	10	1980		150	80						
	20	894	3,000	2,100	70	500	200	20	6	600	20
	35	471	4,000	6,700	25	800	240	30	4	600	30
	80	186	10,000	4,000	20	1,500	180	40	4	600	70
Fine sand	135	104	11,000	2,400	15	2,300	300	25	6	600	90
	200	76			15						
Very fine sand		20		1,000	10	1,800	300	35	10		
Silt			8,000	175		1,700	500	170	24	1200	100
Clay		2		45	3	250	1,500	500	40		

[a]Data by Members of Geochemical Prospecting Research Centre, Imperial College, London.

Mine in Bechuanaland, where calcareous soils have been developed over siliceous metamorphic rocks under a semiarid climate. Similar occurrences have been observed in freely drained latosolic soil derived from calcareous bedrock in central Africa. Primary and secondary copper sulfides, as well as secondary oxy salts occur in the over-burden in the Philippines where juvenile soil has been derived directly from the zone of secondary enrichment, which has been exposed by recent rapid erosion.

Firmly held metal in clay minerals and hydrous oxides accounts for most of the residual metal in areas where unstable ore minerals are oxidizing in a freely drained, thoroughly leached environment. Under these conditions, there is a marked tendency for trace metals of intermediate mobility to be concentrated in the silt and clay-size fractions of the soil, as suggested by the data for Cu, Co and Mo in Table 9-2. White (1957) has carried out experiments on Tennessee soils which indicate that about 50 percent of the zinc in the residuum derived from the weathering of limestone under a humid subtropical climate occurs in the hydrous Fe fraction. Less than 5 percent was found to be readily extractable, and the remainder is assumed to occur in the lattice of the clay minerals. White found a similar partition in both anomalous and background soils. A strong enrichment of firmly bonded anomalous Cu in ferruginous concretions of the B horizon in Rhodesian latosols has been noted by Tooms and Webb (1961); Cu and Co were found to be enriched in manganese wad. Jay (1959) has demonstrated a similar correlation between Co and Mn in the same profiles (Figure 7-5). Concentrations of both As and Mo have been recorded in Fe-rich soils in Sierra Leone, where they probably occur largely as Fe arsenate and ferrimolybdite (hydrated ferric molybdate) respectively (Mather, 1959). Pb also shows a tendency to accumulate with Fe and/or Mn in subtropical soils (Webb, 1958a; Ledward, 1960).

In view of the fact that most of the residual metal in the A and B horizons of freely drained soils is firmly held in this way, the proportion of readily extractable metal (cxMe) is rarely found to exceed 5 to 10 percent of the total metal and often varies erratically down to 1 percent and less.

Adsorption of metal on organic matter in the A_0 and A_1 horizons may account for an important fraction of the total metal. In this case the ratio of cxMe to total metal, though erratic, is commonly higher than in the underlying mineral horizons.

In perennially moist soil horizons, where metal has been introduced or redistributed by dispersion in ground water or soil moisture, very appreciable amounts will be cold-extractable, inasmuch as the bulk of such metal is held by adsorption on clay-size particles and organic matter, or as minor constituents coprecipitated with hydrous Fe and Mn oxides.

Contrast. The primary contrast between bedrock ore and unmineralized host rock will tend to be reflected in the anomaly contrast in the overlying residuum. This tendency is subject to modification

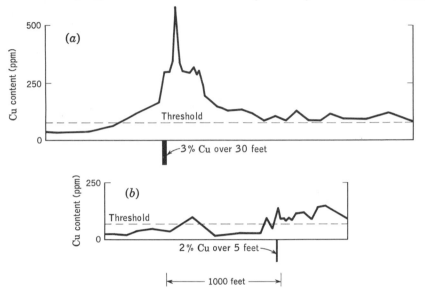

Mineralization: Disseminated chalcopyrite and pyrite in argillaceous ore horizon
Overburden: Freely drained, residual latosol, 20 to 40 feet thick
Relief: Flat peneplain, gentle slope to the south; water table 6 to 20 feet from surface
Sample depth: 18 inches (A_2 horizon)
Analysis: Total Cu, Bisulfate fusion, dithizone/benzene reaction

Fig. 9-1. Relationship between soil anomalies and tenor of underlying mineralization at Baluba, Northern Rhodesia. Data on minus-80-mesh fraction. After Tooms and Webb (1961).

by so many extraneous factors, however, that it is rarely possible to establish any reliable quantitative correlation between anomaly contrast in the soil and the tenor of the bedrock metal source. In the first place, the background metal content is likely to vary as the wall rocks change their character. Secondly, anomaly contrast in the soil can at best reflect the primary contrast at depth only insofar as the latter is preserved in the soil parent material. Consequently, the contrast at surface can vary greatly, even along the strike of the same ore body, solely on account of variations in wall-rock lithology and the degree of subsequent oxidation and leaching at the present-day level of the suboutcrop. To these factors must be added the variations related to changes in the environment of the overburden, particularly with regard to topography, drainage, and the type, depth, and maturity of the soil profile—all of which may vary critically over quite short distances.

Where all the modifying factors are essentially constant, however, the anomaly contrast may correspond roughly with the size and tenor of the underlying mineralization. Figure 9-1 shows an example of such a correlation in areas of similar bedrock geology and soil conditions.

TABLE 9-3.   Accumulation of Niobium as Residual Pyrochlore in Residuum from Carbonatite, Kaluwe, Northern Rhodesia[a]

Depth (inches)	Description	Nb (ppm)
0–3	Brown residual soil	1600
3–6		1000
6–12		800
12–18		600
18–24		500
24–36	Gray-brown calcareous residuum, highly weathered	400
36–48		200
48–60		200
60–72	Weathered carbonatite	400

Source: Watts (1960).
[a]Data for −80-mesh fraction.

Relatively immobile elements such as Sn and Nb suffer little leaching, and to this extent the primary contrast tends to be preserved in the soil. At times, contrast may even be enhanced by residual accumulation of metal in the soil due to solution or eluviation of nonmetalliferous material. Enrichment of this type can be seen over a carbonatite deposit in Northern Rhodesia where solution of the limestone has resulted in the accumulation of stable pyrochlore in the residuum (Table 9-3). With mobile elements such as U, Mo, Zn, and Cu, the anomaly contrast is usually very much less than the primary contrast. Figure 9-2 illustrates the relative preservation of the primary contrast for Pb and the suppression for Zn and Cu in residual soils over a base-metal deposit in North Carolina.

The extent to which the contrast is suppressed or enhanced depends on the total effect at any given point of all the factors influencing mobility and the length of time they have been operative. Briefly, conditions favoring low contrast include deep chemical weathering, mature acid to neutral soil, a siliceous environment, low content of adsorbents (clay, organic matter, and hydrous Fe and Mn oxides), high rainfall, free drainage, and an old stable land form. Conversely, anomaly contrast will tend to be higher where there is a combination of one or more of the following: shallow chemical weathering, juvenile or alkaline soils, a calcareous or highly ferruginous environment, high content of adsorbents, and low rainfall, poor drainage, and active erosion.

Many exceptions to the general trends may be noted. For instance,

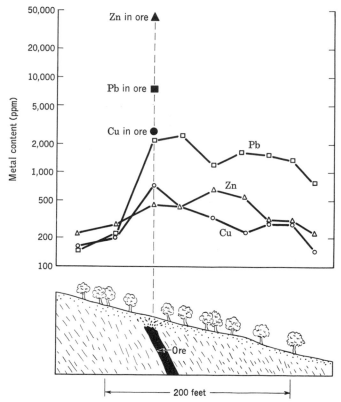

Fig. 9-2. Relationship between residual soil anomalies and ore at Union Copper Mine, North Carolina. Data on minus-2-mm fraction. Data from Huff (1952) and Hawkes (1957).

anomaly contrast for Mo is weak in alkaline soils because of the high mobility of Mo at high pH values. The primary contrast for mobile metals may even be enhanced in the soil if the leached zone has been removed by erosion and the present-day suboutcrop is in the zone of secondary enrichment. Another special case is the marked Cu enrichment that has sometimes been noted in partially leached soils derived from the weathering of calcareous rocks under tropical conditions; in extreme cases 1 to 2 percent Cu occurs in soil derived from bedrock containing only about 0.2 percent Cu.

Anomaly Width and Intensity. As a mineralized structure is weathered, the pattern of distribution of the ore metals will tend to be modified. This modification usually takes the form of simple spreading of the anomalous pattern in the soil so that the anomaly is often substantially wider than the metal pattern in the underlying bedrock. It is important to remember, however, that the presence of

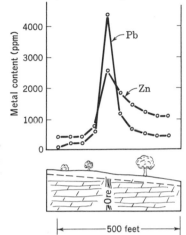

Fig. 9-3. Relationship between residual soil anomaly and lead-zinc vein at Porter's Grove, Wisconsin. Data on minus-2-mm fraction. From Huff (1952).

Mineralization: Fracture-fillings of coarse galena and sphalerite in dolomite
Overburden: Shallow, freely drained residual podzol
Relief: Gentle

a primary dispersion aureole will also contribute to the dimensions of the soil anomaly.

In general, immobile elements tend to give more intense anomalies than do the mobile elements. Figure 9-3 shows the characteristic difference between an intense, sharp Pb anomaly and a weaker, flatter Zn anomaly.

Both mechanical and chemical processes may play a part in dispersing the metal in the soil. Mechanical processes naturally predominate in the case of immobile elements occurring as resistant minerals. Initially, elements of intermediate mobility may be dispersed as aqueous solutions until they are precipitated, whereafter their dispersion is dominated by mechanical rather than chemical factors. The development of the soil anomaly is conditioned, therefore, not only by the relative mobility of the metals concerned but also by the changing balance of all those factors which have a bearing on dispersion. Thus, other things being equal, Cu anomalies formed in a calcareous environment characterized by a high pH will generally tend to be narrower and more intense than those developed in a siliceous environment. The importance of bedrock type in controlling leaching and dispersion is well illustrated in Rhodesia, where broad, diffuse anomalies that may only rise to 1.5 times threshold are characteristic of an arenaceous ore horizon, whereas an anomaly related to

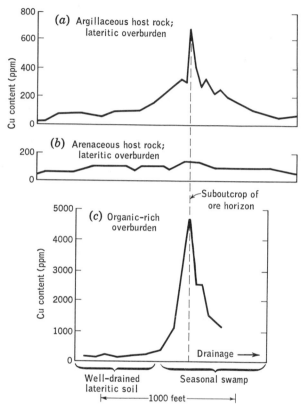

Samples: A_2 horizon in (a) and (b)
          G horizon in seasonal swamp of (c)
Sample depth: 18 inches
Analysis: Total Cu, bisulfate fusion, dithizone/benzene determination; cxCu, cold ammonium citrate (pH 2), dithizone/white spirit determination

Fig. 9-4. Variation in soil anomalies according to host rock and drainage conditions, Northern Rhodesia. After Webb (1958a) and Tooms and Webb (1961).

equivalent mineralization in argillaceous host rock is usually narrower and shows a better-defined peak rising to five to ten times threshold over the ore suboutcrop. The anomaly becomes even more intense where the ore horizon is overlain by poorly drained organic-rich soil, wherein lateral dispersion is retarded by metal adsorption

on organic matter. Anomalies formed under these three conditions
are illustrated in Figure 9-4.

Distortion of Anomalies. Symmetrical halos of dispersed metal
are characteristic of level terrain. On sloping ground, however, anomalies generally tend to fan out asymmetrically in the downslope
direction (Figures 9-2, 9-3, 9-5). Downslope distortion is usually the
effect of physical movement of metal-bearing particles by soil creep

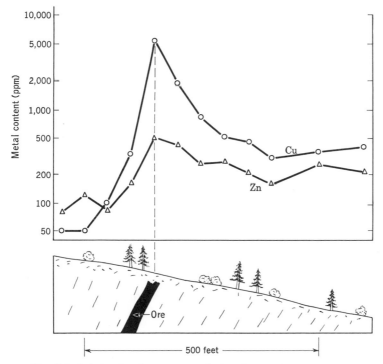

Fig. 9-5. Relationship between residual soil anomalies and ore at
Malachite Copper Mine, Colorado. Data on minus-2-mm fraction.
Data from Huff (1952).

aided by solution and precipitation from laterally moving subsurface waters in the case of soluble metals. Relative mobility is
therefore important in the development of asymmetrical anomalies.
Figure 9-3 shows the difference between the dispersion of Pb and Zn,
where the lower mobility of Pb results in its being dispersed mainly
mechanically by soil creep, whereas the dispersion of Zn has been
aided by chemical solution and precipitation.

As a rule, the steeper the slope, the greater is the distortion. In
extreme cases the anomaly may persist for many hundreds of feet to

the foot of the slope and even beyond into the colluvium (Figure 9-6). However, the relation between relief and the degree of distortion is

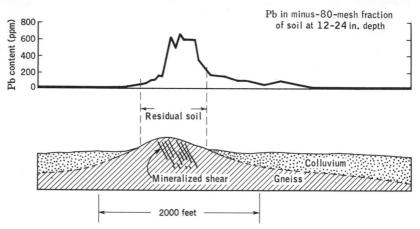

Fig. 9-6. Lateral dispersion of lead from area of mineralized outcrop into soil and colluvium, Mpanda, Tanganyika. After Ledward (1960).

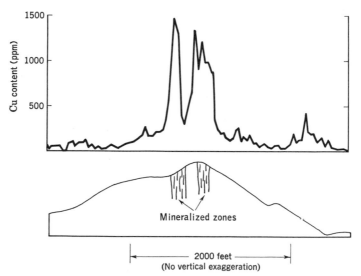

Fig. 9-7. Copper anomalies in near-surface soil, Ruwenzori Mountains, Uganda. Data on minus-80-mesh fraction. After Jacobson (1956).

not always a simple one. For example, in the Ruwenzori Mountains in Uganda, very intense anomalies may occur over the suboutcrop, but extend for only relatively short distances downslope despite gradients of more than 35° (Figure 9-7). The reason for this appears to be that erosion is keeping pace with oxidation, but conditions are such that metal is being leached from the soil as it moves down the slope (Jacobson, 1956). In contrast, if given enough time, a very appreciable degree of distortion can take place on very gentle slopes.

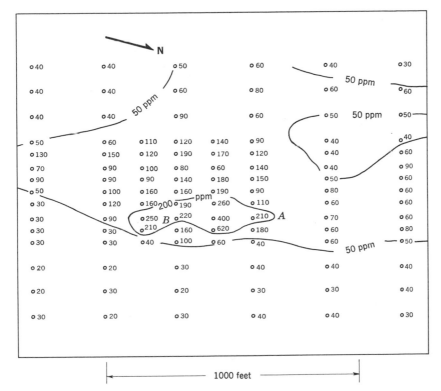

Mineralization: Cu–bearing quartz breccia exposed at *A* and *B*
Climate: Subhumid
Overburden: Residual soil, pH 8.0
Terrain: Essentially flat; general drainage direction is westward
Sample depth: 9 inches
Analysis: Total Cu in minus–80–mesh fraction

Fig. 9-8. Distortion of copper anomaly in residual soil on ancient land surface despite alkaline environment and flat-lying terrain, Bushman Mine, Bechuanaland. After Webb (1958a).

For example, on the mature peneplain of the Rhodesian Copperbelt, anomalies in residual soil may extend for 2000 feet and more on slopes of only one to two degrees (Figure 13-4). The extensive downslope distortion of these anomalies is believed to be due in part to the development of biogenic anomalies over areas of metal-rich ground waters draining the mineralized rock (Tooms and Webb, 1961).

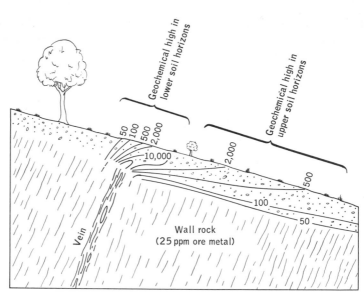

Fig. 9-9. Diagrammatic cross section showing residual soil anomaly resulting from purely mechanical dispersion. From Huff (1952).

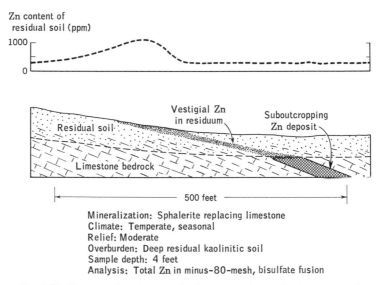

Mineralization: Sphalerite replacing limestone
Climate: Temperate, seasonal
Relief: Moderate
Overburden: Deep residual kaolinitic soil
Sample depth: 4 feet
Analysis: Total Zn in minus-80-mesh, bisulfate fusion

Fig. 9-10. Cross section showing displacement of a residual soil anomaly as a result of compaction during weathering of a gently dipping deposit, Tennessee. After Hawkes and Lakin (1949).

Considerable distortion purely by soil creep can also take place on very old peneplain surfaces if conditions are unfavorable for ground-water dispersion (Figure 9-8).

Where anomalies are distorted by soil creep, it is not uncommon to find that the anomaly peak in the near-surface soil is also displaced downslope from the suboutcrop of the ore (Figure 9-9). The amount of displacement naturally tends to increase with angle of slope and depth of overburden, but in practice is rarely found to exceed 50 feet and is often much less. Displacement of the peak may also occur where the trace of an inclined ore body projects up into the overburden. A case of this kind where the displacement is further accentuated by compaction of the overburden during weathering of the limestone host rock is shown in Figure 9-10.

Homogeneity. The homogeneity or regularity of residual anomalies depends directly on the grain-size and distribution of the soil minerals containing the element in question, and indirectly on the occurrence and distribution of that element in the parent bedrock and/or country rock.

Ore metals which occur as discrete grains of resistant primary or secondary minerals scattered through the soil often show irregular anomalies. On the other hand, much more homogeneous anomalies are characteristic of elements that are pervasively dispersed throughout the body of the soil as minor constituents of the fine-grained clay minerals and hydrous oxides. Thus many of the relatively immobile elements, such as Sn, Be, Pb, tend to give less homogeneous anomalies than Cu, Zn, Co, and other relatively mobile elements. Under certain conditions even the mobile elements may give irregular anomalies if they are preferentially enriched in relatively coarse secondary minerals, concretions, or segregations spotted through the soil.

Despite the very thorough mechanical and chemical homogenization that often occurs in the upper soil horizons, excessively irregular patterns in the bedrock may still persist in the overburden, even in the case of well-dispersed mobile elements. An example of a broad but inhomogeneous Zn anomaly representing the summation of a closely related series of smaller anomalies, each of which by itself may be homogeneous in terms of metal distribution in the individual samples, is illustrated in Figure 4-11. Here the inhomogeneity of the soil anomaly reflects only an inhomogeneous distribution of metal in the bedrock. This is a very different type of inhomogeneity from that described in the previous paragraph, where smoother anomalies could be obtained merely be modifying the sampling technique.

Variations with Depth and Soil Type. Variations in the metal content of the overburden with depth below the surface can come about in three ways: (1) by preservation of the trace of an inclined ore deposit projecting up into the overburden, (2) by physical distortion resulting from soil creep, and (3) by soil formation and profile development.

The palimpsest Zn anomaly shown in Figure 9-10 is an example of the first type. Similar occurrences are also commonly observed in the C horizon of tropical latosols in Rhodesia. Preservation of the inclined attitude can only be expected below the zone of soil mixing and will only assume practical importance in areas of deep and intense weathering, where determination of such variations in metal content with depth may aid in locating the suboutcrop of the primary ore.

In the zone of active soil creep, the metal content varies with depth in a characteristic manner according to the position of the sampling point with respect to the suboutcrop (Figure 9-9). Well downslope from mineralization, the metal content of the soil progressively decreases with depth; on approaching the ore the vertical metal profile shows a maximum at an intermediate depth which becomes progressively deeper until, immediately over the deposit, the metal content increases continuously from surface to bedrock. From Figure 9-9 it will also be seen that the anomaly becomes narrower and more intense with depth. In practice, the ideal sequence is liable to be more or less obscured by slumping, soil homogenization, and the development of soil horizons. Nevertheless, where soil creep is active in moderate to deep overburden, the general trend is usually discernible (Figure 7-12), and the pattern of metal variation down the soil profile can often aid in locating the suboutcrop where conditions are appropriate.

Variation in the distribution of metal with depth is also a natural consequence of weathering and soil formation. The resulting patterns of redistribution in the soil profile depend primarily on the dispersion mechanism, the behavior of the individual metals, and the soil type.

In immature soils, profile variations are not usually important, although under appropriate conditions metals such as Pb, Cu, and Zn, all of which tend to be enriched in humus, may start to accumulate in the organic topsoil. With progressive differentiation of the soil horizons, the pattern of metal redistribution becomes more pronounced.

In mature, freely drained soils, many mobile metals tend to become impoverished in the A horizon and enriched in the B horizon; enrichment in the organic A_0 and A_1 horizons continues erratically. Immediately over the suboutcrop of a deposit the metal content is usually greatest in the C horizon. By contrast, background profiles

and anomalous profiles at a distance from the suboutcrop of the ore
may show a relative enrichment of metal in the B horizon. This type
of redistribution is commonly developed in podzols and podzolic
soils where the dominant agent is downward percolating rain water.
Table 9-4 shows a consistent increase in metal content with depth in

TABLE 9-4.   Metal Content of Anomalous and Background Profiles of Alamance Silt Loam,
North Carolina[a]

Soil Horizon	Average Depth (inches)	Description	Anomalous Profile[b]			Background Profile[b]		
			Pb (ppm)	Cu (ppm)	Zn (ppm)	Pb (ppm)	Cu (ppm)	Zn (ppm)
A_1	0–0.5	Humus	440	150	260	100	20	160
A_2	0.5–2	Gray silt loam	840	300	300	190	24	140
B_1	2–16	Red to yellow silty clay	1000	380	280	230	34	140
B_2	16–29	Same, mottled	1300	750	410	370	57	160
C	>29	Weathered rock	1700	1100	440	180	59	110

Source: Hawkes (1957).
[a]Data for −80-mesh fraction.
[b]Each figure is the average of five samples collected within radius of 4 feet; values rounded to two significant
figures.

an anomalous soil, and a slight enrichment in the B horizon in a
corresponding background soil. The accumulation of metal in the B
horizon has presumably been derived from residual metal leached or
washed out of the A horizon together with any metal that may have
been brought to the surface by plants and subsequently leached from
decaying vegetable matter.

Similar trends are often observed in latosols, where the enrichment
of metals that tend to be precipitated with Fe and Mn may be very
pronounced in the ferruginous B horizon. In this case, in addition to
material derived from the overlying A horizon, ground-water solutions also contribute important amounts of metals dissolved from
the underlying rock. Typical accumulation of Cu and Pb with Fe in
the ferruginous concretionary B horizon and the enrichment of Pb
in organic matter are shown in Table 9-5. Variation in the form of

TABLE 9-5.   Examples of Marked Differentiation of Anomalous Metal in the Different
Soil Horizons of Latosol Profiles, Central Africa[a]

Soil Horizon	Description	Profile Near Cu Deposit Cu (ppm)	Profile Over Cu Deposit Cu (ppm)	Profile Near Pb Deposit Pb (ppm)
A_1	Humic topsoil	130	300	350
A_2	Sandy subsoil	160	300	140
B	Compact with ferruginous concretions	400	1000	880
C	Weathered parent material	200	2000	170

[a]Data for −80-mesh fraction.

copper anomalies in the different horizons of latosolic soils in Rhodesia is shown in Figure 9-11.

In relatively arid environments soluble metals may be expected
to be enriched in horizons formed by evaporation of (1) downward
percolating rain water or (2) ground-water solutions rising into the
capillary fringe zone above the water table. For most semimobile

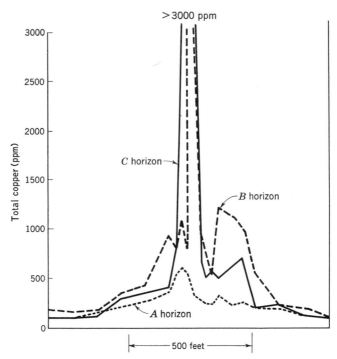

Fig. 9-11. Variation in the form of soil anomalies in different
soil horizons, Northern Rhodesia. After Tooms (1955) and
Tooms and Webb (1961).

metals, however, redistribution in desert environments is likely to
be relatively restricted in view of the characteristically high pH. No
reliable data are available concerning metal distribution in thick
deposits of massive caliche (in Europe, "calcrete") developed in
truly residual overburden. Here, too, mobility is likely to be restricted, with resulting retention or even enrichment of metals in the
zone of precipitation. Metal distribution observed in massive caliche
deposited in overburden of possibly colluvial origin is considered in
the next chapter.

The foregoing has been concerned with freely drained profiles. Where drainage is impeded, the metal distribution in normal hydromorphic soils shows a tendency toward enrichment in the organic-rich A_1 horizon. Directly over mineralization, however, the metal content of hydromorphic soils generally increases progressively with depth (Table 9-6). Similar patterns are observed in tundra profiles where the drainage is impeded by permafrost.

TABLE 9-6.   Profile Distribution of Residual Anomalous Metal in a Poorly
Drained Soil, Northern Rhodesia[a]

Soil Horizon	Description	Background Profile Cu (ppm)	Profile Near Cu Deposit Cu (ppm)	Profile Over Cu Deposit Cu (ppm)
A_1	Organic topsoil	90	360	3250
G	Gley subsoil	80	125	4200

[a]Data for −80-mesh fraction.

9–3. Hydromorphic Anomalies in Residual Soil

Lateral hydromorphic anomalies may be developed in residual soil by precipitation of metal from anomalous ground-water solutions draining a mineralized area. They are most commonly found in seepage areas down the slope of the water table from the bedrock source, at any point where the metal-bearing ground waters approach close to surface. General aspects of seepage anomalies are considered in detail in Chapter 8 and, more specifically, in Chapter 13. Suffice here to compare the features of superjacent and lateral anomalies in residual overburden in terms of their mutual relationship.

Seepage anomalies are, of course, restricted to the group of semi-mobile metals that are soluble in the local ground waters but that are commonly precipitated in the soil of the seepage area. In marked contrast to the metals contained in syngenetic anomalies in residual soil, a substantial proportion of the anomalous metal of seepage anomalies is loosely bonded and therefore readily extractable. In Northern Rhodesia, for instance, the proportion of total Cu that is cold-extractable ranges from 20 to 80 percent in seepage anomalies as compared to less than 10 percent in residual anomalies in freely drained soil (Webb and Tooms, 1959). The cxMe:Me ratio may therefore be used as a criterion for differentiating syngenetic and hydromorphic soil anomalies under these conditions. However, if the ground water recedes and the soil becomes freely drained, both total metal and the cxMe:Me ratio will tend to decline with time as the extractable metal is both removed by leaching and fixed in the course of the drying out of the ground. The background content of mobile metals in seepage soils tends to be higher and to show a greater range of fluctuation than in residual freely drained soils. Thus, both the threshold value and the contrast of threshold to background for seepage anomalies tend to be higher than for syngenetic soil anomalies. Nevertheless, providing the ore is actively undergoing oxidation and leaching, the seepage anomaly may often show a greater anomaly contrast, particularly for cold-extractable metal,

TABLE 9-7. Contrast for Residual and Seepage Anomalies in Areas Underlain by Katanga Sediments, Northern Rhodesia[a]

Location of Anomaly	Metal	Average Threshold (ppm)	Peak Anomaly (ppm)	Contrast
Anomaly in residual soil overlying ore deposit	Cu	75	480	6.4
	cxCu	5	20	4.0
Lateral seepage anomaly 2000 feet downslope from ore	Cu	100	2100	21.0
	cxCu	20	780	39.0

Source: Tooms, personal communication.
[a]Data for −80-mesh fraction.

than does the residual anomaly associated with the same deposit (Table 9-7). This comes about because hydromorphic anomalies are continually being reinforced by precipitation of metal, whereas in residual anomalies the metal is being lost by leaching.

9–4. Anomalies Not Related to Mineral Deposits

Occasionally variations in the bedrock lithology can result in residual patterns simulating those related to mineral deposits. In the Kilembe area of Uganda, for example, the soil over diabase dikes may contain up to 250 ppm Cu and 140 ppm Ni, as compared with the normal background of 50 ppm Cu and 20 ppm Ni over granulites and gneisses (Jacobson, 1956). The Cu anomalies related to copper-cobalt mineralization may be distinguished, however, by their low Ni content and high Co:Ni ratio. In Rhodesia, anomalous soils associated with copper deposits carry more Co than Ni, whereas the reverse holds over gabbroic rocks, although the Cu anomalies in both cases may be identical at 150 ppm compared with the normal background of 20 to 70 ppm Cu.

An interesting example has been recorded from Sierra Leone, where kimberlite and mafic schist can readily be distinguished from

TABLE 9-8. Metal Content of Residual Overburden Derived from Kimberlite and Other Rocks, Sierra Leone[a]

	Depth (ft)	Kimberlite	Mafic Schist	Felsic Schist	Granite
Nickel (ppm)	2	150	160	30	20
	4	260	180	30	20
	8	500	200	30	
Cobalt (ppm)	2	20	10	<10	10
	4	60	80	<10	<10
	8	50	10	<10	
Chromium (ppm)	2	340	900	60	50
	4	400	1050	110	55
	8	1000	1650	35	
Cold-extractable zinc (ppm)	2	7	1	2	1
	4	5	1	1	1
	8	12	1	<1	
Base exchange capacity (meq/100 g clay)	2	8.4	3.6	2.7	6.8
	4	12.0	2.0	1.5	5.7
	8	28.8	2.9	0.5	

Source: Webb (1958a).
[a]Data for −80-mesh fraction.

quartzose bedrock by differences in the Co, Ni, and Cr content. In this area, the kimberlite soil is further characterized by a relatively high cxZn content reflecting the high base-exchange capacity due to the presence of montmorillonitic clay minerals (Table 9-8).

CHAPTER 10

ANOMALIES IN TRANSPORTED OVERBURDEN

Over large areas of the earth, the bedrock is blanketed by relatively recent deposits of glacial debris, alluvium, colluvium, peat, wind-borne material, or volcanic debris. The overlying cover of transported overburden effectively prevents any direct observation of mineral deposits that occur at the surface of bedrock. Just as with residual overburden, however, it has been found that studies of the distribution of traces of the ore metals in the surficial cover may provide clues to the presence of concealed ore.

Geochemical anomalies in transported overburden may be either syngenetic or epigenetic. A syngenetic anomaly is, by definition, an integral part of the matrix, formed at the same time as the deposit of transported material in which it occurs. An epigenetic anomaly, on the other hand, is a dispersion pattern introduced subsequent to the deposition of the matrix. Syngenetic and epigenetic anomalies may, of course, occur together and be mutually superimposed.

10–1. Common Features of Anomalies in Transported Overburden

The geochemical anomalies developed in transported surficial cover have certain features in common that are independent of the origin of the matrix.

Syngenetic Patterns. Syngenetic clastic patterns developed in transported overburden are the effect of purely mechanical movement of solid particles. Irrespective of the nature of the impelling force, be it ice, water, or wind, the general pattern of movement of particulate matter from its source in the bedrock to the site of deposition is the same. As a consequence of this common pattern of movement, all syngenetic anomalies in transported cover tend to be more or less elongated in the direction of movement. This simple pattern due to purely mechanical dispersion may be complicated by a certain amount of local redistribution and reconstitution by ground water or soil moisture that may have taken place during or subsequent to the deposition of the matrix.

As a rule, the concentration of ore materials in the overburden is greatest in the immediate vicinity of the source and decays rapidly with distance as a result of dilution by barren material. Although rapid decay with distance is the rule, special environmental factors in the formation of some kinds of mechanical dispersion patterns may cause feeble traces to persist for very substantial distances.

The mode of occurrence of the ore metals in syngenetic anomalies is in part as relatively resistant fragments of rocks and of primary or secondary minerals, and in part as reconstituted material that has been dissolved and locally reprecipitated. Determination of the metal content of resistant minerals will usually require rigorous chemical extraction. The reconstituted material is likely to consist largely of limonitic precipitates and adsorbed ions, both of which are more readily extractable than the resistant material.

Near the source, the metal content of the overburden will usually increase with depth. If the overburden has been thoroughly mixed, the pattern may decay relatively smoothly with distance from the source. On the other hand, if the overburden is deposited as a series of layers, the syngenetic pattern may persist only in certain horizons, often the bottommost.

Epigenetic Patterns. The hydromorphic and biogenic patterns that may form in transported overburden show no special features beyond those already discussed in previous chapters. Epigenetic anomalies assume special importance in transported cover, however, in view of the fact that syngenetic patterns are not as consistently associated with concealed mineralization as they are in residual overburden. Thus hydromorphic and biogenic anomalies in transported cover may be the only usable geochemical guides to buried ore. In desert areas of low water table where the formation of near-surface hydromorphic dispersion patterns is inhibited, the only surface indication of buried ore may be biogenic anomalies resulting from the uptake of metal by deep-rooted plants.

Anomalies Not Related to Mineral Deposits. Extensive surficial deposits of transported material represent a more or less homogenized sample derived from all the rocks in the source area. As a result, there is often less opportunity for the development of syngenetic patterns that can be traced back to specific rock types of contrasting composition. Except where these rocks occur as major geological units or where the overburden has not moved very far, local patterns not related to ore are more likely to be the result of sorting during the course of transport and deposition than of variations in the composition of the source rocks. Epigenetic patterns, on the other hand, may reflect the presence of quite small-scale lithological units, particularly where the introduced metal is derived from the immediately underlying bedrock.

10–2. Glacial Overburden

The development, detection, and interpretation of geochemical anomalies in glacial overburden are complicated by the diverse nature and origin of glacial deposits, as reviewed in Chapter 7. Sands, clays, gravels, and morainal deposits of varying composition and permeability may be intermixed or stratified. Over short distances the cover may range in depth from a few inches to many tens or even hundreds of feet. Eroded material, scoured and plowed up from the surface over which the ice moved, may have been transported for distances ranging from a few feet to many miles from its place of origin. The glacial debris may have been further subjected to water transport and sorting, and the resultant glaciofluvial deposits distributed over wide areas as outwash fans and lake-bed sediments. The direction of ice movement, which is the principal factor conditioning the form of a glacial anomaly, may change during the course of a single period of glaciation. Complexities in the local deposits and in the local glacial history naturally lead to a corresponding complexity in the dispersion processes and the resulting geochemical patterns. Any or all of these factors can add materially to the difficulties of conducting geochemical surveys in glacial terrain.

Useful syngenetic anomalies normally develop only in moraine deposits, particularly in ground moraine, by mechanical dispersion of ore material eroded by the ice. Where conditions are favorable, epigenetic anomalies of hydromorphic and biogenic origin may be found in any class of glacial or glaciofluvial deposit.

Syngenetic Anomalies.   The particle size of the eroded ore material may range from large boulders down to the finest clays.

Glacially transported boulders are characteristically distributed in fan-shaped patterns extending outward from the bedrock source in the direction of ice movement. Boulder fans have been observed to extend for many miles from the source (Figures 7-19 and 10-1). More commonly, a well-defined boulder fan cannot be traced for more than one or two miles (Figure 10-2).

Fine-grained metal-bearing particles or "micro-boulders," too small or too decomposed to be identified by eye, may likewise be dispersed mechanically to form fan-shaped patterns of abnormally high metal content that are more or less coextensive with boulder fans (Figures 10-2 to 10-5). The homogeneity of such anomalies is dependent on the grain size of the particles and the degree of mixing,

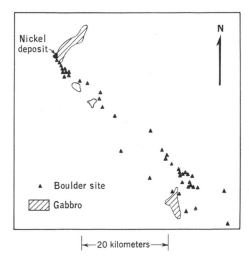

Nickel
deposit

N

▲ Boulder site

▨ Gabbro

Fig. 10-1. Nickel deposit and fan of gabbro boulders containing disseminated sulfide, Storbodsund, Sweden. After Grip (1953).

|←—20 kilometers—→|

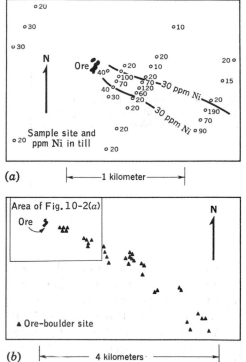

○20

○30   ○10

○30

                N
                          Ore   ○20
                              40○   ○20   ○10   20 ○
                                  ○100 ○20
                                  ○70 ○70 —30 ppm Ni   ○15
                                  ○120
                              40○   ○60
                                  ○30 ○20   ○20
                          ○20   30 ppm Ni ○190
                                                 ○70
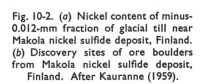
            ○20   Sample site and   ○90
            ○20   ppm Ni in till

                    ○20
                          ○20

(a) |←————1 kilometer————→|

Fig. 10-2. (a) Nickel content of minus-0.012-mm fraction of glacial till near Makola nickel sulfide deposit, Finland. (b) Discovery sites of ore boulders from Makola nickel sulfide deposit, Finland. After Kauranne (1959).

Area of Fig. 10-2(a)   N

Ore ↗ ▲▲▲
            ▲▲
              ▲
              ▲   ▲▲▲
              ▲   ▲▲
                      ▲
                         ▲
                              ▲
                                  ▲▲▲
                                  ▲ ▲

▲ Ore-boulder site

(b) |←————— 4 kilometers —————→|

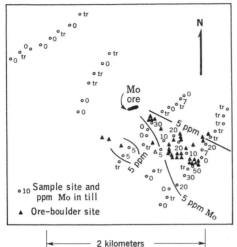

Fig. 10-3. Comparison of molybdenum content of the minus-0.012-mm fraction of glacial till with the distribution of ore boulders, Susineva, Finland. After Kauranne (1958).

○10 Sample site and ppm Mo in till
▲ Ore-boulder site

├─── 2 kilometers ───┤

Fig. 10-4. Distribution of lead in fine-grained fraction of glacial moraine at Korsnäs, Finland. After Hyvärinen (1958).

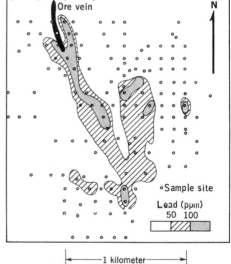

Ore vein

N

○ Sample site

Lead (ppm)
50   100

├──── 1 kilometer ────┤

or sorting, that took place during glaciation. As a rule, fine-grained material will give a more homogeneous pattern than coarser fragments. The homogeneity of a "micro-boulder" pattern may be modified by chemical solution of metals from the larger ore boulders and local reprecipitation in the fine-grained matrix.

Detectable syngenetic anomalies cannot usually be followed as far as boulder fans. In fact, they have rarely been observed extending more than a mile or so from the source. In this connection, Kauranne

(1959) has drawn attention to the importance of the size fraction taken for analysis. He observed that at the Makola Ni deposit in Finland the metal anomaly detectable in the coarser fraction (0.012 to 0.125 mm) had faded to background at 1 kilometer, while at the

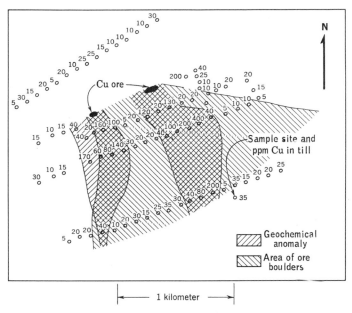

Fig. 10-5. Comparison of copper content of minus-0.05-mm fraction of glacial till with area of glacial ore boulders, Outokumpu, Finland. After Kauranne (1959).

same distance the Ni content of the fine fraction (<0.012 mm) was at a maximum. The experiments by Lundegårdh (1956) near the Sala lead deposits in Sweden and by Dreimanis (1960) near the Noranda copper sulfide deposit in Canada similarly indicated that a well-developed and homogeneous geochemical pattern could be traced only for about 1 mile from the source (Figures 10-6 and 10-7). At Mount Bohemia in northern Michigan, where the observation of glacial boulders of chalcocite-bearing amygdaloid and the subsequent mapping of Cu in the glacial till led to an important discovery, the syngenetic glacial pattern extends hardly more than 500 feet from the source in the bedrock (Figure 10-8).

Hydromorphic Anomalies. Accurate interpretation of geochemical data from glaciated terrain is not possible without some way of distinguishing syngenetic patterns from hydromorphic patterns. One criterion is the form of the pattern. Whereas the form of a syngenetic

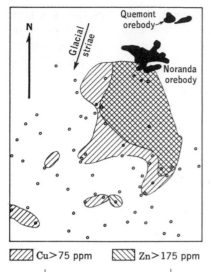

Fig. 10-6. Copper and zinc content of moraine near Noranda Cu deposit, Quebec. Data on minus-80-mesh fraction. After Dreimanis (1960).

Cu>75 ppm   Zn>175 ppm

|—— 2 kilometers ——|

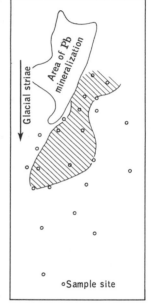

Fig. 10-7. Lead content of fine-grained fraction of till near bedrock mineralization, Sala, Sweden. After Lundegårdh (1956).

Pb>50 ppm

|—— 5 kilometers ——|

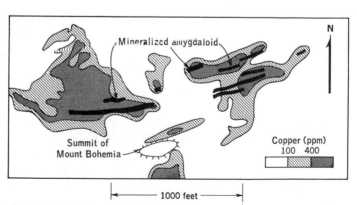

Fig. 10-8. Copper content of glacial till near Mount Bohemia chalcocite deposit, Michigan. After Pollock et al. (1960).

glacial anomaly is related to the direction of ice movement, hydromorphic patterns are related to the direction of ground-water flow, a
fact that may be used to discriminate between these anomalies providing the two directions do not coincide. Another criterion is the
presence or absence of certain resistant ore minerals which can only
be of syngenetic origin. Hydromorphic anomalies are, of course, more
highly developed for the more mobile constituents of the ore. The
intensity of a hydromorphic anomaly depends in the first instance on

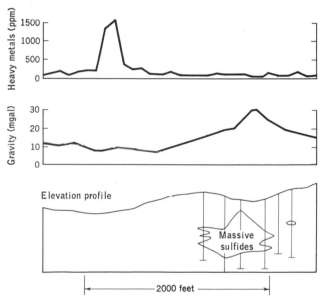

Fig. 10-9. Cross section showing seepage anomaly in glacial
overburden downslope from ore, Vangorda Mines, Yukon
Territory. Data on bulk samples. After Chisholm (1957).

the rate of oxidation of the primary ore minerals. It is a common
observation that in many glaciated areas, bedrock deposits have
been eroded by the ice down to the relatively compact and impermeable fresh primary ore. The slow rate of oxidation of such material
militates against the formation of strong epigenetic anomalies in the
glacial cover. As a rule, the strongest patterns are developed in silty
overburden, where the permeability is adequate to permit access of
solutions, but where at the same time sufficient fine material is
present to adsorb metal. Downslope from the suboutcrop of a vein,
hydromorphic anomalies in glacial overburden tend to be restricted
to the bottom few feet. Koehler *et al.* (1954) have reported high concentrations of Co in relatively permeable deposits of sandy clay near

the bottom of a 15-foot blanket of glacial overburden in the Cobalt District of Ontario. Patterns of this kind may extend for several hundred feet downslope from the source before they eventually come to the surface as anomalous springs and seepages.

Seepage anomalies or, more strictly, lateral hydromorphic anomalies, are commonly by far the most prominent of all the patterns occurring in glacial overburden. At the Vangorda Mines, Yukon Territory, for example, a strong seepage anomaly in Zn was observed

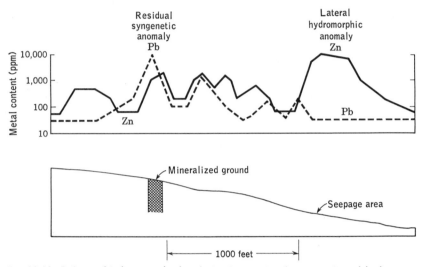

Fig. 10-10. Relationship between lead and zinc in associated syngenetic and hydromorphic anomalies, Charlotte Prospect, New Brunswick. Data on minus-80-mesh fraction.

in a topographic depression 1000 feet from the nearest known ore as indicated by drilling and gravity surveying (Figure 10-9). Anomalous concentrations of Pb and Zn have been observed in boggy spring areas downslope from vein deposits on the Isle of Man (Webb, 1958b). In the case of deposits containing two or more metals of differing mobilities, the ratio of the metals in the seepage anomaly generally favors those which are the more mobile. The converse relationship holds in the syngenetic anomaly (Figure 10-10).

Biogenic Anomalies. Concentration of metal at the surface rather than at depth is reported over the Van Stone ore body in eastern Washington, where the glacial cover immediately overlying Zn ore in the bedrock ranged from 15 to 50 feet in thickness (Cox and Hollister, 1955). Inasmuch as the anomalous pattern was most strongly developed in the top foot and disappeared with depth, it is almost certainly of biogenic origin.

Superjacent Anomalies of Complex Origin. Anomalous patterns of probable complex origin have been reported in morainal material immediately over mineralized bedrock in a number of areas. Figure 10-11 illustrates a pattern of dispersed Cu in till overlying essentially fresh pyrrhotite-pentlandite-chalcopyrite ore at Kiuruvesi, Finland. Figure 10-12 shows anomalous patterns detectable by surface sampling of till ranging in thickness from 6 inches to 12 feet at the Chollet

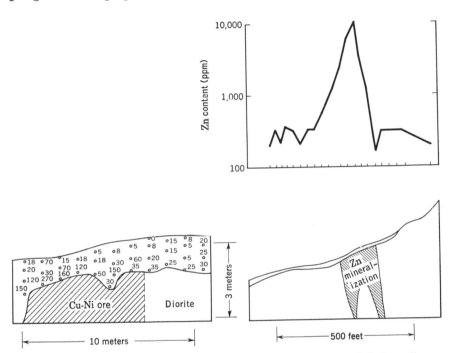

Fig. 10-11. Section showing copper content of glacial till over copper-nickel ore, Kiuruvesi, Finland. Data on minus-0.05-mm fraction. After Kauranne (1959).

Fig. 10-12. Zinc content of shallow till over zinc mineralization, Chollet Prospect, Washington. Data on minus-2-mm fraction. After Cox and Hollister (1955).

prospect in eastern Washington. The anomalous patterns at these localities are probably the combined effect of syngenetic and epigenetic material.

10–3. Colluvium and Alluvium

Colluvium is generally taken to include all those deposits of local origin built up at the base of slopes as the result of gravity movement assisted by frost action, soil creep, and sheet wash. It ranges from poorly sorted angular rock fragments to fine clays, according to the nature of the bedrock material supplied from above. Although as a rule colluvial deposits are limited in extent, on ancient land surfaces they may cover very large areas, locally filling the old valleys to depths of some hundreds of feet.

Alluvial deposits include an equally wide range of material. They are, however, commonly better sorted and are more likely to be stratified than is colluvium. In confined valleys, alluvial deposits are necessarily restricted in their lateral extent, but in open valleys and on flat, mature surfaces, vast areas may be covered by thick accumulations of water-borne material.

The anomalies formed in both kinds of overburden possess many features in common and are conveniently considered together.

Syngenetic Anomalies. In both colluvium and alluvium the form of the anomalous patterns will depend on the origin and mode of transport of the anomalous material. Colluvial deposits below residual soil anomalies commonly show a broadly spreading, fan-shaped pattern of anomalous values. Fanglomerate deposits built up by streams draining mineralized outcrops commonly show a somewhat similar spreading pattern. The patterns in the alluvial deposits of confined valleys take the form of alluvial trains. These processes have been discussed and illustrated in more detail in Chapter 8.

The mode of occurrence of the metal may vary greatly according to the element concerned and the mechanism of dispersion. In colluvial anomalies the syngenetic material will occur in essentially the same form as in the parent soil anomaly. In alluvial anomalies the metal may be derived by the erosion of residual soil anomalies or of upstream anomalous seepage areas. Alluvial anomalies of this type are discussed in Chapter 13.

Epigenetic Anomalies. Hydromorphic halos may develop in barren colluvium and alluvium overlying buried ore by the upward movement of metal-bearing solutions. They are subject to the same conditions and controls that are common to similar hydromorphic patterns developed in other materials.

The anomalies detected by Fulton (1950) in Tertiary alluvium overlying mineralized bedrock in the Apallachian zinc district are almost certainly of hydromorphic origin. A small but well-developed halo over lead-zinc ore in Nigeria was observed in an alluvial deposit that was dated archaeologically as 400 years old (Figure 10-13). The vertical, pipelike shape of the Pb pattern in the Nigerian example contrasts strongly with the broader halo of decreasing Zn values in the same material. It is possible that the Pb anomaly is biogenic and formed by the growth and decay of grass roots in which the Pb had been concentrated.

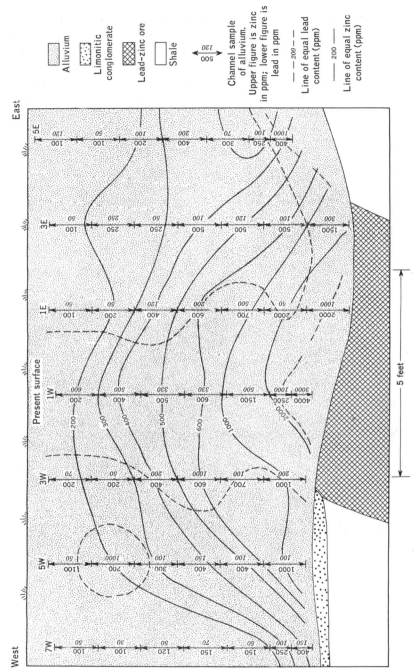

Fig. 10-13. Distribution of lead and zinc in alluvium overlying lead-zinc ore in bedrock, Nyeba district, Nigeria. Data on minus-80-mesh fraction. From Hawkes (1954).

In arid and semiarid environments it is reasonable to expect a substantial upward movement of ground water to replenish the moisture lost by evaporation and transpiration from the fringe zone above the water table. Secondary Cu has, in fact, been reported in the post-ore conglomerates overlying the San Manuel deposit in Arizona (Schwartz, 1949). A similar pattern has been observed in Tertiary gravel deposits immediately overlying the Mission deposit, also in Arizona. In neither of these areas, however, has the pattern been observed more than a few tens of feet above the bedrock sur-

TABLE 10-1.   Metal Distribution in Caliche Overlying
Mineralized Dolomite, South-West Africa

Description	Depth (ft)	Zn (ppm)	Pb (ppm)
Brown topsoil	0–1	75	70
	1–2	125	120
	2–3	115	20
	3–4	240	50
Massive caliche	4–5	150	20
	5–6	95	15
	6–7	300	35
	7–8	240	55
	8–9	850	120
Mineralized dolomite	9–10	6400	290
Background for caliche over unmineralized dolomite		20–100	5–30

face. In South-West Africa, on the fringe of the Kalahari Desert, erratically anomalous contents of Zn and, to a lesser degree, Pb have been detected in massive caliche overlying mineralized dolomite. The data of Table 10-1 shows a sharp rise in metal values toward the base of the caliche layer. The environment is inimical to leaching, and the pattern of distribution suggests that the metals have been introduced from below. Nevertheless, the possibility that they are in fact residual cannot be entirely discounted.

Lotspeich (1958) has recorded enrichment of Cr, V, P, and Zn in colluvium $1\frac{1}{2}$ to 4 feet thick overlying phosphatic beds containing abnormal amounts of these metals (Table 10-2). Under semiarid conditions and in the absence of vegetation, upward movement of moisture is considered to be the dominant dispersion mechanism. In a subhumid environment, biogenic metal derived from deep-rooted vegetation is believed to contribute to the epigenetic pattern developed in the overburden.

In Rhodesia, lateral superimposed patterns for Cu have been

TABLE 10-2.   Enrichment of Metals in Colluvium Overlying Phosphatic Bedrock[a]

Element	Content in Phosphatic Bedrock (ppm)	Content in Overlying Colluvium (ppm)		Content in Barren Colluvium (ppm)
		Arid Environment	Subhumid Environment	
V	5,000	800	150	65
Cr	5,000	500	200	35
Zn	3,500	500	500	100
P	10,000	7,000	12,000	1,000

[a]Mean values computed from data by Lotspeich (1958).

observed in river flood plains below mineralized ground, on the surrounding valley slopes, and around the mouths of tributary streams draining mineralized catchment areas. These features are described in detail in Chapter 13.

10-4. Organic Deposits

Organic deposits accumulate in any situations where vegetable matter is formed faster than it decomposes. In this class of overburden are included peat, muck, and muskeg bogs of moist, cool climates, and the mangrove and other organic swamps of the tropics.

For the most part, organic deposits accumulate by the growth and decay of vegetation in place. Although such deposits are usually confined to swampy, stagnant depressions, in certain environments they can occur also in upland areas.

Rarely, organic deposits are formed in basins of sedimentation by the accumulation of clastic plant debris and mineral matter washed in from the surrounding higher ground.

Where ore lies beneath the organic cover, superjacent hydromorphic patterns may be formed by artesian flow or by the natural slow circulation of ground water up from the underlying bedrock to feed the transpiration of the surface plants. Salmi (1955), for example, has found a close relationship between the distribution of Fe, Ti, and V in a bog and the composition of underlying titaniferous magnetite ore (Figure 10-14). From similar studies of bogs over different kinds of ores in the underlying bedrock, Salmi has concluded that Ti, V, Ni, and Al tend to be precipitated at the bottom of the organic layer, whereas Fe, Mn, Mo, and Pb are enriched at the top surface of the bog. Cu and Zn do not appear to be concentrated in any particular horizon.

Iron precipitated in deposits of organic matter may also be derived from the decomposition of Fe sulfides in the underlying bedrock. Figure 10-15 shows the epigenetic pattern of Fe that has been solubilized from a Cu-bearing Fe sulfide deposit buried beneath a peat bog in New Brunswick, Canada. This pattern apparently is the result of both upward and lateral movement of Fe-bearing swamp water. The

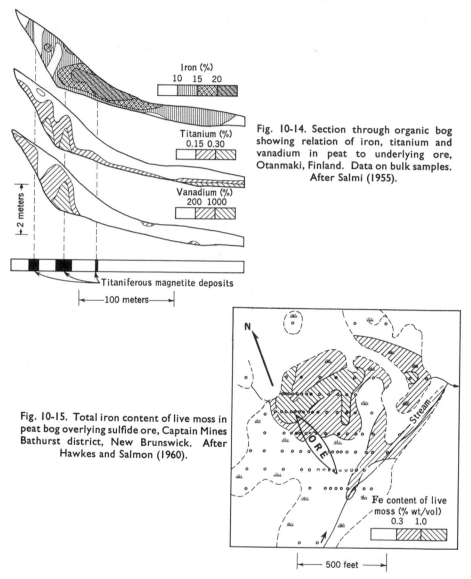

Iron (%)
10 15 20

Titanium (%)
0.15 0.30

Vanadium (%)
200 1000

Fig. 10-14. Section through organic bog showing relation of iron, titanium and vanadium in peat to underlying ore, Otanmaki, Finland. Data on bulk samples. After Salmi (1955).

2 meters

Titaniferous magnetite deposits

100 meters

Fig. 10-15. Total iron content of live moss in peat bog overlying sulfide ore, Captain Mines Bathurst district, New Brunswick. After Hawkes and Salmon (1960).

N

ORE

Stream

Fe content of live moss (% wt/vol)
0.3 1.0

500 feet

strongest pattern is shown by the Fe content of the live moss. The pattern of Fe in the organic matter at a depth of 12 inches was closely parallel, suggesting that the dispersion has been the combined effect of both ground-water movement and plant activity.

Lateral patterns in organic swamps formed by ground water draining from mineralized ground beneath the surrounding uplands are extremely common. These are discussed in detail in Chapter 13.

Finally, syngenetic anomalous patterns could conceivably be developed in bogs also by the washing in of anomalous soil eroded from the surrounding higher ground. Such anomalies would, of course, be found on the margins nearest the mineralized ground or near the mouths of inlet streams carrying anomalous sediment.

10–5. Lake and Marine Sediments

Sedimentary material deposited in bodies of quiet water varies greatly, depending on the source of the material and on the chemical and physical environment of deposition. Normally, lake sediments consist of muds with a variable amount of admixed fine-grained organic debris. Lake sediments deposited in areas of vigorous mechanical erosion may be largely silty or even sandy. In areas characterized by slow chemical weathering of calcareous rocks, they may consist predominantly of marl. In cold climates, where organic matter can accumulate, the lacustrine deposit may be largely mucky or organic. Marine deposits characteristically contain saline solutions in the pore spaces, and often include precipitates or evaporation residues derived from the salt water.

The only known example of a superjacent syngenetic anomaly in quiet-water sediments is reported by Huff (1955). He has correlated the Cu content of the basal sandstone of Cambrian age in the Jerome area of Arizona with Precambrian Cu ore exposed in the sea floor at the time the sandstone was deposited. Numerous localities where the sandstone contains more than 80 ppm each of Cu and Zn occur within a radius of 2 miles from the exposure of the United Verde ore body on the Precambrian erosion surface. The background for Cu and Zn is less than 40 ppm (Figure 10-16). This pattern is interpreted as the result of lateral dispersion of Cu by water currents and waves washing back and forth over Cu ore exposed in the floor of the shallow marine basin.

Lateral syngenetic anomalies may occur in the deltaic sediments that build up at the mouths of anomalous tributary streams (Figure 10-17). The higher metal contents in these sediments extend for no more than a few hundred feet into the lake, although feebly anomalous values may persist for considerable distances. Sediments deposited in the center of large lakes may represent a chemical average of the finer material brought in by all the inlet streams, together with metals precipitated by organic activity in the lake

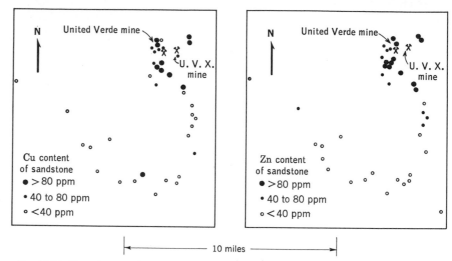

Fig. 10-16. Distribution of copper and zinc in basal Paleozoic sandstone unconformably over-lying United Verde base-metal deposit, Arizona. After Huff (1955).

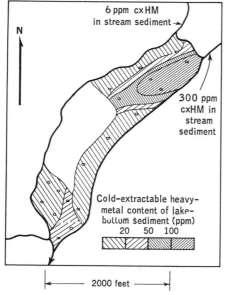

Fig. 10-17. Lake-sediment anomaly, Second Portage Lake, New Brunswick. Data on minus-80-mesh fraction. After Schmidt (1956).

environment. Marine sediments apparently may also serve as host to geochemical drainage anomalies. H. V. Warren (personal communication) has reported that the metal content of modern sediments dredged from marine inlets on the coast of British Columbia shows a correlation with the occurrence of ore in the tributary areas.

Hydromorphic anomalies overlying ore can develop wherever there is upward movement of metal-bearing ground water into the lake. Although no well-defined example of this phenomenon has been reported in the literature, the writers have observed dispersion patterns of Pb and Zn in lake-bottom sediments in New Brunswick that are almost certainly the result of deposition from metal-rich spring water entering from the bottom of the lake.

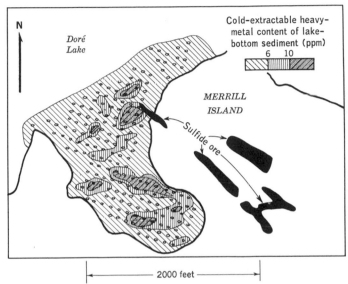

Fig. 10-18. Lake-sediment anomaly, Doré Lake, Chibougamau district, Quebec. Data on minus-80-mesh fraction. After Schmidt (1956).

Lateral hydromorphic anomalies can develop wherever there is movement of metal-bearing ground water into the lake. Where the ore lies in the surrounding drainage area, lateral patterns may be formed in the lake-bottom sediments near the shore. Figure 10-18 shows a pattern of metal-rich lake sediment offshore from known sulfide deposits. Presumably most of the metal in these anomalies was derived by erosion from the adjoining land area, although an undetermined fraction may have been precipitated from metal-rich solutions rising as springs in the lake floor.

10–6. Other Types of Transported Overburden

Relatively few attempts have been made to investigate dispersion patterns in aeolian deposits. Some evidence of syngenetic dispersion in wind-blown sand has been reported from the Sahara. Here the pattern of values in the sand surrounding a mineralized hill is distorted asymmetrically in the direction of the prevailing wind (Lambert, personal communication). No evidence of epigenetic anomalies. in wind-borne material has been reported. In Wisconsin, Kennedy (1956) found no pattern of Zn developed in a 10-foot layer of Pleistocene loess over known Zn mineralization in the underlying bedrock. However, there is no reason to doubt that, given shallow groundwater conditions, epigenetic anomalies could be formed in an aeolian deposit.

Like the wind-blown sands of the desert, post-ore volcanic cover presents a major prospecting problem. The possibility of the development of superimposed anomalies through volcanic cover has not been investigated.

CHAPTER II

GEOCHEMICAL SOIL SURVEYS

Sampling and analysis of residual soils is by far the most widely used of all the geochemical methods described in this book. The popularity of residual-soil surveying as an exploration method is a simple reflection of the reliability of soil anomalies as ore guides. General experience in many climates and in many types of geological environments has shown that where the parent rock is mineralized, some kind of chemical pattern almost always can be found in the residual soil that results from the weathering of that rock. Where residual-soil anomalies are not found over known ore in the bedrock, further examination usually shows either that the material sampled was not truly residual or that an unsuitable horizon or size fraction of the soil was sampled, or possibly that an inadequate extraction method was used. In other words, when properly used, the method is exceptionally reliable in comparison with most other exploration methods.

Residual-soil surveys have been found particularly applicable in areas of deep residual cover and sparse outcrops, where other exploration methods are either too expensive or are technically ineffective. Thus, the areas of deep weathering in the southern Appalachians of the United States and in east and central Africa have been found to be well suited for geochemical soil surveying. Although any of the common ore metals may form pronounced anomalous patterns in residual soil, the strongest contrast is developed for the relatively immobile elements such as Pb.

In areas of transported cover, geochemical soil surveys have not proved to be so generally applicable. This is not altogether surprising in view of the more complicated dispersion processes involved in the development of anomalies in transported soil. Nevertheless, under favorable conditions, near-surface superjacent anomalies have been reported in glacial till and alluvial overburden where the bedrock is buried to depths of as much as 50 feet. As compared with areas of residual cover, relatively little orientation work has been directed to the study of the dispersion of weathering products in transported overburden over known metalliferous deposits. It is certain that the scope and reliability of geochemical surveying techniques in areas of transported soil will be increased as a result of further experimentation. Meanwhile, the applicability of transported-soil sampling as an exploration method could be materially extended simply by taking advantage of what is now known about the use of cold-extraction techniques, the significance of lateral hydromorphic anomalies, and the various kinds of anomalies that may be developed in transported cover immediately above the surface of bedrock.

11–1. Orientation Surveys

As with all geochemical surveys, the first step in attacking an operational problem is to conduct an orientation survey. Such a survey normally consists of a series of preliminary experiments aimed at determining the existence and characteristics of anomalies associated with mineralization. This information may then be used in selecting adequate prospecting techniques and in determining the factors and criteria that have a bearing on interpretation of the geochemical data.

Although the orientation study will provide the necessary technical information upon which to base operational procedures, the final choice of methods to be used must also take into account other factors, such as cost of operation, availability of personnel, and the market value of the expected ore discoveries. These considerations are discussed in Chapter 16, and only the technical aspects of orientation are considered here.

If possible, these preliminary experiments should be undertaken in the vicinity of known deposits that have not been disturbed or contaminated by human activity, so that the natural geochemical pattern can be observed. As a rule, only vein extensions or minor subeconomic deposits will be available for these experiments. It is important, however, that orientation should be conducted in areas where the geological and geomorphological characteristics are representative of those likely to be encountered during prospecting.

Determination of the distribution of metal values in unmineralized terrain is of equal importance. Background studies must be carried out well away from the possible influence of known mineralization. They should also cover the full range of environmental conditions that exist in the exploration area.

The nature of the overburden, whether it is residual or is of glacial, alluvial, or wind-borne origin, is the first question that must be answered by the orientation survey. Sometimes it is surprisingly difficult to discriminate between residual and transported soil. The safest method, therefore, is to make critical and careful examinations of complete sections of the overburden at the start of every new field survey. If road-cut exposures are not available, the soil profile should be examined by pitting or augering.

Although the basic procedure in conducting an orientation survey is the same not only for residual but also for many kinds of transported soil, there are some differences in detail to which attention is drawn below.

Residual Soil.   A completely thorough orientation survey in a new area starts with the collection of a series of vertical sections through the soil profile, arranged as a traverse across the suboutcrop of the mineralized ground. Comparable profiles from background areas should be sampled at the same time. The initial traverse over the deposit should extend for a substantial distance on either side of the suboutcrop. Along the line of traverse, pits are dug at close intervals; if the deposit is narrow and the ore metals are relatively immobile, a complete trench section may be required. Every attempt should be made to sink the orientation pits to bedrock, particularly if any doubt remains as to whether the overburden is of residual or transported origin. If bedrock cannot be reached by pitting, deep samples may be collected with the aid of specialized augering equipment.

The next step is to log the pits in detail and establish the residual or transported origin of the overburden at all depths. The complete profile should then be channel sampled. No sample should represent a section of more than 1 to 2 feet, or should include material from more than one visibly distinguishable horizon. Background soil profiles should be sampled in a similar manner at selected points over representative types of unmineralized rock in otherwise comparable environments. A typical example of an orientation pit log, including the results of subsequent analysis, is shown in Figure 11-1.

Preliminary analysis of the minus 80- or minus 100-mesh fraction for the predominant ore metal or associated pathfinder elements will usually suffice to show whether an anomaly is present or not. Analytical determination should include the total metal content (Me) and, in the case of relatively mobile elements, the readily extractable metal content (cxMe) as well; the choice of extractants is based on the possible modes of occurrence of the metals in question. Selected anomalous and background samples should then be subjected to a series of experiments to determine the range of concentration of the key elements, as well as the size fraction and analytical method that shows the greatest contrast between anomaly and background. When dealing with the elements that characteristically occur in the soil as components of readily identifiable clastic minerals, the heavy-mineral fraction of the soil should be examined mineralogically. On the basis of these experiments, procedures of preparation and analysis that show the maximum contrast of anomaly over background are selected. Further pitting may be necessary to cover fully the width of the

AREA: Kiswami River		Location: Trav 2 (see map)		Pit No. 2/6			
Sampler: L. M. James		Date: 20 Aug 59		Analyst: R. Hickman			
Description of site: Residual overburden on granite bedrock on 5-degree slope, 20 feet below presumed suboutcrop. Grass and shrub vegetation (secondary growth? Ground may have been cultivated). No possibility of contamination from old trench spoil 200 feet east.				Date: 2 Sep 59 Methods: Minus 80 mesh Pb } KHSO₄ fusion; dithizone Zn } exHM: citrate, dithizone			
Soil horizon	Depth in feet	Pictorial log	Sample No. Depth (in.)	ppm			
				Pb	Zn	exHM	
A₁ Gray, humic	10		7642 10	800	400	40	
A₂ Buff, sandy			7641 24	500	350	15	
	36		7640 36	400	180	5	
B Red-brown, concretionary, sandy loam matrix	50		7639 50	400	750	20	
B/C Transition			7638 61	250	600	30	
C Mottled clay-sand mottling decreasing in depth. Limonitic qtz vein.			7637 75	110	400	40	
			7636	30	250	30	
Transition to decomposed granite	90		90 7635 96	20	200	30	
Limonitic qtz vein at	72		7643	5000	1000	>80	

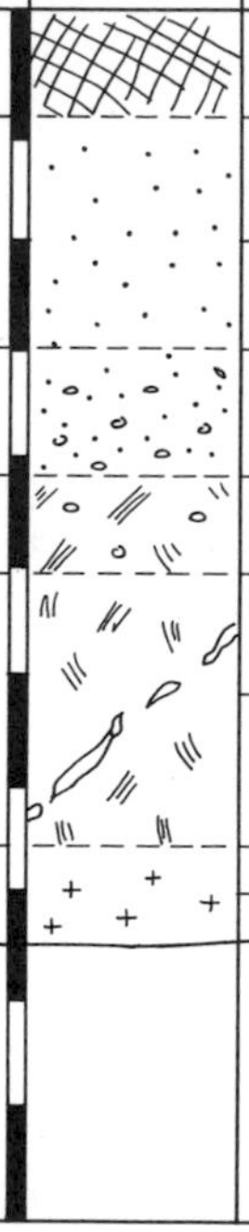

Fig. 11-1. Typical example of an orientation pit log.

anomalous pattern. Analysis of the complete suite of samples by the selected procedures provides the basic information upon which to choose the most practicable horizon for sampling, i.e., the minimum depth at which an adequate anomaly contrast is obtained over the greatest width.

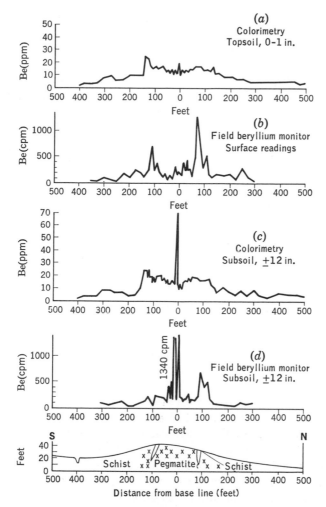

Fig. 11-2. Example of orientation traverse to determine spread and homogeneity of a residual soil anomaly at two depths and by two analytical methods. After Debnam and Webb (1960); Be-monitor readings by K. C. Burke. Chemical data on minus-80-mesh fraction.

Pit traverses are now supplemented by traverses along which closely spaced samples are collected from the selected optimum depth, in order to determine the shape, spread, and homogeneity of the anomaly (Figure 11-2). Replicate samples at selected points may be collected to determine sampling error. In addition to examination of the superjacent anomalies, tests should also be carried out on the base-of-slope colluvium and in seepage areas downdrainage from mineralization, to determine the characteristics of the lateral anomalies, if any. Determination of the ratio of readily extractable to total metal (cxMe:Me) in the various kinds of material is particularly important at this stage.

Similar experiments should be made in each type of environment present in the exploration area. Particular attention should be given to ascertaining, if possible, the effect on metal content of variations in the grade and oxidation of the deposit, depth of overburden, soil type, and bedrock lithology. The metal content of mineralized and nonmineralized gossans, if present, should also be investigated.

While the foregoing is generally applicable to most soil surveys in a new area, each problem will usually call for some special modifications and additions in the design of the orientation experiments. Pitting may not always be practicable, or even necessary, if adequate information is available from a closely comparable area. In such cases, the orientation study may be restricted to determining the metal content only of the near-surface soil horizons, preferably including the B horizon.

Transported Soil. In transported overburden the metal content of the surface soil and of the deeper horizons of the overburden may be of special importance, in view of the possibilities of dispersion via deep-rooted plants and ground-water solutions respectively.

Glacial cover presents a number of additional problems, notably the need to understand the nature of the glacial deposits and the glacial history of the area. The direction of ice movement and the existence of possible syngenetic fans should also be determined. The development of lateral seepage anomalies also assumes special importance in areas covered by glacial debris.

Organic soils should, if possible, be test sampled in both anomalous and background areas in the same way as described above for residual soils. The distribution of metals at different depths in the profile and the cxMe:Me ratios of the mobile elements should be determined. Careful attention should be directed to possible relationships between metal content, pH, Eh, and organic matter. The degree of decomposition of the organic matter may be an important factor in this connection. The influence of internal ground-water drainage on the pattern of anomalies should be studied in three dimensions if possible. Anomalies should be sought not only immediately above the suboutcrop of the mineralized ground but also down-drainage. Where mineralization occurs on the higher ground surrounding an area of organic soil, all likely seepage areas should, of course, be tested for lateral anomalies.

Lake-bottom sediments similarly should be test sampled along traverses across the suboutcrop of a known mineralized body. If possible, samples should be taken of the mineral sediment rather than the flocculent organic material that commonly forms the upper layer of the lake bed. Tests for cxMe as well as total metal are clearly essential. The principal factors that would need to be considered include nature of the sediment, pH, Eh, ground-water movement beneath the lake bottom, bedrock lithology, oxidation of the ore, and seasonal changes in the lake environment. If the mineralization occurs on the higher ground surrounding the lake or in the catchment areas of inlet streams, near-shore sediments and deltaic deposits around the mouths of inlet streams should be tested for lateral anomalies.

Contamination.   A thorough orientation study of a new area should also include appropriate sampling to determine the extent of possible contamination arising from human activity.

As a rule, contamination from trash, fertilizers, road metaling, and farming or industrial installations is very localized and is generally restricted to the surface horizons. Leaching from old, oxidized spoil and mine dumps can disperse the metal deeper and may even contaminate seepage areas some distance downslope. Orientation studies of the effect of these sources of contamination are a simple matter of systematic sampling at progressively greater distances from a known source and noting any systematic decay in metal concentration.

Contamination by condensation from smelter fumes can be a more extensive feature and can sometimes be difficult to recognize and make corrections for. One key to smelter contamination is the fact that the effect is usually confined to the top few inches of the soil. For example, within a mile of the copper smelter at Superior, Arizona, the Cu content of surface soil is 5000 ppm but decreases rapidly to the normal background of about 20 ppm at a depth of 6 inches. Canney (1959) found that evidence of contamination existed in the upper 2 inches of the soil 18 miles downwind from the Kellogg smelter in the Coeur d'Alene district, Idaho. Nevertheless, subsoil at a depth of 6 inches even in the immediate vicinity of the smelter was not enough contaminated to interfere seriously with geochemical prospecting operations. Rather deeper penetration has been recorded for As (Table 11-1) where the effect is still noticeable at a depth of 12 inches at a point one-half mile downwind from a smelter in Southern Rhodesia.

Ancient smelting sites can present a far more serious problem. In the Bawdwin Mine area in Burma, for example, the soil has been extremely contaminated with Pb, often to depths of several feet (Table 11-2a); here the proportion of cxPb is more than twice as much as in natural anomalous soils. Strong contamination to a depth of

TABLE 11-1. Contamination of Soil Profile One-Half Mile
Downwind from Smelter, Southern Rhodesia[a]

Description	Depth (in.)	As (ppm)
Sandy layer transported by sheet wash	0–2	560
Brown loam subsoil	2–8	200
	8–13	120
Red loam with rubble	13–18	50
Soft, mottled decomposed greenstone	18–28	45

Source: Webb (1958a).
[a]Data for −80-mesh fraction.

about 30 inches has also been noted at the Bushman Mine in Bechuanaland in an area where the evidence of ancient smelting has been
almost completely eradicated; much deeper contamination would
have occurred but for the high soil pH (Table 11-2b).

TABLE 11-2. Intense Contamination of Soil
Beneath Ancient Smelting Sites[a]

(a) Bawdwin Mine, Burma

Sample	Depth (ft)	Pb (ppm)
Residual overburden	0–1	4700
	1–2	1400
	2–3	1300
	3–4	1100
	4–5	900
	5–6	450
	6–7	400
	7–8	300
Sandstone bedrock	8–9	50

(b) Bushman Mine, Bechuanaland[a]

Description	pH	Depth (in.)	Cu (ppm)
Brown-black topsoil	8.0	0–6	7500
		6–12	1600
Brown-black clay subsoil	8.4	12–31	200
Brown sandy clay, some CaCO₃ spots	9.0	30–52	50
Main zone of calcification with bedrock fragments	9.0	52–63	40
Decomposed granite gneiss with patches of CaCO₃	9.2	63–82	40

Source: (a) Ledward (1960); (b) Webb (1958a).
[a]Data for −80-mesh fraction.

Orientation work is almost always needed in the vicinity of modern
or ancient smelters for the purpose of establishing a sampling technique that avoids the collection of contaminated samples. Inasmuch as

the intensity of contamination falls off with both horizontal distance from the smelter site and vertical distance below the surface, the experimental samples should be collected as a series of vertical profiles of equivalent soils taken at progressively increasing distances from the source. The results should then indicate the minimum depth for uncontaminated samples at any given distance from the smelter.

11–2. Field Operations

An operational prospecting survey to be successful must have two qualifications: it must be based on valid principles, and it must be efficiently carried out. Establishing and confirming the validity of the principles is the function of the orientation survey, as already discussed. The actual mechanics involved in the operational survey procedure then is only a matter of determining the cheapest and most efficient means of gathering the required data. Although to a large degree the systems used in sampling, analysis, and preparing the geochemical data maps are simply a matter of common sense, a summary of the systems most widely used might be instructive.

Sampling Pattern. The selection of the best sample pattern is determined primarily by the size and shape of the target. In looking for superjacent anomalies, the most suitable pattern is a simple rectilinear grid of samples taken at equal intervals along evenly spaced lines. Rectilinear grids are preferred because of the ease in supervising the field work and in plotting the data.

If the strike direction is known, the traverse lines should be laid out at right angles to the ore structure, at intervals such that every anomaly of interest will be intersected by at least two lines. This means that the traverse-line interval should be not more than one-third of the minimum economic strike length. Sample points along the line should then be spaced at intervals that ensure that at least two points fall within every important anomaly. Thus the interval is fixed by the probable minimum width of the expected anomalies. If the anomalies are not homogeneous, a correspondingly closer sampling interval will be required, so that statistically at least two samples and preferably more will exceed threshold within the anomalous area.

Linear, elongated, or fan-shaped dispersion patterns should be sought by systems of traverses laid out at right angles to the long dimension of the pattern. If the strike direction of elongated targets is not known, or if the anomalies are expected to be equidimensional or irregular, the most economical pattern is a square grid. Here the dimensions of the grid and the sample interval should be chosen so that at least four samples will fall within the limits of the smallest

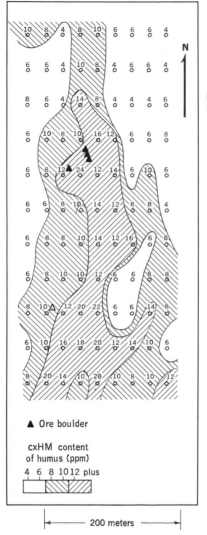

Fig. 11-3. Rectilinear sampling grid, Petolahti, Finland. From Kauranne (personal communication, 1959).

▲ Ore boulder

cxHM content
of humus (ppm)

4 6 8 10 12 plus

|← 200 meters →|

Fig. 11-4. Square grid used where strike direction of elongated targets is not predictable.

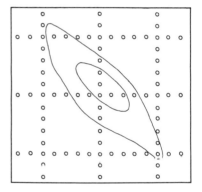

expected anomaly. Typical examples of rectilinear patterns are illustrated in Figures 11-3 to 11-5.

Where the terrain is very steep it may be desirable to lay out a simple pattern to conform to the topography. Under these circumstances, soil sample traverses following the crests and spurs of ridges have been used successfully on a number of occasions (Figure 11-6). In order to obtain adequate coverage, it may be necessary to supplement ridge-crest traversing with contour or base-of-slope traverses. If down-slope distortion of soil anomalies is extreme, it may be possible

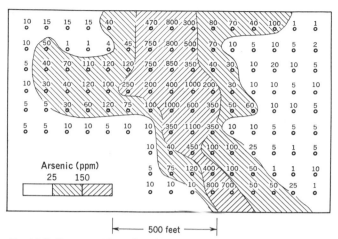

Fig. 11-5. Square grid used to detect irregular patterns of arsenic in residual soil overlying arsenical gold mineralization, Sierra Leone. Data on minus-80-mesh fraction. After Mather (1959).

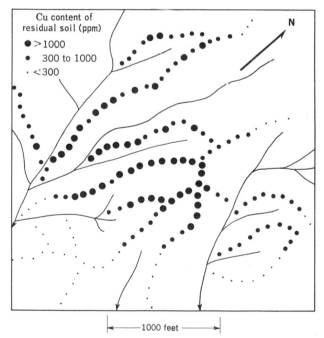

Fig. 11-6. Example of ridge-and-spur soil-sampling pattern, Cebu Project, Republic of Philippines. Data on minus-80-mesh fraction. Reproduced by courtesy of Newmont Mining Company.

to detect any important anomaly on the higher ground by sampling only the base-of-slope colluvium (Figure 11-7).

Sampling patterns designed for mapping lateral hydromorphic anomalies are necessarily determined by the distribution of seepage areas. These are most commonly found in topographic depressions, at the base of slopes and along the margins of swamps and flood plains.

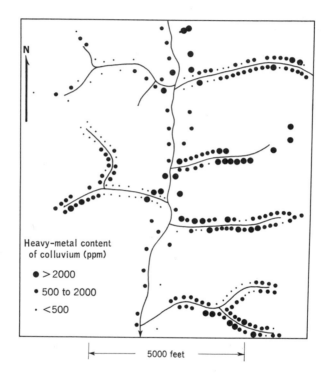

Fig. 11-7. Example of base-of-slope sampling pattern, Lemieux District, Quebec. Data on minus-½-inch fraction After Riddell (1954).

Spring and seepage areas may also occur, of course, at any point along the outcrop of aquifers, such as faults and permeable horizons, that may be carrying water under hydrostatic pressure.

Sampling Procedure. As a rule, 20 to 50 grams of sample will provide enough material after sieving for analysis. Probably the best all-purpose containers are 3- by 5-inch water-resistant kraft paper envelopes that may be fastened by folding over a noncontaminating metal tab attached to the open end. The advantages of such envelopes are low cost, convenience in handling, and the fact that wet samples may be dried out without removing them from their containers. With very wet samples, it is advisable to pack the envelopes into a narrow, lightweight cardboard box, in order to prevent chafing during transport.

Soil samples at depths up to 1 or 2 feet may easily be collected from small pits. Deeper samples of loamy soils can usually be collected more economically be means of a soil auger. The simple type shown in

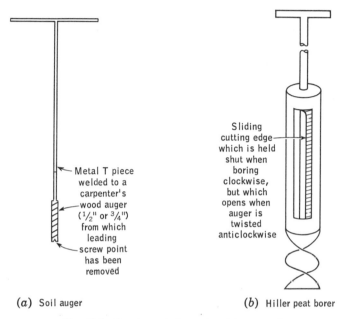

Metal T piece welded to a carpenter's wood auger (1/2" or 3/4") from which leading screw point has been removed

Sliding cutting edge which is held shut when boring clockwise, but which opens when auger is twisted anticlockwise

(*a*) Soil auger   (*b*) Hiller peat borer

Fig. 11-8. Simple tools for soil and peat sampling.

Figure 11-8 has been found satisfactory up to depths of 4 to 6 feet. Augering to a predetermined depth is greatly facilitated if a hole is first made with a crowbar. When deep holes are required, light power augers may prove economical and have been used for taking samples as deep as 30 feet. Special augers, such as the Hiller peat borer (Figure 11-8), are often more convenient than conventional soil augers when sampling organic overburden at depths greater than 2 feet below the surface.

Lake-bottom sampling also presents special technical problems. In shallow water, conventional soil- or peat-sampling equipment may be suitable. For fine-grained samples a baler device may be used, either attached to a string of rods for sampling in shallow water, or on the end of a line for deep-water sampling (Figure 11-9). Lake-bottom sampling is usually undertaken from a boat, which presents certain difficulties from the point of view of sample location; in northern latitudes, however, it may be convenient to sample in winter when the lakes are frozen over.

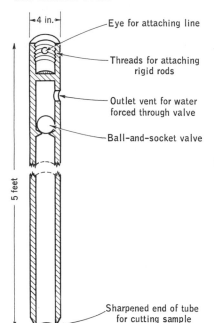

Fig. 11-9. Cut-away section of sample bailer for lake-sediment sampling.

Locating and Identifying Samples. Location of sample sites or sample traverses need only be accurate enough to enable any anomalous sites to be revisited in the field. Inasmuch as precise surveying is not necessary, pace-and-compass traverses, without the cutting of lines beyond those necessary for access, are normally quite adequate. Samples collected on irregular patterns, such as along ridge crests and contours or in seepage areas, may be located directly on aerial photographs or topographic maps if available.

Knowledge of the local topography is usually essential when interpreting soil surveys. If published contour maps are not available, the necessary information may be obtained by taking aneroid barometer readings along the traverse lines, or by measuring and recording the direction and angle of slope at each sample point. Providing the traverses are close enough together, approximate form lines can then be drawn on the geochemical map.

It is almost always desirable to mark the sample site in such a way that it can be found again when revisiting the area. Along traverse lines it is rarely necessary to identify more than every third or fourth site. Stakes or blazes, marked with weatherproof crayon, are usually adequate to ensure legibility for the period of the survey. Baselines and other critical points may be identified by more permanent metal tags or cairns.

Two systems of numbering are in common use. On geometric grids, samples are usually identified by the grid coordinates with reference to the baseline. When the sampling net is irregular, the best procedure is to number the samples consecutively in the order in which they are collected. Duplication of samples can be avoided by prenumbering the containers, which can readily be done with a standard office-type automatic enumerator. A similar system can usefully be employed when grid sampling, to serve as a safeguard against errors in assigning grid coordinates.

The field notebook should record the traverse number, sample number, sample interval, and depth, together with a description of the material collected and any special information such as whether the ground is freely or poorly drained, topographic situation and so on.

Sample Preparation and Analysis. Preparation of samples for analysis is usually carried out at base camp or in the laboratory. If the overburden is particularly stony, however, it may be desirable to sieve the samples to minus 2 millimeters on the spot and discard the coarse fraction. Generally speaking, samples are too moist to pass through a fine mesh without being dried. In some climates samples will dry out by evaporation through the paper walls of their containers if laid out in the sun or stored in a dry room for a few days. Otherwise it is necessary to use some form of low-temperature oven, which may be improvised in the field.

The optimum system for sample preparation should be determined as part of the orientation experiments. For most problems, it is usually necessary only to sieve the sample, discard the coarse fraction, and retain the fines for analysis. Crushing at any stage of preparation of soil samples here is generally avoided. Rarely, the element sought may occur preferentially as clastic grains, such as Be in the mineral beryl; in this case, it may be found preferable to retain and crush one of the coarse fractions for analysis. Noncontaminating sieves should always be used. The principal danger of contamination is from Cu and Zn in standard brass sieves, where samples are to be analyzed for these metals. A sieve made of stainless steel, nylon, or bolting silk set in a plastic or wooden frame is satisfactory.

The choice of analytical procedure will depend to a large extent on the form in which the element is held in the overburden. Determination of both the total and readily extractable metal is helpful in differentiating between syngenetic and hydromorphic anomalies.

The choice of the element to be determined is generally based on considerations of relative mobility, together with suitability of available analytical techniques. Thus, because Zn tends to form broader dispersion patterns than Pb, it is usual to analyze for Zn in initial stages of exploration surveys for Pb-Zn ores, and for Pb when a more precise location of the bedrock metal source is desired. The precision of the analytical procedure should be high enough that the analytical errors will be small compared with the natural range of background fluctuation. Some of the chemical procedures most commonly employed in soil analysis are listed in Table 3-3; factors in the organization of an analytical program are discussed in Chapter 16.

Preparation of Geochemical Maps. Two different kinds of maps are commonly prepared in the course of recording and interpreting the data of geochemical prospecting surveys. One of these, the data map, is simply a vehicle for the chemical data. The other is an interpretation map that embodies a greater or less degree of graphical generalization of the data.

The purpose of the data map is to record the actual observations and to show their relationship to observed features of geology, topography, drainage, and possible sources of contamination. Where this cannot be done on a single sheet without causing congestion, then a series of transparent overlay maps should be prepared. Inasmuch as the map should present the data objectively and in full, all sampling points and the actual analytical values obtained should always be given, together with a note as to the analytical method used. The scale of the map should be chosen so that the minimum distance between symbols for sample sites is not less than a quarter of an inch.

Data may be plotted as profile curves where it is desired to emphasize the distribution of metal along separate lines of samples. As a rule, curves are used on maps when the traverse lines are too far apart to justify joining anomalies from one line to another. Figure 11-10 illustrates some common conventions for plotting data in the form of profile curves.

Interpretation maps usually involve the grouping of the data in ranges of concentration. These ranges then may be represented by simple graphical symbols such as lines of equal concentration, sometimes called geochemical contours or *isograds* (Figures 11-3 to 11-5), and shaded or colored circles (Figures 11-6 and 11-7). When selecting contour intervals or group concentration ranges for bringing out the pattern and relative significance of anomalies on the geochemical map, it is usual to select the intervals as factorial multiples of the threshold value, e.g., for a threshold of 100 ppm and a factor of 2, the intervals would be 100, 200, 400, 800, 1600 ppm, and so on. Generally speaking, contours should only be employed where anomalies are homogeneous and where there is adequate data to ensure validity of the contours. Graphical presentation of nonhomogeneous anomalies is best done by means of a graduated series of circles or other appropriate symbols. The selection of contour intervals or concentration ranges is determined by inspection of the data and the estimated threshold value, as discussed below.

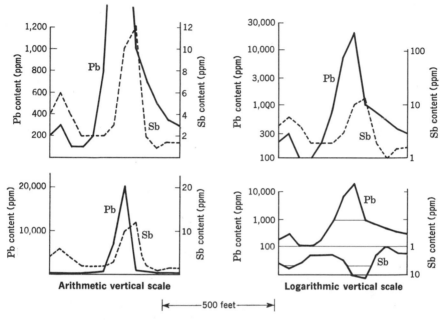

Arithmetic vertical scale   **Logarithmic vertical scale**

|←————500 feet————→|

Fig. 11-10. Systems for plotting geochemical data as profile curves. Data on minus-80-mesh fraction. From Hawkes (1954).

In addition to the geology, either topographic contours or form lines should also be plotted to facilitate interpretation. The pattern of surface drainage and areas of ground-water seepage should be indicated to help distinguish between hydromorphic and syngenetic anomalies. For the same reason it is desirable to show the boundaries of spring areas, lakes, swamps, and flood plains. Appropriate symbols should be used to distinguish soil samples collected in freely drained ground from those collected in seepage areas. In glaciated terrain the direction of ice movement and the distribution of glacial deposits of different origin should also be plotted. In lake-sediment sampling the map should show the depth of water at each sampling point and the location of inlet and outflow streams, the direction and flow of currents, and any other information that may have a bearing on the pattern of sedimentation.

II-3. Interpretation of Data

In general terms the interpretation of geochemical soil data involves four main problems: (1) estimation of background and threshold values; (2) distinguishing between significant and nonsignificant anomalies; (3) distinguishing between lateral and superjacent anomalies, and (4) appraising the significance of anomalies in terms of possible ore, with a view to selecting those that merit further investigation.

It is naturally extremely difficult to generalize on interpretation, as each area presents its own problems. No attempt is therefore made in the following paragraphs to indicate more than a general philosophy, in the knowledge that any instructions as to interpretative techniques will often be found incomplete in detail and may well need to be modified in practice to suit the needs of particular problems.

Estimation of Background and Threshold Values. The general approach to this problem has been outlined in Chapter 2. In practice, the principal difficulty lies in recognizing the different background patterns that are related only to bedrock types or to variations in overburden and drainage and that are not connected with mineralization. Geological or geomorphic features responsible for major variations in geochemical patterns may easily pass unnoticed at the time the samples are collected. This problem assumes increasing importance as anomaly contrast diminishes and peak anomalous values related to significant mineralization approach the threshold value. The best practice is to study the over-all geochemical pattern on the data map with a view to recognizing any correlations that exist between the "geochemical relief" and the observed and recorded features of geology and geomorphology. It will be remembered that the units comprising the geochemical landscape are defined not only by differences in the mean level of the values but also by differences in scatter, or deviation about the mean. The boundaries of these geochemical units should be outlined on the data map and studied as an overlay to the geological, topographical, and such geophysical maps as may be available. In this way, not only is attention drawn to the more obvious anomalies but also the broader features of the background pattern. Provisional correlations between geochemical features and the geology or topography provide a basis for determining the background and threshold values that should be assigned to each component geochemical unit of the over-all background pattern. A review of the geochemical pattern within each unit may then disclose anomalies that would not have been apparent had the data been assessed against the yardstick of a uniform threshold value. Other advantages of this approach are that it can provide additional information on the general geology of the area, as well as facilitating the subsequent interpretation of the anomalies.

Recognition of Nonsignificant Anomalies. Recapitulating from Chapter 8: the principal types of anomalies that are not related to mineral deposits include those resulting from (1) barren rock types characterized by a relatively high background metal content; (2) human contamination, and (3) sampling and analytical errors.

Anomalies resulting from the weathering of high-background rocks may be suspected wherever the patterns cover very large areas compared with the expected dimensions of an ore deposit. Such anomalies are particularly suspect where these broad patterns lie parallel to the known trend of the regional geological structure. Associations of elements that are characteristic of certain specific rocks, such as the Ni-Co-Cr association in ultramafic rocks, may also be useful as clues to the origin.

Contamination as a cause of anomalous patterns is immediately suspect where the anomalies are located near mine dumps and smelters or are related to some recorded pattern of agriculture, roads, or railways. Difficulties in interpretation can occur, however, in old mining areas where visible evidence of past activities may be lacking or inconspicuous. In these circumstances it is necessary to rely on the geometry of the anomalies, the fact that there is a general tendency for values to decrease with depth and that, for mobile elements in freely drained residual overburden, the cxMe:Me ratio is commonly higher than would be expected if the anomalous metal were truly residual. As mentioned earlier, however, biogenic anomalies also commonly decrease with depth, and all epigenetic anomalies, both biogenic and hydromorphic, are characterized by a high cxMe:Me ratio.

False anomalies due to the inadvertent collection of samples that contain a natural enrichment of metal may be difficult to recognize unless the field area can be revisited. They most commonly reflect unnoticed variations in (1) the nature of the sample material, particularly with regard to the content of organic matter, clays, or hydrous oxides; (2) the depth of the different soil horizons in relation to the sampling depth (Figure 11-11); (3) the nature of the vegetation and its influence on the accumulation of biogenic metal in the soil, and (4) local drainage conditions. False anomalies due to analytical errors are more readily spotted and can easily be corrected by repeat analyses. Erratic high values are obviously suspect, as are patterns that are related to particular batches of samples. Inasmuch as samples are usually analyzed in the order in which they are

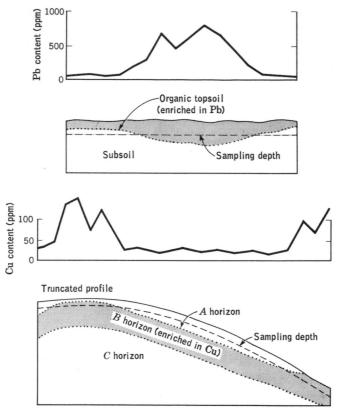

Fig. 11-11. Hypothetical examples of false anomalies due to inadvertent collection of samples from more than one soil horizon.

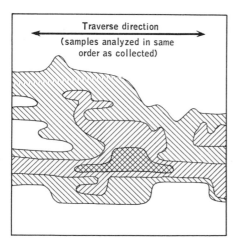

Fig. 11-12. Typical example of a false anomaly (or a false trend in a real pattern) due to variation in analytical bias.

collected, batch variation shows immediately as a pattern that trends parallel to the traverse direction (Figure 11-12).

Distinction Between Superjacent and Lateral Anomalies.   Many costly errors in interpreting geochemical data have occurred because the assumption was made that the source of metal lay immediately beneath the anomaly. In other words, the anomaly was assumed to be superjacent when in reality it was a lateral anomaly developed by horizontal movement either of ground water or of the soil itself.

The two principal kinds of superjacent dispersion patterns are the relic patterns in residual soil due to simple weathering in place and hydromorphic or biogenic patterns in transported cover resulting from upward movement of metal-rich solutions. Residual patterns are of course syngenetic, and may be recognized by the presence of diagnostic primary minerals and by a low cxMe:Me ratio in freely drained overburden; only under rare circumstances is the cxMe:Me ratio high, such as when the concealing overburden is poorly drained or organic-rich, or where the anomalous metal occurs in the superjacent pattern as relatively soluble secondary minerals. Superjacent patterns of hydromorphic or biogenic origin, on the other hand, are characterized by the predominance of more mobile metals and a high cxMe:Me ratio. In this respect they are generally indistinguishable from lateral patterns, since the latter are nearly always hydromorphic in origin. A more certain criterion is given by the location and geometry of the pattern. Thus, after allowing for any distortion that may have taken place during dispersion, a soil anomaly whose shape and trend shows little or no correlation with land forms yet is consistent with a probable geological trend is more likely to be a superjacent anomaly. Lateral anomalies, on the other hand, will usually show a close relationship with local land forms.

Fossil anomalies related to past topography and drainage conditions may offer considerable difficulty in interpretation. Thus, one-time seepage areas can become freely drained, leading to a decrease in the original ratio of readily extractable to total metal. Occurrences are known (Mather, 1959) where downslope extensions of residual anomalies have become isolated from the rest of the anomaly by erosion of the intervening ground, giving the impression of two anomalies related to two bedrock sources. Relic patterns of anomalous terrace alluvium on valley slopes can be another source of difficulty. Past changes in the climate, ground-water level, and other features of the environment can leave their mark on the present-day dispersion pattern. Such effects have been noted in the central African peneplain where, in the past, there have been at least five alternating arid and pluvial periods.

Appraisal of Anomalies. The principal considerations in assessing the possible economic significance of geochemical anomalies are: (1) the magnitude of the values, often expressed as the contrast between the peak values and threshold; (2) the size and shape of the anomalous area; (3) the geological setting; and (4) the extent to which the local environment may have influenced the metal content and the pattern of the anomaly.

It must be emphasized that the contrast between anomalous values and threshold constitutes no more than a provisional guide to help in the first stages of interpretation. Classification of anomalies solely on the basis of metal content tacitly assumes a reliable correlation between anomaly contrast and primary tenor of the bedrock source—an assumption that is rarely justified in practice.

As a general rule, all anomalies whose dimensions are consistent with the possibility of a sizable deposit should be listed for further investigation. Priorities will generally depend on the favorability or otherwise of the geological setting. It will be appreciated, however, that shallow overburden, restricted mobility, and many other factors may lead to local enhancement of metal values and to the development of a relatively strong anomaly from a low-grade bedrock source. At the same time, a local variation in the environment, such as a deeper overburden, more intensive leaching, and so on, can result in relatively feeble values that are in fact related to a high-grade source. Consequently, providing that the geological setting is not entirely unfavorable, even weak anomalies of adequate extent should never be discounted without first considering the possibilities of local suppression of the values.

II–4. General Procedure for Follow-Up

The object of the follow-up investigation is to provide further information as to the possible significance of the selected anomalies and to pinpoint targets for drilling or other means of direct subsurface exploration. The first obvious step is to revisit the area with a view to (1) confirming the cause and seeing whether there is any evidence for local enhancement or suppression of anomalous values and (2) planning the follow-up work. If practicable, it is useful to recheck the anomalous pattern on the spot with a field chemical test. In the case of hydromorphic patterns, this can easily be done with a pocket cold-extraction kit. With residual or other types of anomaly, where the cxMe content is low, this test can give very unreliable results.

The source of lateral anomalies will be sought upslope, upglacier, or updrainage, according to the mechanism of dispersion. Lateral geochemical anomalies almost never provide drill targets without further work. Usually an elaborate system of follow-up involving

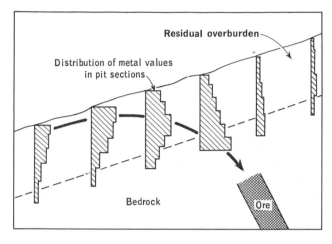

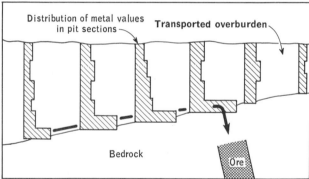

Fig. 11-13. Idealized diagrams illustrating the manner in which distribution of metal with depth may assist in locating bedrock source.

geochemical soil surveys, geophysical surveys, or conventional prospecting will be necessary before a decision can be made regarding the chances of ore and the desirability of drilling.

Superjacent patterns may be followed up by close-spaced sampling aimed at delineating the axis of the anomaly. This may be facilitated by taking deep samples, insofar as the intensity of such patterns often increases with depth. Where deposits contain associated metals of contrasting mobility, a sharper pattern may be obtained by analyzing the samples for the relatively immobile constituents. The more promising sections of the anomaly may be opened up by pitting, trenching, or stripping, preferably to bedrock if possible. Pits should be logged and channel-sampled vertically, in the same manner as described for the orientation survey. The distribution of metal values down the pits may then aid in pinpointing the location of the bedrock source (Figure 11-13). Trench exposures may be horizontally channel-sampled with the same end in view.

Where the nature of the deposit responsible for a superjacent geo-chemical anomaly cannot be readily determined, it may be helpful to carry out an appropriate geophysical survey in order to come to decisions regarding the desirability of drilling and the selection of drill sites. Inasmuch as drilling is usually the most expensive stage in the follow-up sequence, every possible means should be taken to localize suitable targets before drilling is undertaken.

CHAPTER 12

ANOMALIES IN NATURAL WATERS

Anomalous patterns of elements contained in ground and surface water are known as hydrochemical anomalies. The elements most likely to travel in solution in natural waters are, by definition, the relatively mobile elements. In approximate order of decreasing mobility, those which have received most attention in prospecting by water analysis are SO_4, Mo, U, Zn and Cu. Experimental studies, particularly in the U. S. S. R., have also drawn attention to the distribution in natural waters of many other minor elements, including Pb, Cr, Be, Co, Ni, Sn, W, Ag, Bi, Sb, and As. The development of hydrochemical methods of prospecting has been hampered by technical difficulties in determining the extremely low concentrations of the trace elements in natural waters, which are commonly in the order of parts per billion (ppb, micrograms/liter, or 10^{-9} g/ml). There can be little doubt, however, that as analytical techniques improve, the scope of water analysis as a prospecting method will continue to broaden.

The present chapter reviews the characteristics of hydrochemical anomalies. Chapter 13 will cover the characteristics of anomalies in seepage soils and stream sediments. Chapter 14 will review technical aspects of geochemical reconnaissance surveys based on sampling components of the drainage pattern.

12–1. Mode of Occurrence of Elements

Inorganic material can occur in natural water in a variety of forms. If an element is to move with the water, it must occur either in soluble form or as a component of a stable suspension. The following are the most important of these mobile phases.

1. Cations. Most of the water-soluble ore metals occur in natural water apparently as simple cations. Examples are Zn^{++}, Cu^{++} and Co^{++}. One exception is U, which is mobile as the complex UO_2^{++} cation under certain conditions. Some of the soluble cations can be measured by simple colorimetric tests; others, because of their very

low concentrations in natural water, require a preliminary separation by ion-exchange resins, chromatography, or coprecipitation.

2. Anions. A number of elements under appropriate conditions travel as anions. For example, S and Mo are stable in mildly oxidizing waters as the anion oxide complexes SO_4^{--} and MoO_4^{--}; As and Se in natural waters are probably always present as anions. The evidence suggests that U can occur as the $UO_2(CO_3)_3^{4-}$ anion complex. With proper buffering, most anion complexes can be measured by the common colorimetric procedures, either directly or after pre-concentration by one of the separation procedures mentioned for cations.

3. Ions Adsorbed on Suspended Matter. The small particle size and resulting large surface area of suspended matter give it a high exchange capacity. An active equilibrium is maintained between ions in solution and ions adsorbed to the surfaces of the suspended particles. Thus, most of the standard procedures that depend on determining the ionic content of aqueous solutions will also measure a substantial fraction of the ions adsorbed on suspended particles, just as if they occurred as free ions.

4. Undissociated Inorganic Solutes. Many inorganic compounds can occur in aqueous solution as undissociated and nonionized molecules. The principal undissociated solute of molecular dimensions that occurs commonly in natural water is silica in the form of the H_4SiO_4 molecule. The extent to which dispersed ore constituents may occur in this form is not known. Determination of undissociated solutes generally requires evaporation of the sample and re-solution of the residue in an appropriate reagent.

5. Soluble Organic Matter. Metal in simple ionic form may react with the organic matter of humus or peat to form undissociated water-soluble metallo-organic complexes. Determination of the metal held in this form normally requires evaporation of the water sample followed by destructive ashing or wet oxidation of the residue before analysis.

6. Suspensoids. The quantity of metal traveling in natural water as relatively insoluble components of suspended matter varies greatly as a function of the turbulence of the water, the abundance of finely divided and easily suspended sediment, the amount of organic activity with the resulting growth of floating organisms, and the factors tending to stabilize colloidal dispersions of the hydrous Fe, Mn, Si, and Al oxides. The trace-element content of nonionic suspended matter can normally be determined only by evaporation of the water and analysis of the residue.

The partition of minor elements between these six mobile phases is conditioned in part by the over-all geochemical behavior of the element in question and in part by the stability of each phase in the natural water. The geochemical peculiarities of the individual elements are summarized in the Appendix. The stability of the various phases with which the minor elements travel depends to a large extent on the local environment.

Ground water carries most of its load of metal in one of the ionic phases, with lesser proportions traveling as stabilized colloidal sols.

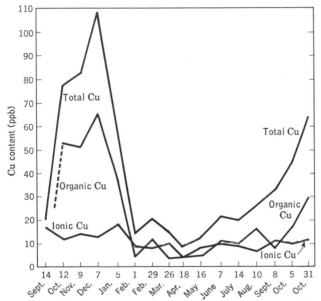

Fig. 12-1. Seasonal variation in the various fractions of copper in surface water from Lake Quonnapaug, Connecticut. From Riley (1939).

Surface water, on the other hand, because of the effect of both sunlight and increased aeration and turbulence, carries a large, variable, and unpredictable fraction of its metal content in nonionic form, principally as constituents of soluble organic matter and of both inorganic and organic suspensoids. Sunlight and warmth promote the growth of both rooted plants and floating organisms, which may absorb ionic constituents from the water and which serve as the source material for both dissolved and suspended organic matter. The organic content of the water is also liable to vary according to the amount of organic-rich soil in the spring area or along the banks of the stream; seasonal variation in the decay of vegetation is another important factor in this connection. The amount of suspended inorganic matter in natural water also depends on the environment and tends to increase with increased turbulence of the water and availability of a source of fine-grained material. Figure 12-1 shows an example of variations with time of year in the fraction of the total Cu content of lake water that occurs respectively in ionic and soluble organic forms.

12–2. Persistence of Anomalies

The usefulness of hydrochemical anomalies in exploration depends to a large extent on how far they extend downstream from the source before they are lost in the normal range of background variations. The length, or *persistence*, of a hydrochemical anomaly is conditioned largely by (1) contrast at the source, (2) dilution, and (3) precipitation.

Contrast at Source. Both the background metal content and anomaly contrast can vary widely according to local conditions (Table 12-1). A high contrast at the source is favored by rapid solution of

TABLE 12-1. Metal Contents of Natural Waters in Mineralized and Unmineralized Areas, U. S. S. R.

	Average Metal Content (ppb) of Ground Water			
	Zn at Pb-Zn Deposits		Cu at Cu Deposits	
District	Background	Anomalous	Background	Anomalous
Transcaucasia	200	200–500	—	—
Altai	10	50–300	4	20
The Sayans and Kuznetzk Altau	1	40–90	1	10–100
Central Kazakhstan	80–200	300	30	130
Central Asia	—	—	20	50
Ural	—	—	30	80

Source: Brodsky, quoted by Ginzburg, 1960, p. 202. Reprinted with permission from I. I. Ginzburg, Principles of Geochemical Prospecting, copyright 1960 by Pergamon Press Incorporated.

the ore minerals. The rate of solution of most primary ore minerals is largely dependent on the stability of the minerals under weathering conditions, the accessibility of the ore to percolating solutions, and the solubility of the secondary products.

The stability of many ore minerals is a matter simply of their relative solubility in water. Thus the stability of the mineral components of most oxide ores is relatively high, whereas that of the soluble minerals of saline deposits is correspondingly low. Most sulfide minerals, in spite of their relative insolubility in pure water, are vulnerable to attack in the oxygen-rich environment of weathering because of the high solubility of the products of their oxidation. The free oxygen content of the water affects the rate of oxidation. Also, the

rate of decomposition of sulfides may be accelerated if pyrite or marcasite is present, as these minerals on oxidation liberate extremely
corrosive solutions of free sulfuric acid that then can attack the
other primary ore minerals. Thus, other factors being equal, an ore
high in pyrite will release metal into solution at a very much higher
rate than an ore of equivalent grade that is low in pyrite. Similarly,
strongly pyritized rock containing only minor quantities of the ore
metals may release as much or more metal into the ground water as

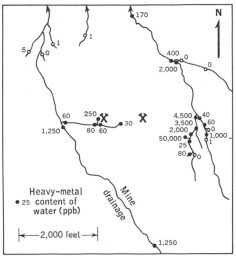

Fig. 12-2. Heavy-metal anomalies in streams of the Gambler Gulch area, Keno Hill, Yukon Territory. After Boyle et al. (1955).

high-grade ore containing no pyrite. Rapid discharge of metals into the
drainage is inhibited by calcareous country rock that either neutralizes
the acids before they have a chance to attack the ore minerals quickly,
or that causes the precipitation of the metals in secondary minerals.

Fracturing promotes the liberation of soluble metals by increasing
the reactive surface between the ore and the oxidizing solutions. A
similar effect is seen in the case of fine-grained sulfides disseminated
in a permeable host rock. Water draining highly sheared or disseminated, permeable ores will therefore tend to show stronger anomalies
than water from compact, massive ores of equivalent grade and size.
The high contrast at the source illustrated in Figure 12-2 results largely
from the occurrence of sulfides exposed to oxidation and leaching in
mine workings or in fissure zones.

The rate of flow of water through an oxidizing deposit also can
have a pronounced effect on the intensity of a hydrochemical anomaly. A low rate of flow will provide more time for the weathering
products of the ore minerals to go into solution and hence will result
in a higher metal content of the water.

The solubility of an element may also be governed by the presence of other ions in solution. For example, the concentration of uranium in a solution is dependent not only on the availability of a source of the metal but also on the concentration of HCO_3^-, with which it reacts to form the soluble uranyl-carbonate complex (Illsley et al., 1958). In these circumstances, it may be necessary to determine not only the metal content but also the concentration of relevant major constituents in order to obtain a better guide as to the distribution of the metal in the bedrock of the catchment area.

The contrast of anomalous values over background in any given area will reflect the balance of these bedrock factors as conditioned by the local geomorphic environment. Topographic relief and climate are particularly important in this connection. Other things being equal, maximum contrast will normally be expected in areas of moderate rainfall and moderate relief. High rainfall and strong relief both tend to decrease contrast by increasing the flow of water and hence the chances that the anomaly will be swamped by water of background composition. In areas of strong relief, the rate of erosion may be so rapid as to keep pace with or even outstrip the rate of oxidation, so that the amount of solubilized metal available for leaching is restricted. Much depends, however, on the depth of effective oxidation. In areas of weak relief, the increased contrast resulting from a slow rate of flow of ground water is often offset by the fact that the water table and hence the zone of active oxidation lies close to the surface. Nevertheless, even in areas of low relief, appreciable solution of metal may still take place from ores that have been deeply oxidized during an earlier climatic cycle when the water table stood at a lower level. Climate can have an effect also on the pH and hence indirectly on the corrosive power of the percolating solutions. Thus, in northern temperate regions, near-surface waters tend to be more acid than in tropical and desert areas.

Decay by Dilution. The pattern of decay of anomalous metal contained in waters draining an oxidizing ore deposit is in part the effect of simple dilution by water from unmineralized areas. Where this dilution by gradual small increments of barren water is the only factor in the decay of a hydrochemical anomaly, the anomalous pattern may be traced for a considerable distance, until it is lost in normal background fluctuations. Anomalous water may, however, be diluted abruptly by a very great volume of background water at a point relatively close to the source. Catastrophic dilution of this kind may obliterate anomalous patterns before they reach a point where they would normally be sampled, and thus make it difficult to detect them without excessively detailed sampling patterns.

Figure 12-3 from the classic work of Sergeyev shows the decay of the heavy metal content of an anomalous stream as the result of dilution by relatively small increments from side tributaries and stream-bed seepage derived from unmineralized ground. The lowest sampling point is from a large river and illustrates the destruction of the anomalous pattern by catastrophic dilution.

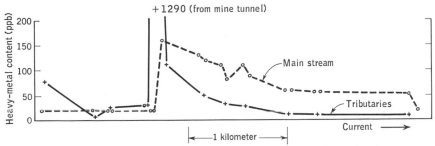

Fig. 12-3. Heavy-metal content of water, Berezov Brook, U. S. S. R. After Sergeyev (1946).

Decay at Precipitation Barriers. Hydrochemical anomalies normally decay more rapidly than can be accounted for by simple dilution. Metal-rich water, as it moves away from the source of the metal, ordinarily soon comes into an environment where changing conditions of some kind cause precipitation of part or all of the metal from the water.

Precipitation barriers characteristically occur in spring and seepage areas where ground waters coming to the surface encounter an environment of increased availability of oxygen, sunlight, and organic activity. Soluble ferrous iron derived from the oxidation and leaching of Fe sulfides tends to be further oxidized to ferric iron and precipitated as limonite. Other ore metals may be either coprecipitated with the limonite or with the organic matter that accumulates in the swampy soil of spring areas. This effect is illustrated by the distribution of Zn around a Zn-rich spring in the southwestern Wisconsin Zn district, as shown in Figure 12-4. Here, in a distance of less than 200 feet, the Zn content of the water is reduced by a factor of 20.

A precipitation barrier may also occur where acid waters emerge from the reducing environment of an organic swamp into the oxidizing environment of an open stream channel. This change in environment commonly causes the precipitation of hydrous Fe and Mn oxides in the stream bed and the consequent removal of dissolved metals from the solution by coprecipitation.

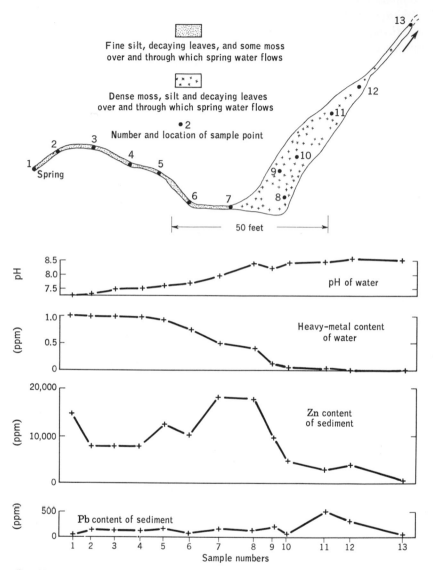

Fig. 12-4. Precipitation of heavy metals from spring water, Potosi area, southwestern Wisconsin zinc district. Data on bulk samples. After Kennedy (1956).

The mixing of waters of two confluent streams of contrasting chemical composition may result in a chemical reaction and a resulting precipitation of material in the stream bed. Theobald *et al.* (1958), observing the point of mixing of a stream water of pH 3.5 with a stream of pH 8.0, found heavy precipitates of hydrous Fe and Mn

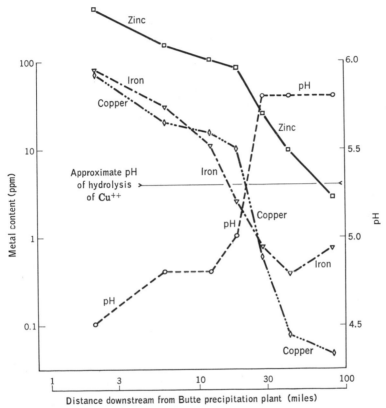

Fig. 12-5. Copper, zinc and iron content and pH of drainage water below copper mines at Butte, Montana. Data collected by L. C. Huff.

oxides together with large concentrations of other metals immediately below the confluence. Aluminous precipitates were observed in the stream bed for several miles below the confluence. The pH of the mixed water is 6.5.

A similar decay in metal content was observed in the highly contaminated drainage below the mines at Butte, Montana, where acid, metal-rich mine water is progressively diluted by background water of normal pH. Figure 12-5 shows the sudden decay in the Cu content of the water as the pH is increased beyond 5.3, the point at which Cu normally begins to precipitate as insoluble basic salts. Presumably the more regular decline in the Zn content of the same series of samples is the result of simple dilution, uncomplicated by precipitation.

Ground water, as a result of the lower content of free oxygen and the absence of sunlight and the biological activity that goes with it, is not as much at the mercy of precipitation barriers as surface waters. Even so, conspicuous examples of precipitation of metal from ground water as it moves into a chemically reactive environment, such as the zones of secondary enrichment in copper deposits, are well known.

The most mobile elements are the ones that are the least likely to be affected by precipitation barriers as they are carried away from their source in the bedrock. However, even the extremely mobile elements may be immobilized on occasion. Sulfur, for example, may be precipitated as sulfide in a strongly reducing environment. Similarly, molybdate may be precipitated as the insoluble ferric molybdate in Fe-rich solutions. It is important to appreciate that precipitation of a particular metal will depend on the mode of occurrence of the element. Thus, the fraction of the total content of a metal that is traveling in an ionic form may be precipitated by adsorption or co-precipitation, while the nonionic fraction may be unaffected.

Re-Solution at Precipitation Barriers. The chemical environment at any given spot may change with time. A site that at one time was a precipitation barrier may, as a result of changing conditions, become a site of re-solution of precipitates of anomalous material originally derived from the leaching of an ore deposit. Precipitated material thus subjected to later solution may consist of relatively insoluble secondary ore minerals, anomalous residual soil or material precipitated in hydromorphic and biogenic anomalies. Hydrochemical anomalies, therefore, can be of complex origin insofar as they may comprise soluble materials derived both directly from the leaching of the primary ore and indirectly by way of a number of intermediate materials, as illustrated diagrammatically in Figure 8-2.

The secondary release of Cu in soluble form appears to be an important factor in the development of the drainage anomalies of the Rhodesian Copperbelt. Here, as a result of extremely deep oxidation during an earlier epoch, no primary sulfide minerals now occur within several hundred feet of the present surface. At the same time, the present-day ground-water level and zone of active chemical leaching is relatively shallow. Thus, the Cu moving in the ground waters draining mineralized ground in these areas must come from re-solution of metal from the zone of past oxidation rather than from the underlying zone of Cu-bearing sulfides (Tooms and Webb, 1961).

Secondary release of major quantities of soluble metals can also result from the natural decay or burning of metal-rich organic matter.

12–3. Time Variations

Hydrochemical anomalies show a very strong tendency to change in intensity with changes in weather. The resulting instability of geochemical anomalies in water is one of the most serious problems in practical prospecting work based on water analysis.

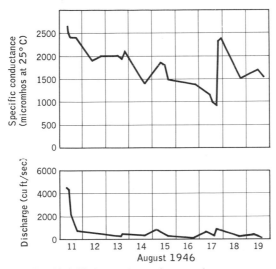

Fig. 12-6. Variations in conductance (proportional to content of ionized salts) and discharge of Rio Grande River, New Mexico. From Hem (1959).

Rainfall and runoff have a marked effect on the intensity of water anomalies, particularly in climates where the rainfall is highly seasonal. Normally the composition of ground and surface water is relatively stable during dry periods. At the first rain immediately after a period of dry weather, two factors come into play. One is simple dilution. The other is the leaching and flushing effect of the percolating rain water removing the soluble salts that have accumulated in the soil over the previous dry period. The result is a relative increase in the salt content of the surface water with increasing discharge and a decline to normal as the water level falls. This relationship is illustrated by the data for the Rio Grande River for August 15 and 17, 1946, as presented in Figure 12-6.

Metal derived from the leaching of mineral deposits normally shows a similar increase at the beginning of a period of increased rainfall and runoff. At this time the metal content of the water, in addition to being higher, tends to be somewhat erratic. With continuing rain the metal content may settle down to a value less than

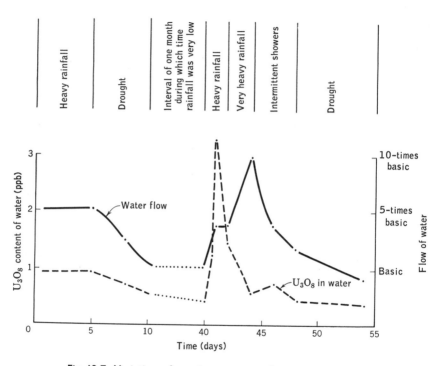

Fig. 12-7. Variation of uranium content of stream water with changing weather conditions. After Wodzicki (1959).

the peak at the start of the rains, but still somewhat higher than that during the previous dry season.

This rather complex correlation between the metal content of water and the incidence of rainfall and runoff has been noted in many parts of the world. Webb and Millman (1950) in Nigeria were the first to note the characteristic pattern of erratic variation in the anomalous heavy metal content of stream waters at the onset of the rainy season as compared with other times of the year. Later work in the same area showed that the contrast between anomaly and background is sharpest in the latter half of the rainy season (Webb, 1958a). The distribution of copper in stream water shows the same seasonal trends in Angola (Atkinson, 1957). Wodzicki (1959) in New Zealand measured a marked variation in the U content of surface water with rainfall over a period of 55 days (Figure 12-7). Polikar-pochkin *et al.* (1958) in the Transbaykal region of Siberia find a stable heavy-metal content of river water at periods of low discharge and a high and erratic content at periods of high discharge (Figure 12-8).

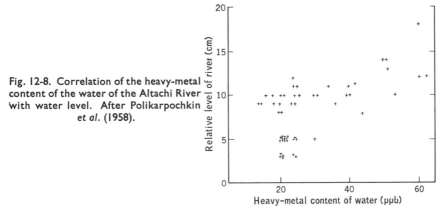

Fig. 12-8. Correlation of the heavy-metal content of the water of the Altachi River with water level. After Polikarpochkin *et al.* (1958).

Other factors in addition to the combined flushing and diluting effect of rain water may play a part in the variability of water anomalies. Melting snow in the springtime may cause dilution. In arid climates, evaporation during dry weather results in an increase in the content of metals as well as other salts dissolved in the water (Fix, 1956). According to Ginzburg (1960, p. 211), the contents of sulfate and chloride tend to vary sympathetically with rate of flow. An unusually high $SO_4^{--}:Cl^-$ ratio in ground or surface water, therefore, may provide a better indication of a sulfur-rich bedrock source than the absolute content of sulfate alone. Changes in weather may be reflected in the biological activity, with resulting changes in the partition of metal between the various ionic and nonionic aqueous phases (Figure 12-1).

12–4. Ground-Water Anomalies

The form of ground-water anomalies depends on the flow pattern of the water, which in turn depends on the permeability and geometry of the aquifers through which the anomalous water moves.

Systems of unconnected fissures in the bedrock result in irregular flow patterns that cannot be contoured or otherwise handled in a routine manner. Systems of interconnecting pore spaces in uniformly permeable rock or overburden result in a smooth, easily contoured water table. In shallow bedrock covered by unconsolidated alluvial or residual material, the ground water often follows channels defined by the bedrock surface.

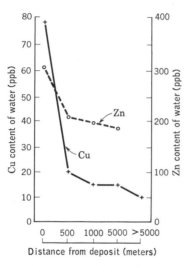

Fig. 12-9. Variation in the copper and zinc content of subterranean waters in relation to distance from deposit (Central Asia). Reprinted with permission from I. I. Ginzburg, Principles of Geochemical Prospecting, copyright 1960, Pergamon Press Incorporated.

The composition of aerated water descending through well-defined cracks and fracture zones will in general reflect the chemical character of the wall rock of the fractures. Lovering (1952) has shown that the metal content of descending water in the relatively dry mines of the Tintic district, Utah, reflects the presence or absence of ore in the channels through which the water has passed. He concluded that the composition of this water has been modified by the chemical character of the rocks adjoining the channels and by the distance traveled by the solutions. Work in Japan showed a correlation between the content of Fe, Zn, and SO_4 in fracture-zone waters and the occurrence of known ore above the underground workings in which the samples were collected (Kimura et al., 1951). On the basis of data of this kind, the discovery of at least one body of ore has been claimed (T. Watanabe, oral communication, 1953).

For some elements at least, the relative mobility is the same in ground water as in surface water. Figure 12-9, for example, shows a more rapid decay with distance from the source in the Cu content of ground water than in the Zn content. This trend parallels that found for surface water, as shown in Figure 12-5.

Fan-shaped hydrochemical anomalies normally develop wherever the permeability of the matrix is such that a smooth and uniformly sloping water table can develop. Fan-shaped patterns are characteristic of long, gentle slopes underlain either by recent alluvium or by unconsolidated, relatively porous rocks. They also occur in many areas where the aquifer is a metamorphic or igneous rock, but where the fracturing is sufficiently pervasive to permit a homogeneous pattern. Figure 12-10 shows the fan-shaped distribution of Mo-rich

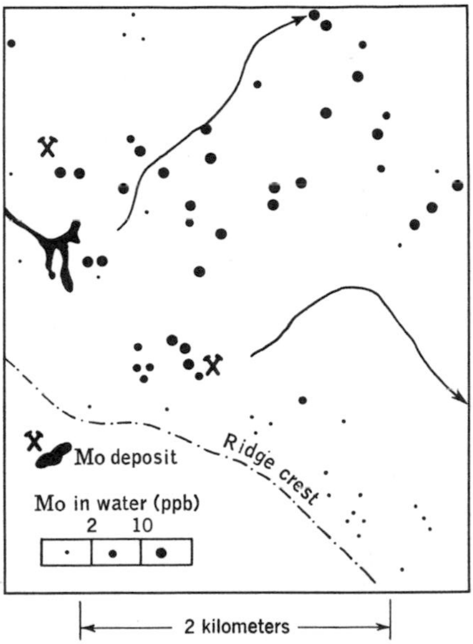

Fig. 12-10. Distribution of molybdenum in ground and spring water near the Lyangar molybdenum deposit, U. S. S. R. After Vinogradov (1957).

springs issuing from a biotite granite downslope from a series of contact metamorphic molybdenite deposits in the mountainous terrain of the Caucasus. A somewhat similar pattern exists downslope from a disseminated molybdenite deposit in the desert climate of Central Asia (Figure 12-11). Figure 12-12, drawn on a considerably smaller scale, shows the relation between the heavy-metal content of ground water and known Pb-Zn deposits in the semiarid Transbaykal region. Here, because of the wide scattering of many small deposits, the fan-shaped distribution of the anomalies shown in Figures 12-10 and 12-11 is lacking, and the boundary of the area where anomalous water samples were found is effectively coextensive with the boundary of the mineralized district.

Linear hydrochemical anomalies occur in the underflow of streams and rivers where they may be detected by sampling shallow wells in modern valley alluvium. The relation between anomalous fans on

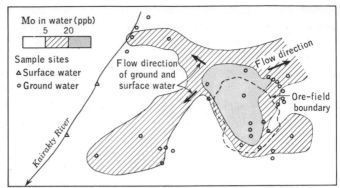

Fig. 12-11. Fan-shaped patterns of molybdenum-rich ground water downslope from Upper Kairakty molybdenum deposit, Kazakh S. S. R. After Belyakova (1958.).

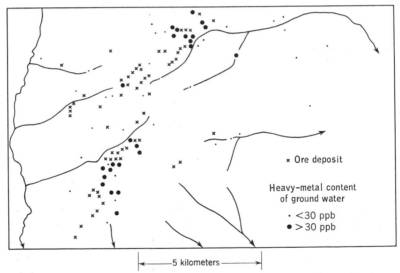

Fig. 12 12. Distribution of metal-rich ground water in the Nerchinsky Zavod district, eastern Transbaykal region, U. S. S. R. After Polikarpochkin et al. (1958).

valley slopes and anomalous underflow in valley bottoms is shown diagrammatically in Figure 8-8.

12–5. Stream-Water Anomalies

Stream water and the load of solid material that is dissolved or suspended in it come primarily from three sources: direct surface

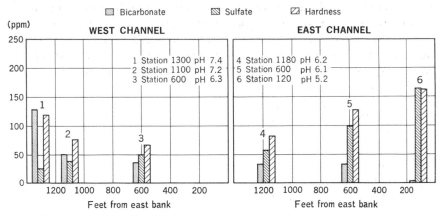

Fig. 12-13. Bicarbonate, sulfate, hardness, and pH of water samples collected in cross section of Susquehanna River at Harrisburg, Pennsylvania. From Hem (1959).

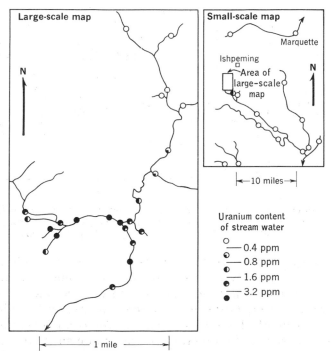

Fig. 12-14. Uranium content of stream water, Ely Creek Area, Michigan. After Illsley et al. (1958).

runoff, springs, and ground-water seepage. The soluble salts carried by the streams include all the constituents originally dissolved in the ground water that have escaped being precipitated, together with any soluble constituent picked up from the stream bed itself. Anomalous metal in any of the materials through which the water has flowed may dissolve in the water and produce an anomalous hydrochemical pattern in the stream water.

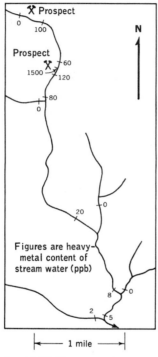

Fig. 12-15. Heavy-metal content of Missouri Creek, Colorado. After Huff (1948).

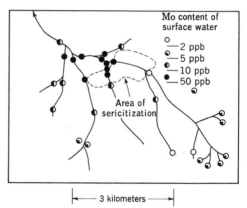

Fig. 12-16. Molybdenum content of surface water near the Yangokly molybdenum deposit, U. S. S. R. After Vinogradov (1957).

The homogeneity of stream water is one of its outstanding characteristics. As a rule, only a minor amount of turbulence is needed to mix waters of contrasting chemical or physical characteristics. Where turbulence is absent, however, or where the stream is wide in proportion to its depth, lateral variations in the composition of stream water may persist for considerable distances downstream. A lack of homogeneity of this kind is particularly common in the broad, shallow channels of the larger rivers (Figure 12-13).

Anomalous metal may enter a stream at the headwater spring (Figure 12-14) or at some point along its course (Figure 12-3). In the latter event, the transition from anomalous to background values in the upstream direction is referred to as the *cutoff*. Where there is a strong influx of metal at a single point, the anomaly will tend to show a progressive increase in values to a well-developed peak and a sharp cutoff. More commonly, the metal enters at a number of points along a section of the stream course, in which case the anomalous pattern tends to be more erratic, and no single, well-defined cutoff point should be expected (Figures 12-2, 12-15, and 12-16).

12–6. Lake-Water Anomalies

Lake-water anomalies presumably can be derived from anomalous tributary streams, from seepage of ground water around the shores

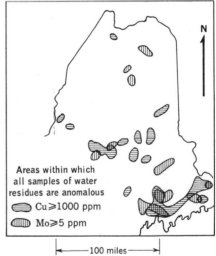

Fig. 12-17. Lake-water anomalies for copper and molybdenum in northern Maine. After Kleinkopf (1960).

Areas within which all samples of water residues are anomalous

⊖ Cu⩾1000 ppm

⬭ Mo⩾5 ppm

|←——— 100 miles ———→|

and from ground water entering by way of springs in the lake bottom. The chemical composition of lake water is complicated by thermal stratification of the water and by the resulting heterogeneities in oxygen supply, organic activity, pH, and Eh. The principal immediate cause of variations in the chemical composition of lake water is the scavenging effect of floating organisms, which are particularly active in the sunny, oxygen-rich environment of the surface layers of most lakes.

Chisholm (1950), working in Ontario, was the first to report that the metal content of lake water could be correlated with mineralization in the surrounding terrain. More recently, a systematic survey of lakes in northern Maine was carried out by Kleinkopf (1960), who analyzed a total of 439 samples for 12 minor elements. The principal geological correlation found here was between the Cu and Mo content of the lake waters and the occurrence of known Cu and Mo sulfides in the southwestern corner of his map area, as shown in Figure 12-17.

12–7. Anomalies Not Related to Mineral Deposits

Variations in the bulk composition of normal unmineralized rocks may cause variations in the composition of the drainage waters similar to those resulting from the weathering of ore deposits. Sulfate-rich waters identical in many respects to water draining actively oxidizing sulfide ores, for example, have been observed draining areas of disseminated pyrite and of gypsum. Although few reliable data are available, it is probable that the minor-element content will be similarly affected and that anomalous patterns can develop in waters in the vicinity of any rock characterized by unusually high background metal values.

Any condition promoting a local increase in the rate of decomposition of normal rocks can lead to the release of trace constituents in higher than normal amounts. Marmo (1953) has described well waters with as much as 500 ppb Cu and 5000 ppb Zn resulting from intense leaching by acid solutions derived from the weathering of a pyritiferous but otherwise unmineralized granite. The metal content of natural waters may be enhanced under arid climatic conditions by evaporation and the resulting concentration of all the dissolved solids. It may also vary in response to variations in the content of soluble organic matter. Finally, anomalous patterns have been found in areas of thermal activity that are apparently the effect of solutions of deep-seated origin.

CHAPTER 13

ANOMALIES IN DRAINAGE SEDIMENTS

Clastic stream sediments are composed predominantly of the residual and hence relatively insoluble products of weathering. Dispersion of the immobile elements that make up a large part of this clastic material is accomplished primarily by the mechanical erosion of metal-rich overburden by surface waters. The relatively mobile elements may occur in stream sediments, in part as original components of strictly clastic material and in part as material precipitated as hydromorphic patterns from the aqueous solutions in contact with the sediments. A particularly strong development of hydromorphic anomalies normally occurs in areas of ground-water seepage at the precipitation barrier defined by the boundary between the underground and the surface environments.

As discussed in Chapters 8 to 10, consideration of hydromorphic anomalies in seepage areas is necessarily an integral part of the study of anomalies developed in residual and transported overburden. These same anomalies, however, are an equally integral component of dispersion patterns in drainage sediments, inasmuch as they serve as a source of a large fraction of the anomalous clastic material that goes to make up stream-sediment anomalies. It is from this point of view that relevant features of seepage anomalies are recapitulated and further described in this chapter.

13–1. Spring and Seepage Areas

Precipitation of insoluble compounds in areas where natural waters pass from one chemical environment into another tends to remove metal from solution, and thus cause an accelerated decay of hydrochemical anomalies. Updrainage from a precipitation barrier of this kind, hydromorphic anomalies show up more clearly in the water. Below the barrier, they are stronger in the clastic material with which the water is in contact. Within the area where precipitation is actively taking place, anomalous values arising from material precipitated in the clastic matrix will be at a maximum.

The immediate source of the anomalous concentrations of metal in the soil and muck of seepage areas is, of course, the ground water that comes to the surface at these points. The ultimate source of the metal, however, must be sought somewhere along the route traversed by the ground water. Where the ground water flows through generally pervious, unconsolidated overburden, the route is determined by the slope of the water table and the topography of the bedrock surface. Where the ground water issues directly from the bedrock, the route is determined by the pattern of fissures, fractures, caverns, and high-pressure artesian channels in the bedrock.

The mode of occurrence of anomalous metal in seepage anomalies is commonly as components of precipitated hydrous oxides and as readily soluble components of the fine-grained fraction of the matrix. A close correlation of extractable metal with the organic content of many seepage soils suggests precipitation of an organic complex of some kind. The high base-exchange capacity of organic matter is undoubtedly a factor in this connection.

The location and form of seepage anomalies is controlled by the local relationships between the relief and water table and by the flow of water within the seepage area. Thus, seepage anomalies commonly occur in hollows and low places in sloping terrain, where the ground water emerges or comes relatively near the surface. Figure 8-6 and 8-7 illustrate some of the characteristic relations of spring and seepage areas to land forms.

Chemical precipitates of strictly inorganic origin are characteristic of many spring areas. Hydrous Fe oxides are commonly precipitated from iron-rich spring water. If these waters were also rich in ore metals, the limonitic material will be correspondingly enriched in these metals. Lead in amounts as high as 1 percent has been found occurring in an unidentified white, chalky mineral coating pebbles near the discharge of an acid spring in the Judith Mountains of central Montana. Accumulations of Pb up to 2 percent and probably more have been observed in organic-rich spring areas in the United Kingdom.

The edges of organic swamps are especially favorable sites for the development of seepage anomalies (Figure 13-1). This distribution results from the fact that the organic matter of swamps tends to precipitate many of the ore metals out of ground-water solutions at the points where they first encounter the swamp environment. As the ground water moves toward the center of the swamp, it becomes progressively impoverished in metal, with the consequence that the anomalies are commonly restricted to the edges of the bogs. Figure 13-2 shows Zn anomalies of this kind resulting from precipitation of metal where Zn-rich ground and surface water enters the immobilizing organic environment. The Zn in the water here has been derived from the leaching of Zn-rich beds in Silurian dolomites. The oval patterns in the middle of the bog are related to springs rising from the Zn-rich bedrock. A deposit of native Cu of somewhat similar origin has been observed in a peat bog where Cu-rich water from neighboring mines enters the reducing environment of the swamp

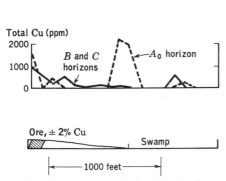

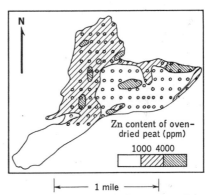

Fig. 13-1. Seepage anomaly developed in humus horizon at edge of swamp, downslope from source of metal, Campbell-Merrill ore zone, Chibougamau district, Quebec. Data on minus-80-mesh fraction. After Ermengen (1957).

Fig. 13-2. Distribution of zinc in peat bog near Manning, New York. From Staker and Cummings (1941).

(Forrester, 1942). Here the precipitation of the Cu appears to be related to the low redox potential of the swamp rather than to chemical reaction with organic matter.

Although seepage anomalies have been used extensively in prospecting, it is only in Rhodesia that they have received intensive study. The following description of the distribution of Cu in the seepage areas, or dambos, of this area is therefore quoted at length from Webb and Tooms (1959).

The sub-tropical climate is markedly seasonal, with an annual rainfall of 40 to 55 inches. For the most part, the vegetation is relatively thin forest savannah, except for small scattered areas of grassland known as "dambos," the majority of which are seasonal swamps.

The country is drained by an open dendritic pattern of well-graded streams and tributaries which commonly rise in irregular pan-shaped "head-water" dambos. During the wet season these dambos are waterlogged and the outflow is considerable. Although some of the swamps may dry out completely at the surface as the ground-water level falls during the dry season, there is often a continual, though diminished, flow of water from

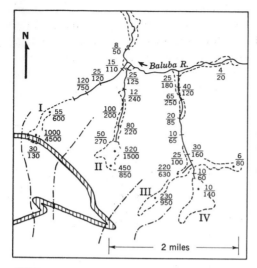

Fig. 13-3. Map showing relation of copper in dambos and outlet-stream sediments to location of ore horizon, Baluba area, Northern Rhodesia. Data on minus-80-mesh fraction. After Webb and Tooms (1959).

Ore-bearing shale horizon

Dambo (seasonal swamp) $\frac{65}{250}$ ppm cold-extractable Cu / ppm total Cu

Approx. boundary between catchment areas

Fig. 13-4. Section showing relation of copper in Dambo I (Fig. 13-3) to underlying ore horizon. Data on minus-80-mesh fraction. After Webb and Tooms (1959).

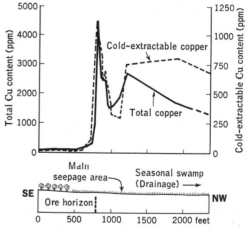

the outlet of the dambo into the conventional stream channel below. The latter are generally moderately incised and may be flanked by narrow dambos more or less continuously along their course.

Over 500 samples of dambo soil, stream sediment and stream banks were collected from the Baluba River and its tributaries in the area shown in Figure [13-3].

In barren areas the metal content of poorly drained organic-rich dambo soil ranges from 30 to 200 ppm Cu and 4 to 20 ppm cxCu. These wide ranges in values are probably due to the sporadic distribution of very minor mineralization such as may occur in most of the rocks of the area. In dambo I, which overlies the Baluba ore-horizon, the metal content of the soil within 18 inches from surface exceeds 4000 ppm Cu and 1000 ppm cxCu. Strongly anomalous values up to about half these figures are recorded in the adjoining dambo II, which at its nearest point is over 2000 feet from the suboutcrop of the deposit. Even dambo III is moderately anomalous, despite the fact that only a small section of the mineralized horizon projects beyond the watershed into this particular catchment area.

The peak values immediately over the ore-horizon in dambo I (Figure [13-4]) are no doubt largely of residual origin, being derived by weathering of the deposit *in situ*, which was almost certainly subject to oxidation before the advent of swamp conditions. The prolongation of peak values down-drainage from the ore suboutcrop is probably due to additional copper precipitated from ground waters, enriched in metal leached from the deposit

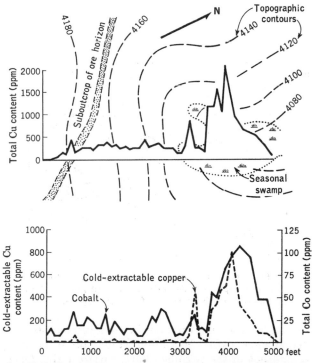

Fig. 13-5. Plan showing copper and cobalt in Dambo II (Fig. 13-3) where soil is derived from ore horizon located outside of swamp area. Data on minus-80-mesh fraction. After Webb and Tooms (1959).

rising in the main zone of seepage towards the centre of the dambo. Much less equivocal evidence of metal deposition from ground waters draining mineralized ground is shown in Figure [13-5], where a moderate copper anomaly in freely drained soil extends down-slope from the ore-horizon towards dambo II. On entering the dambo, the total copper content rises

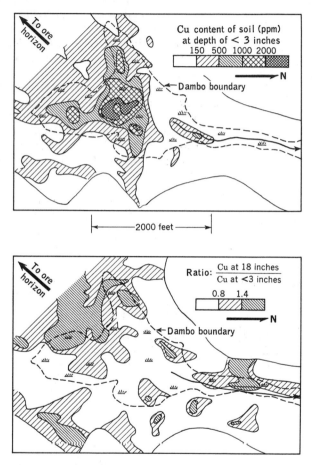

Fig. 13-6. Plans showing relative increase in copper content of dambo soil with depth on side of dambo nearest source. Data on minus-80-mesh fraction. After Govett (1958).

from about 250 ppm to 1500 ppm Cu, and the cold-extractable content from <5 ppm to over 800 ppm cxCu. Maximum values occur in the principal zone of seepage and not in the peripheral areas nearest the deposit. Occasionally small saucer-shaped depressions may occur in the broad head of the dambo, through which the ground waters emerge preferentially as the water-table rises during the wet season. In anomalous dambos, peak copper values are concentrated around these incipient springs—and also around more obvious springs, should any exist.

Although subject to considerable variation, the ratio of cold-extractable to total copper increases from 5 to 10 percent in background samples to 20 to 50 percent (occasionally up to 80 percent) in anomalous dambos. It follows that, although there is a degree of proportionality between the total and cold-extractable metal contents, the latter gives appreciably the greater contrast between anomaly and background. This observation does not apply to nearly the same extent in the areas of freely drained soils surrounding the dambos, where the cxCu : Cu ratio is consistently very much lower in samples collected at a comparable depth.

As a rule, the Cu content of anomalous soils in Rhodesia tends to decrease with depth from surface except in the immediate vicinity of the main points of seepage from suboutcropping mineralization (Table 13-1). Dispersion of Co follows a broadly similar pattern to that of Cu (Jay, 1959). According to Govett (1958), Cu values may also increase with depth away from the main seepage areas in the direction from which the Cu-rich waters are entering the spring area (Figure 13-6). The general validity of this trend has not been established. In some dambos, the seepage anomalies are developed only at the break of slope along the dambo margin (F. H. Cornwall, personal communication).

13-2. Active Stream Sediments

The metal contained in anomalous stream sediments may have reached its present position by one or more of a number of different routes, as suggested diagrammatically in Figure 8-2. Some may have been contributed from the erosion and transport of metal-rich soils, gossans, or other anomalous weathering products that originate very near to the parent ore deposit. Some may come from the erosion of clastic material from hydromorphic anomalies in spring and seepage areas or in the upper reaches of the stream. And finally, some metal may have been locally precipitated from the stream waters directly on to the clastic particles of the sediment.

Mode of Occurrence. Anomalous metal in stream sediments can occur as primary ore minerals, resistant secondary minerals, and precipitates of various kinds. The resistant primary ore minerals commonly have a high specific gravity and hence travel with the heavy-mineral fraction of stream sediments. An outstanding exception is beryl, which has about the same density as quartz and thus tends to travel with the light-mineral components of stream sediments. Heavy clastic fragments of limonitic material or other

TABLE 13-1. Metal Distribution in Typical Soil Profiles from Background and Anomalous Dambos[a]

Soil Horizon	General Description	Average Depth (ft)	Background Profile (1)			Anomalous Profiles					
						(2)			(3)		
			Cu (ppm)	cxCu (ppm)	cxCu:Cu (%)	Cu (ppm)	cxCu (ppm)	cxCu:Cu (%)	Cu (ppm)	cxCu (ppm)	cxCu:Cu (%)
A	Black organic-rich topsoil containing 2–5% organic carbon; pH 4.7–5.4	0–1½	90	4	4.4	550	110	20.0	960	220	23.0
G	Blue-gray, orange-spotted sand/clay subsoil containing 0.07–0.4 percent organic carbon; pH 5.8–6.4	1½–6+	80	4	5.0	750	170	22.6	480	45	9.4

Source: Webb and Tooms (1959).
[a] All determinations carried out on minus-80-mesh fraction. Profiles. (1) draining unmineralized basement granite; (2) in main seepage area of dambo II draining mineralized ground; (3) 5000 feet downdrainage from mineralized ground.

secondary ore minerals also may contribute to the stream-sediment anomaly. The residual weathering products of ore deposits that are normally retained in the clay-sized components of residual soils are liable to be swept away in suspension on being eroded. Nevertheless, most sediments usually contain some of this fine-grained material, though the proportion is generally very much smaller than in the parent material. All these materials, being ultimately of residual origin, will tend to show a low cxMe:Me ratio, generally less than 5 percent.

Hydromorphic sediment anomalies consist of material precipitated from aqueous solutions on the surface of clastic fragments. The anomalous metal is liable to be concentrated in the finer size fractions as adsorbed ions on mineral surfaces and organic matter, in metallo-organic compounds or as components of precipitates that coat the detrital grains. The cxMe:Me ratio in this material of hydromorphic origin tends to be moderately high, generally more than 5 percent.

In any given anomaly, the relative proportions of these different materials will depend on a number of factors, including the nature of the primary bedrock source, the previous dispersion history of the anomalous constituents, the origin of the stream sediment, and the degree of sorting of material within the stream channel. For instance, sulfide-free ores containing minerals like cassiterite, wolframite, columbite, pyrochlore, and beryl commonly yield sediment anomalies comprised predominantly of eroded primary ore minerals. Many of the Cu sediment anomalies in Rhodesia are thought to be due mainly to the erosion of anomalous seepage-area soils. In the Kilembe area of Uganda, the sediment anomalies are apparently largely derived from the erosion of anomalous residual soils. In this case, nearly 50 percent of the anomalous metal is incorporated in precipitates of secondary Fe oxides; about the same amount is "lattice-held" presumably in clay minerals, while only a small fraction, usually less than 5 percent, may be present as adsorbed ions (Table 13-2). In the background streams, however, the overwhelming majority of the metal content is lattice-held. These results are similar to those obtained by White (1957) on Zn-rich residual soil in Tennessee, although here the partition of the metal was found to be much the same in both anomalous and background samples.

In other areas, the major proportion of the anomalous metal has probably been precipitated directly from metal-rich stream waters. Clear-cut examples of this may be seen where contaminated water from mine workings discharges into an otherwise normal drainage channel. Here, stream sediments showing cxMe:Me ratios greater than 50 percent are not uncommon. With time, the readily extractable metal tends to become fixed, with a resulting decline in the cxMe:Me ratio.

TABLE 13-2.   Partition of Cu in Stream Sediments, Kilembe, Uganda[a]

Location of Sample	Exchangeable[b]	Presumed Mode of Occurrence Incorporated in Secondary Fe Oxides[c]	Lattice-Held[d]
		Copper content (ppm)	
Anomalous stream			
Near mineralization	15	120	135
1100 ft downstream	12	50	68
1750 ft downstream	5	15	65
Background stream	1	3	26
	2	3	30
		Presumed Partition (%)	
Anomalous stream			
Near mineralization	6	44	50
1100 ft downstream	9	39	52
1750 ft downstream	6	18	76
Background stream	3	10	87
	6	9	85

Source: J. S. Webb and R. E. Stanton, unpublished data.
[a]Data on minus-80-mesh fraction.
[b]Cu released by cold-citrate extraction at pH 7.3.
[c]Additional Cu released by dithionite extraction by method of White (1957).
[d]Additional Cu released by $KHSO_4$ fusion, after citrate and dithionite extraction.

Contrast.   While anomaly contrast in stream sediments is certainly dependent ultimately on the primary contrast at the bedrock source, it is a more direct function of the contrast at the point where the anomalous material is being fed into the stream channel. Where sediment anomalies are derived by the erosion of anomalous residual or seepage soil, the contrast in the sediment will simply reflect the contrast in the parent soil anomaly. Similarly, where the anomalous

TABLE 13-3.   Content of Zinc and Exchangeable Heavy Metal[a] of Different Size Fractions of Stream Sediments, New Brunswick

Size Fraction	Weight Percent	Total Zn (ppm)	cxHM (ppm)
−8 + 32	65	500	6
−32 + 80	25	500	15
−80 + 115	4	800	25
−115 + 200	3	800	45
−200	3	1000	75

Source: Hawkes and Bloom (1956).
[a]Undifferentiated Zn, Pb, and Cu.

pattern in sediments results from precipitation from metal-rich stream water, the sediment anomaly contrast will depend most directly on the contrast between anomalous and background waters. In either case, the contrast in a stream-sediment anomaly will decrease with increasing distance between the bedrock source and the point of entry into the stream channel, as a result of dilution with barren material.

Contrast also varies with the mode of occurrence of the anomalous metal in the sample, and thus with the methods used to detect it. Depending on the mineralogy of the primary ore, the anomalous metal of stream sediments may be preferentially concentrated in the fine-grained fraction, the coarse-grained light fraction, or the coarse-grained heavy fraction.

Most of the anomalous metal in stream sediments is usually concentrated in the finer size fractions. Thus an inverse relationship between metal content and grain size is observed under a wide

TABLE 13-4. Copper Content and Particle Size in Stream Sediments, Northern Rhodesia

Size Fraction (B.S.S. mesh)	Weight Percent of Minus-2-mm Fraction		Total Cu (ppm)			cxCu (ppm)		
	Sample B	Sample A	B Background Sediment	A Anomalous Sediment	Contrast A/B	B Background Sediment	A Anomalous Sediment	Contrast A/B
−20 + 35	5.4	24.1	80	180	2.3	8	80	10.0
−35 + 80	64.4	43.5	40	160	4.0	2	35	17.5
−80 + 135	21.1	21.4	40	210	5.2	3	70	23.3
−135 + 200	5.4	4.6	80	250	3.1	12	110	9.2
−200	1.7	0.6	110	360	3.3	22	170	7.7
−80			50	220	4.4	4	80	20.0

Source: Webb (1958a).

variety of climates, as illustrated by the data of Tables 13-3 to 13-5. Where comparable figures for anomalous and background samples were reported, it is seen that maximum contrast is brought out by analysis of the intermediate grain sizes, between 80 and 200 mesh, even though these sizes do not show the maximum absolute values. These experiments also show that the contrast may be markedly greater for cxMe than total Me.

TABLE 13-5. Copper Content of Different Size Fractions of Stream Sediments, Ruwenzori Mountains, Uganda

Size-Fraction (B.S.S. mesh)	Weight Percent of Minus-2-mm Fraction		Total Cu (ppm)			cxCu (ppm)		
	Sample B	Sample A	B Background Sediment	A Anomalous Sediment	Contrast A/B	B Background Sediment	A Anomalous Sediment	Contrast A/B
−20 + 35	27.7	23.0	30	100	3.3	0.2	5	25
−35 + 80	26.6	13.8	30	150	5.0	0.4	9	22
−80 + 135	9.8	7.8	30	210	7.0	0.4	16	40
−135 + 200	4.8	5.0	40	260	6.5	0.6	30	50
−200	3.0	2.8	90	500	5.5	2.5	55	22
−80			45	280	6.2	0.8	28	35

Source: Webb (1958a).

Primary resistant minerals often tend to be concentrated in the coarser size fractions of the sediment. An example of this relationship is illustrated in Figure 13-7. Here the higher contrast for Be in the coarser fractions is due to beryl, whereas the values in the finer fractions are probably due largely to the presence of Be in clay

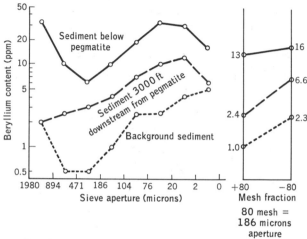

Fig. 13-7. Beryllium content of different size fractions of stream sediments, Ishasha Claims, Uganda. From Debnam and Webb (1960).

minerals. Most of the primary resistant ore minerals are relatively heavy and tend to be enriched in the heavy-mineral fraction of the sediment. Thus in prospecting for Sn and Nb, much higher relative values may be obtained by analyzing only the heavy-mineral fraction in which the detrital cassiterite and columbite have been concentrated. The extent to which contrast will be enhanced in this way will depend on whether the same detrital mineral also occurs as a normal accessory of the host rocks. Thus, the background level for Sn in detrital cassiterite, which often occurs in the bedrock only as an ore mineral, may be relatively low, whereas the background for Cr in chromite, a mineral that occurs as a minor accessory in ultramafic rocks, may be fairly high.

Decay Patterns.   The general form of the decay pattern of sediment anomalies is more or less the same whether the anomaly occurs as residual detrital minerals or as precipitates of hydromorphic origin. The principal factors affecting the persistence of these anomalies are (1) the contrast at source as discussed above, (2) the input of metal along the stream course, and (3) dilution by erosion of the bank material and by confluence with barren tributaries.

A type case is illustrated by the sediment anomaly at Nash Creek, New Brunswick, as shown in Figures 13-8 and 13-9. At site 1, upstream from the mineralized area, the metal content of the sediments

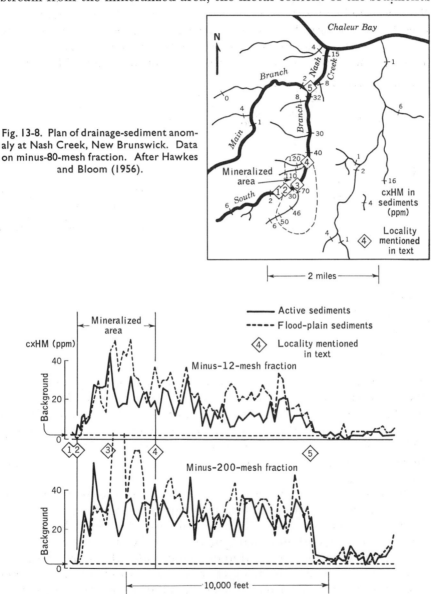

Fig. 13-8. Plan of drainage-sediment anomaly at Nash Creek, New Brunswick. Data on minus-80-mesh fraction. After Hawkes and Bloom (1956).

Fig. 13-9. Longitudinal diagram of drainage-sediment anomaly at Nash Creek, New Brunswick. After Hawkes and Bloom (1956).

is near the background value. The content of metals increases sharply as the stream enters the source area (site 2). As the stream flows through the source area, the metal content fluctuates in response to local increments from lateral drainage, ground water, and springs. Metal-rich tributary streams are known to enter the main channel at sites 3 and 4, where they can be correlated with local increases in the metal content of the flood-plain sediments. Further downstream the decay in metal content is largely a reflection of simple dilution. At

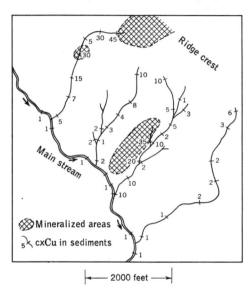

Fig. 13-10. Dispersion of copper in stream sediments draining copper mineralization, Uganda. Data on minus-80-mesh fraction. From Research Report for 1954–57, Royal School of Mines, Imperial College, London.

site 5 the anomalous South Branch of Nash Creek is joined by the Main Branch, with about four times the drainage area. The ratio of the discharge of the two streams almost exactly accounts for the drop in metal content of the sediments. Very commonly, the dilution effect where a small anomalous tributary enters a large stream is enough to obliterate the anomalous pattern completely, as illustrated in Figure 13-10.

The metal content of the banks alongside the active stream channel is a factor of obvious importance in determining the persistence of sediment anomalies. In most cases, this factor is related to the alluvial or colluvial origin of bank material. At Nash Creek the streams are bordered by flood-plain alluvium containing about the same concentration of anomalous metal as the active sediment. In this and similar areas, the persistence of an anomaly is determined in large measure simply by the distance between confluences with barren streams and the size of these streams relative to the anomalous stream. Where the banks are composed of colluvium derived from the adjoining valley slopes, on the other hand, continuous progressive dilution of the sediment anomaly begins as soon as the anomalous stream leaves the source area. Under these circumstances, drainage trains may be drastically curtailed. Figure 13-11 shows an

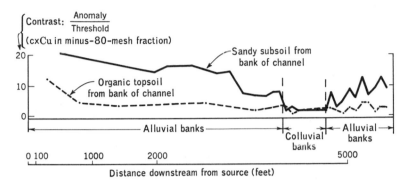

Fig. 13-11. Longitudinal diagram of drainage anomaly in alluvial sediments from bank of active channel, Baluba, Northern Rhodesia. Data on minus-80-mesh fraction. After Govett (1960).

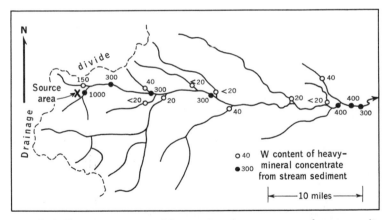

Fig. 13-12. Tungsten content of heavy-mineral concentrates of stream sediments, Clear Creek, Colorado. After Theobald and Thompson (1959).

example of dilution of anomalous patterns by erosion of barren bank material.

According to the mode of occurrence of the metal, the effect of dilution may sometimes be reduced by treatment of the samples to separate the barren diluents from the anomalous components of the sediment. For example, very persistent W anomalies were obtained in streams draining huebnerite deposits by analyzing the heavy-mineral fraction (Figure 13-12). Heavy-mineral anomalies are liable to decay more rapidly in areas where the local barren rocks contain abundant heavy accessory minerals, such as magnetite, ilmenite, garnet, zircon, and monazite. Where this happens, it may sometimes

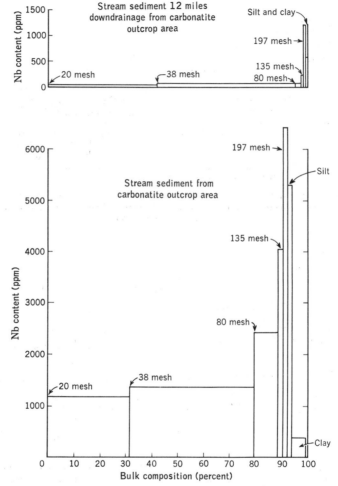

Fig. 13-13. Diagrams showing changes in niobium content of individual size fractions of stream sediments with distance from source, Kaluwe pyrochlore carbonatite, Northern Rhodesia. After Watts (1960).

be possible to improve the persistence of anomalies by electromagnetic or electrostatic separations or by procedures involving selective chemical attack. Some detrital minerals are preferentially enriched in the fine-grained clastic fraction of stream sediments. Figure 13-13 shows the greater contrast and persistence of anomalous Nb, which occurs as pyrochlore, in the fine-size fractions of sediments downstream from a carbonatite deposit in Northern Rhodesia. Analysis of the minus-80-mesh fraction of the local drainage disclosed a sediment anomaly extending for 12 miles to the confluence with a major river (Figure 13-14). The persistence of this anomaly is due in large measure to the fact that the anomalous stream flows for

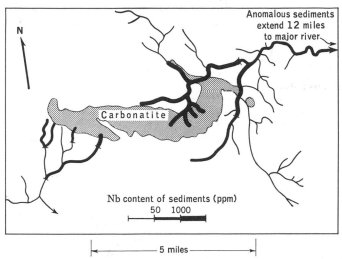

Fig. 13-14. Distribution of niobium in stream sediments draining pyrochlore carbonatite, Kaluwe, Northern Rhodesia. Data on minus-80-mesh fraction. After Watts (1960).

much of its course through flood-plain alluvium. Light detrital minerals, such as beryl, cannot be so readily separated from the quartz which serves as the principal diluent mineral in most sediments. Even so, under appropriate conditions, the anomalous metal content may be detected for appreciable distances downstream (Figure 13-15).

Enhancement of Anomalies at Precipitation Barriers. Most ore metals tend to be soluble in the acid environment of an oxidizing sulfide deposit. As the acidity of the waters draining a deposit is progressively reduced with distance, the metals tend to be precipitated as hydroxides or basic salts. The distribution of metal in the stream sediments thus will naturally be strongly conditioned by the pH of the stream water in contact with it. The effect in the sediments will be precisely the reciprocal of that in the drainage water. An example

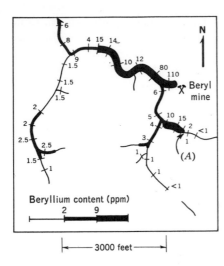

Fig. 13-15. Distribution of beryllium in stream sediment, Ishasha area, southwestern Uganda. (A) indicates position of undisturbed pegmatite discovered by sediment sampling. After Debnam and Webb (1960).

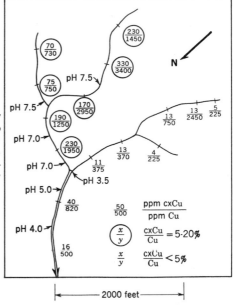

Fig. 13-16. Plan of drainage anomaly showing relation of pH of water to ratio of cold-extractable copper (cxCu) to total copper in stream sediments, Cebu Project, Republic of Philippines. Data courtesy of Newmont Mining Company (Coope and Webb, in preparation).

is provided by the partition of Cu in the stream sediment below the disseminated Cu deposits of Cebu in the Philippines (Coope and Webb, in preparation). Where the pH is below 4.0 as a result of the strong acid coming into the surface drainage from the oxidation of pyrite, the ratio of cxCu to total Cu is extremely low, as shown in

Figure 13-16. As the pH increases past 5.0, this ratio also increases to a value of about 10 percent.

Reference has already been made to the precipitation of metal below the confluence of two streams of contrasting composition (Theobald *et al.*, 1958). Similar effects can be expected at any point along a stream course when abrupt changes in the chemical environment contrive to produce a precipitation barrier, as discussed in Chapter 12. For example, in an area of Northern Rhodesia the sediment of certain streams draining mineralized ground is not anomalous. Where these streams feed into the main river, anomalous cxCu patterns are developed in the swampy ground bordering the river. It is presumed that Cu traveling in the tributary stream water either in suspension or solution is deposited in the sluggish organic-rich environment alongside the main river (D. R. Clews, personal communication).

Homogeneity. The homogeneity of stream-sediment anomalies is governed (1) by the distribution of the points of entry of metal into the stream channel, (2) by the mode of occurrence of the anomalous metal, and (3) by variations in the nature of the sediment along the stream course.

A single point of entry of anomalous metal into a drainage system results in a progressive building up of values to a well-defined and sharp cutoff. More commonly, metal-rich material is fed into the stream at a number of points, with the result that the anomalous pattern in the source area may be fairly complicated, as illustrated in Figures 13-9 and 13-17.

The occurrence of anomalous metal as a principal constituent of one or more specific minerals results in a lack of homogeneity both in samples and in anomalous patterns. Samples tend to be more homogeneous where the metal is pervasively impregnated through the finer fractions, as in hydromorphic patterns.

Variations from one sample to another in the relative proportions of coarse and fine material and of organic matter may reduce the chemical homogeneity. Where the metal is concentrated in the silt or clay fraction, sieving to remove the coarser barren sand will often suppress some of the apparent irregularities in the anomalous pattern (Table 13-6). Uneven patterns due to variations in sediment type are for the most part related to local variations in the velocity and flow of the stream waters. Coarse-grained heavy minerals tend to be sorted and concentrated at depth in stream sediments, commonly directly on the surface of bedrock. Such concentrations may be patchily distributed along the stream bed according to variations in the currents around bends in the stream course or by the "riffle" action of irregularities in the stream-bed topography. When the metal occurs in the fine fractions, the apparent homogeneity may be reduced where increased stream velocity prevents deposition of all

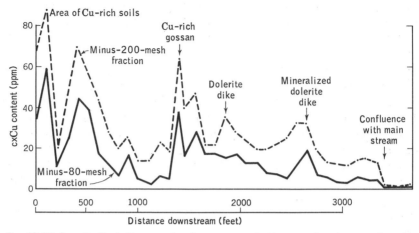

Fig. 13-17. Longitudinal diagram of sediment anomaly showing distribution of readily soluble copper in minus-80- and minus-200-mesh fractions, Uganda. From Webb (1958a).

TABLE 13-6.   Variation in Metal Content with Sediment Type, Nash Creek, New Brunswick

| | cxHM^a (ppm) | |
Sediment Type	Minus-12-Mesh	Minus-200-Mesh
Site A		
Silt	74	60
Sand	20	50
Gravel	30	55
Site B		
Organic ooze	47	50
Silt	37	40
Gravel	13	40

Source: After Hawkes and Bloom (1956).
^{a}Exchangeable heavy metal (undifferentiated Zn, Pb, and Cu).

but the coarser barren material. Stream-bed sediments are sometimes stratified, so that the metal content may vary with depth in the sediment profile. In Rhodesia, for example, it is not uncommon to find alternating layers of coarse sandy material and fine organic sediment. In this case, the metal content of the fine material can be appreciably higher than in the coarse layers. (Govett, 1958).

Time Variations. Our knowledge of the variation of the metal content of sediments with time is limited to only two series of systematic observations. One was a study of the cxCu content of anomalous sediments collected from active stream channels in Northern Rhodesia (Govett, 1958), where seasonal variations up to a factor of about 3 occur near the source and increase to more than 5 as the pattern decays downstream (Figure 13-18). This variation thus reduces the effective length of the dispersion train during the wet season. The reason for this seasonal variation is thought to be the

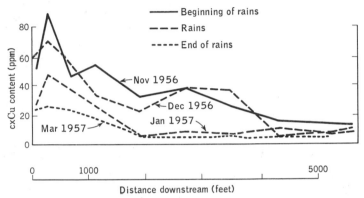

Fig. 13-18. Effect of rain on cold-extractable copper content of sandy stream sediment, Baluba area, Northern Rhodesia. Data on minus-80-mesh fraction. After Govett (1958).

accumulation of fine-grained metal-rich material during the period of minimum, extremely sluggish flow in the dry season.

A similar study of variation in the Cu content of anomalous and background stream sediments was made in the Highland Valley Cu area of British Columbia by Gower and Barr (personal communication). Here, determinations of both cxCu and total Cu in a wide variety of sediments throughout a period of four summer months showed no significant variation, in spite of a decline in volume of runoff over the period of the experiment by a factor of more than 20. No information is available, however, concerning the mode of dispersion of the metal or whether the drop in velocity had any marked effect on the mechanical composition of the sediment.

13–3. Flood-Plain Sediments

The pattern of anomalous metals in flood-plain sediments will reflect their distribution in the abandoned channels previously followed by the stream. As a rule, therefore, the part of the flood-plain anomaly that is due to detrital minerals will tend to be most pronounced toward the base of the alluvium. Where the anomalous metal is dispersed in the finer-sized fractions, however, other factors intervene. Flood-plain sediments normally are characterized by a

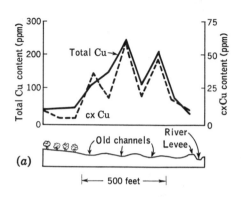

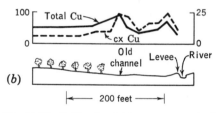

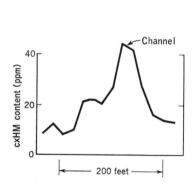

Fig. 13-19. Cold-extractable heavy-metal content of sediments from traverse across flood plain, Nash Creek, New Brunswick. Data on minus-80-mesh fraction. After Hawkes and Bloom (1956).

Fig. 13-20. Cold-extractable copper content of sediments from traverses across flood plain, Baluba River, Northern Rhodesia. Data on minus-80-mesh fraction. After Webb and Tooms (1959).

higher proportion of fine material, and thus may carry a greater content of anomalous metal than active sediments from an equivalent site. This effect may be offset by the fact that flood-plain sediments are more subject to leaching by rain water or by barren ground water entering the channel from the side, whereas the metal content of active sediments may be maintained by chemical exchange with the anomalous water in contact with it.

The lateral distribution of anomalous metals across the flood plain varies somewhat depending on local conditions. For example, in eastern Canada, anomalous patterns of exchangeable heavy metal in the minus-200-mesh fraction of sediment collected immediately on the bank of the active channel will be roughly the same as that of samples of equivalent organic content from the channel itself, although the values normally decay with distance from the active channel (Figures 13-9 and 13-19). Observations in Northern Rhodesia indicate a clear correspondence between the metal content of flood-plain sediments and the location of abandoned channels. In the levee separating the flood plain from the active channel, the values are relatively low compared with the finer-grained, organic-rich flood-plain sediments beyond the levee (Figure·13-20). Experience in

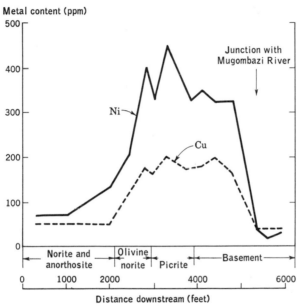

Fig. 13-21. Longitudinal diagram of sediment anomaly resulting from erosion of ultramafic rocks, Kungwe Bay, Tanganyika. Data on minus-80-mesh fraction. After Coope (1958).

Borneo has shown anomalous sediments in the active channel incised into flood-plain sediments, the near-surface horizons of which are completely negative (Fitch and Webb, 1958). Here the flood-plain alluvium was derived from the barren headwater areas at times of excessive floods and now stands well above the normal water table. As a result, Cu-bearing ground waters draining from a deposit on the valley slopes feed into the active channel without passing through the upper parts of the alluvium (P. Walker, personal communication).

The profile distribution of metals in flood-plain sediments is liable to be affected by soil-forming processes. In Rhodesia, for example, the Cu content tends to be higher in the organic-rich topsoil and is not so much influenced by seasonal leaching as the sandy subsoil (Govett, 1958).

13–4. Anomalies Not Related to Mineral Deposits

Insofar as barren rocks characterized by a high background metal content may give rise to distinctive anomalous patterns in either the soil or ground water, so may they affect the metal content of stream sediments that are derived by erosion of the metal-rich soil or that come in contact with the metal-rich water. In prospecting surveys in Uganda, for instance, dolerite dikes containing trace amounts of disseminated sulfides can give rise to Cu anomalies in the sediments similar in many respects to those associated with the Cu mineralization (Figure 13-17). Sediment anomalies in Ni and Cu are commonly developed from the erosion of ultramafic rocks with their characteristically high content of these metals (Figure 13-21). Under appropriate conditions, this relationship between the metal content of stream sediments and the geology of an area promises to be one of the most useful guides in regional geochemical mapping (Webb and Tooms, in preparation).

CHAPTER 14

GEOCHEMICAL DRAINAGE SURVEYS

The two outstanding areas of applicability of geochemical drainage surveys are (1) primary reconnaissance, as a method of locating both individual deposits and entire mineralized districts, and (2) in the appraisal of prospects, geophysical anomalies, and favorable geological features.

Very large areas can be scanned for their mineral potentialities by drainage surveys because of the great distances over which the weathering products of ore bodies are carried by ground and surface waters. At least one representative of the group of mobile (S, Mo, U) and semimobile (Zn, Cu, Ni, Co) elements occurs characteristically either as a principal component or a minor constituent of many types of ore. If to these we add the ore metals that occur in the heavy-mineral fraction of stream sediments (Au, Sn, W), then almost every type of ore should give some kind of a recognizable drainage anomaly.

Appraisal of mining prospects or of anomalous areas found by other prospecting methods is becoming an increasingly important application of drainage studies. Under favorable conditions, field tests of sediments from seepage areas and small drainage channels can provide an on-the-spot indication of the mineral possibilities of the area under examination.

This chapter is devoted primarily to a review of the techniques of planning, conducting, and interpreting the data of geochemical drainage surveys that have been found effective under a wide variety of conditions throughout the world. These discussions represent the conclusions of a considerable number of experimental and operational surveys. Many or most of the conclusions will be pertinent in any new area that is being considered for a geochemical drainage survey. However, it is not safe to assume that the applicability of techniques necessarily will carry over from one area to another. For this reason, an experimental orientation survey in an area known to be mineralized is strongly recommended as a prelude to routine exploration work in an unknown area.

14–1. Orientation Surveys

Orientation preparatory to undertaking a geochemical drainage survey will be concerned mostly with determining the relative merits of sampling water, alluvial sediment, and soil from seepage areas. The known deposits that provide the source of anomalous metal in the orientation experiments need not be of economic grade. In fact, noneconomic deposits are generally preferable because of the usual absence of serious contamination resulting from mining operations.

Water.   Opportunities may exist in known mineralized districts for sampling ground waters in mine workings, bore holes, and wells, and for sampling surface waters in springs, streams, and lakes. Providing contamination can be avoided, none of these opportunities should be neglected. In general terms, samples should be taken at the following locations: (1) updrainage from a known, preferably undisturbed metal source, (2) at or near the deposit, and (3) at every point downdrainage where a tributary stream or a change of environment may modify the composition of waters draining the known deposit. Intermediate samples should be taken where the distance between these critical points exceeds, say, 500 feet. If the deposit has been opened up by underground workings, it is necessary to bear in mind that the resulting accelerated oxidation may lead to enhancement in anomaly contrast relative to what might be expected had the deposit been undisturbed. Background samples should be collected in barren areas to represent all variations in bedrock type and other conditions of environment.

Analysis should include the determination of pH, total salinity, and appropriate major constituents in addition to the assemblage of ore metals. The processing of the sample should be planned with due regard for the fact that the content of ionic constituents may change during storage. Tests suitable for analysis directly in the field are available for some metals; usually, however, it is preferable to concentrate the ionic metal at the sample site by solvent extraction, coprecipitation, or treatment with ion-exchange resins, followed later by comprehensive analysis in the laboratory. The water, after the deionizing treatment, should be retained for determination of the nonionic fraction. Total analysis of an acidified sample of the untreated water can be used as a check. All determinations should be carried out with maximum precision and sensitivity. This is particularly important in comparing ratios of the different constituents at the extremely low concentration levels commonly encountered in natural waters. In view of the concentration level and the number of different constituents that may need to be determined, water samples for an orientation survey will usually need to be quite large, say 1 to 5 liters. Where filtration is necessary, the fine suspended matter may be removed by using micropore filters and a simple hand-operated vacuum pump.

The downstream decay pattern of metals may be the effect of either dilution or precipitation. As a first approximation, the dilution effect may be estimated by analyzing and determining the discharge rate of all sources of water from unmineralized areas entering the anomalous drainage pattern. For a more nearly complete study it is necessary to take into account ground-water seepage via the stream bed by carrying out similar determinations at intervals along the main stream. The possibility of precipitation may be investigated by sampling stream sediment, swamp soil, or other solid material in contact with the waters. Particular attention should be given to possible relationships between the metal content of the water and the presence of organic matter, ferruginous scums, and other precipitates that may have scavenged ionic metals from the water.

The effect of seasonal variations commonly related to rainfall or melting ice and snow should be investigated by periodic resampling of critical sites at different seasons of the year. Particularly in lakes, variations in metal content and anomaly contrast due to seasonal changes in organic activity and thermal turnover should be watched for. Analysis of repeated samples taken at the same sites may provide a correction factor to apply to operational data collected during different weather conditions.

Drainage Sediment. In orientation studies of metal in drainage sediments, experimental samples should be collected from both the flood plain and the active channel at intervals no more than 200 feet for the first 1000 feet or so downstream from sources of anomalous metal. The interval may be progressively expanded with increasing distance from the metal source. In this phase of the program, samples should be taken much closer together than would be necessary for routine exploration; on the basis of these results, the optimum sample spacing may then be selected (Figure 14-1). Sediment from all tributary streams and seepage areas must be sampled. At each location, the various types of sediment represented, e.g., sand, silt, clay, and ooze, should be sampled separately. Sediment samples from the active stream channel should be collected well away from the banks to avoid dilution from collapsed bank colluvium of local origin. At each sediment sampling point, bank samples should be taken on either side of the stream and a record kept of the alluvial or colluvial origin of the bank material at that point. The metal content of flood-plain soils should be investigated by transverse soil-sample traverses.

The variation of metal content with depth in all kinds of sediments, whether from seepages, active channels, or flood plains, should be checked by collecting samples from a number of experimental vertical profiles.

When dealing with metals that may occur in readily extractable form, both cxMe and the total metal content should be determined

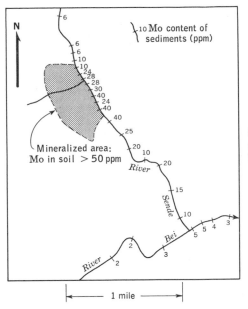

Fig. 14-1. Reconnaissance stream sediment survey of River Sende, Sierra Leone. Data on minus-80-mesh fraction. After Mather (1959).

and the ratio computed for purpose of interpretation. The optimum sieve size should be determined by analyzing different size fractions of representative material from both anomalous and background areas and observing which fraction gives the strongest contrast of anomaly over background, as well as the most homogeneous and the most persistent pattern. Mineralogical and chemical examinations should also be carried out on the heavy minerals, particularly when dealing with metals such as Sn and W.

Contamination. Surface drainage samples, particularly water, are far more susceptible to contamination than soil samples, and careful attention must be given to this problem during the orientation survey.

Contamination may come from trash, metal-rich drainage from factories and mechanized farms, metalliferous insecticides and algicides, roads and railway beds graded with mine waste, and condensates from smog and industrial fumes. The most common industrial and domestic contaminants are Zn and Cu. In wells where pumping machinery has been installed, it is virtually impossible to obtain water samples that are not severely contaminated with these metals. Spring water is almost always free of contamination; the only exceptions reported are very rare cases of springs that drain old mine workings.

Mining and smelting activity constitutes one of the most serious sources of contamination of surface water. Extremely high metal concentrations normally occur in water draining old workings and ore piles where the primary sulfide minerals have been artificially exposed to the air and the oxidation process thereby greatly accelerated. It has been estimated that the metal content of such waters may be 10 or even 100 times higher than if the deposits had not been opened up.

Contaminated stream water often contaminates the sediments with which it is in contact. Except where the metal content of the water is extremely high, such as in areas of past mining activity, the contamination passed on to the sediment is often not nearly as severe as in the water. Sediment surveys have been conducted in well-populated areas where satisfactory water sampling would have been impossible because of contamination.

14–2. Choice of Material to Be Sampled

The choice of material to be sampled, whether water, seepage soils, fine-grained sediments, or heavy-mineral concentrates from the sediments, must naturally be made on the basis of which medium gives the strongest and most reliable pattern that at the same time can be readily detected by the techniques at hand. The principal factors in this connection are (1) the mobility of the constituents of the ore being sought, (2) the influence of local conditions on the dispersion pattern, (3) opportunities for sampling, and (4) availability of a suitable analytical method. While it is often possible to carry out a reliable drainage survey on the basis of a single sample medium, however, for complete and reliable coverage it may be found profitable under some conditions to collect samples of more than one kind of material.

Water. Water sampling is naturally most effective where the elements sought are the relatively mobile ones that would not normally be carried with detrital material. The elements that have been used with greatest success in hydrochemical prospecting are the mobile Mo, U, and SO_4. Alkaline, calcareous, ferruginous, and organic-rich environments tend to reduce the general effectiveness of water sampling. A humid climate coupled with moderate to strong relief and a relatively low pH provide the most favorable conditions.

The principal advantage of water over other kinds of geochemical samples is its physical homogeneity. Difficulties are the time variations and other factors affecting the composition of the water, combined with practical problems in transporting, analyzing, and storing water samples.

Seepage Soils.   The soils of swamps, seepages, and spring areas are commonly enriched in the same elements as the ground water that comes to the surface in these areas. By virtue of the hydromorphic origin of the anomalies, seepage-soil surveys are limited to the semimobile metals. By far the greatest amount of work has been concerned with prospecting for Cu and Zn. Sampling soils from spring and seepage areas is usually preferable to sampling the spring water at the same localities because (1) soils can be sampled when water is difficult to collect or even completely absent in the seepage areas, (2) the composition of the soil in the seepage anomaly is not as strongly affected by changes in weather as the composition of the water, (3) in some areas seepage soils show a stronger contrast of anomaly over background than water samples, (4) in most cases trace analysis of soil presents fewer technical problems than does water, and (5) soil samples may be easily shipped or stored for future reference. Under rare conditions, spring water will be preferable to seepage soils, particularly where the element sought does not tend to precipitate from the water or where the composition of the soil has been shown to be excessively unreliable or lacking in homogeneity.

The anomalous patterns in seepage soils will be somewhat different depending on whether they are analyzed for total or for readily extractable metals (cxMe). Experience in the dambo areas of Northern Rhodesia, for example, favors cxCu over total Cu. Here the principal factor in the choice is the substantially greater contrast of anomaly over background for cxCu as compared with total Cu. In other problems, the principal points in favor of cxMe may be greater speed and economy of the determination and the possibility of making the analyses either at the base camp or directly at the sample site. Patterns defined by the distribution of total metal, however, tend to be more homogeneous. They also are not as susceptible to changes with the seasons as the cxMe content. A determination of total metal in addition to cxMe may be desirable as a confirmatory check. Furthermore, the cxMe:Me ratio may be very helpful in determining the origin of an anomalous pattern. With certain exceptions, a high cxMe:Me ratio suggests a hydromorphic anomaly, whereas a low ratio suggests a residual pattern.

Stream Sediments.   The semimobile and immobile elements are the ones best suited for stream-sediment surveying. Under some conditions, however, sediment sampling may also be used for elements that are normally highly mobile, such as Mo. Anomalous stream sediments are not necessarily accompanied by an anomaly in the water with which they are in contact (Figure 14-2). Even where there is a corresponding hydrochemical anomaly, stream sediment sampling may be preferable because of the scarcity of water

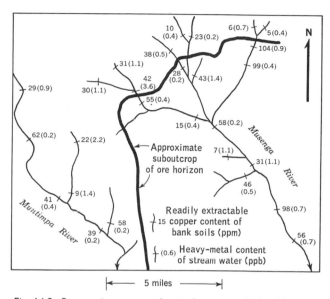

Fig. 14-2. Reconnaissance geochemical survey of the Musenga and Muntimpa drainage systems, Northern Rhodesia. After Govett (1958).

in the drainage channels, excessive seasonal variations in the composition of anomalous water, and the greater ease of collecting, analyzing, shipping, and storing sediment samples. However, where anomalies occur in both sediment and water, both media should be sampled concurrently if maximum information from each sample site is desired, particularly if the partition of the metal between water and sediment is variable. Data on the dispersion of semimobile and immobile elements in the sediment anomalies will also complement the data on the mobile elements from the water anomalies.

In some areas equally strong anomalies occur in both the active sediment and the flanking flood plain. If the banks are made up either wholly or in part of barren colluvium, then the choice is limited to the active sediment. Flood-plain sediments have the advantage of containing a higher proportion of fine material and are usually easier to collect. Generally speaking, however, they are liable to give more erratic results than the active sediment, particularly in the case of semimobile metals. In spite of its shortcomings, flood-plain sampling has been used extensively in Canada with satisfactory results. In seasonal swamps there may not always be a well-defined surface channel, and in this case samples of the soil should be collected along the preferred drainage lines within the swamp.

Immobile elements usually must be determined by total-metal analysis. For mobile and semimobile elements, the choice between total and cold extractable metal as the most useful ore guide is much the same for stream sediments as for seepage soils. With sediments, a high cxMe:Me ratio suggests chemical precipitation either directly in the stream bed or in a seepage area undergoing erosion further upstream; a low cxMe:Me ratio indicates that the anomaly may be derived by the mechanical erosion and dispersion of metal-rich residual soil.

Heavy Minerals in Stream Sediments.   Heavy-mineral surveys are mostly restricted to the immobile elements, Au, Sn, W, Hg, and Ta-Nb, although in exceptional circumstances some of the more mobile ore elements may also occur in the heavy fraction.

Heavy-mineral patterns often have the advantage of giving a longer dispersion train than that obtained by chemical analysis of sediment samples. Sometimes, however, the heavy-mineral grains are too small to be readily separated from the light fraction.

The choice between chemical analysis and mineralogical examination of heavy-mineral concentrates depends on the ability to identify the diagnostic constituent and on the technical facilities available. In some ways, mineral studies are simpler, but they are subject to errors both in identifying the mineral species and in estimating the relative abundance of the different minerals. Chemical analysis, particularly of fine-grained fractions that cannot be easily examined optically, tends to reduce such errors. Chemical analysis also may bring out patterns that cannot be appraised by optical examination, such as the Cu content of magnetite from magnetite-bearing Cu deposits.

14-3. Sample Layout

Ground-Water Patterns.   The layout of sampling points in ground-water surveys will depend not only on the dimensions of the patterns that are being sought but also on the distribution of available wells, springs, and seepage areas. Where these are densely distributed, surveys can be run by systematic cross-country traversing to collect samples at all wells, springs, and seepage areas that can be seen from the traverse lines. In other areas, it may be preferable to traverse along certain land forms that are especially likely to represent a line of effluence of ground water, as for example at the break in slope where the terrain begins to flatten and along the edges of swamps, lakes, and the flood plains of streams.

Figure 14-3 shows the results of a survey based in part on the sampling of a series of springs located along one of these topographic lines. In this survey, mineralized areas were found to lie within a threshold contour of 10 ppb over a background of 0.1 ppb uranium. Anomalous values up to 250 ppb led to the discovery of ore deposits in areas not otherwise thought to be favorable.

Springs may also be sought along geological features such as faults and the contacts between permeable and impermeable rocks. The sample interval along traverses of this kind must necessarily depend on the natural spacing of the spring and seepage areas, as well as on the probable size, shape, and geological control of the ore that is being sought.

Where the seepage areas are very large, as for example the seasonal swamps of Northern Rhodesia, it is necessary to sample the internal drainage at the main points of entry of ground water and along the lines of preferential flow within the seepage area as a whole. Where the internal drainage is not evident, it may be necessary to resort to systematic soil sampling within or around the periphery of the seepage area, depending on the most likely points of inflow.

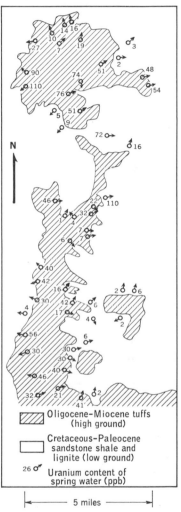

Fig. 14-3. Distribution of uranium in spring water, Slim Buttes, South Dakota. After Denson (1956).

Drainage-Channel Patterns. The sample layout for drainage surveys depends on (1) the length of the decay pattern that can be anticipated downstream from a significant deposit and (2) the size of the largest stream, conveniently expressed as the maximum area of the catchment basin in which such an anomaly may be detectable. The decay distance, determined in the orientation experiments, is commonly found to lie between 1000 feet and 2 miles and the limiting catchment area between 5 and 20 square miles. In streams up to this size, the sample interval should be set close enough to ensure that at least two adjoining samples will fall within every significant anomaly. For complete coverage of areas flanking rivers that exceed the

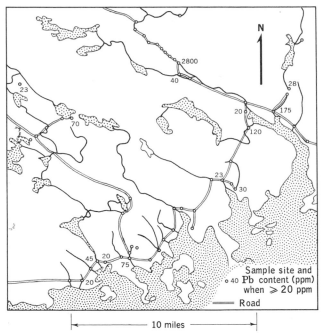

Fig. 14-4. Example of stream sediment survey based on road traverses, Nova Scotia. Data on minus-80-mesh fraction. From Holman (1959).

limiting catchment area, it will be necessary to sample all the tributary streams, springs, and seepages no matter how local and insignificant they may appear to be.

Complete coverage is not always possible or even desirable in areas where access is difficult or where the geology is not particularly favorable. Inasmuch as most of the cost of a geochemical drainage survey is the cost of personnel time and expenses traveling to the sample site, optimizing the ratio of cost to completeness of coverage may justify confining traverses to roads, trails, navigable streams, or coastlines (Figure 14-4).

14-4. Collection and Processing of Samples

Water. Polyethylene bottles are usually employed for water samples; lightweight collapsible polyethylene containers, which are now available, save considerably on volume. Collecting a sample of well water or deep lake water may require special equipment. A device easily improvised is an empty polyethylene bottle fitted with a friction stopper. The bottle is weighted and lowered to the desired depth on a length of line, and the sample collected by pulling out the stopper which is attached to a separate line.

The use of polyethylene containers eliminates the risk of contamination by metals dissolved from the walls of the container—a hazard that is always present in the case of soft-glass vessels. Containers should always be rinsed out at the sample site with the water to be collected. A loss of trace metals from the sample solution by precipitation or adsorption on the walls of the container presents a somewhat more serious problem. Trace elements can be coprecipitated with products of hydrolysis, principally hydrous Fe oxides, which coagulate and collect on the walls of the vessel. Air introduced into water samples at the time of collection may stimulate the growth of algae or bacteria, which absorb many trace elements from the water. The CO_2 produced by bacterial action may then be responsible for other complicating reactions. Acidification of the sample with metal-free acid to about pH 2.0 at the sample site will prevent the precipitation of hydrous Fe oxides and at the same time inhibit the growth of microorganisms. The addition of a few milliliters of chloroform to a water sample at the time of collection will also inhibit organic activity.

Any kind of container, after it has held an anomalous sample, must be thoroughly cleansed of possible precipitates before it is refilled. Strong, metal-free HCl, which will solubilize precipitated hydrous Fe oxide, is a good cleaning agent. Polyethylene bottles that have been used for storing metal-rich chemical reagents should never be used because, despite the most vigorous cleaning, potential contaminants may remain in the walls of the vessel.

Chemical analysis of fresh water for traces of metal may be carried out according to a variety of systems. Each of the systems has its respective advantages and disadvantages which must be considered in planning a program.

Analysis directly at the collection site is possible with a number of analytical methods (Chapter 3). These include tests for SO_4, Mo, Zn, and heavy metals. When they are present in concentrations exceeding 10 ppb, Cu and Pb in water may also be determined in the field;

values as high as this, however, are rarely found in background areas. Field determination of total salinity and pH may be made with portable electrometric instruments. The advantage of analysis at the sample site is that the sample does not have a chance to change composition either by contamination or by precipitation of trace metals in the course of the time lapse between collection and analysis. Furthermore, the cost and inconvenience of shipping bulky water samples is eliminated. The pH and CO_2 content of water samples are extremely unstable, so that immediate determination of these values at the sample site is mandatory. The disadvantages of sample-site analysis are that in general these methods are less precise; they measure only the ionic content of the water, and they can be time-consuming.

Pre-enrichment of the material dissolved in the water has been widely practiced in recent years. Pre-enrichment may be carried out at the sample site by adsorption on ion-exchange resins, by solvent extraction, or by filtering after coprecipitation with some suitable collector such as cadmium sulfide or aluminum phosphate. These methods of pre-enrichment recover only the ionic constituents of the water sample. Where a determination of the total content of a trace element in both dissolved and suspended forms is desired, evaporation is necessary. This operation can be carried out conveniently only in the laboratory or base camp. The concentrates prepared in the field or in base camp are then shipped to a central laboratory for analysis. As with chemical analysis at the sample site, the advantages of pre-enrichment are that the sample does not have a chance to change composition on shipment and that the cost of shipment of the sample to the laboratory is greatly reduced. An added advantage is the considerably greater precision and economy in having the analysis made under controlled conditions in a well-organized laboratory. The disadvantages are the technical difficulties and the time involved in carrying out the pre-enrichment procedures in the field.

Swamp Soil and Sediment. As the metal content of soil and stream sediment may vary considerably with grain size and the amount of organic matter present, it is very desirable that material of about the same fineness and content of organic matter be collected. Even so, the composition of the samples may be so erratic that a single sample at each site will not be properly representative, particularly for cxMe. Depending on the results of the orientation study, it may be necessary to collect two, three, or even four samples at each site. Where samples are collected along a longitudinal stream traverse rather than at individual isolated sites, the same effect may be achieved by taking single samples at a reduced sampling interval. Samples so collected may be analyzed either individually or later mixed and analyzed as composite samples.

At all sample points, care must be taken to avoid sampling collapsed bank material of local origin, particularly when the banks are composed of colluvium derived from the adjoining slopes.

No specialized tools are necessary for collecting samples of seepage soils or stream sediments. Small samples of from 10 to 50 grams are normally adequate, inasmuch as most of the chemical procedures do not require more than a fraction of a gram. For relatively coarse-grained samples from fast flowing streams, however, it may be necessary to collect 100 to 200 grams or more in order to obtain sufficient fine material for analysis. Sediment samples, even when very wet, can conveniently be collected in envelopes made of heavy kraft paper, waterproof glue, and a metal fold-down tab. A light, rigid carrying box will prevent chafing of the paper in transit. Plastic, aluminum, or steel containers have been used on some surveys with varying degrees of success.

Most of the problems in processing sediment samples are the same as already discussed in connection with soil samples, and need not be repeated in detail. Sieving to about minus-80-mesh and retaining only the fines for analysis is desirable for the purpose of homogenizing the samples and enhancing the anomalous values. Sieves should always be made of noncontaminating material. If the samples as collected are dry enough, they may be dry sieved at the sample site. If water is available, moist samples may be wet sieved on the spot; a simple design for a wet sieve is illustrated in Figure 14-5. Wet sieving in general is not recommended, because of the loss of the ultrafine fraction which may contain a high proportion of the anomalous metal. Except for wet sieving, moist samples cannot be sieved directly, but must be dried in some way. In sunny weather, samples in paper envelopes will dry through the porous paper in a few days; otherwise a low-temperature oven may be used to accelerate the drying process.

Heavy Minerals. Heavy detrital minerals characteristically occur in greatest abundance near the base of a sequence of alluvial sediments, usually just above the surface of bedrock. Collecting samples from the surface of bedrock involves either digging pits or sinking holes with augers or post-hole diggers. The heavy-mineral fraction then may be either separated in the field by panning, or shipped to the laboratory for whatever system of mineral separation or chemical

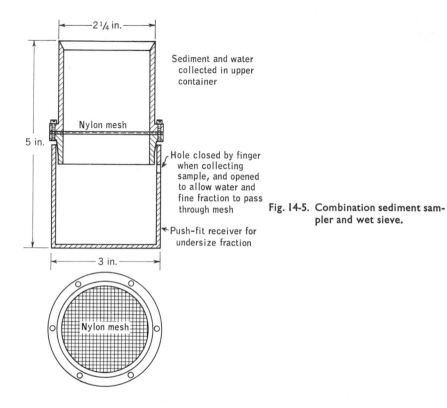

Sediment and water collected in upper container

Nylon mesh

Hole closed by finger when collecting sample, and opened to allow water and fine fraction to pass through mesh

Push–fit receiver for undersize fraction

Nylon mesh

Fig. 14-5. Combination sediment sampler and wet sieve.

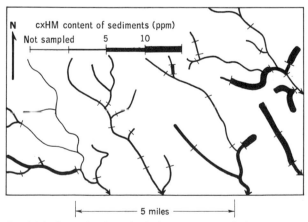

N

cxHM content of sediments (ppm)

Not sampled   5   10

5 miles

Fig. 14-6. A graphical method of representing drainage anomalies. Data on minus-80-mesh fraction of sediment samples. After Hawkes et al. (1956).

analysis is called for. Techniques of collecting and panning heavy-mineral concentrates from sediments are discussed by Raeburn and Milner (1927), Mertie (1954), Theobald (1957), and Griffith (1960).

14–5. Preparation of Maps

Most of the comments made in Chapter 11 regarding the preparation of geochemical soil maps also apply to geochemical drainage maps. The principal difference is the considerably greater complexity of much of the information that must be presented on a drainage map.

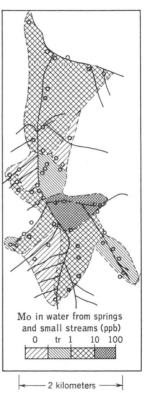

On a small-scale reconnaissance map, the symbols must be highly simplified if all the necessary information is to be plotted on a single map. Where more than one chemical determination is made on each sample, a system of transparent overlays is usually desirable. Normally a scale such that sample points are not separated by less than one-quarter inch results in an attractive and legible map.

With particular reference to water data, the results may be plotted in terms of the metal content of the water or of the total dissolved salts (total salinity). At other times it may be preferable to plot the ratio of the metal to some major constituent, such as $U:HCO_3^-$, and $SO_4^{--}:Cl^-$. The choice is made according to which method gives the most significant and reliable guide to ore.

A wide variety of different symbols has been used in representing the data of water and sediment analysis. The direction of flow of the water, if it is known, should be indicated by arrows, unless it is already apparent from the drainage pattern. Appropriate symbols should be used to distinguish the data of different kinds of samples, such as active or flood-plain sediments, swamps and seepage soils, water, plants, and residual soils, where they are all shown on the same map. Separate symbols may also be used to distinguish anomalous from background values. Examples of different methods of plotting geochemical drainage data are shown in Figures 14-1 to 14-4 and 14-6 to 14-8.

Mo in water from springs and small streams (ppb)

0   tr 1   10   100

|← 2 kilometers →|

Fig. 14-7. A graphical method of representing drainage anomalies. After Dolukhanova (1957).

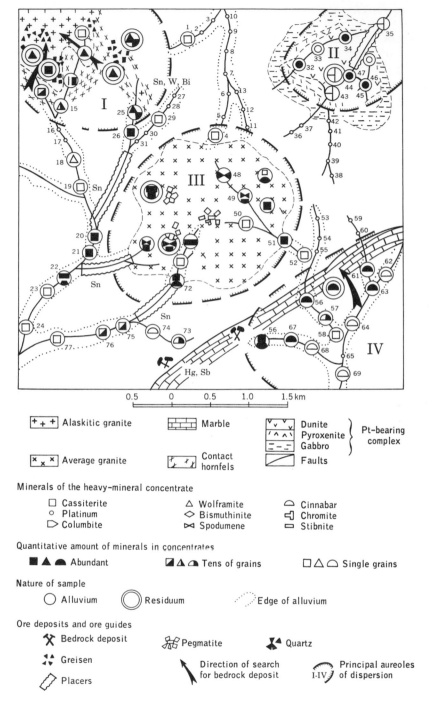

Fig. 14-8. System of symbols suggested by Zhilinsky (1956) for representing data of heavy-mineral surveys.

0.5   0   0.5   1.0   1.5 km

+̲+̲+̲ Alaskitic granite	
x̲x̲x̲ Average granite	
▦▦ Marble	
⸝⸝⸝ Contact hornfels	
ᵛᵛᵛ Dunite / ^^^ Pyroxenite / ‒‒‒ Gabbro	⟩ Pt-bearing complex
⟋ Faults	

Minerals of the heavy-mineral concentrate

☐ Cassiterite   △ Wolframite   ⌓ Cinnabar
○ Platinum   ◇ Bismuthinite   ⊐ Chromite
▷ Columbite   ⋈ Spodumene   ⊐ Stibnite

Quantitative amount of minerals in concentrates

■▲⬤ Abundant   ◪◭◖ Tens of grains   ☐△⌓ Single grains

Nature of sample

◯ Alluvium   ◎ Residuum   ⸴⸴ Edge of alluvium

Ore deposits and ore guides

⚒ Bedrock deposit   ⚒⚒ Pegmatite   ⚒ Quartz
⚒ Greisen   ↑ Direction of search for bedrock deposit   ⌒ Principal aureoles I-IV of dispersion
◇ Placers

14–6. Interpretation of Data

The general approach to interpretation is common to all kinds of geochemical anomalies and has already been discussed in Chapter 2. With drainage data, however, it is especially important to determine the range of background fluctuations related not only to bedrock geology and sample type but also to changes in environmental factors, such as pH and bulk composition of the water.

Distinguishing between significant and nonsignificant anomalies is always one of the more difficult tasks in interpretation. Before any time is spent in follow-up work, every anomaly should be carefully examined to see whether it may be considered as a possible bona fide indicator of ore or dismissed as the result either of natural accumulations of metal unrelated to ore, of artificial sources of contamination, or of errors in technique. First, it is advisable to reanalyze all the critical samples and to check the field description against the sample material as a guard against simple mistakes. At the same time, it may be possible to recognize assemblages of associated elements that may help to indicate the nature of the parent source. Available maps and air photos should be examined with a view to the possibility both of contamination and of correlation of the anomaly with recorded topographic and geologic features. In many cases, it may be necessary to revisit the sample site before it is possible to decide whether an anomaly is significant or not.

Appraisal of significant anomalies, once they have been identified, calls for a critical review of the intensity and form of the anomaly taken in the context of the general favorability of the geological environment, together with consideration of all those environmental factors that may enhance or suppress anomalous patterns. A simple study of the geochemical data alone is never enough to warrant any kind of a prediction as to the grade and tonnage of the bedrock metalliferous deposit responsible for a drainage anomaly. The intensity of a drainage anomaly is a function only of the total amount of metal that has been leached from the catchment area, minus what has already been precipitated before the water enters the surface drainage.

A strong anomaly, therefore, may mean (1) a very large area of low-grade mineralization, (2) swarms of very small deposits of high-grade metalliferous material, (3) small deposits of weakly mineralized but highly fractured rock that is unusually accessible to the leaching action of circulating ground water, or (4) one or more large deposits of ore grade. Furthermore, the absence of a strong anomaly does not necessarily mean the absence of an ore body. It may be only the effect of a low rate of chemical attack on the bedrock. Just as commonly, the absence of an anomaly may be caused by either dilution or precipitation of the metal somewhere along the drainage system between the source and the sample site.

14-7. Follow-Up Techniques

The technique of following up anomalies disclosed during a geochemical drainage reconnaissance will of course depend very much on local conditions. Opportunities for detailed sampling aimed at further delimiting ground-water patterns are often lacking, and the follow-up then passes directly to geological examinations, coupled with geophysical investigations and detailed geochemical soil surveys when conditions are appropriate. However, careful study of the ground-water pattern in relation to the local topography and other factors that may be influencing the subsurface drainage may help to define the area of maximum interest wherein to concentrate the detailed follow-up work.

With regard to anomalies detected in the surface drainage, the following outline presents many of the steps that have come into common use under a variety of different operating conditions.

After confirming the original reconnaissance indication, traverse upstream from the discovery site to find the cutoff. This may be done either by field analysis with a portable test kit or by sampling at close intervals and submitting the samples for laboratory analysis. The choice between these two methods will depend on local conditions of accessibility, personnel, analytical methods used, etc. Figure 12-2, for example, shows the data of a follow-up survey based on field analysis of water samples.

When using the field-test kit, it is often found that values are erratic owing to variable proportions of coarse and fine material in the unsieved samples. In very gravelly streams, it may even be difficult to confirm laboratory analyses which are carried out on the fine fraction. In the field, reproducible determinations giving a better-defined picture of the anomaly may often be obtained by sieving the sample on the spot.

At the cutoff, check carefully for possible contamination, natural enrichment, and any visible evidence of mineralization. Determine the principal points at which anomalous metal is entering the drainage system. According to the nature of the problem, this may best be done by collecting samples at close intervals along both banks of the active channel, along the zones of seepage and spring areas on opposite edges of the flood plain, or along the base-of-slope colluvium.

The most highly anomalous samples will normally indicate the side of the valley from which most of the metal is coming. Where spring or seepage anomalies are caused by near-surface water, the source will normally occur directly up the slope of the valley side. Where the anomaly is the result of water flowing from bedrock channels, the source will lie somewhere along the upslope projection of the water-bearing fracture or other aquifer. Such a source may be deeply buried and not come to the surface of bedrock.

As a result of these studies, it is often possible to delimit, quickly and more or less precisely, the area of interest wherein to concentrate detailed exploration by more intensive geological, geophysical, and geochemical surveys.

CHAPTER 15

VEGETATION

Chemical analysis of systematically sampled trees and shrubs for traces of ore metals was one of the first geochemical methods to be investigated. In the early 1930s, V. M. Goldschmidt, pioneer in geochemistry, made the observation that the humus of forest soils was very much enriched in most of the minor elements. From this he deduced that the same trace elements must be correspondingly enriched in the plants from which the humus was derived. He made the first suggestion that analysis of plant material might be an effective method of prospecting. In later years this method of exploration came to be known as the *biogeochemical* method, following the terminology of the Russian geochemist Vernadsky.

Visual observation of plants, when used as a guide to buried ore, is known as *geobotanical* prospecting. Whereas biogeochemical methods require chemical analysis of plant organs, the geobotanical methods depend on direct observations of plant morphology and the distribution of plant species. Where applicable, therefore, geobotanical methods have very great advantages over other geochemical methods of prospecting in that the results of the survey are immediately available without further treatment of the samples.

15–1. Uptake of Mineral Matter by Plants

The principles underlying both biogeochemical and geobotanical studies of vegetation as methods of locating buried ore deposits are basically simple. The root systems of trees act as powerful sampling mechanisms, collecting aqueous solutions from a large volume of moist ground below the surface. These solutions then serve as a source of inorganic salts that may be deposited in the upper parts of the plant, or that may stimulate, inhibit, or otherwise modify the growth habits of the plant.

In detail, however, the internal circulatory systems of terrestrial plants are by no means simple. A vast and complex set of equilibrium relationships is active from the time the soil solution comes within the influence of the root tip until the water is discharged into the atmosphere. Whether or not a metal-rich nutrient solution will result in an easily measured variation in the composition of the plant, or in a diagnostic variation in plant morphology or ecology, depends on the balance of these many relationships.

In reviewing the factors causing plant anomalies, it is pertinent to consider (1) the availability of elements in the soil, (2) factors in plant nutrition, and (3) the chemical and biological effects of the nutritional process that can be used as ore guides.

Availability of Elements in Soil. Agricultural scientists refer to *available* nutrients. These consist of ions that are either dissolved in the soil moisture or that are adsorbed on the clay minerals of the soil in readily exchangeable form. These nutrients constitute the mineral content of the soil that is immediately available for uptake by the plant. They make up only a small proportion of the total mass of the soil, the remainder of which consists of ions tightly bonded within the lattice structures of the stable soil minerals.

Availability of an element to plants is measured either by determining the amount of the element that can be removed from a soil by leaching with chemical reagents, or by growing a plant in the soil and determining the amount of the element taken up by the plant.

Availability is a concept closely related to mobility in the surface environment. It can be regarded as the mobility with respect to plant activity. The ratio of the available to the total content of an element in the soil is a function principally of the soil pH, redox potential, exchange capacity, and presence of complexing agents. Artificial modification of one or more of these factors can, under many conditions, change the nutritive value of a soil.

Plant Nutrition. The root tips of a growing plant can absorb the salts dissolved in the soil moisture. Under certain conditions, they also have the capacity to mobilize and absorb mineral matter that is more or less firmly bonded in the clastic soil particles. According to currently held concepts, the surface of the root tip of a plant and the immediately surrounding solutions are characterized by a relatively high acidity. This effect is so local that it is not generally apparent from a measurement of the pH of the soil as a whole. The cause of the acid conditions here is probably the hydrolysis of CO_2, which escapes through the roots in substantial quantities. The effect of the abundance of hydrogen ions is to set up active cation-exchange reactions between the clay minerals of the soil and the surface of the roots, which have been shown to have a high exchange capacity (Figure 15-1). On the surface of clay minerals, hydrogen ions exchange for metal ions, which are then free to diffuse through the soil moisture to

TABLE 15-1. Uranium and Vanadium Content of Roots Compared to Tops of Vegetation in the Thompson District, Utah

Plant Species	Uranium (ppm U) in Ash			Vanadium (ppm V_2O_5) in Ash		
	Tops	Roots	Ratio, Roots:Tops	Tops	Roots	Ratio, Roots:Tops
Deep roots collected from mine workings						
Juniperus monosperma	7.8	1600.0	200.0	20	3000	150.0
Juniperus monosperma	2.0	140.0	70.0	50	4000	80.0
Quercus gambeli	10.0	190.0	19.0	90	1700	19.0
Near-surface roots						
Juniperus monosperma (average of 40 samples)	1.2	7.0	5.6	54	110	2.0
Atriplex confertifolia	3.0	5.0	1.6	10	90	9.0
Oryzopsis hymenoides	30.0	40.0	1.3	70	1600	23.0
Artemisia spinescens	3.0	5.0	1.6	70	100	1.4
Artemisia bigelovi	2.0	2.0	1.0	50	5	0.1
Astragalus preussi	70.0	70.0	1.0	3000	2600	0.8
Aplopappus armerioides	40.0	20.0	0.5	260	180	0.7

Source: Cannon (1960a).

the roots. When the metal ions reach the outer surface of the root tip, they exchange for hydrogen ions, which are released to repeat the process (Jenny and Overstreet, 1939; Keller and Frederickson, 1952; Mehlich and Drake, 1955).

Empirical observations have shown that the local but extremely corrosive environment near the root tips of plants can extract mineral matter well in excess of what is present in readily exchangeable form.

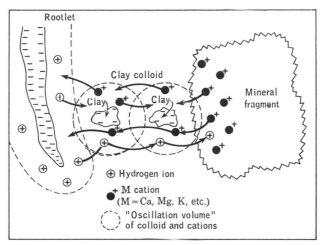

Fig. 15-1. Diagram illustrating cation exchange reactions near root tips. After Keller and Frederickson (1952).

Even the primary silicate minerals can be broken down and their components made available to the plant (Lovering, 1959). A spectacular example of the dissolving effect of roots is the *converter* plant, which takes up Se from stable and relatively insoluble Se compounds in the soil. With the death and decay of the plant, the Se returns to the soil in soluble form and is then available for uptake by other plants that lack the power to solubilize Se (Beath *et al.*, 1939, p. 266).

Movement of inorganic constituents into the plant is selectively controlled in such a way that some elements are freely admitted while others are impeded to a greater or lesser degree. Pb, for example, is an element that is apparently largely immobilized by precipitation in the root tissues of some plants (Hammett, 1928). Thus, toxic excesses of Pb may not reach the active centers of growth in the upper parts of the plant. If the quantity of Pb in the soil solution is too great, the precipitated Pb salt apparently impedes the flow of solutions, and the plant does not grow normally. U and V, elements which are also toxic, are apparently precipitated in the roots in the same way, as suggested by the data of Table 15-1.

Nutritive elements are commonly accepted freely into the plant's system up to a point where the nutritional requirements are satisfied, after which additional quantities of these elements may be rejected. As a result, the concentration of such elements in a plant may indicate only the nutritional needs and may bear little or no relation to the amount available in the soil.

Although the toxic elements, such as U and Pb, are largely precipitated in the root cells, enough reaches the upper parts of most

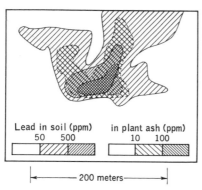

Fig. 15-2. Coincident lead anomalies in plants and soil over an ore deposit in the Rudny Altay region, U. S. S. R. After Nesvetaylova (1955a).

Lead in soil (ppm)   in plant ash (ppm)
   50   500   10   100

|← ——— 200 meters ——— →|

plants to be readily detected. They normally occur in plant ash in lower concentrations than in the supporting soil (Figure 15-2). In spite of this impoverishment, however, the geochemical patterns formed by the toxic elements may be a more faithful reflection of the composition of the soil moisture than the patterns of some of the more readily accepted nutrient elements.

The movement and storage of mineral matter within plants is controlled by many factors. These include free and restrained diffusion, movement of the solvent, electrical and thermal effects, exchange reactions and, perhaps most important, the accumulation of mineral nutrients in metallo-organic molecules (Broyer, 1947). Of the last type of reaction, the entrance of Mg into the chlorophyll molecule is a familiar example. Many other elements play a similar dominant role as components of enzymes and other catalysts that speed the many vital reactions in a growing plant.

Stated in a different way, the movement of inorganic matter throughout the structure of a plant is a response to the plant's nutritional requirements. In the upper part of the plant, the nutritive elements are commonly enriched in the actively growing cells, particularly in the seed structures and growing tips. As the cells mature, the concentration of these elements declines. There is abundant evidence that the distribution of nutrient elements changes with changing requirements and that the circulatory systems of plants maintain a dynamic balance whereby inorganic material can be supplied to fulfill the nutritive needs and also removed when it is no longer needed. The specific nutritive or toxic effect of any one element may depend on the over-all composition of the nutrient solution. The uptake of one element in a plant may thus be suppressed or increased by the presence of other elements in the solution (Evans et al., 1951; Ahmed and Twyman, 1953).

Each species of plant has its own individual nutritive requirements that differ somewhat from those of every other species. Thus different species of plants all supported by identical nutrient solutions will contain widely varying concentrations of many of the minor elements.

For whatever reasons the elements are needed by plants, it has been definitely established that in addition to the common nutritive elements—N, K, P, S, Ca, and Mg—most plants require small quantities of many minor elements, including principally Cu, Zn, Fe, Mo, Mn, and B (Mitchell, 1955). If the soil solutions do not contain adequate quantities of these elements, the plant will be unhealthy or may not survive. Some workers have even postulated that plants require a certain small amount of every element in the periodic table, but perhaps in quantities so small that the need would be extremely difficult to demonstrate in greenhouse experiments.

At the other extreme, an excess of a particular element above a critical level in the nutrient solution will impair the health of the plant or may even kill it. In this case, the element is present in such quantities that it interferes with rather than assists the normal metabolism of the plant and thus has an over-all toxic rather than a nutritive effect.

For some elements there is an optimum range for the composition of the nutrient solution. If the concentration of an element in the solution is either greater than the upper limit of this range or less than the lower limit, the plant will not grow normally. Boron is an example where the available concentration level is extremely critical; very small quantities are necessary for the growth of many plants, whereas only slightly higher concentrations cause injury. With many plant species the range between these two levels is only a few parts per million of B (W. O. Robinson, personal communication). For some other elements, such as Zn and As, plants can tolerate a wider range without conspicuous damage. For still others, the existence of either one or both of the limits has not been demonstrated. It is quite possible, however, that further research will eventually show that an optimum range of concentration exists for every element of the periodic table.

15-2. Biogeochemical Anomalies

Biogeochemical anomalies are areas where the vegetation contains an abnormally high concentration of metals. If the metal content of a sample of plant material is to be useful in prospecting, it should bear a fairly simple relationship to the metal content of the supporting medium. Considerations of solubility of the ore metals in the nutrient solution, together with the many vital and nonvital processes affecting the movement of ions into and through the plant, indicate that the relationship may not be as simple as might be desired. In general, however, if other factors do not interfere, a useful degree of correlation will exist. The problem is to determine what irrelevant factors are most likely to mask the correlation between plant composition and the composition of the supporting soil and soil moisture.

Variations Between Plant Species.   Different species of plants take up different amounts of inorganic material from the soil. The closest

TABLE 15-2.   Average Metal Content (ppm) in the Ash of Five Types
of Vegetation Growing in Unmineralized Ground[a]

	Vegetation					
Element	Grasses (above ground)	Other herbs (above ground)	Shrubs (leaves)	Deciduous trees (leaves)	Conifers (needles)	Averages and totals
Cr	19 (30)	10 (139)	14 (67)	5 (100)	8 (120)	9 (462)
Co	10 (30)	11 (192)	10 (70)	5 (101)	<7 (119)	9 (512)
Ni	54 (28)	33 (226)	91 (182)	87 (209)	57 (213)	65 (858)
Cu	119 (102)	118 (429)	223 (853)	249 (293)	133 (370)	183 (2047)
Zn	850 (62)	666 (355)	1585 (735)	2303 (278)	1127 (333)	1400 (1763)
Mo	34 (32)	19 (217)	15 (104)	7 (118)	5 (145)	13 (616)
Pb	33 (29)	44 (311)	85 (877)	54 (339)	75 (352)	70 (1908)
V	25 (4)	23.5 (39)	25 (46)	16 (14)	21 (77)	22 (180)

Source: Cannon (1960b). Reprinted from *Science* by permission.
[a]Figures in parentheses show the number of analyses used in the calculations.

correlation between the composition of the plant with that of the supporting medium is not necessarily found in the plant that is the most highly enriched in a given element. Each plant has its own peculiar habits that must be determined empirically. An example of contrasting uptake of certain minor elements by different types of plants all living in essentially the same climate and all growing in an unmineralized environment is shown in Table 15-2. An extreme example of selective enrichment is the Arctic dwarf birch, in which the background Zn content of the ash of mature twigs is commonly about 1 percent (Warren *et al.*, 1952). It would obviously be extremely misleading, therefore, to attempt geologic interpretations of the minor-element content of plant samples taken without regard to species. In a given environment, a group of species may have a similar response to certain elements, and where this can be established it is permissible to include two or perhaps more species in one set of comparable samples.

Depth of Root Penetration. Deep-rooted plants that habitually obtain their water from the zone of saturation below the water table

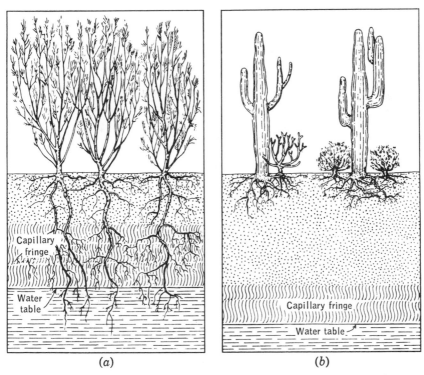

Fig. 15-3. Distinction between phreatophytes (a) and xerophytes (b) shown by their occurrence in relation to the water table. After Robinson (1958).

are defined as *phreatophytes*, in contrast to the shallow-rooted *xerophytes* that can survive exclusively on vadose water derived from rainfall (Figure 15-3). Observations in areas of transported overburden under a variety of climatic conditions have clearly demonstrated that many species of plants not uncommonly take up anomalous metal from ore bodies buried at depths of 30 to 50 feet. In the mine workings of the Shasta copper district of northern California, a live root was observed in a mine tunnel at a depth of 150 feet below the surface. In the arid climate of the Colorado Plateau area, live juniper roots have been observed in uranium mines at depths of several hundred feet (Cannon and Starrett, 1956). A field survey in the desert of New Mexico showed a positive correlation between the U content of the branches of piñon and juniper trees and the location of U mineralization in a flat-lying horizon 65 feet below the surface (Figure 15-4). A few scattered observations of similar

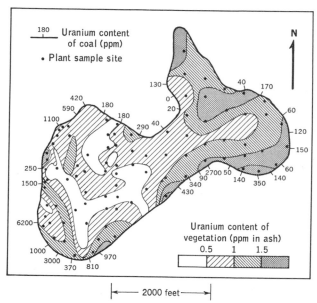

Fig. 15-4. Uranium content of dead piñon and juniper branches from top of La Ventana Mesa, 65 feet above uranium-rich coal horizon. After Cannon and Starrett (1956).

responses at depths of 150 feet or more have been reported by Russian observers (Vinogradov, 1954).

Variation Between Plant Parts. The part of the plant selected for analysis is an especially critical factor. As a result of vital processes, the metal content of different organs of the same plant may be widely divergent. The Zn and Cu content of mature twigs and wood have generally been found to be more stable than the content in immature green tips, leaves, or seed structures in which the composition depends on the rate of metabolism of the actively growing part (Warren et al., 1952). Dead branches of piñon and juniper have been reported as more satisfactory than live branches in biogeochemical sampling for uranium (Cannon and Starrett, 1956). The branches on a given side of a tree are connected most directly with roots on the same side. Thus the metal content may vary greatly even from one side of the tree to the other, and to be properly representative, samples should be taken from all sides of an individual tree (Cannon, 1957).

Variation with Other Factors. In well-drained soils, the roots of plants must go deeper for their water. Drainage conditions also affect the relative acidity of the soil. Variations in soil pH will cause variations in the relative solubility of elements in the soil and hence the availability of those elements for uptake by the plants. The movement of mineral nutrients into plants varies with the amount of sunlight received. Thus, the composition of plants on a sunny slope will be somewhat different from that of the same plants growing on the same soil on a shady slope. Plants may also change in composition with time of year, the mineral content often increasing in the spring during the active growing period, followed by a gradual decline in mineral content with maturity.

Contrast. The contrast of anomalous biogeochemical values against the normal background content appears to be related to the

TABLE 15-3. Contrast of Anomaly to Background Shown in Pb and Ag Content of Trees from Nyeba Pb-Zn District, Nigeria

	Metal Content of Oven-Dried Twigs					
	Pb (ppm)			Ag (ppm)		
Species of Tree	Background	Anomaly Peak	Ratio, Peak : Bg	Background	Anomaly Peak	Ratio, Peak : Bg
Afzelia africana	0.8	140	175	0.05	0.31	6
Baphia nitida	0.4	16	40	<0.03	0.06	>2
Albizzia zygia	0.4	23	57	0.04	0.07	2
Vitex cuneata	0.6	6	10	0.04	0.08	2
Parkia oliveri	0.4	13	32	<0.03	0.05	>2
Millettia sp.	0.3	7	23	<0.03	0.04	>1

Source: Webb and Millman (1951).

mobility of the element in soil solutions. Of the metals for which reliable data are available, Mo shows a fairly consistently high contrast. Expressed as the ratio of anomaly to average background, the contrast in Mo anomalies ranges from 10 up to as much as 100 to 1 (Warren et al., 1953; Baranova, 1957; Malyuga, 1958). For Co, Pb, Fe, and U the contrast is normally in excess of 5 to 1 (Webb and Millman, 1951; Nesvetaylova, 1955a; Cannon and Kleinhampl, 1956; Goldsztein, 1957; Warren and Delavault, 1957), and Cu, Zn, and Ag usually show contrasts of 2 or 3 to 1 (Webb and Millman, 1951; Warren et al., 1952). Table 15-3 shows the relatively greater contrast of Pb as compared with Ag in plants from an area of Pb-Zn mineralization in Nigeria. Figure 15-5 illustrates the same relationship graphically. For some elements, the contrast in soil anomalies is equal to or greater than that in the corresponding biogeochemical anomaly, whereas the reverse has been reported for some other elements. These two relationships are illustrated in Figures 15-6 and 15-7 respectively.

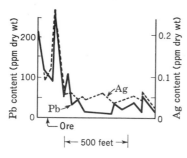

Fig. 15-5. Lead and silver content of oven-dried twigs of *Rubiaceae sp* over ore, Nyeba lead-zinc district, Nigeria. After Webb and Millman (1951).

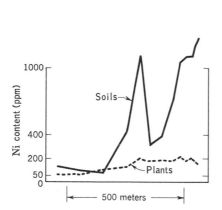

Fig. 15-6. Nickel content of plant ash as compared with corresponding soils at the Novo-Tayketken deposit, U.S.S.R. After Vinogradov and Malyuga (1957).

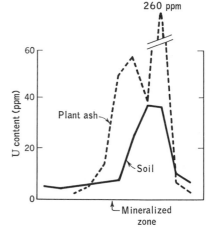

Fig. 15-7. Uranium content of ash of pine needles as compared with corresponding soils, Estérel region, France. After Goldsztein (1957).

Homogeneity. The mineral content of plants is the combined effect of a great many unpredictable variables, of which only a very few are related even indirectly to the composition of the underlying rock. It is therefore not surprising to find that biogeochemical anomalies, at least for the mobile elements, are generally more irregular than the corresponding residual soil anomalies. An example showing the relative homogeneity of soil and plant samples collected from the same traverse is presented in Figure 15-8.

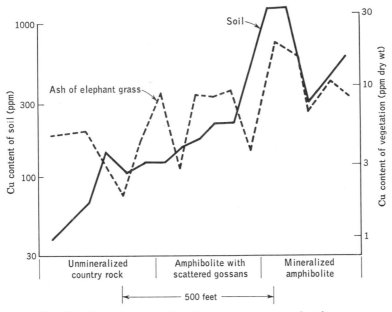

Fig. 15-8. Copper content of elephant grass as compared with corresponding soils, suggesting greater homogeneity of soil pattern, Kilembe area, Uganda. Data on minus-80-mesh fraction. After Jacobson (1956).

Form of Anomalies. Subject to the several modifying factors previously discussed, variations in the chemical composition of the upper parts of the plant correspond with variations in the composition of the solutions tapped by the root system. Thus the form of biogeochemical anomalies is merely a composite of the form of the combined syngenetic, hydromorphic, and biogenic anomalies in the underlying soil together with whatever ground-water anomalies may be present. Where the plant is either rooted directly in ore or in a superjacent soil anomaly, the biogeochemical anomaly will also be superjacent. Where the parent anomaly is a lateral ground-water or hydromorphic soil anomaly, the resulting biogeochemical anomaly will show a corresponding displacement with respect to the ore. An example of the characteristic coincidence of plant and soil anomalies is shown in Figure 15-9.

15–3. Biogeochemical Surveying Techniques

Operating conditions vary from area to area so much that a universally applicable system of biogeochemical surveying cannot be recommended. The general rule of starting with a review of previous

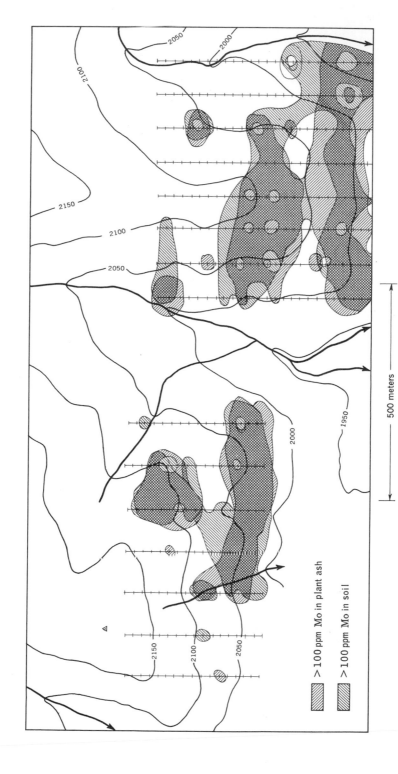

Fig. 15-9. Plan showing molybdenum content of plant ash as compared with corresponding soils, Okhchi River, Armenian Republic, U. S. S. R. After Malyuga (1958).

> 100 ppm Mo in plant ash

> 100 ppm Mo in soil

500 meters

experience in similar problems and following with a carefully planned orientation survey will, however, apply in most areas.

Orientation Survey. The system of preliminary orientation experiments preparatory to biogeochemical survey work in the Colorado Plateau follows a pattern that could profitably be copied in other areas. According to Cannon and Kleinhampl (1956), the orientation study "should include observations on the extent, depth and inclination of the ore-bearing strata, the size and habits of the ore bodies, the probable grade of the ore, the presence or absence of a chemical

TABLE 15-4. Contamination of Junipers Near a Uranium Mill

Distance from Mill	No. of Samples	U Content (ppm ash)
2000–4000 feet	6	40 (av.)
800–1500 feet	4	150 (av.)
Adjacent to the mill	2	700 and 1100

Source: Cannon (1952).

halo in the surrounding barren rock, and the relation of the ore-bearing bed to the water table and the plant roots. Botanical studies should be made of the growth habits of species available for sampling. Preliminary samples should be collected on both mineralized and barren ground and then analyzed to determine the amount of uranium absorbed by trees in the area under study. Finally, from this geological and botanical information, the sampling medium, the sampling pattern, and sampling interval may be determined."

The possibility of contamination should receive special attention in the course of the orientation study. Contamination of plant samples most commonly results from airborne material such as automobile exhaust, industrial gases, smelter fumes, and dust from ore-processing mills. An example of the latter is shown in Table 15-4. Biogeochemical surveying in general should not be attempted in seriously contaminated areas.

Choice of Sampling Medium. Deep-rooted plants are generally preferable to shallow-rooted species. For adequate coverage, a common and uniformly distributed species is desirable. If it can be demonstrated that under the same conditions, two or more species take up proportional amounts of metal, then they may be included in the same set of samples. The first or second year's growth of twigs from high shrubs or trees has been used successfully in many different climatic environments. The metal content of mature twigs does not vary appreciably through the growing season, in contrast to the fruit, leaves, needles, or other actively growing parts; furthermore, twig samples are easier to collect and process than samples of bark or wood. The taller shrubs and trees are less likely to be contaminated by rain splatter than low shrubs and nonwoody plants. In bog areas, however, where rain splatter is not a danger, mosses and low shrubs may be successfully used (Salmi, 1956; Hawkes and Salmon, 1960).

Collecting and Processing of Samples.   In areas densely populated by the species to be sampled, sampling points may be laid out on geometrical grids of profile lines. In areas of widely scattered individuals, it may be necessary to sample plants wherever they can be found and to survey the location of each sample separately. Standard pruning tools are quite satisfactory for collecting twig samples. A sample of 20 grams is large enough to yield the 1 gram of ash normally needed for analysis. The most commonly used containers are small envelopes or paper bags. Maps should be prepared to show location of sample sites, species sampled and pertinent aspects of the bedrock geology and of land forms. Standard procedures call for the drying, pulverizing, and homogenizing of plant samples before analysis. In relatively dry climates, samples collected in paper containers will normally dry out sufficiently in the course of the two weeks or so that usually elapse between collection and analysis. In moist climates, oven-drying of samples before shipment may be necessary to prevent the development of mold and the disintegration of the paper containers.

Choice of Analytical Method.   A problem in the chemical analysis of plant material is the possible loss of trace elements on burning the sample to its ash. If losses of this kind are suspected, it may be preferable to use wet-ashing methods. Other than this, the choice of the analytical method depends only on economy of method as balanced against precision and sensitivity. Normally, plants cannot conveniently be analyzed for trace elements in field laboratories, but must be sent to a central laboratory set up with adequate equipment for pulverizing and ashing.

The analytical results may be expressed in terms of the metal content of the ash or of the dry plant material, according to which method gives the most significant pattern.

Interpretation of Data.   The first problem in interpretation of biogeochemical data, as with other geochemical prospecting data, is distinguishing between significant anomalies that are related to bedrock mineralization and that can be used as exploration guides, and similar patterns that arise from irrelevant natural or artificial factors.

Nonsignificant anomalies may appear as the result of normal variations in soil pH, drainage conditions, or exposure to sunlight. Under some conditions, variations in the metal content of plants due to such factors may be partially eliminated by determining the ratio of two elements that have a similar response to the various non-geologic factors. Warren *et al.* (1949, 1952) report that, although the absolute content of Cu and Zn in plants in an unmineralized area may vary through a wide range due to variations in local conditions, the ratio will remain fairly constant. This otherwise constant ratio would be modified by the presence of either Cu ore or Zn ore within the reach of the plant roots. They consider that a Cu:Zn ratio above 0.23 would indicate Cu ore in the bedrock, and a ratio below 0.07 would indicate Zn ore.

15–4. Geobotanical Indicators

All living plants respond in one way or another to the chemical, physical, and biological environment in which they find themselves. This response normally takes the form of a characteristic habit of growth. For example, plants in a warm, moist, and nutritive environment may grow much more luxuriantly than the same species in a more rigorous and less fertile environment. Where conditions are too rigorous, the plant cannot develop at all. In the same area, other species will be more tolerant of, or may even prefer, the more rigorous environment. Thus by a process of natural selection, the distribution pattern of plant species becomes adjusted to local variations in the environment.

Geobotany is the study of plants as related specifically to their geologic environment. Many factors that have little or no relation to the geology can have a major influence on the health and distribution of plants. Chief among these are sunlight, length of growing season, elevation, forest fires, blights, and insect pests. Many important factors in the natural development of plants do, however, arise either directly or indirectly from their geologic environment.

A plant may respond to its geologic environment by showing characteristic variations in its form, size, color, or rate of growth. The abnormal colors and morphological features of a plant caused by a poisonous element in the nutrient solution are collectively referred to as toxicity symptoms. Between the level where a plant can tolerate the concentration of a given element in the soil solutions and the level where it cannot survive is a fringe zone where the plant can live but where it shows visible injury as a result of the poisoning effect of the toxic element. Most commonly, the toxemia takes the form of a simple stunting of growth that cannot be uniquely associated with any specific cause. A few plants, however, develop peculiarly diagnostic symptoms that can be interpreted directly in terms of probable excesses of a particular element in the soil (Table 15-5).

Geobotanical indicators are either plant species or characteristic variations in the growth habits of plants that are restricted in their distribution to rocks or soils of definite physical or chemical properties. Geobotanical indicators have been used in locating and mapping ground water, saline deposits, hydrocarbons and rock types, as well as ores.

TABLE 15-5. Physiological and Morphological Changes in Plants Due to Metal Toxicities

Element	Effect
Aluminum	Stubby roots, leaf scorch, mottling
Boron	Dark foliage; marginal scorch of older leaves at high concentrations; stunted, deformed, shortened internodes; creeping forms; heavy pubescence; increased gall production
Chromium	Yellow leaves with green veins
Cobalt	White dead patches on leaves
Copper	Dead patches on lower leaves from tips; purple stems, chlorotic leaves with green veins, stunted roots, creeping sterile forms in some species
Iron	Stunted tops, thickened roots; cell division disturbed in algae, resulting cells greatly enlarged
Manganese	Chlorotic leaves, stem and petiole lesions, curling and dead areas on leaf margins, distortion of laminae
Molybdenum	Stunting, yellow-orange coloration
Nickel	White dead patches on leaves, apetalous sterile forms
Uranium	Abnormal number of chromosomes in nuclei; unusually shaped fruits; sterile apetalous forms, stalked leaf rosette
Zinc	Chlorotic leaves with green veins, white dwarfed forms; dead areas on leaf tips; roots stunted

Source: Cannon (1960b). Reprinted from *Science* by permission.

Indicators of Ground Water.   Desert plants respond in a very spectacular manner to the availability of water. Phreatophytes, the plants that habitually obtain their water supply from the zone of saturation, indicate a water table within reach of their root systems. Representatives of this group in the western United States are alfalfa, mesquite, greasewood, and paloverde (Meinzer, 1927; Robinson, 1958). In water-supply work, phreatophytes are important because of their effective wastage of ground water by transpiration. In contrast to phreatophytes are the xerophytes, which depend on occasional rain water and have only shallow roots (Figure 15-3). Most other desert plants are indiscriminate in their choice of water and are grouped as mesophytes.

Many plants cannot grow in a soil that is saturated for any length of time, while other plants may thrive under these conditions. In eastern Canada, for example, alders, willows, and some ferns indicate waterlogged soil or ground-water seepage areas. Most other areas of the world also have their water-indicating plant assemblages. In prospecting, these botanical indications are important in that they point to areas where hydromorphic anomalies may have developed as a result of precipitation of ore metals from shallow ground water.

Indicators of Saline Deposits. Many desert plants tolerate or even prefer a nutrient solution with a high content of dissolved salts. Specific indicators of high salinity, or *halophytes*, are useful to stockmen in recognizing areas unsuitable for grazing cattle. Borate-rich

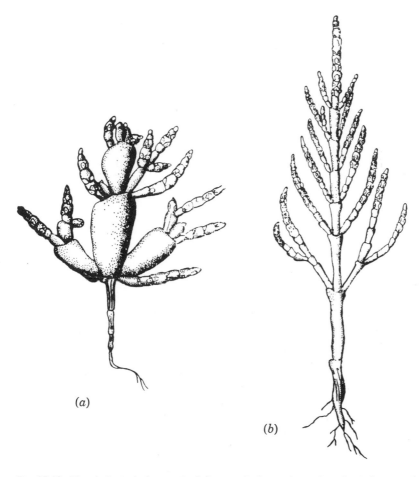

(a)

(b)

Fig. 15-10. Morphological changes in *Salicornea herbacea* L. under the influence of boron. (a), *Salicornea* grown on soil with an increased boron content; (b), grown on control sections which contained practically no boron. After Buyalov and Shvyryayeva (1955).

saline deposits in Central Asia are indicated by a series of plant species that are highly tolerant to B. Where the B content exceeds 100 ppm, many plants show deformities (Figure 15-10) or are subject to diseases such as rotting of the roots, increased gall formation, and chlorosis (Buyalov and Shvyryayeva, 1955).

Indicators of Hydrocarbons. Experimental investigations have shown that plants rooted in bituminous soils tend to have peculiar forms, distinguished by gigantism and deformity (Viktorov, 1955). Some of these plants show a tendency for abnormal repeated blooming (Kartsev *et al.*, 1959). These responses are not often seen under field conditions, and no immediate applications of indicator plants to petroleum exploration seems likely.

The population of microscopic plant indicators in surface materials may under favorable circumstances be useful as a guide in petroleum exploration (Kartsev *et al.*, 1959). The most successful microbiological methods are based on the identification of bacteria that can obtain their vital energy only from the oxidation of certain hydrocarbons, principally propane. According to Russian workers, the light hydrocarbon gases dissolved in the connate water of sedimentary rocks can diffuse upward from their source in deep-lying oil pools. Under the same conditions, the heavier hydrocarbons and the water itself are held firmly in a static condition. The Russian authors claim further that propane is a specific indicator of liquid or gaseous hydrocarbons and cannot be derived from bituminous sediments or black shales. They have reported the observation of a dynamic flow of light hydrocarbons extending continuously from an oil pool buried at depths of several thousands of feet directly to the surface of the earth. Where hydrocarbons reach the zone of oxidation, they are met by oxidizing bacteria, among which are the specific propane-oxidizing bacteria. These bacteria are determined by incubating a culture of soil or soil water in an atmosphere of propane mixed with sterile air. After a period of 10 days, the cultures are examined and appraised qualitatively. The development of bacteria of any kind, as evidenced by a scum on the surface of the cultured samples, is an indication of propane bacteria, inasmuch as no other bacteria could survive or multiply in this environment. A success ratio of 65 percent in obtaining petroleum from wells drilled on the basis of microbiological anomalies is reported. Of these discoveries, a large number are reported to have developed into commercially producing oil fields (Mogilevsky, 1959).

Indicators of Rock Types. Limestone soils commonly support a diagnostic assemblage of indicator species. It is not always clear whether this response is due to soil pH, or to the calcium content of the soil solutions. Recognition of limestone indicators may be helpful both in geologic mapping and in prospecting for ores that occur preferentially in limestone country rock.

Areas of rock alteration and pyritization may support a characteristic plant assemblage (Billings, 1950). Here again it is not clear whether the geobotanical response is from the acid environment of the oxidizing pyrite, from the abundance of some minor element, or from the texture of the material.

Ultramafic rocks in virtually all climates have a very profound influence on the ecological assemblages of plants growing on them. In general, the vegetation in areas underlain by ultramafic rocks is conspicuously stunted and thinly developed. This relationship is ordinarily so clearly defined that the contacts of ultramafic rocks can be sketched accurately on aerial photographs. It is not known whether this relationship is the effect of poisoning by the Ni, Cr, Co, or Mg of the ultramafic rock, from starvation for one of the important plant nutrients such as K or Mo, or perhaps simply from the poor drainage conditions often associated with the characteristic clay-rich overburden.

Indicator assemblages have been noted over many other rock types, such as granite, quartzite, shale, or basalt. In virtually all of these associations, the cause seems to be clearly a matter of relative drainage and availability of water rather than chemical composition of the soil.

Indicators of Ore. Long lists of indicator plants for specific elements have been compiled by various authors. These lists include specific indicators for virtually all the ore metals (Lidgey, 1897; Dorn, 1937; Vinogradov, 1954; Nesvetaylova, 1955b). Unfortunately only a very few of all the plants listed are now, or ever have been, of any real help in prospecting. The reason is that most of these species were recorded from the unnaturally acidified and contaminated soils in the vicinity of old mine workings rather than from virgin areas.

Indicator plants that are definitely known to have been used in prospecting are listed in Table 15-6. Here, plants that are restricted exclusively to rocks or soils of a definite mineral content and not found under any other conditions have been defined as *universal* plant indicators (Cannon, 1960b). Those that are common plants of wide distribution but that in local situations have served as useful ore guides are noted as *local* indicators.

The first of the indicator plants to be used in prospecting was the "calamine violet," which thrives only on Zn-rich soils in the Zn districts of central and western Europe. In the early days of development of these districts, the distinctive yellow blossoms of this plant are reported as having led to the discovery of many zinc deposits buried under shallow cover.

Selenium indicators were first described by Beath *et al.* (1939). These are a group of plants, chiefly species of *Astragalus*, in the Rocky Mountain states that will grow only on soils containing an

TABLE 15-6. Plants That Have Been Used as Indicators in Prospecting

Element	Universal (U) or Local (L)	Family	Genus and Species	Common Name	Locality
Bitumen	L	Goosefoot	Anabasis salsa	Saltwort	Caspian Sea
	L	Goosefoot	Salsola spp.	Onion	Caspian Sea
	L	Lily	Allium sp.		California
Boron	L	Goosefoot	Salsola nitraria	Saltwort	U. S. S. R.
	L	Goosefoot	Eurotia ceratoides	Winter fat	U. S. S. R.
	L	Plumbago	Limonium suffruticosum	Statice	U. S. S. R.
Copper	U	Pink	Gypsophila patrini	Kachim	U. S. S. R.
	L	Pink	Polycarpea spirostylis	Pink	Australia
	L	Mint	Acrocephalus roberti		Katanga
	L	Mint	Elsholtzia haichowensis	Elsholtzia	China
	U	Mint	Ocimum homblei	Basil	Rhodesia
	U	Moss	Merceya latifolia	Copper moss	Sweden and Montana
	L	Poppy	Eschsholtzia mexicana	Calif. poppy	Arizona
	L	Plumbago	Armeria maritima	Thrift	Scotland
Gypsum	L	Buckwheat	Eriogonum inflatum	Desert trumpet	Western U. S.
	L	Loasa	Mentzelia spp.	Blazing star	Western U. S.
Iron	L	Birch	Betula sp.	Birch	Germany
	L	Guttiferae	Clusia rosea	Copey clusia	Venezuela

Lead	L	Grass	*Erianthus giganteus*	Beardgrass	Tennessee
Phosphorus	L	Morning-glory	*Convolvulus althaeoides*	Bindweed	Spain
Selenium	U	Legume	*Astragalus bisulcatus*	Poison vetch	Western U. S.
	U	Legume	*Astragalus racemosus*	Poison vetch	Western U. S.
	U	Legume	*Astragalus pectinatus*	Poison vetch	Western U. S.
	U	Sunflower	*Oonopsis* spp.	Goldenweed	Western U. S.
	U	Sunflower	*Aster venustus*	Woody aster	Western U. S.
	U	Mustard	*Stanleya* spp.	Princesplume	Western U. S.
Selenium and uranium	U	Legume	*Astragalus pattersoni*	Poison vetch	Western U. S.
	L	Legume	*Astragalus preussi*	Poison vetch	Western U. S.
	L	Legume	*Astragalus* sp.	*Garbancillo*	Andes
Silver	L	Buckwheat	*Eriogonum ovalifolium*	Eriogonum	Montana
Zinc	U	Violet	*Viola calamineria (lutea)*	Zinc violet	Belgium and Germany
	L	Saxifrage	*Philadelphus* sp.	Mock orange	Washington

Source: Cannon (1960b). Reprinted from *Science* by permission.

excess of Se. This relationship is so consistent that it is possible to make accurate maps of seleniferous geologic formations simply by outlining the distribution of Se indicators. Inasmuch as Se-rich forage is highly toxic to sheep and other livestock, the recognition of seleniferous areas by means of the Se-indicator plants is of considerable practical importance. In prospecting, the Se indicators are valuable because they point to the location of the Se-rich uranium ores of the Colorado Plateau. Here a substantial ecological assemblage of Se-indicators and also sulfur-indicators has been described (Cannon 1957). Deep-rooted members of this association of indicator plants have been found over uranium ore buried at depths up to 70 feet.

The "copper flower," *Ocimum homblei* de Wild, discovered in Northern Rhodesia in 1949 by G. Woodward, has been perhaps the most successful of all the ore indicators. This plant, an herb of the *Labiatae* family, grows to a height of 18 inches to 2 feet. Although it has a characteristic flower and leaf form that can be recognized by careful examination, it is very similar in appearance to another species of *Ocimum* that is not exclusively associated with Cu-rich soils. Field studies have shown that the minimum Cu content of soils in which *Ocimum* will grow is 100 ppm, but that it will tolerate and thrive in soils containing 5000 ppm and more. The readily extractable Cu content of the soil appears to be more critical here than the total Cu content. Thus, because of the high cxCu:Cu ratio in swamp soils, *Ocimum* tends to come in at a lower total Cu content than in freely drained soils. Greenhouse studies have demonstrated that the seeds will not germinate in culture solutions unless 50 ppm Cu is present, with optimum growth conditions reached in solutions containing 600 ppm. General experience with exploration work based on the copper flower shows that flower-chart outlines are almost identical with the outlines of either underlying Cu deposits or lateral seepage anomalies (G. Woodward, personal communication; Horizon, 1959).

Another copper flower, *Acrocephalus robertii*, has been described from the Katanga area in the Congo, immediately north of the Rhodesian Copperbelt (Duvigneaud, 1958). This is reported as a small annual mint whose resistance to toxicity appears to be infinite. This also is an herb of the *Labiatae* family of the Ocimoideae tribe and may in fact be identical to *Ocimum homblei* de Wild (Cannon, personal communication).

Still another copper flower, *Gypsophila patrini*, or "kachim," is associated with Cu in the Rudny Altay deposits of Central Asia (Nesvetaylova, 1955b). Kachim grows so selectively on Cu-bearing rocks that even small Cu-bearing dikes may be marked by a strong growth of this Cu indicator.

A local indicator of Cu in Arizona is the California poppy, observed over the outcrop of the San Manuel copper deposit. Here the distribution of this species is confined to Cu-rich soil, and its population density is closely proportional to the Cu content of the soil. In neighboring areas of slightly different climate, the poppy can grow almost anywhere, whereas in other areas not too far distant it cannot grow at all even where Cu is abundant (Lovering *et al.*, 1950).

Chlorosis, or the yellowing of the leaves of plants, has been a useful though nonspecific guide to ore. Ni, Cu, Co, Cr, Zn, and Mn are all antagonistic to Fe in the plant metabolism. Excesses of these elements produce a deficiency of Fe necessary in the formation of chlorophyll, with a resulting decoloration of the leaves (Cannon, 1960b). Chlorosis can result from a variety of other causes, including plant infections, improper drainage, and excess acidity in the soil. At the same time, abnormally colored leaves always deserve the attention of the prospector, inasmuch as chlorotic symptoms, particularly in the grasses and small flowering plants growing in seepage areas, are common in many mineralized areas.

The absence of normal vegetative cover rather than the presence of specific geobotanical indicators may, under some conditions, be useful as an ore guide. Acid from the oxidizing pyrite of sulfide deposits or toxic excesses of soluble metals may prevent the development of a normal plant ecology. In Rhodesia, some of the big deposits were originally discovered because of lack of tree growth over the suboutcrop. This may have been due to sterility arising from acid leaching of nutrients rather than from the acidity or toxicity of the soil itself.

15–5. Geobotanical Surveying Techniques

Unless the indicator species are relatively conspicuous (which is rarely the case) the identification of reliable geobotanical guides is a difficult task, requiring specialized skill. As with other methods, the first step is to carry out a preliminary orientation study involving the preparation of population maps of all plant species growing both in the vicinity of known but undisturbed mineralization and in barren areas of otherwise similar characteristics. Cannon (1957, p. 408) describes her experimental technique as follows: "The information on indicator plants was established by marking off 10 × 5 foot areas over known ore bodies in a number of districts, and similar areas over unmineralized parts of the same bed with similar exposure and slope. Complete lists of plants in each plot were made, and final lists of indicator and tolerant plants were derived from them. When any of these plants are observed in a new area, a careful study of their distribution should be made to determine whether and how they can be used in prospecting."

Indicator plants are best found and mapped when they are in bloom. Mapping plants at other times of year can, of course, be done, but the work progresses at a very much slower rate and with very much greater danger of overlooking an occurrence of indicator plants. Once a system of identifying geobotanical indicators has been established, a geobotanical survey consists merely in plotting their occurrence on a map and then sketching the outlines of areas where they occur.

15–6. Photogeologic Mapping

Photogeology is the art of interpreting in terms of geology the patterns both of land forms and of vegetation that are visible in air photographs. Patterns of vegetation reflecting glacial features, alluvial deposits and the location of water-bearing faults and fissures in the bedrock can often be mapped more easily on air photographs than on the ground. In the Precambrian shield areas, granites and metasedimentary rocks can be easily identified photogeologically by their characteristic types of vegetative cover. The structures in folded sedimentary sequences can, under favorable conditions, be easily followed by their characteristic plant patterns. In gravel-covered areas in the deserts of southwestern United States, the plant patterns may reflect the suboutcropping bedrock geology through many feet of overlying Tertiary cover.

The techniques of photogeology and its application in exploration are subjects considerably beyond the scope of this book. For further discussion, the reader should consult the standard references listed below.

SELECTED REFERENCES ON USE OF VEGETATION IN EXPLORATION

General   Cannon (1960b)
Plant nutrition   Truog (1951)
                                 Mehlich and Drake (1955)
Biogeochemical prospecting   Cannon and Kleinhampl (1956)
                                 Cannon (1960a)
Indicator plants   Cannon (1957, 1960b)
Photogeology   Ray (1960)
                                 American Society of Photogrammetry
                                    (1959)
                                 Lueder (1959)

CHAPTER 16

GEOCHEMICAL METHODS IN MINERAL EXPLORATION

To help him in the increasingly difficult task of locating concealed mineral deposits, the present-day exploration geologist has at his disposal a wide selection of geological, geophysical, and geochemical techniques. At the same time he has generally better maps and mapping equipment and vastly improved facilities for transport and communication. As a result of the multiplicity of new techniques and facilities, modern exploration has become a complex and often costly business. With the rising cost of field operations, maximum efficiency in the application of the modern technical aids is demanded in order to reduce the financial risk to reasonable proportions. This can be achieved only where adequately skilled personnel are using appropriate methods in carefully chosen areas at the most opportune time. To do this with legitimate economy requires that expenditure of funds must be correctly balanced against the chances of success and the possible financial return. Quite apart from technical considerations, it is important that the economic factor be given its full weight in each successive step in the evolution of a modern exploration program.

Figure 16-1 illustrates in diagrammatic form the sequence of administrative decisions normally followed in the planning and early operational stages of a mineral exploration program.

A detailed discussion of all aspects of mineral exploration is beyond the scope of this book. This chapter attempts only to put geochemical methods in perspective with other aids to exploration as an introduction to a discussion of problems in the planning and organization of geochemical surveys. Suffice to emphasize at this point that the objective of all components of an exploration system is the same, namely, to detect and record any feature or property of the earth's crust that, when correctly interpreted, can serve as a guide to ore. The geological, geophysical, and geochemical surveys differ only with respect to technique. The basic philosophy of each is the same.

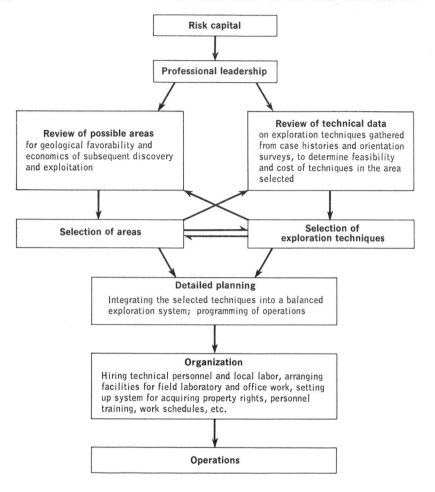

Fig. 16-1. The evolution of an exploration program.

16–1. Professional Leadership

Many exploration surveys have fallen short of expectations through lack of experience and technical training in the professional personnel responsible for planning and supervising the program. The essential requirements are a sound background in exploration geology, specialized skill in the different exploration techniques, and a natural flair for ore finding. Rarely are these to be found in any one man. More often it is necessary to build up a team, the members of which cooperate to provide the necessary virtues. The inability to obtain the services of a supervising geologist or of a specialist with the requisite experience and training may well be sufficient reason for ruling out a particular technique, no matter how much it may otherwise be appropriate for the problem on hand. Not all techniques make the same demands on professional personnel. Full-time professional attention is certainly needed for most geological studies, but geochemical and geophysical surveys usually involve a considerable amount of routine work which can be done by trained teams of artisans and local labor, working under part-time professional supervision. The critical phases of orientation, planning, and interpretation, however, can be done effectively only by an appropriately qualified and experienced professional geologist.

16–2. Selection of Area

The initial selection of areas must be based on the most thorough review of the known geology and record of past mining and prospecting activity. Particular attention should be given to the possible types of deposit, the distribution of favorable rocks and structures, the nature of the overburden, and other conditions which may mask the surface manifestations of bedrock mineralization; the study of air photographs can also be an invaluable source of information at this stage. In addition to the technical considerations, other relevant aspects include the political environment, ground ownership, markets and taxation, communications, and labor. Preliminary visits to likely field areas may well be necessary before a well-founded final selection can be made.

16–3. The Exploration Sequence

A large exploration program is commonly organized as a logical sequence of operations. Each stage in this sequence involves the study of an area by whatever exploration method or combination of methods is most effective for the purpose of delimiting smaller areas for more intensive study in the next stage (Figure 16-2). Thus, the first stage may be broad-scale reconnaissance for regional criteria, to help decide which parts of a large area of interest have the best mineral potential and which parts can be eliminated as relatively unfavorable. The most promising regions constitute local areas of interest that are then followed up by more detailed surveys for more restricted aspects of the ore environment, in order to determine whether an intensive exploration survey of some kind is desirable. This process of elimination of unfavorable areas and of increasingly detailed study of the favorable areas is continued step by step up to

the ultimate proving of a deposit by drilling and underground exploration. It is a process of progressively reducing the size of the target,
where at each step the target is the area having the highest probability
of containing ore. The ultimate purpose of a technical exploration

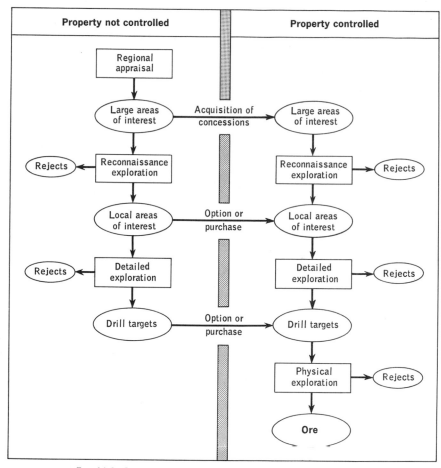

Fig. 16-2. Sequence of operations in an exploration program.

program is the selection of drill sites. Almost invariably, the cost of
drilling is by far the largest part of the exploration budget. The price
of one hole saved will pay for a great deal of preliminary survey work.

16-4. Choice of Exploration Methods

Normally, several ore guides with their corresponding methods of
detection will be found to be more or less applicable for any given

problem. The degree of usefulness of a particular exploration method will, of course, be different for each method and for each successive stage in the exploration sequence. For greatest over-all effectiveness, it is necessary to strike an optimum balance between the various methods that are known to be applicable. After the initial choice of area, the choice of methods and of the plan of operations that will result in this optimum balance is by far the most critical decision that must be made by the geologist in charge. This choice must of necessity be based on relevant previous experience and case-history data, supported by the results of preliminary orientation surveys in the areas under consideration.

A few volumes devoted primarily to exploration case histories are listed at the end of this chapter. In addition, the journal literature, particularly in mining, carries frequent articles describing field experience gained in production geochemical surveys. References to case histories of particular interest are marked in the Bibliography with an asterisk. A few examples that may be helpful in planning are presented in the following chapter.

Case-history studies and previous personal experience are useful only as suggestive guides in the choice of methods in a new area. The more nearly the past experience matches the new situation, the more reliable will be the conclusions that are drawn. However, the diversity of factors controlling metal dispersion is such that no two field problems are ever exactly alike. Quite subtle variations in the local environment can so radically change the course and pattern of metal dispersion as to demand more or less drastic modifications in technique and, particularly, in interpretation.

Preliminary orientation surveys should therefore be considered mandatory if any degree of success is to be expected from a geochemical survey. In fact, an orientation study as an initial step in planning an exploration program should be a completely general rule. As an important corollary, the effectiveness of a geochemical survey must rest initially on the thoroughness and competence with which the orientation has been carried out. In addition to the vital preliminary studies, supplementary orientation may also be required from time to time as new conditions are encountered in the course of field operations.

The principal factors bearing on the selection of exploration methods are the size of the exploration target, property control, the reliability of the method under the local conditions, the cost of the survey, and the expected value of the ore deposit to be found. Except for the expected value of the ore, these factors insofar as they apply to some of the more important ore guides are summarized in Table 16-1 and Figure 16-3. It will be appreciated that the applicability of

TABLE 16-1. Principal Geological, Geophysical, and Geochemical Ore Guides

Ore Guide	Explanation	Example
Favorable Geological Features		
Ore provinces	Preferential occurrence of some kinds of ore deposits in certain well-defined areas.	Porphyry-copper deposits of the southwestern United States
Regional structures	Ores preferentially located with respect to structural features of continental scale	Epigenetic precious metal deposits in the Basin and Range structural province, western United States
Igneous rock associations	Preferential association of some kinds of ores with certain kinds of igneous rocks	Nickel sulfide ores associated with gabbros and norites
Proximity to known ore	Better chances of finding additional ore near a known deposit than at a distance from it	Discovery of Mission deposit near Pima and Banner deposits, Twin Buttes district, Arizona
Host rock	Ores preferentially localized in specific rock types or in specific stratigraphic horizons	Rhodesian Copperbelt ores localized in the Mines Series
Local structures	Ores preferentially located with respect to the crests, troughs or flanks of folds, or to certain features of fracture systems	Proximity of ore to Osborne Fault in the Coeur d'Alene district
Mineral zoning	Changes in grade or type of ore either laterally or with depth as indicated by changes in mineralogy	Zoning of Pb ore at surface to Zn ore at depth in southwestern Wisconsin Zn district
Glacial ore boulders	Ore buried by glacial debris indicated by glacially transported ore boulders (see Chapter 10)	Ore boulders south of Steep Rock Lake iron deposit, western Ontario
Geophysical Anomalies		
Airborne geophysical anomalies	Geophysical anomalies related to ore that can be detected by airborne equipment	Discovery of magnetite deposits by airborne magnetic surveys in southeastern Pennsylvania
Ground geophysical anomalies	Geophysical anomalies related to ore that are mapped instrumentally at the surface of the ground	Discovery of New Brunswick massive sulfide deposits with electromagnetic surveys
Geochemical Anomalies		
Geochemical provinces	See Chapter 4	
Hydrothermal dispersion patterns	See Chapter 4	
Drainage anomalies	See Chapters 12–14	
Lateral soil anomalies	See Chapters 9–11	
Superjacent soil anomalies	See Chapters 9–11	
Biogeochemical anomalies	See Chapter 15	
Geobotanical indicators	See Chapter 15	

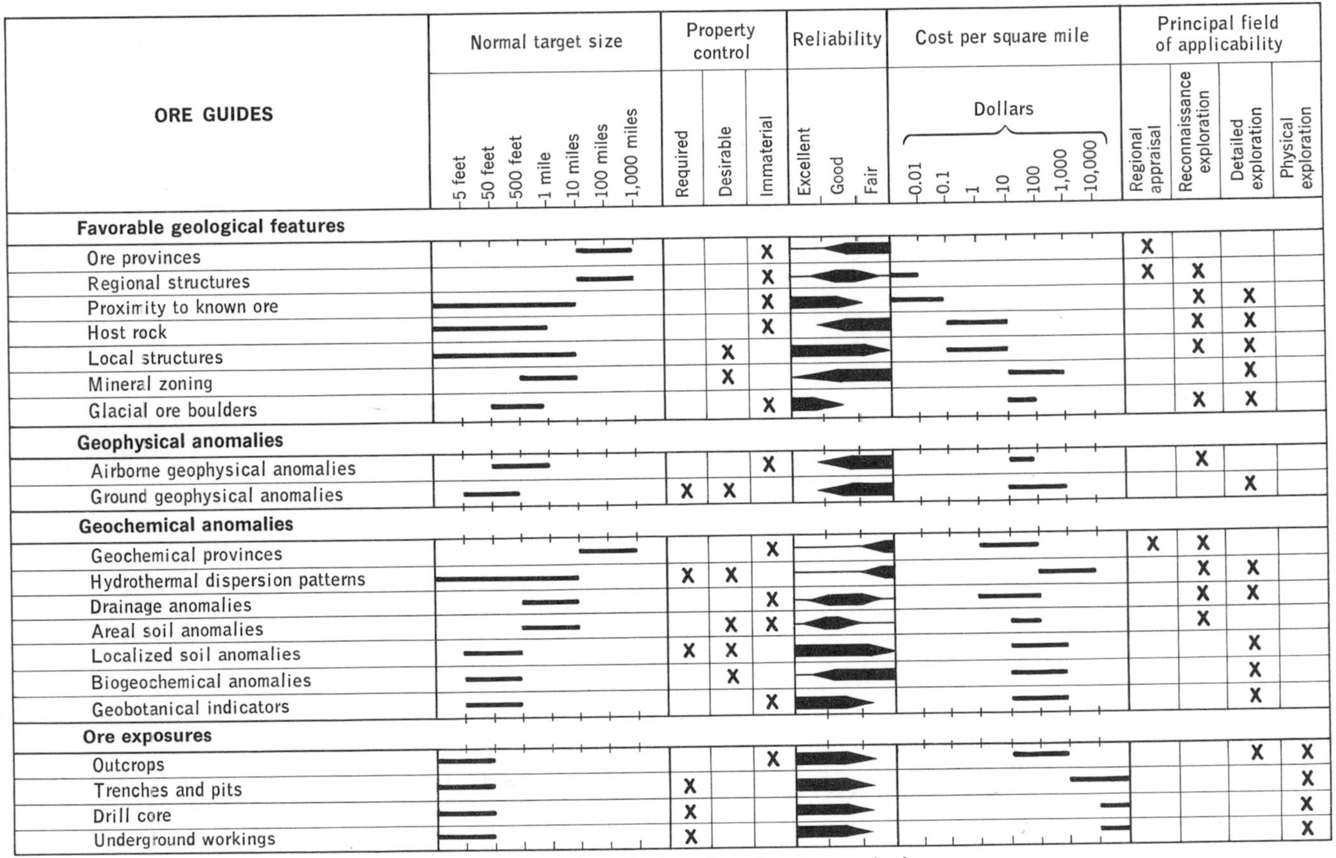

Fig. 16-3. Factors in the selection of exploration methods.

ORE GUIDES	Normal target size	Property control — Required	Desirable	Immaterial	Reliability	Cost per square mile (Dollars)	Regional appraisal	Reconnaissance exploration	Detailed exploration	Physical exploration
Favorable geological features										
Ore provinces				X	Fair		X			
Regional structures				X	Fair		X	X		
Proximity to known ore				X	Good			X	X	
Host rock				X	Good			X	X	
Local structures			X					X	X	
Mineral zoning			X						X	
Glacial ore boulders				X	Excellent			X	X	
Geophysical anomalies										
Airborne geophysical anomalies				X	Fair		X	X		
Ground geophysical anomalies		X	X						X	
Geochemical anomalies										
Geochemical provinces			X		Fair		X	X		
Hydrothermal dispersion patterns		X	X		Good			X	X	
Drainage anomalies				X	Good			X	X	
Areal soil anomalies				X	Excellent			X		
Localized soil anomalies		X	X		Good				X	
Biogeochemical anomalies			X		Fair				X	
Geobotanical indicators				X	Fair				X	
Ore exposures										
Outcrops				X	Excellent				X	X
Trenches and pits		X			Excellent					X
Drill core		X			Excellent					X
Underground workings		X			Excellent					X

any given method or combination of methods to a particular problem will naturally depend on the balance of all these factors.

Target Size. Just as the center of the marksman's target is surrounded by concentric rings, so most ore deposits are related, more or less closely, to a series of larger target areas, each characterized by some geological, physical, or chemical feature that is diagnostic of the ore environment. The relationship between these features and the ore may be either direct or indirect. Thus, some features of the ore environment, such as favorable host rocks, geologic structures, or geochemical provinces, are related to the genesis and localization of the ore but are not in themselves necessarily indicative of mineralization. Other features, such as most geophysical anomalies, are a direct response to some unusual physical property of the ore body itself. Still others, as for example gossans, leached outcrops, and secondary geochemical anomalies, result from the weathering and dispersion of the primary components of the ore.

Each geological, geophysical, and geochemical feature of the ore environment defines a target area of characteristic size, shape, and relationship to the ore. Some extend over large areas, forming targets that may be detected by widely spaced observations. Others are more restricted in their extent and require more detailed examinations for their detection.

The figures for "target size" given in Figure 16-3 refer to the longest dimension of the favorable area or target. Examination of regional structural trends on a geologic map of the United States, for example, may show that the Appalachian belt is a favorable ore province. This presents a large target. Airborne magnetic surveys, on the other hand, will not indicate a magnetic anomaly much more than 1000 feet from the magnetic body responsible for the anomaly, whereas ground magnetic observations must usually be made within 100 feet of the deposit in order to detect it. These are small targets. The normal sequence of operations in a large exploration program consists of surveys for progressively smaller targets by techniques capable of progressively greater resolving power.

Property Control. The acquisition of property rights, in most countries, is an extremely tedious and expensive phase of mineral exploration. Where this situation exists, the general pattern of exploration may be modified or even dominated by property considerations. Exploration methods that can be applied to appraising a tract of land *without* acquisition of property or of trespass rights are at a very definite premium. Subject to the local mining laws, airborne geophysical surveys and most geological and geochemical reconnaissance methods fall into this category. For detailed ground surveys of any type, and all physical exploration except for simple outcrop examination, property and trespass rights are usually desirable or required by law.

Reliability of Method. The reliability of a method refers to the probability of obtaining *and recognizing* indications of an ore body or mineralized district by the method being used. Reliability depends not only on whether a readily detectable target exists and how effective the exploration method is in locating it, but also on the extent to which the anomaly is specifically related to ore and the extent to which it is possible that nonsignificant anomalies may confuse the interpretation. As a simple illustration, a resistivity survey would not normally detect Zn deposits where the nonconducting sphalerite is the only ore mineral. At the same time, the resistivity survey might record strong anomalies due to graphitic horizons or water-filled fractures that are of little or no prospecting significance and that would confuse the interpretation. Resistivity surveying, therefore, would not be considered a reliable method of prospecting for this kind of Zn deposit. Geochemical soil anomalies, however, are present over virtually all base-metal deposits that occur in the bedrock immediately beneath a cover of residual soil. Here the chances of finding a target are much greater, and the interpretation of the anomalies is likely to be fairly straightforward. In other words, residual soil sampling under these conditions would be a relatively reliable ore guide for Zn.

Cost. The cost of an exploration survey is the only one of the critical factors that can be estimated with any degree of accuracy. Costs should be compared on a unit-area basis. High total cost and high cost of capital equipment do not necessarily imply a high unit-area cost. Airborne geophysical surveys, for example, although they represent a high cost of overhead and hourly operation, are often relatively inexpensive when computed in terms of cost per square mile, providing, of course, that the area surveyed is sufficiently large.

Value of Expected Ore. The expected value of the ore body being sought and the chances of success may have an appreciable bearing on the applicability of a given method. Thus, a high-cost survey such as detailed geochemical soil sampling is justified if large ore bodies are expected and there is relatively little chance of overlooking a deposit. Conversely, a low-cost survey, such as the airborne magnetic, can sometimes offset small target size, poor chances of finding a target, or a low probability for the occurrence of large ore bodies.

16–5. The Role of Geochemistry in an Exploration System

It should be apparent from the foregoing discussion that geochemical methods have no unique claim to general applicability in mineral exploration. For any given problem, the pros and cons of the appropriate geochemical methods must be weighed against those of the other available prospecting methods, and a proper place assigned to each in the schedule of reducing the target size. The areas of particular applicability of geochemical methods, together with those of other exploration methods, are summarized in the right-hand column of Figure 16-3.

Scale of Operations. Ore guides that present large target areas commonly constitute the basis for regional appraisal and preliminary reconnaissance surveys. Here the aim is to determine the mineral potential of a relatively large area, eliminate the barren ground, and draw attention to local areas of interest. Small targets closely associated with mineralization, on the other hand, are usually of most value in detailed surveys of highly promising areas. In this case, the aim of the survey is to pinpoint the bedrock metal source with the greatest possible precision, often preparatory to physical exploration by drilling or underground work.

In a sense, the principle of reconnaissance is strategic, while that of detailed surveys is tactical. Thus, the collection of a few sediment samples in the vicinity of an old prospect is just as much a reconnaissance, in that it is done to assess the mineral potential of the prospect, as is the systematic collection of drainage samples over an area of 10,000 square miles. Conversely, a soil survey aimed at locating all the deposits within an extensive area may be just as much a detailed survey as soil sampling to pinpoint the bedrock source in a more limited area of interest.

Regional Appraisal. To date, the pattern of distribution of known ore deposits taken together with their associated regional geologic structures has been the principal guide in the selection of areas worthy of systematic reconnaissance exploration. Of the geochemical ore guides, the geochemical province shows the most promise as a method of regional appraisal. If a correlation can be established between the probability of ore and the chemical composition of some widely distributed rock or mineral, regional geochemical mapping may serve to focus attention on areas that might otherwise be passed over.

Reconnaissance Surveys. In reconnaissance, the aim of the geochemical survey is to aid in appraising the mineral potential of an area of substantial size by determining the broad picture of metal distribution, with a view to focusing attention on the relatively more promising parts of the area. Although the same techniques of geochemical reconnaissance may be used in the initial examination of small areas, as for example in prospect appraisal, they are more characteristically employed as a rapid preliminary method of scanning relatively large tracts of ground. For this purpose, large target areas, permitting a low sample density, are desirable in order to give a high rate of coverage at low cost per unit-area. Broad patterns are most likely to be formed by metal dispersion in the drainage system, by glacial transport, or by the development of regional primary patterns in the bedrock. Large size of target is not essential for the success of a reconnaissance method, as evidenced by the effective use of residual soil surveys and geobotanical studies in appraising extensive areas.

The effectiveness of reconnaissance based on the search for drainage anomalies in stream water and sediments and for lateral hydromorphic anomalies in spring and seepage areas has been amply demonstrated in many parts of the world. While stream-sediment sampling is applicable for most metals, exploration based on analysis of natural water and seepage soil is necessarily limited to the more mobile elements. Ease of operation and low cost per unit-area combined with a relatively high reliability place drainage surveys in an outstanding position as a reconnaissance tool. Mapping the distribution of glacially dispersed ore boulders has proved to be a successful method of reconnaissance in Scandinavia. Chemical analysis of moraine for glacially dispersed ore material, although it has not yet been widely used, will probably become equally important as it is better understood.

Residual soil anomalies related to the weathering of suboutcropping deposits are normally of very local extent. Nevertheless, despite the consequent high cost per unit-area, soil surveys have been widely used in reconnaissance because of their relatively high dependability. In the Soviet Union systematic soil sampling, or "metallometric" surveys, are applied as a matter of routine to all areas that are being mapped on the regional scale, either geologically or geophysically. More usually, however, soil sampling is applied in detailed surveys in areas where the ground is already known to be promising.

For the most part, useful biogeochemical and geobotanical anomalies are similarly localized in the immediate vicinity of the deposit and are most useful in detailed surveys. Of the two methods, geobotany has the wider scope in reconnaissance, largely on account of the rapidity with which observations can be made and the fact that no sampling or analysis is required.

Detailed Surveys. In order to localize the bedrock metal source with the greatest possible precision, a relatively high sampling density is usually required. On grounds of cost alone, therefore, the application of detailed surveys is mostly restricted to limited areas of particular interest, selected on the basis of other geochemical, geophysical, or geological information. To be most useful, the anomalies should be well defined and developed in close proximity to the ore.

Systematic sampling of residual soil in search of superjacent anomalies has been outstandingly successful in detailed exploration. The method has been widely used under a variety of conditions for locating suboutcropping deposits of many kinds, appraising geophysical anomalies and other features of interest, tracing vein extensions, and in property examinations. The points in favor of residual soil sampling are its dependability and simplicity.

Much the same can be said of soil surveys as a method of locating superjacent anomalies in transported overburden. Here the dependability factor is much lower, inasmuch as deposits concealed by a blanket of transported cover are not so consistently accompanied by readily detectable superjacent anomalies. Nevertheless, the dependability can often be improved by deep sampling, though with a consequent steep rise in cost. It may, therefore, be more profitable to confine soil surveying in areas of transported overburden to small target areas already delimited by other cheaper methods, such as seepage reconnaissance or airborne geophysical surveys.

Plant sampling is in general applicable only in problems where for one reason or another soil sampling is unsatisfactory. The erratic distribution of individuals of the appropriate plant species together with the relatively erratic distribution of anomalous metal from one plant individual to another serves to reduce the homogeneity of plant anomalies as compared with soil anomalies. Furthermore, biogenic soil anomalies tend to be the more homogeneous because of the accumulation, and hence the averaging, of metal derived from the individual plants of many generations. Plant sampling also presents certain technical problems not encountered with soil sampling. Personnel trained in recognizing plant species are needed for plant work, whereas soil sampling can be carried out by relatively untrained labor. More highly specialized supervision is necessary in a biogeochemical survey. The collecting, shipping, drying, pulverizing, and ashing of plant samples are all procedures that are either much easier or that are completely eliminated with soil samples. Virtually the only circumstances where plant sampling is technically more satisfactory than soil sampling are in the winter in snow-covered or permafrost areas and in areas where for one reason or another soil is absent.

Primary geochemical patterns that can be used as ore guides in detailed surveys include leakage anomalies and primary aureoles. Leakage anomalies may be sought by sampling the cap rocks or the residual soil derived therefrom. Dispersion patterns developed in the wall rock of the ore are particularly applicable in detailed surveys underground, where rock sampling may be used to detect proximity to ore during crosscutting and drilling. Although primary anomalies have shown some spectacular associations with ore, their application in commercial exploration has not been widespread.

Resolution of Detailed Surveys. The ultimate purpose of all geological, geophysical, or geochemical methods is to serve as a guide in the physical exploration operations of trenching, pitting, drilling, or underground work that are necessary to establish grades, tonnage, and viability of a deposit. Geological features such as vein projections and the extensions or intersections of well-defined structural features have long been accepted as guides in laying out physical exploration campaigns. Under certain conditions, mineral zoning may indicate favorable ground for drilling in depth. The apices of glacial fans are sometimes so clearly defined that sites for subsurface exploration by pitting or drilling can be selected immediately. Ground geophysical surveys, particularly since 1950, have played an increasingly important part in providing targets for the final phase of exploration. Of the geochemical methods, detailed soil surveys most commonly provide the resolving power necessary for pinpointing targets in areas where superjacent anomalies are developed. Under certain favorable conditions, such as in Rhodesia, geobotanical observations may also serve as an immediate prelude to physical exploration. With the exception of some wall-rock aureoles, hydrothermal dispersion patterns are not as a rule directly useful in siting drill holes. Leakage patterns, in particular, usually need to be supplemented by geological or geophysical information in order to determine the target in depth.

In general terms, irrespective of the nature of the principal ore guide employed, it is invariably wise to seek confirmatory evidence from all possible sources before embarking on the costly ultimate phase of drilling.

16-6. Organization and Operations

The best kind of organization for a geochemical exploration survey depends not so much on the nature of the problem as on the scale of operations. At one extreme is the quick reconnaissance appraisal of a prospect involving only a limited number of samples and simple analytical equipment. At the other extreme, large scale operations involving comprehensive exploration over an extensive area may well require a complex organization comprising numerous field teams, centralized and mobile laboratories and the services of specialized personnel. An enterprise of this kind presents a major problem in coordination. An example of the integration of geochemical exploration operations within a mining company is illustrated in Figure 16-4.

Every geochemical survey organization, irrespective of its scale, is based on three main functional units: (1) the field party, engaged primarily in sampling, (2) the laboratory, and (3) the technical direction responsible for decisions on personnel, technique, operation, and interpretation of the results. The detail of organization within the functional units is largely a matter of circumstance and common

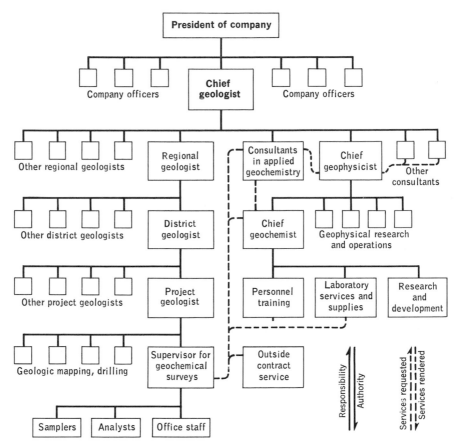

Fig. 16-1. Example of organization of applied geochemistry within administrative structure of a mining company.

sense. In the following paragraphs, however, attention is drawn to a few of the most critical factors in the organization of geochemical exploration.

Field Operations. In a sampling program, maximum efficiency requires that lower grade personnel be used in preference to professional geologists wherever possible. Most operations in a systematic sampling program can be carried out by teams of local labor working under the supervision of trained field assistants. In some surveys, however, proper selection of the material to be sampled and adequate recording of information needed in later interpretation may demand the experience and training of a member of the junior professional staff. The most rigid systematization of the sampling procedure is, of course, essential in order to ensure adequate reliability. Fullest efficiency also requires that all nonessential operations be eliminated and that the time required for each remaining operation be reduced to a minimum. Under no circumstances should time be wasted in unnecessarily precise surveying. The exact location of negative samples is of no interest. All that is required is enough information that any site can be revisited if it eventually proves to be anomalous. Productivity depends very largely on the time taken in traveling between sample points. Before a decision is made on the mode of operation of a sampling survey, careful estimates should be made of the relative combined cost of transport plus personnel time for travel on foot, by jeep, by helicopter, and by any other available means. Not infrequently, such studies show that an apparently expensive system of transport may actually be the cheapest in terms of cost per sample site.

Laboratory. In the analytical phases of a geochemical survey, the principal problems are: (1) location of the laboratory, (2) the nature and number of the personnel employed, and (3) systematization of the laboratory routine.

The promptness with which analytical data are required varies with the nature of the operation. In an orientation survey preparatory to laying out a program, data are often needed within a day or so from the time of collecting the sample, and can best be provided by a mobile analytical unit at the field camp. When following up anomalies already detected by drainage reconnaissance, it is also very desirable to be able to carry out determinations on the spot. Most of the colorimetric procedures listed in Table 3-3 can, if necessary, be set up under crude field conditions, and a few of the procedures are even adaptable for use at the sample site. Mobile spectrographic laboratories have also been designed for field use.

For large routine surveys, however, where there is no call for immediate day-to-day decisions, it is usually best to ship the samples to a central laboratory. In general, the most efficient, reliable, and economical analytical work is done in an established laboratory. The centralized laboratory may, if desirable, be supplemented by a forward field laboratory, where samples can be scanned rapidly before being sent back for more reliable or comprehensive analysis.

For most of the analytical techniques used in geochemical prospecting the bulk of the cost is salaries and wages. Experience has shown that when they are properly trained and organized, nonprofessional operators can be trusted with the entire laboratory routine. In many African laboratories, for example, sample preparation and analysis is performed by locally recruited African labor, working under trained nonprofessional supervisors. The services of a professional chemist are, of course, necessary for analytical development work and for any technical difficulties that may arise in the course of operations. The laboratory should be organized to handle about 30 percent productivity over and above the anticipated sampling rate, in order to cope with check samples, repeat determinations, and contingencies.

The reliability of routine laboratory operations may be checked and controlled by repeated analysis of selected samples at periodic intervals. Good control of analytical precision can be maintained with systematic replicate analysis of (1) samples selected at random from the previous day's work, (2) all samples exceeding the threshold value, and (3) samples from a prepared series, as described by Craven (1954).

Supervision. The interpretation of the data of a geochemical prospecting survey in terms of possible mineral deposits is fundamentally a geological rather than a chemical problem. For this reason it is essential that the direction of geochemical surveys should always be the responsibility of one who is first an experienced exploration geologist, and second a man with sound training in geochemical techniques. His responsibilities will include (1) orientation to establish both field and laboratory technique, (2) maintenance of technical efficiency and coordination throughout the operation, (3) interpretation of data, and (4) prompt follow-up of anomalies and preparation of recommendations for further work.

Larger organizations, such as the one illustrated in Figure 16-4, may have their own research and development section; more usually, however, commercial exploration relies on the published literature and the specialized services of consultants for the development and application of new concepts and techniques. It goes without saying that in every case there must be the closest continuing liaison between the geochemical staff and all other technical groups that may be concerned in the exploration.

SELECTED COLLECTIONS OF EXPLORATION CASE HISTORIES

International Geological Congress, XX Session (1956, 1958)
International Geological Congress, XXI Session (1960)
Sixth Commonwealth Mining and Metallurgical Congress (1957)
United Nations (1956, 1958)
Krasnikov (1957)

CHAPTER 17

CASE HISTORIES OF INTEGRATED EXPLORATION PROGRAMS

The following three case histories have been selected for detailed discussion because they appear to illustrate particularly clearly the advantages of combining a variety of geological, geophysical, and geochemical ore guides into a well-balanced system of mineral exploration. Although these examples represent areas where climates and operational conditions are strikingly different, the same basic philosophy underlies the exploration program used in each area.

17-1. New Brunswick, Eastern Canada

In New Brunswick and the Gaspé peninsula of eastern Canada, the authors of this book participated in an exploration enterprise that started with a regional reconnaissance and was followed successively with detailed work and physical exploration. In 1954 and 1955, Selco Exploration Co. Ltd. of Toronto sponsored a program of geochemical stream-sediment reconnaissance that led to the delineation of a number of local areas of interest. In one of these areas, known as the Charlotte prospect, the New Jersey Zinc Company (Canada) Ltd. has subsequently carried out detailed exploratory drilling leading to the discovery of a base-metal sulfide deposit. The authors are indebted to T. Parks of Selco Exploration Co. and William Callahan of the New Jersey Zinc Company for permission to use the following information.

Description of Reconnaissance Area. Following is a summary of the significant features of the areas covered by the reconnaissance survey.

1. Relief: New Brunswick, flat to moderate; Gaspé, moderate to rugged with maximum elevations in central Gaspé of more than 4000 feet.

2. Drainage: Well developed.

3. Climate: Northern temperate, with annual rainfall approximately 40 inches. Average temperature: January, 15° F, July 65° F.

4. Vegetation: Secondary growth, largely broadleaf trees with scattered conifers that are harvested for pulpwood.

5. Surface features: Although the entire area was covered by continental glaciation, much of it still retains a fairly deep cover of residual soil and weathered rock that is essentially in place. Freely drained soils show well-developed podzol profiles.

6. Sulfide mineralization: In Gaspé, disseminated Cu deposits in country rock adjoining intrusive stocks, and coarse-grained galena-sphalerite fracture fillings in Middle Paleozoic shales. In New Brunswick, very fine-grained massive Fe sulfide deposits containing sphalerite and galena as the principal ore minerals.

The first major discoveries made in the Bathurst district of New Brunswick in 1952 and 1953, inasmuch as they had not been disturbed by any previous mining or development work, provided especially suitable areas for orientation experiments. Table 17-1

TABLE 17-1. Results of Orientation Survey with Cold-Extractable Heavy Metals in Stream Sediments as a Reconnaissance Ore Guide in New Brunswick

Deposit	Observed Length of Anomaly[a] (miles)	End of Anomaly Defined by
Heath Steele Mine	6	Background values at 8 mi
Anacon Mine	4	Marginal indication at 5 mi
Brunswick Mine	4	Confluence of stream with large river
Pioneer Prospect	4	Confluence with contaminated stream
Nash Creek Prospect	2.4	Ocean
Keymet Mine	1.0	Background values at 1.5 mi

Source: Hawkes et al. (1956).
[a]Defined as length of stream course in which the exchangeable heavy-metal content exceeds 10 ppm.

summarizes the results of this program of orientation work with stream-sediment analysis as a method of reconnaissance exploration. In 1954, drainage reconnaissance by stream-sediment sampling was carried out on an operational basis over most of New Brunswick and the Gaspé Peninsula. This part of the program was planned for maximum coverage in the time available, with only minor consideration for the relative geologic favorability of the various parts of the area. Sampling, therefore, was confined almost entirely to passable roads and major waterways. During this season, a total of thirty major anomalies were found, one of which led to the development of the Charlotte prospect described below.

In 1955, reconnaissance was confined to areas chosen for geologic favorability, principally in the Bathurst district of northern New Brunswick. A review of the geologic setting of the known deposits and major geochemical anomalies showed that, with only minor exceptions, no important deposits occurred (1) in areas underlain by predominantly sedimentary rocks, (2) within bodies of plutonic

rocks, and (3) in areas of low magnetic relief as shown on the aero-
magnetic map series of the Geological Survey of Canada. A composite map showing the distribution of these controlling features so
far as they were known at the time was prepared and used as a guide
in selecting areas for geochemical reconnaissance (Figure 17-1).

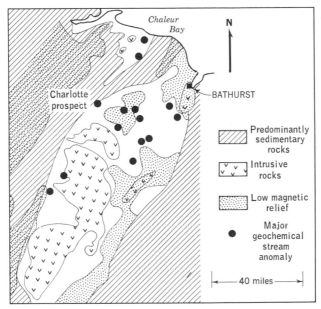

Fig. 17-1. Geologic favorability map of Bathurst district, New
Brunswick. After Hawkes *et al.* (1956).

Table 17-2 presents an operational summary of the geochemical
reconnaissance work of the 1954 and 1955 seasons.

Confirmation and follow-up of reconnaissance anomalies was based
mainly on sampling stream sediments and seepages. Where results
were favorable, the ground was staked and then examined in detail
by geologic mapping, soil sampling and electromagnetic surveying.
Table 17-3 summarizes the results of follow-up work of this kind
carried out at the five principal anomalies. Of these five, the Charlotte prospect was explored most thoroughly and will therefore be
described in detail.

Detailed Survey—Charlotte Prospect.   Following is a summary of
the principal features of the Charlotte prospect.

1. Relief: Moderate, ridge crests 500 to 1000 feet above surrounding
valleys.
2. Drainage: Well developed.

TABLE 17-2. Operational Summary of Geochemical Reconnaissance,
New Brunswick and Gaspé, 1954–1955

	1954	1955	Total
Reconnaissance survey			
Area, square miles	27,000	6,000	33,000
Number of sample sites	3,266	1,671	4,937
Number of man-days, field[a]	184	131	315
Number of anomalies found	30	13	43
Follow-up surveys			
Number of man-days[a]	230	61	291
Number of recommended properties	4	5	9
Analytical work			
Number of samples	9,200	6,100	15,300
Number of man-days	305	224	529
Office work, administration			
Number of man-days	276	306	582
Equipment			
Trailer laboratory	1	1	
Canoes, boats	1	2	
Cars	3	3	

Source: Hawkes et al. (1956).
[a]Figures for number of man-days are for technical personnel only exclusive of local labor hired as field assistants.

3. Vegetation: Mixed coniferous and broadleaf trees.

4. Geology: Gently dipping and moderately folded mid-Paleozoic volcanic and sedimentary rocks.

5. Sulfide mineralization: None known at start of survey.

6. Weathering and overburden: Outcrops generally confined to ridge crests. A common type of overburden consists largely of angular fragments of rocks of local derivation, indicating little glacial movement. Freely drained soils show characteristic podzol profile.

Strong geochemical reconnaissance anomalies in two streams both led into the same general area. A detailed exploration program was carried out in the parts of the area where the reconnaissance anomalies were the most intense. This work consisted of a geochemical soil survey for Cu, Pb, and Zn, and an electromagnetic survey of an area of about 600 acres. Five drill holes were put down and traces of base-metal sulfides found in all holes. The most highly mineralized intersection consisted of about 15 feet of 3 percent combined Pb and Zn in zone A in Figure 17-2.

At this point (1957) the property was optioned to the New Jersey Zinc Exploration Company (Canada) Ltd. The following details of subsequent exploratory work were kindly supplied by E. A. Goranson and William Callahan of that company.

Preliminary investigation by New Jersey Zinc involved an airborne electromagnetic survey on $\frac{1}{8}$-mile spacing under contract with

TABLE 17-3. Data on Principal Anomalies Found by Geochemical Reconnaissance, New Brunswick and Gaspé, 1954–1955

| | Geochemical Indications | | | | |
Anomaly	Metals	Source Areas	Geophysical Indications	Geology	Mineralization
Charlotte, Restigouche Co., New Brunswick	Zn Pb Cu	Distributed throughout area 12,000 ft long and 4000 ft wide	Strong electromagnetic indications apparently unrelated to mineralization	Altered pyroclastics and sedimentary rocks	Massive pyrite containing fine-grained base-metal sulfides
Jacquet River, Restigouche Co., New Brunswick	Zn Pb	At least three separate sources in zone 5 mi long	Well-defined resistivity anomalies indicative of mineralized shear zones	Rhyolite and rhyolitic pyroclastics	Pyrite, sphalerite, galena and chalcopyrite in mineralized shear zones
Lemieux Township, Gaspé-Nord Co., Quebec	Zn Pb Cu	Restricted to three well-defined spring areas	Not surveyed	Sedimentary rocks intruded by dikes of syenite	Unknown
Mount Pleasant Charlotte Co., New Brunswick	Cu Zn Pb	Distributed throughout area 2 mi long and 1 mi wide	Essentially featureless electromagnetic pattern	Altered rhyolytic tuffs and breccias	Small lenses of high-grade sphalerite; pervasive disseminations of fine-grained sulfides with fluorite and cassiterite
O'Hearn's Brook, Northumberland Co., New Brunswick	Zn Pb	Distributed principally along single 2800-ft zone	Featureless electromagnetic pattern	Quartz-sericite schists	Unknown

Source: Hawkes et al. (1956).

Aerophysics of Canada Ltd., in the summer of 1956, prior to optioning the property in 1957.

Surface exploration consisted of laying out an east-west baseline and cutting north-south picket lines at 400-foot intervals for control purposes, and conducting geological mapping, soil sampling and testing, prospecting and some digging, and electromagnetic surveying over the cut lines. Geological mapping consisted mainly of examining

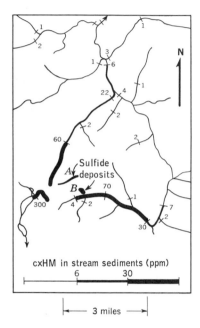

Fig. 17-2. Follow-up pattern in stream sediments, Charlotte property, New Brunswick. Data on minus-80-mesh fraction. After Solow (1959). Based on a map by Max Gschwind in the February 1959 issue of *Fortune*, by special permission.

float, as outcrops are very sparse, and the resulting map showed the general distribution of the rock types consisting of east-west bands of metamorphosed sediments, tuffs, and volcanics of Ordovician age, succeeded on the north by less metamorphosed sediments and volcanics of Silurian and Devonian ages. Several soil anomalies were found, some new and some coinciding with earlier located ones. A number of electromagnetic conductors were outlined with the more continuous ones suggesting graphitic or carbonaceous horizons. Little coincidence was obtained between the two types of anomalies.

In the fall of 1958, two of the more prominent soil anomalies (*A* and *B* on Figure 17-2) and two electromagnetic anomalies were investigated by surface diamond drilling. Interesting amounts of base metals were intersected in the soil anomaly areas, and graphite and carbonaceous material in the electromagnetic anomaly areas. Self-potential surveys were then conducted over parts of the soil anomalies, and a self-potential anomaly of -300 millivolts was obtained in the southeasterly soil anomaly area (B). Further drilling in 1958 in this area indicated a massive sulfide body carrying base metals within altered acidic volcanic rocks.

Surface diamond drilling was resumed on the property in 1959, and an ore body was outlined consisting mainly of fine-grained massive pyrite with sphalerite, galena, and some chalcopyrite, pencil-shaped in form and plunging from 12° to 15° to the north. It apparently outcrops under 10 to 15 feet of surficial material under and south of the stream in which the earlier reconnaissance survey had shown the initial silt values. Fragments of oxidized sulfides were found in 1959 in the stream near this suboutcrop.

The ore body strikes about N33° W, has a strike length of about 1500 feet, widths up to 300 feet, an average thickness of about 35 feet, and occurs in altered acidic lavas, locally termed dacites, and minor tuffs, with some more acidic interbands to the north. The structure of the deposit is as yet not known.

From drilling, done mainly on 100-foot centers, the ore body is estimated to contain over 1,000,000 tons averaging about 31 percent iron, 39 percent sulfur, 0.034 ounce gold, 2.92 ounce silver, 0.35 percent copper, 5.49 percent lead, and 6.76 percent zinc.

17–2. Northern Rhodesia

Details of the following case history illustrating the successive stages of a geochemical soil survey were kindly supplied by F. H. Cornwall and are published with the permission of the Chartered Exploration Company.

The system of exploration employed by the Chartered Exploration Company presents an excellent illustration of the phased program. The object of the program is to assess the mineral potential of concession areas totaling 120,000 square miles. In the first instance, regional geological maps are prepared based on air photographs and previous geological reports supplemented by geological reconnaissance as required. From this information, the more favorable areas are selected for prospecting. Primary reconnaissance is then carried out by airborne geophysical surveys (magnetic, electromagnetic, and radioactivity) and/or geochemical reconnaissance by drainage or soil sampling, according to the possible types of deposit and the nature of the terrain. Anomalous indications obtained by any of these methods are followed up by detailed geological and geochemical soil-survey methods. After first delimiting the anomalous area in the soil, closely spaced traverses are run to locate the peak values. The axis of the anomaly is then investigated by pitting, followed by drilling, in the event of encouraging results being obtained.

Physical features of the area:

1. Relief: Essentially flat-lying, peneplain topography. Elevation 4500 feet.

2. Drainage: Open, dendritic pattern of streams and dambos or vleis (seasonal swamps).

3. Climate: Subtropical, seasonal. Annual rainfall 45 inches.

4. Vegetation: Thin forest and grassland.

5. Geology: Sedimentary series of Katanga shales, sandstones, limestones, dolomites, phyllites, and quartzites with minor intrusions of syenite.

Tabular deposits of disseminated copper sulfides in sedimentary series. Weathering extends to a depth of 150 to 200 feet. Sulfides completely oxidized down to 150 feet.

6. Overburden: Deep residual cover over entire area. Fully to partially developed lateritic profiles, 20 to 30 feet thick, on interfluves. Gley profiles in seasonal swamps.

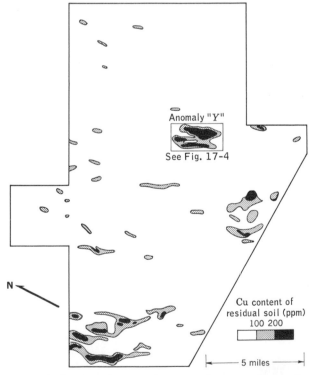

Fig. 17-3. Results of reconnaissance soil survey for copper, Mumbwa area, Northern Rhodesia. Data on minus-80-mesh fraction.

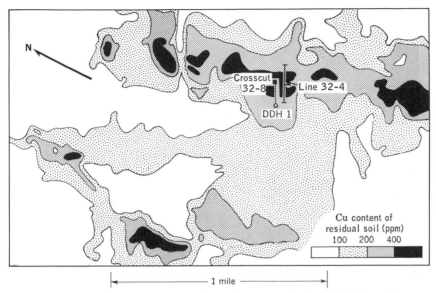

Fig. 17-4. Detail soil grid, anomaly "Y", Mumbwa area, Northern Rhodesia. Data on minus-80-mesh fraction. For location, see Figure 17-3.

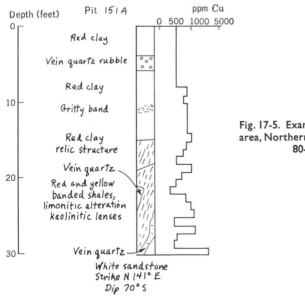

Fig. 17-5. Example of pit profile, Mumbwa area, Northern Rhodesia. Data on minus-80-mesh fraction.

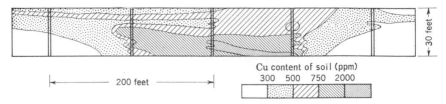

Cu content of soil (ppm)

300   500   750   2000

|← —————— 200 feet —————— →|

Fig. 17-6. Example of pit-profile section, Mumbwa area, Northern Rhodesia. Data on minus-80-mesh fraction.

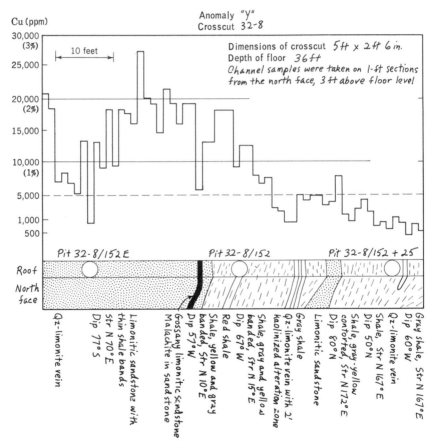

Fig. 17-7. Example of geological and geochemical section along crosscut, Mumbwa area, Northern Rhodesia. Data on minus-80-mesh fraction.

Geochemical Soil Surveys.   The initial soil grid covered an area of about 170 square miles. Samples were taken at 18-inch depth at intervals of 200 feet on lines 2000 feet apart. Analysis of the minus-80-mesh fraction for Cu by dithizone following KHSO$_4$ fusion disclosed several anomalies, some of which were quite extensive (Figure 17-3).

The results obtained on Anomaly "Y" by close sampling at 100 feet intervals on lines 200 feet apart are shown in Figure 17-4. The axis of the anomaly thus defined was investigated by pitting (Figures 17-5 and 17-6).

The plotted analytical results of channel samples from these pits indicated the approximate position of the suboutcropping mineral

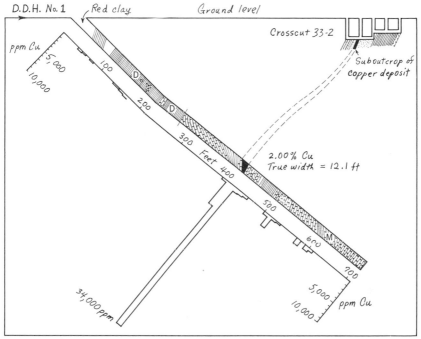

Fig. 17-8. Example of geological and geochemical drill-hole section, Mumbwa area, Northern Rhodesia.

horizon, which was specifically located by crosscutting between selected pits (Figure 17-7).

The structure and lithology were mapped by geological examination of the highly weathered rocks exposed in the pits and crosscuts. Drilling based on the geological and geochemical information disclosed 2 percent Cu over a width of 12 feet (Figure 17-8).

Technical Details. Reconnaissance sample lines were run by teams of eight to ten Africans under the supervision of a European sampler. A normal day's sampling for a sampling team on reconnaissance soil sampling is eight line miles or 200 samples at 200-foot intervals.

The samples were prepared and analyzed in a field laboratory by a team of about ten Africans under the supervision of a European laboratory assistant. Approximately 400 to 600 samples were analyzed in this laboratory daily.

17–3. Cebu, Republic of Philippines

An area of 7 square miles on the island of Cebu was investigated in detail by geological, geophysical, and geochemical surveys. The authors are greatly indebted to the Newmont Mining Corporation and the Atlas Consolidated Mining and Development Corporation for permission to publish this extract of information compiled by J. A. Coope.

Description of area:

1. Relief: Rugged, variations up to 1000 feet. Maximum elevation 2300 feet.
2. Drainage: Numerous deeply incised tributary streams feeding two main river systems.
3. Climate: Humid tropical; annual rainfall averages 60 inches; indistinctly seasonal.
4. Vegetation: Originally tropical forest, now mainly replaced by a secondary growth of tall grass and scrub following native cultivation.
5. Geology: Irregular stocklike diorite bodies intrusive into volcanic series of andesites, tuffs, etc.; both are Mesozoic and are overlain unconformably by Tertiary limestones and coal measures which cap the higher ground surrounding the field area.
6. Sulfide mineralization: Chalcopyrite with minor bornite, the principal Cu minerals, are distributed throughout the Mesozoic rocks, but concentrations of possible economic interest are present as veinlets and disseminations of porphyry copper type only within or closely associated with silicification in a coarse-grained micaceous facies of the diorite. Chalcopyrite, with sphalerite, also occurs as narrow veins in the Mesozoic rocks. Molybdenite associated with pyrite in gypsum veins, does not appear to be closely related to the occurrence of chalcopyrite. Pyrite is the most common sulfide, and drilling and geophysical (induced polarization) results have indicated that it occurs in all rocks, sometimes making up to 8 percent of the volume in the volcanic formations adjacent to the intrusive diorite bodies. Magnetite is disseminated throughout the dioritic and volcanic series.
7. Weathering: In many areas, weathering extends to more than 100 feet. Oxidation of sulfides is more variable. According to locality, either leached rock, oxidized minerals (including malachite and chrysocolla) or fresh sulfides may occur at surface.
8. Overburden: Dominantly residual, with base-of-slope colluvium; soil creep, slumping, and landslip are active. Depth variable, commonly 4 to 6 feet increasing to 20 feet and more toward the base of slope. Generally immature soils, profiles often truncated by erosion.

Geochemical Drainage Reconnaissance. Systematic sampling of active stream sediments, followed by analysis of the sediment samples for total Cu, was successful in outlining several distinctly anomalous areas in which the values exceed 300 ppm Cu (Figure 17-9). Although background was established at 100 ppm, it was found that anomalies in which values ranged from 150 to 300 ppm Cu were related to no more than insignificant mineralization. The length of the significant dispersion patterns ranged from 1000 feet to over a mile.

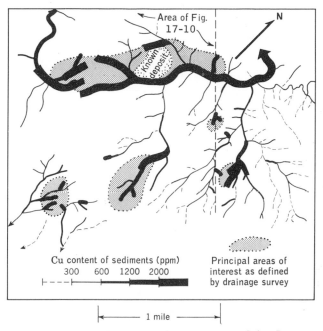

Fig. 17-9. Results of stream sediment survey, Cebu Project, Republic of Philippines.

The samples were also analyzed for cxCu and cxZn. A belt was disclosed wherein the cxZn content ranged from 20 to 500 ppm as compared with 2 to 20 ppm over the rest of the area. All the known vein-type mineralization occurred within this belt.

Interpretation of the cxCu:Cu ratio was complicated by marked variations in the pH of the stream waters, which ranged from about 3.5 to 8.5. The acidity was found to depend primarily on the amount and intensity of oxidation of pyrite; the more alkaline streams were draining calcareous rocks.

Geochemical Soil Survey. Systematic soil sampling was carried out along ridge crests and spurs and by close traversing in the principal areas of interest. Background for the area was established at

50 to 100 ppm Cu, and significantly anomalous areas were delimited by the 300 ppm contour (Figure 17-10). Within the anomalies, peak values ranged from 1000 ppm to 6000 ppm and more. Detailed follow-up by close sampling and pitting showed that the anomaly peaks were in part related to metal accumulation in seepage areas at

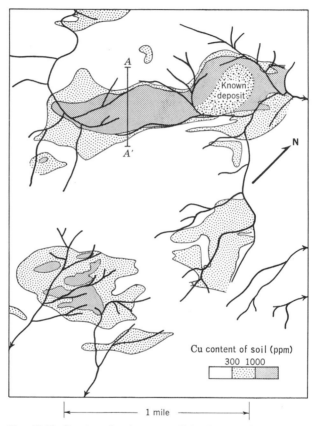

Fig. 17-10. Results of soil survey, Cebu Project, Republic of Philippines. Data on minus-80-mesh fraction.

the base of slope, in part to the presence of oxide Cu enrichment, and in part to variations in the tenor of the primary mineralization. High cxCu:Cu ratios were recorded in seepage areas and in profiles where oxide Cu minerals occurred. Conspicuous blue-green precipitates of Cu salts were found at some seepages.

Analysis for Zn showed that feebly anomalous values of 250 ppm Zn accompanied Cu in the significant Cu areas, while over Cu-Zn veins the Zn anomalies were more pronounced.

Mo, on the other hand, was present only in background amounts (about 1 ppm) within the areas of significantly anomalous Cu, but rose to 280 ppm near the boundaries of the Cu anomalies and over pyritic zones surrounding the copper mineralization.

Technical Details. The sampling and analytical routines were based on the results of preliminary orientation surveys. Sediment samples were collected at 500- to 1000-foot intervals and at all stream confluences. Soil samples were taken at 18-inch depth at intervals of 100 feet along the traverses. All samples were dried and sieved to minus-80-mesh. Analysis was carried out using the following standard colorimetric tests: biquinoline procedure for total Cu; dithiol for Mo; dithizone in benzene for total Zn, cxZn, and cxCu.

Philippine labor was used for all sampling and analytical routine. In difficult country, three 2-man teams could collect 100 samples per day. Sediment sampling was carried out by one team under supervision, at a rate of up to 55 samples per day.

Four local men were trained to operate the laboratory; one was engaged on sample preparation, two on total metal determinations, and one on cold-extraction tests. The maximum daily productivity was 245 determinations.

Including setting up, training, orientation, and detailed follow-up by pitting, the entire geochemical operation was completed in 7 months, of which rather less than half was spent on systematic soil and sediment surveys. A total of 13,420 analytical determinations were carried out on 7200 samples.

Integration with Other Methods. The geochemical surveys were carried out in conjunction with contemporaneous geological and geophysical surveys. In the early stages of the program, the geological and geochemical reconnaissance coverages were carried out independently, while geophysical methods were used to explore an area of promising geological indications. Following the termination of the primary geological and geochemical (stream-sediment) surveys, geophysical programs were outlined to examine thoroughly the possibly significant areas defined. Geological information and principles were carefully considered when interpretation of geochemical and geophysical anomalies was made.

Because of the size and nature of the disseminated deposits being sought, selected anomalies were drilled systematically without special regard to the distribution of peak values. Core examination provided valuable information concerning the distribution of sulfide minerals within the various rock facies, and, supplemented by detailed geological examination, further conclusions concerning the significance of geophysical and geochemical anomalies could be made.

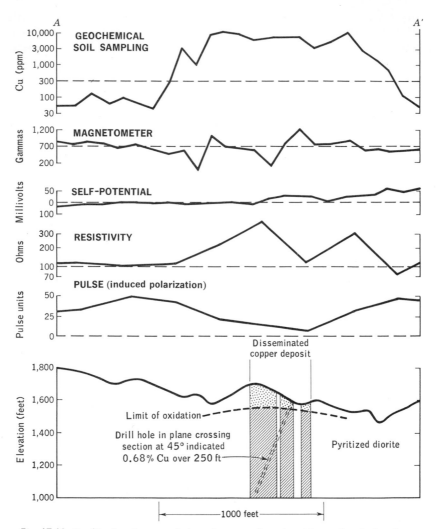

Fig. 17-11. Profile showing correlation of copper deposit with geochemical and geophysical data, Cebu Project, Republic of Philippines. Data on minus-80-mesh fraction. For location see A-A', Figure 17-10.

These conclusions were then considered in the evaluation of undrilled anomalies.

Results.   Copper sulfide mineralization was discovered in the bedrock beneath all the geochemical soil anomalies which were drilled. The mineralization was variable, however, confirming the results of detailed follow-up methods, and the amount of Cu in the soil was often twice as much as the amount of the same metal in the unweathered bedrock at depth, suggesting a concentration process in near-surface horizons. The presence of mineralization of ore grade is reported beneath the largest and most significant geochemical anomaly. This anomaly is characterized by many soil values greater than 6000 ppm Cu, although relevant figures on the size and over-all grade of the occurrence are not available.

The degree of correlation between the geochemical and geophysical results on a single traverse across this deposit are shown in Figure 17-11. Over the area as a whole, the geophysical results were influenced by the distribution and oxidation of barren pyrite mineralization, the presence of which does not seriously interfere with the geochemical interpretation.

A diamond-drill hole, collared in an area where Cu and Zn anomalies overlap, proved the presence of sphalerite and chalcopyrite at depth. Small amounts of galena occurred with the sphalerite in veins up to 1 inch in width. The chalcopyrite occurred as disseminations throughout the core, and also in association with the Pb and Zn sulfides.

Comparison of the geochemical and the final geological maps indicates that there is a close correlation throughout the area between the position and extent of the larger geochemical soil anomalies and the distribution of the facies of the diorite with which the disseminated Cu mineralization is closely associated.

CHAPTER 18

CURRENT RESEARCH AND FUTURE TRENDS

In bringing this book on the applications of geochemistry in mineral exploration to a close, it is perhaps instructive to speculate on just what particular aspects of the subject are the most likely to change and develop in the foreseeable future. To a certain degree, of course, the growth of any area of science or technology will depend on factors that cannot be forecast, such as the spectacular discovery of some new basic principle or the unexpected development of some new research tool. At the same time, a reasonably dependable short-term forecast can be made by projecting present trends insofar as they can be determined.

The future of geochemistry in mineral exploration does not depend alone on "applied" research that is directed specifically toward the solution of industrial problems. Advances in both pure geochemistry and in other fields of applied geochemistry, together with changes in the technology and economics of the minerals industry, all are likely to play a major role in future developments. Conversely, the experience gained in perfecting the art of geochemical prospecting will almost certainly contribute materially to progress in the other specialized fields of pure geochemistry. A brief summary of current research both in geochemical prospecting and in allied subjects is therefore presented as a background against which to view the future trend.

18–1. Current Research in Geochemical Prospecting

Coordinated research activity in geochemical prospecting is divided principally between private mining company groups and the government-supported laboratories listed in Table 1-2. To this co-ordinated work should be added the independent research conducted by the staff and advanced students of a substantial number of academic institutions throughout the world.

Primary geochemical dispersion in all its ramifications is under

348

intensive examination by many diverse research groups. In Canada, trace analysis of systematically collected rock samples is being studied as a means of determining broad-scale geochemical variations. In Rhodesia, regional geochemical maps showing the distribution of a comprehensive range of trace metals in the fine-grained fraction of modern stream sediments are being prepared for the purpose of bringing out patterns related to primary geochemical provinces. In Malaya, the distribution of minor elements in stream sediments is being studied as a means of establishing district variations within a well-defined Sn province. In several areas, studies of the areal distribution of minor elements in the individual mineral phases of plutonic rocks show what appear to be strong positive correlations with hydrothermal mineralization in the surrounding areas. Particularly significant data are being obtained for Cu and Zn in the ferromagnesian minerals of plutonic rocks. Smaller-scale primary patterns of pathfinder elements closely associated with mineralization are also being investigated as an aid in detecting the presence of blind deposits.

Anomalies in residual overburden continue to receive particular attention. Present emphasis is on the behavior in weathering of the less common ore metals and associated elements, and on improving criteria for interpreting the results of soil-survey data. In addition, both private and governmental groups are carrying out orientation work directed toward determining the applicability of standard methods of residual-soil surveying in areas where they have not previously been tried.

Anomalies in transported overburden are of particular importance because in many areas they are providing our first opportunity for economical exploration for deposits hidden beneath post-ore cover. In the glaciated terrain of Scandinavia and Canada, experimental field work is showing that well-defined dispersion fans detectable by trace analysis of the fine-grained fraction of glacial till are the rule rather than the exception. In the peaty material of organic swamps, epigenetic patterns developed by the upward movement of metal-rich solutions from suboutcropping ore also appear to be far more common than was originally suspected. In the desert terrain of the western United States, epigenetic dispersion patterns in the gravels of pediment areas are being investigated. Gaseous dispersion of Hg in the interstitial air of post-ore gravels and wind-blown sand is under consideration as a guide to Hg-rich sulfide deposits in the bedrock.

Anomalies in surface water and water-borne sediment are the subject of particularly intensive study by a number of research and development groups because of the extreme economy of the drainage survey as a method of geochemical reconnaissance. After a period of relatively little activity, the metal content of ground and surface water is again attracting attention, and current field experiments in North America suggest that certain components of natural water may be extremely diagnostic of mineralization in the vicinity. Orientation work with both total and cold-extractable metals in stream sediment is continually extending the known fields of applicability of drainage-sediment surveys in mineral reconnaissance.

Vegetation as a guide to ore, except for the outstanding work of one or two laboratories, is not receiving the concerted attention of research workers that the other geochemical methods have enjoyed. With growing recognition of the potentially important role of botanical methods in exploration, there will undoubtedly be a corresponding increase in the scale of geobotanical research.

Fundamental problems in systematizing and interpreting large volumes of geochemical field data are currently under study, particularly in commercial laboratories. These studies are leading to an increased application of the principles of statistics to problems in data handling. A parallel trend is the search for additional independent criteria to assist in appraising geochemical anomalies. This is reflected in the growing volume of research work on the factors that influence dispersion and in an increased awareness of the importance of pathfinder elements, particularly Se, Sb, As, Bi, Hg, Ag, and Mo, that are associated with ore deposits and that can be used as auxiliary guides to economic mineralization.

Methods of trace analysis used in geochemical prospecting are undergoing continual improvement. New chemical methods are being developed for the semiquantitative determination of those elements where adequate analytical procedures have not previously been available. A substantial amount of effort is also being devoted to the application of relatively new instrumental techniques to the routine semiquantitative analysis of large volumes of samples. New or improved techniques particularly in emission spectrometry, X-ray fluorescence analysis, and atomic absorption are currently under active study and development. An increased application of natural or induced nuclear reactions will probably grow out of current research in gamma-ray spectrometry. This type of work has already led to new instrumental methods for Be and Hg.

18–2. Current Research in Pure Geochemistry

The level of research activity in pure geochemistry has increased in recent years probably faster than in any other field of earth science. The sudden expansion of general interest in this field is evidenced by the growth of The Geochemical Society to an international body of 1700 members in the first three years of its existence. A comprehensive review of the status of current research in pure geochemistry would be far beyond the scope of this book. At the same time, a very brief summary of the relative levels of research activity in the various specialized fields of pure geochemistry will be helpful in attempting to view geochemical prospecting in proper perspective (Table 18-1).

TABLE 18-1. Relative Levels of Research Activity in Pure Geochemistry

	Deep-Seated Environment[a]	Surficial Environment[a]
Abundance and distribution of the elements	High (23)	Low (5)
Geochemical mapping	Very low (0)	Very low (0)
Stability fields of minerals	Moderate (10)	Low (5)
Dynamics of fractionation and migration of elements	Low (6)	Moderate (10)
Fractionation and distribution of isotopes	Moderate (7)	Low (4)
Geochronology	Moderate (11)	Low (4)
Chemical oceanography	—	Moderate (7)
Organic geochemistry	—	Moderate (11)
Chemistry of meteorites	Very high (41)	

[a]Numbers in parentheses indicate numbers of papers appearing in Volumes 14 through 19 of Geochimica et Cosmochimica Acta.

Many of the major advances in geochemical prospecting are a direct outgrowth of research in pure geochemistry. In this regard, particular mention should be made of the fundamental data on the abundance of minor elements, mineral stabilities, and the fractionation of elements between various earth materials. Unquestionably, advances in pure geochemistry will continue to provide new tools and new ideas for the further development of geochemical methods of mineral exploration.

Geochemical mapping, very significantly, was not the subject of a single paper in the volumes scanned for Table 18-1. Geochemical mapping is, of course, the aspect of geochemistry of most importance in geochemical prospecting. The development of this aspect of geochemistry, involving the techniques of systematic collection and processing very large numbers of samples and presenting and interpreting the resulting analytical data, has been the contribution almost entirely of the research workers in geochemical prospecting.

The ultimate significance of geochemical mapping, however, goes far beyond its application in mineral exploration. Regional patterns in the distribution of major and minor elements are as much a part of our study of the earth as the patterns in the distribution of soils, rock types, or tectonic and metamorphic features that are normally recorded as parts of conventional mapping projects. At the present time, at least three research projects in pure geochemistry, all aimed at regional geochemical mapping and all based on methods originally developed for use in mineral exploration, are in progress.

18-3. Other Fields of Applied Geochemistry

Exploration for mineral deposits is only one of a number of fields where the principles of geochemistry can be put to practical use in the service of mankind. Industrial applications of geochemistry in some fields are already well established. In many others, applications are the subject of active research. Following are a very few of the most important fields of applied geochemistry.

Petroleum Exploration. Geochemical methods of exploration for petroleum have been the subject of more or less intensive research for many years, as discussed elsewhere in this book and as summarized in an extensive literature. So far, exploration methods based on the formation of dispersion patterns of hydrocarbons over oil pools have not been generally accepted by the petroleum industry. Research is still active in some quarters, particularly in the Soviet Union. The possibility still remains, therefore, that geochemistry may find an important place in petroleum exploration.

Petroleum Production. Studies of the nature and genesis of reservoir rocks and of the organic compounds that comprise crude petroleum are leading to improved methods of secondary recovery. This field, now known as organic geochemistry, is the subject of active research in many industrial petroleum laboratories.

Agriculture. The geochemical environment plays a dominant role in the fertility of soils. The relationship between geochemistry and fertility starts with the major- and minor-element composition of the parent rock and may be traced through all the dynamic processes of weathering and soil formation and the internal metabolism of plants. In spite of the obvious character of this relationship, agricultural geochemistry has received far less attention than it deserves. Exceptions to this general neglect may be seen principally where some situation has become desperately acute, such as with Se poisoning of cattle or Mo deficiency in soils under leguminous crops. As the demand for food in the world increases, it is probable that studies of agricultural geochemistry will be intensified.

Public Health. Statistical studies of the geographical incidence of certain human diseases are showing an apparent correlation with certain geological formations and hence probably with the abundance or deficiency of certain elements in the diet. The causative relation between iodine deficiencies and goiter has been known for many years, and a corrective treatment has been developed. More recent work suggests that cancer and multiple sclerosis also may be correlated with the geochemical environment. Future research in the geochemistry of public health will almost certainly include studies of the composition of water supplies as well as agricultural products.

Raw Materials from the Ocean. The oceans of the world offer untapped reserves of both minerals and food. Of the potentially useful minerals, special mention should be made of phosphorite in relatively shallow water, and of the virtually inexhaustible reserves of manganese concretions on the floor of the deep sea. For food, the oceans offer unexplored opportunities for artificially controlled marine farming, by either changing the patterns of circulation or by adding chemical nutrients. Research in marine geochemistry, or chemical oceanography as it is more commonly called, is currently increasing in both magnitude and scope. The future will certainly see the growth of marine industry as a result of this research activity.

18-4. The Future of the Minerals Industry

In the long term, the outlook for geochemical prospecting is clearly dependent on its continued capacity to serve the mineral industry despite inevitable changes in the kinds of ore deposits that will be sought in the future. Here again, a review of present trends can help in forecasting. Following is a review of various kinds of ore bodies classified according to ease of discovery and economics of operation.

1. Deposits that crop out conspicuously at the surface. Almost all of these have already been discovered and worked to considerable depths. Many of them are essentially exhausted (Examples: Butte; Franklin Furnace).

2. Blind high-grade deposits found by exploring favorable structures near known ores. Progressively fewer of these are now being found and developed as exploration of high-grade districts reaches saturation and as deep mining becomes progressively less attractive (Example: United Verde Extension).

3. Outcropping deposits, usually low grade, that have escaped discovery because of surface leaching or because of the inconspicuous nature of the ore minerals. With more thorough testing of all geological possibilities, these are currently being identified and developed (Examples: Topaz Mountain beryllium deposit, Utah; Atlas copper deposit, Philippines).

4. Blind deposits obscured by transported overburden, deep residual

soil, or a moderate cover of barren cap rock. These are rapidly being discovered with modern exploration methods and are currently coming into production (Examples: Pima; Ambrosia Lake).

5. Known deposits where development has been delayed because of low grade, technical difficulties in processing or lack of demand for the product (Examples: chromite deposits of the Stillwater Complex, Montana; Cuban lateritic iron ores).

6. Normal rocks occurring in essentially inexhaustible quantities that can be processed to yield metals (Examples: sodium products from rock salt; magnesium from dolomite).

Exploration for conventional ore deposits can confidently be expected to continue for many years to come. This expectation is particularly valid for blind deposits in poorly exposed or little explored terrain such as exists in many tropical and desert areas, and in the polar land masses. There is, however, a general trend in the mineral industry toward bulk treatment of low-grade material. As a result of this trend, shallow deposits of large horizontal dimensions that can be handled by open-pit methods are at a premium over underground operations. Probably many of the underground mines of the past century could not be operated at a profit now because of the increase in the cost of underground operations relative to the value of the product. Conversely, it is highly probable that an increasing number of metal producers of the future will be processing what to us now is simply "ordinary rock," such as for example black shale, serpentine, or carbonatite.

18-5. The Future of Geochemistry in Mineral Exploration

Forecasting future trends in geochemical prospecting involves now a composite of the foregoing forecasts of research trends in the sciences, and of technical trends in the mining industry. A second-order forecast of this kind is admittedly dangerous, but still perhaps useful in some respects.

First, geochemical reconnaissance based on stream water and sediments will undoubtedly continue at current or increased scales until all the geologically favorable areas of the world wherein these methods are applicable have been covered. As techniques are improved, it may be necessary to cover many areas with reconnaissance surveys more than once. The goal will be the discovery of indications not only of new deposits but also of new mineralized districts that for one reason or another had escaped previous discovery. Within a finite period of time, this task will be essentially finished, unless new methods of primary reconnaissance are unexpectedly developed.

Detailed geochemical surveys based on sampling soils or vegetation will be applied in many areas of the world where the mineralized bedrock is masked by either residual or transported soil. To an increasing degree, detailed geochemical work will be carried out in conjunction with geological and geophysical studies as a component of integrated exploration systems aimed at pinpointing targets for trenching or drilling. This type of work will probably continue for many years before declining as promising areas are progressively eliminated.

Primary dispersion patterns associated with known ore will receive increased attention, and more will come to be mapped on a routine basis along with rock types, geologic structures, alteration patterns, and mineralization. At the same time, systematic geochemical mapping in conjunction with regional geological surveys will become an increasingly important phase of the services offered by government geological survey departments. The aim will be both to find indications of new ore deposits and to gather basic information for use in deciphering the geologic history of a region. The scale of this work, after it has become standard practice, may essentially parallel the scale of regional geologic mapping.

Finally, the most effective application of the principles and practice of geochemical exploration will require personnel with a more extensive background in all related disciplines than is common today. Their training will include not only the essential foundation of economic geology but also applied geophysics, photogeology, diamond drilling, and other methods of direct subsurface investigation.

While the demand for specialists in each particular field will undoubtedly remain, the continuing rapid growth in modern techniques raises a more general problem, concomitant with the trend toward ever greater complexity and scope. The task of securing optimum planning and efficiency in the conduct of exploration programs will become increasingly difficult without an intimate up-to-date knowledge of the over-all technology. It is evident that coordination in mineral exploration must inevitably become a specialized field in itself.

For these reasons, therefore, we may expect to see a more widespread trend in the earth science departments of our educational institutions toward advanced courses of study that combine all aspects of mineral exploration technology in fully integrated curriculums.

APPENDIX

GEOCHEMICAL CHARACTERISTICS
OF THE ELEMENTS

In the following sections, the geochemical characteristics of the individual elements are reviewed insofar as they are important in the development of secondary geochemical anomalies.

Unless specifically noted otherwise, the sources are as follows:

IGNEOUS ROCKS: Av (average) from Green (1959). Umaf (ultramafic rock), Maf (mafic, or basic rock), and Fels (felsic, or acid rock) from Vinogradov (1956a, Table 4).

SEDIMENTARY ROCKS: Ls (limestone and dolomite), Ss (sandstone), Sh (shale), BkSh (black shale) from Krauskopf (1955, Tables 1 and 2, p. 416, 417). Question marks in Krauskopf's original have been omitted.

SOILS: Av (average) from Vinogradov (1959, Table 126, pp. 183–184). Range from Swaine (1955).

PLANT ASH: Average from Cannon (1960b), rounded to 2 significant figures.

FRESH WATER: Range selected from data quoted by Gill and Denson (1957, Table 4, p. 168–169), Hawkes (1957, Table 2, p. 229) and John P. Miller (personal communication).

ASSOCIATIONS: Goldschmidt's system of geochemical classification of elements according to their major associations into siderophile (iron phase), lithophile (silicate phase), and chalcophile (sulfide phase) is followed. Outstanding specific associations within these groups are mentioned.

MINERALS: The mineral components of rocks, primary ores, and weathering products in which each element is normally enriched are listed, with a note as to the stability of the deep-seated minerals in the surficial environment. This list is not restricted to minerals containing the element as a major constituent.

SOIL AND AQUEOUS PHASES: The known constituents of soils and fresh waters in which each element is enriched are given. Many metals may occur in the aqueous phase as unknown organic and inorganic complexes in addition to those mentioned in review.

BIOLOGICAL RESPONSE: Outstanding effects of the element on the metabolism and distribution of living organisms are mentioned. The general relationships outlined here are discussed at greater length in Chapter 15 and in standard references such as Bear (1955).

SUPERGENE MOBILITY: The relative mobility of each element in weathering is indicated qualitatively, and the principal limiting factors controlling its mobility are mentioned.

GEOCHEMICAL PROSPECTING APPLICATIONS: Mention is made of the most widely used and the most promising geochemical prospecting methods, based on secondary dispersion patterns, with references to the principal published papers describing each of these methods.

ANTIMONY

IGNEOUS ROCKS: Av 0.3; Umaf 0.1; Maf 0.15; Fels 0.4 ppm.
SEDIMENTARY ROCKS: Ss 1; Sh 3 ppm.
ASSOCIATIONS: Chalcophile; Ag and Au in complex precious-metal sulfide deposits.
MOBILITY: Probably low.
GEOCHEMICAL PROSPECTING APPLICATIONS: The Sb content of residual soils and stream sediments has been successfully used in locating bedrock stibnite deposits (Sainsbury, 1957). Sb in soils has also been reported as a pathfinder for Au (Anthony and Mukherjee, 1956; James, 1957a; Chapman, 1958; Webb, 1958a). A high content of Sb in stream sediments of the Transbaykal region has been claimed by Polikarpochkin et al. (1958) as a positive indication of a sulfide deposit in the immediate vicinity.

ARSENIC

IGNEOUS ROCKS: Av 2; Umaf 2.8; Maf 2; Fels 1.5 ppm.
SEDIMENTARY ROCKS: Sh 4; BkSh 75–225 ppm.
SOILS: Av 5; Range 1–50 ppm.
FRESH WATER: 1–30 ppb.
ASSOCIATIONS: Chalcophile; Au, Ag, Cu, Co in sulfide deposits; strong association with epigenetic Au ore.
ROCK MINERAL: Pyrite (unstable).
PRIMARY ORE MINERALS: Principally arsenopyrite, also complex sulfarsenides of ore metals (all unstable).
SECONDARY MINERALS: Limonite, iron arsenates.
SOIL PHASE: Limonite, to a minor degree organic matter.
BIOLOGICAL RESPONSE: Plants apparently tend to solubilize As to a certain extent, inasmuch as As is somewhat enriched in the humus horizon of soils. The As content of coal ash is extremely high. As a result, burning of coal releases As to the air and causes contamination of surficial material throughout the surrounding country.
MOBILITY: Generally low, limited by coprecipitation as AsO_3^{-3} with limonite and as $FeAsO_4$ (scorodite); in iron-poor environments, As becomes more mobile and may even form detectable dispersion trains in stream waters (Mather, 1959).
GEOCHEMICAL PROSPECTING APPLICATIONS: The As content of soils has been used experimentally in geochemical prospecting as a pathfinder for Co (Canney et al., 1953), for W (Granier, 1958), and for Au and Ag (Martinet, 1956; James, 1957a; Chapman, 1958; Miesch and Nolan, 1958; Webb, 1958a; Mather, 1959).

BARIUM

IGNEOUS ROCKS: Av 640; Umaf 15; Maf 270; Fels 830 ppm.
SEDIMENTARY ROCKS: Ls 20–200; Ss 100–500; Sh 300–600; BkSh 450–700 ppm.

SOILS: Av 500; Range 100–3000 ppm.

FRESH WATER: 4–35 ppb.

ASSOCIATIONS: Lithophile; K in felsic igneous rocks; accompanies many Pb-Zn sulfide ores as barite.

ROCK MINERAL: K-feldspar (moderately stable).

PRIMARY ORE MINERAL: Barite (relatively unstable).

SOIL PHASE: Probably barite.

AQUEOUS PHASE: Probably ionic Ba^{++}.

MOBILITY: Probably high, limited primarily by solubility of Ba sulfate.

GEOCHEMICAL PROSPECTING APPLICATIONS: Ba may be a useful pathfinder for deposits of Pb, Zn, and Ag because of its association with Pb-Zn deposits. Barium in both soils and plants has been shown experimentally to be a good indicator of Ba-rich bedrock deposits (Roberts, 1949, as reported by Harbaugh, 1953, pp. 24–25).

BERYLLIUM

IGNEOUS ROCKS: Av 4.2; Umaf 0.2; Maf 1.5; Fels 5.5 ppm.

SEDIMENTARY ROCKS: Ls < 1; Ss < 1; Sh 1–6; BkSh 1 ppm.

SOILS: Av 6 ppm.

PLANT ASH; <2 ppm.

FRESH WATER: Order of 0.1 ppb (Merrill et al., 1960).

ASSOCIATIONS: Lithophile; Al and Si in silicate minerals; Li, B, Nb, Th, and U in pegmatite veins; W veins.

ROCK MINERAL: Beryl (very stable), mica (stable), feldspar (moderately stable).

PRIMARY ORE MINERAL: Beryl (very stable).

SECONDARY MINERALS: Not known.

BIOLOGICAL RESPONSE: Be anomalies in plants show approximately the same contrast as in soils (Zalashkova et al., 1958; Kuzin, 1959).

MOBILITY: Probably low, limited by insolubility of beryl in weathering.

GEOCHEMICAL PROSPECTING APPLICATIONS: Experimental work on the Be content of residual soils shows some promise (Karayeva and Chesnokov, 1958; Zalashkova et al., 1958; Debnam and Webb, 1960). Analysis of stream sediments may also be useful in reconnaissance surveys (Debnam and Webb, 1960).

BISMUTH

IGNEOUS ROCKS: Av ± 0.1 ppm.

SEDIMENTARY ROCKS: Ss 0.3; Sh 1 ppm.

ASSOCIATIONS: Chalcophile; Sb and As in sulfide deposits.

MOBILITY: Probably low, limited by coprecipitation with limonite.

GEOCHEMICAL PROSPECTING APPLICATIONS: Bi might be useful as a pathfinder for sulfide ores. Its use has been retarded by lack of an adequately sensitive analytical method.

BORON

IGNEOUS ROCKS: Av 13; Umaf 40; Maf 10; Fels 15 ppm.
SEDIMENTARY ROCKS: Ls 18; Ss 155; Sh 130 ppm (Green, 1959).
SOILS: Av 10 ppm.
PLANT ASH: 700 ppm.
FRESH WATER: 1–10,000 ppb (Hem, 1959).
SEA WATER: 4600 ppb.
ASSOCIATIONS: Lithophile; Be, Li, Nb, Th and U in pegmatite veins; as a
   result of the enrichment of B in sea water, the B content of marine shales
   is very much higher than in fresh-water shales and may be used as a
   criterion of origin (Keith and Degens, 1959).
ROCK MINERALS: Tourmaline (very stable); most primary igneous silicates
   (variable stability).
PRINCIPAL MINERAL OF EPIGENETIC DEPOSITS: Tourmaline (very stable).
SECONDARY MINERALS: Clay minerals, soluble borates.
SOIL PHASE: Clay minerals, tourmaline, soluble borates.
AQUEOUS PHASE: Soluble borates.
BIOLOGICAL RESPONSE: At a low level of concentration, B is a necessary
   nutrient for most plants; at a somewhat higher level of availability in the
   soil it is generally toxic (Mitchell, 1955). Boron toxicity may take the form
   of recognizable symptoms that can be used as guides to B deposits (Buyalov and Shvyryayeva, 1955).
MOBILITY: Extremely high, except for B in stable silicates, particularly in
   tourmaline.
GEOCHEMICAL PROSPECTING APPLICATIONS: Experimental studies of the
   distribution of B in soils, plants and water show an apparently useful
   correlation with B-rich saline deposits (Sergeyev, 1936; Shvyryayeva,
   1957; Smith, 1960).

CADMIUM

IGNEOUS ROCKS: Av 0.13; Maf 0.19; Fels 0.1 ppm.
SEDIMENTARY ROCKS: Sh 0.3 ppm.
SOILS: Av 0.5 ppm.
ASSOCIATIONS: Chalcophile; Cd shows an almost universal association with
   Zn. The Zn : Cd ratio does not deviate by much more than a factor of 2
   from an average of 500 to 1 in igneous, metamorphic, and sedimentary rocks.
ROCK MINERALS: Same as for Zn.
PRIMARY ORE MINERALS: Same as for Zn.
SECONDARY MINERAL: Greenockite (relatively unstable).
MOBILITY: Cd follows Zn in weathering except during the oxidation of Zn
   sulfide. Here the secondary Cd sulfide tends to remain behind after the Zn
   sulfide has been solubilized by oxidation.
GEOCHEMICAL PROSPECTING APPLICATIONS: Cd in stream sediments has
   been reported as a possible pathfinder for Zn deposits (Polikarpochkin
   et al., 1958).

CHROMIUM

IGNEOUS ROCKS: Av 117; Umaf 2000; Maf 300; Fels 25 ppm.

SEDIMENTARY ROCKS: Ls 5; Ss 10–100; Sh 100–400; BkSh 10–500 ppm.

SOILS: Av 200; Range 5–1000 ppm.

PLANT ASH: 9 ppm.

FRESH WATER: 0.5–40 ppb.

ASSOCIATIONS: Lithophile; strong association with Ni, Mg in ultramafic rocks; Fe and Al in sedimentary cycle.

ROCK MINERAL: Chromite (very stable).

PRIMARY ORE MINERAL: Chromite.

SECONDARY MINERALS: None.

SOIL PHASE: Chromite, if present in parent rock; limonite.

AQUEOUS PHASE: Ionic CrO_4^{--} at high pH and Eh.

MOBILITY: Generally low, except for conditions of high pH and Eh where the mobile CrO_4^{--} chromate ion is stable.

GEOCHEMICAL PROSPECTING APPLICATIONS: Successful experiments based on plant analysis for Cr have been reported. The analysis of residual soils for Cr may also be an effective method in the event that the mineral itself cannot be readily identified or, as in Great Dyke in Southern Rhodesia, where narrow seams of chromite are concealed by overburden containing eluvial chromite over ore and country rock alike (James, 1957b; Webb, 1958a). Under most conditions, however, the geochemical anomaly is defined by detrital grains of chromite, which generally are so conspicuous that a chemical method of determination is not necessary.

COBALT

IGNEOUS ROCKS: Av 18; Umaf 200; Maf 45; Fels 5 ppm.

SEDIMENTARY ROCKS: Ls 0.2–2; Ss 1–10; Sh 10–50; BkSh 5–50 ppm.

SOILS: Av 8; Range 1–40 ppm.

PLANT ASH: 9 ppm.

FRESH WATER: 0.03–10 ppb.

ASSOCIATIONS: Siderophile, to a lesser degree chalcophile; Mg and Ni in ultramafic and mafic rocks; Fe, As, Sb, Cu, Ni, Ag, and U in sulfide deposits.

ROCK MINERALS: Ferromagnesian minerals (moderately stable).

PRIMARY ORE MINERALS: Complex As and Sb sulfides, sometimes also the simple sulfides carrolite and linnaeite (unstable).

SECONDARY MINERALS: Limonite, MnO_2, erythrite ($3CoO \cdot As_2O_5 \cdot 8H_2O$), heterogenite ($CoO \cdot 2Co_2O_3 \cdot 6H_2O$).

SOIL PHASE: Limonite, MnO_2.

AQUEOUS PHASE: Probably ionic Co^{++}.

BIOLOGICAL RESPONSE: Important in animal nutrition.

MOBILITY: Probably moderately high, limited in early stages by coprecipitation with limonite and MnO_2.

GEOCHEMICAL PROSPECTING APPLICATIONS: The analysis of residual soils for Co has proved to be a very useful method of locating bedrock deposits of Co-bearing ore (Canney et al., 1953; Hawkes, 1959). Co also may migrate into and be precipitated in transported overburden, where it may serve as a guide to buried Co deposits (Koehler et al., 1954). Although cobalt anomalies have been demonstrated in soil and stream sediment in Uganda and on the Copperbelt in Northern Rhodesia, the associated copper is the more useful indicator element in prospecting (Tooms, 1955; Webb, 1958a; Jay, 1959). Experimental biogeochemical prospecting for Co shows promise (Warren and Delavault, 1957). Under favorable conditions, Co should be useful in prospecting by stream-water or stream-sediment analysis. Although adequate analytical methods are available, reconnaissance prospecting surveys based on Co in drainage patterns have not been tried on a large scale.

COPPER

IGNEOUS ROCKS: Av 70; Umaf 80; Maf 140; Fels 30 ppm.
SEDIMENTARY ROCKS: Ls 5–20; Ss 10–40; Sh 30–150; BkSh 20–300 ppm.
SOILS: Av 20; Range 2–100 ppm.
PLANT ASH: 180 ppm.
FRESH WATER: 0.2–30 ppb.
ASSOCIATIONS: Chalcophile; Pb, Zn, Mo, Ag, Au, Sb, Se in sulfide deposits; Cu-Ni-Pt; Cu-Co-As.
ROCK MINERALS: Ferromagnesian minerals (moderately stable), chalcopyrite (unstable).
PRIMARY ORE MINERALS: Chalcopyrite, bornite, complex Cu-As-Sb-S minerals (all unstable).
SECONDARY MINERALS: Sulfides, oxides, basic carbonates, sulfates, and silicates.
SOIL PHASE: Limonite, MnO_2, organic matter.
AQUEOUS PHASE: Ionic Cu^+ and Cu^{++}, floating organisms, and soluble organic matter.
BIOLOGICAL RESPONSE: Cu is one of the important plant nutrients. Where the Cu content of soil falls below 10 ppm, deficiency symptoms may develop in the vegetation. Somewhat higher concentrations of Cu in soils may be toxic to plants. A number of very useful indicator plants for Cu have been reported from various parts of the world (Nesvetaylova, 1955b; Duvigneaud, 1958; Horizon, 1959).
MOBILITY: High where pH is below about 5.5, low at neutral to alkaline pH; mobility limited primarily by pH, to lesser extent by coprecipitation with limonite and by sorption to organic matter and clay minerals.
GEOCHEMICAL PROSPECTING APPLICATIONS: Sampling of residual soil has become a widely used method of locating Cu deposits (Sokoloff, 1950, 1951; Huff, 1952, 1956; Williams, 1953; Tooms, 1955; Jacobson, 1956; Malyuga and Makarova, 1956; Boyle and Cragg, 1957; Volobuyev, 1957; Hawkes et al., 1957; Webb, 1958a; Govett, 1960). Although considerable

experimental work has been done on biogeochemical prospecting for Cu (Warren *et al.*, 1952), the method has not found wide favor. The contrast of anomaly over background is relatively low, and generally the same patterns can be obtained more easily and cheaply by soil sampling. Copper also forms useful superimposed anomalies in transported over-burden (White and Allen, 1954; Ermengen, 1957; Yardley, 1958; Hawkes and Salmon, 1960). Except in spring areas, the Cu content of fresh sur-face water has not been very useful because of the limited mobility of Cu (Huff, 1948; Brodsky, 1956). Where Cu-rich residual soils are actively eroding or where Cu-rich ground water comes to the surface, the Cu con-tent of stream sediments may be a useful method of reconnaissance pros-pecting (Lovering *et al.*, 1950; Tooms, 1955; Holman, 1956b; Webb, 1958a; Govett, 1958; Webb and Tooms, 1959). As a result, surveys of readily extractable Cu in stream sediments have been effectively used in many parts of the world.

FLUORINE

IGNEOUS ROCKS: Av 660; Umaf 100; Maf 370; Fels 800 ppm.
SEDIMENTARY ROCKS: Ls 51; Ss 290; Sh 590 ppm (Green, 1959).
SOILS: Av 200 ppm.
FRESH WATER: 50–1000 ppb (Hem, 1959).
ASSOCIATIONS: Lithophile; follows phosphate in apatite; F^- proxies for OH^- in primary and secondary minerals.
ROCK MINERALS: Apatite (very stable), micas (stable).
PRIMARY ORE MINERAL: Fluorite (moderately stable).
SECONDARY MINERALS: Secondary phosphates.
SOIL PHASE: Secondary phosphates.
AQUEOUS PHASE: Ionic F^-.
BIOLOGICAL RESPONSE: None known in plants; in animal nutrition, F plays a part in the structure of teeth and bones.
MOBILITY: Not highly mobile; limited by abundance of phosphate.
GEOCHEMICAL PROSPECTING APPLICATIONS: The F content of soils may be useful as a guide in locating fluorite deposits (Nackowski, 1952). As a pathfinder for deposits of Pb and Zn, however, F will probably not be as useful as the distribution of the ore metals themselves.

GOLD

IGNEOUS ROCKS: Umaf 0.1; Maf 0.035; Fels 0.01 ppm.
SEDIMENTARY ROCKS: Ls 0.005–0.009; Ss 0.03; BkSh 0.01–1 ppm.
PLANT ASH: <0.007 ppm.
FRESH WATER: 0.0001–0.0073 ppb.
ASSOCIATIONS: Siderophile; Ag, As, Sb in precious metal deposits; also Fe, Zn, and Cu in many other sulfide deposits.
PRIMARY ORE MINERAL: Native Au (stable), Au tellurides (unstable).
SECONDARY MINERAL: Dissolved and redeposited native Au.

AQUEOUS PHASE: Not known, but thought to be a complex ion such as $AuCl_4^-$, a soluble organic complex, or a stable colloidal dispersion.

BIOLOGICAL RESPONSE: Au can enter the circulatory system of plants where it is deposited in the leaves and twigs in reported concentrations up to 2 ppm (ash basis).

MOBILITY: Possibly moderately high, depending on conditions favoring solubilization of primary grains of native Au; empirical observations suggest substantial transport of Au by natural fresh waters.

GEOCHEMICAL PROSPECTING APPLICATIONS: Experiments with the direct determination of Au in water, soils, and plants as a method of prospecting have been reported (Safronov et al., 1958). This method has not been used on a large scale because of the lack until recently of a suitable method of chemical analysis for traces of Au. Field studies have indicated that As, Sb, Zn, Cu, Pb, and Ag can be used at times as pathfinders in geochemical prospecting for Au.

HELIUM

ASSOCIATIONS: Atmophile; a radioactive daughter product of U and Th.

MOBILITY: Extremely mobile as a noble gas and as a chemically unreactive dissolved constituent of ground and surface water.

GEOCHEMICAL PROSPECTING APPLICATIONS: Atmospheric He contains a small proportion of He^3 in addition to He^4. It may be possible to distinguish He generated by the decay of U and its daughters from He of atmospheric origin by the $He^3 : He^4$ ratio. The He in natural gas from the Texas Panhandle led to the discovery of Rn and eventually to U-bearing asphalt above the gas-producing zones (Faul et al., 1954).

IRON

IGNEOUS ROCKS: Av 4.65; Umaf 9.85; Maf 8.56; Fels 2.7 percent.

SEDIMENTARY ROCKS: Ls 1.3; Ss 3.1; Sh 4.3 percent (Green, 1959).

SOILS: Range 1.4–4.0 percent (Lawton, 1955).

PLANT ASH: 0.67 percent.

FRESH WATER: 40–1500 ppb.

ASSOCIATIONS: Siderophile; enriched in mafic igneous rocks.

ROCK MINERALS: Ferromagnesian minerals (moderately stable), pyrite (unstable).

PRIMARY ORE MINERALS: Pyrite (unstable), magnetite (stable).

SECONDARY MINERALS: Limonite, jarosite.

SOIL PHASE: Limonite.

AQUEOUS PHASE: Ionic Fe^{++} at low Eh and Fe^{3+} at low pH; colloidal suspensions of hydrous Fe oxides at normal pH.

BIOLOGICAL RESPONSE: Fe is necessary for the enzymatic synthesis of chlorophyll in plants. Deficiencies of iron cause a breakdown of the chlorophyll mechanism and a yellowing of the leaves known as chlorosis. Fe-rich soils may suppport a characteristic plant assemblage, some members of which may be useful as Fe indicators (Buck, 1951).

MOBILITY: Fe^{++} moderate; Fe^{3+} low, limited by precipitation of limonite, but under some conditions colloidal suspensions of undissociated hydrous Fe oxides or Fe-bearing organic complexes may be stable (Hem, 1960).

GEOCHEMICAL PROSPECTING APPLICATIONS: Fe is important in geochemical prospecting mainly because of the very large number of trace elements whose mobility is limited by coprecipitation or adsorption on limonitic material. Measurement of the Fe precipitated in swamps, spring areas, and stream beds below Fe-rich deposits may serve as a direct ore guide (Salmi, 1955; Kvashnevskaya, 1957; Hawkes and Salmon, 1960). The Fe content of vegetation also shows promise as a guide to pyrite-bearing ores (Tkalich, 1953).

LANTHANUM

IGNEOUS ROCKS: Av 40; Maf 27; Fels 46 ppm.

SEDIMENTARY ROCKS: Ss 17; Sh 40 ppm (Green, 1959).

SOILS: Av 40 ppm.

PLANT ASH: 16 ppm (for total rare earths).

ASSOCIATIONS: Lithophile; universal association with the other rare earth elements, together with Sc, Y, Th; Nb, P, U in alkaline rocks; Al in weathering products.

ROCK MINERALS: Allanite (unstable), apatite, monazite (both stable).

SECONDARY MINERALS: Clay minerals.

SOIL PHASE: Probably the clay minerals.

MOBILITY: Probably low.

BIOLOGICAL RESPONSE: No known nutritive effect, although certain plants can apparently solubilize large quantities of La and the other rare earths (Robinson et al., 1958).

GEOCHEMICAL PROSPECTING APPLICATIONS: No example is known where geochemical sampling and analysis for La or other rare earth elements have been used in prospecting.

LEAD

IGNEOUS ROCKS: Av 16; Maf ± 12; Fels 48 ppm (Green, 1959).

SEDIMENTARY ROCKS: Ls 5–10; Ss 10–40; Sh 20; BkSh 20–400 ppm.

SOILS: Av 10; Range 2–200 ppm.

PLANT ASH: 70 ppm.

FRESH WATER: 0.3–3 ppb.

ASSOCIATIONS: Chalcophile; Ag in precious metal deposits; Fe, Zn, Cu, Sb in many other sulfide deposits. K in rock-forming silicates.

ROCK MINERALS: Micas (stable), K-feldspars (moderately stable).

PRIMARY ORE MINERAL: Galena (relatively unstable).

SECONDARY MINERALS: Cerussite, anglesite, pyromorphite ($Pb_4(PbCl)(PO_4)_3$).

SOIL PHASE: Unknown; enrichments of more than 1000 ppm Pb in organic-rich soil developed from normal parent rock under certain types of vegetation have been reported. Pb also has been observed enriched in the ferruginous horizon of lateritic soils.

AQUEOUS PHASE: Probably ionic Pb^{++}.

BIOLOGICAL RESPONSE: Pb is generally toxic to vegetation when present in ionic form.

MOBILITY: Generally low, in part limited by precipitation with organic matter and limonite, but probably higher in chloride (semiarid) environment.

GEOCHEMICAL PROSPECTING APPLICATIONS: Pb in residual soils gives a very strong indication of Pb-rich deposits because of its relative immobility (Huff, 1952; Hawkes, 1954; Riddell, 1954; Boyle and Cragg, 1957; Miesch and Nolan, 1958; Webb, 1958b). Reconnaissance prospecting based on the Pb content of stream water and sediment (Polikarpochkin et al., 1958; Webb, 1958b) shows considerable promise.

LITHIUM

IGNEOUS ROCKS: Av 50; Umaf 2; Maf 15; Fels 70 ppm.

SEDIMENTARY ROCKS: Ls 2–20; Ss 7–29; Sh 50; BkSh 17 ppm.

SOILS: Av 30; Range 5–200 ppm.

FRESH WATER: 0.3–3 ppb.

ASSOCIATIONS: Lithophile; Mg in silicate rocks; Be, B, La, Nb, Th, and U in pegmatite veins.

ROCK MINERALS: Ferromagnesian minerals (moderately stable).

PRIMARY ORE MINERALS: Spodumene $(LiAl(SiO_3)_2)$ and amblygonite $(LiAl-(F,OH)PO_4)$ (both stable), Li-mica (moderately stable).

SECONDARY MINERALS: None known.

SOIL PHASE: Probably clay minerals.

MOBILITY: Probably high.

GEOCHEMICAL PROSPECTING APPLICATIONS: Li in surface fresh water or soil may serve as a pathfinder for pegmatite deposits (Miller and Danilov, 1957; Karayeva and Chesnokov, 1958).

MANGANESE

IGNEOUS ROCKS: Av 1000; Umaf 1300; Maf 2200; Fels 600 ppm.

SEDIMENTARY ROCKS: Ls 1300; Ss 385 ppm (Green, 1959).

SOILS: Av 850; Range 200–3000 ppm.

PLANT ASH: 4800 ppm.

FRESH WATER: 0.3–300 ppb.

ASSOCIATIONS: Lithophile; Mg and Fe in silicates.

ROCK MINERALS: Ferromagnesian minerals (moderately stable).

PRIMARY ORE MINERALS: Carbonates (unstable).

SECONDARY MINERALS: Hydrous Mn oxides.

SOIL PHASE: Hydrous Mn oxides.

AQUEOUS PHASE: Probably Mn^{++}

BIOLOGICAL RESPONSE: Mn is an essential nutrient for most plants.

MOBILITY: Very low, limited by low solubility of Mn^{4+} oxides at normal pH; in acid pH range, Mn may be mobile as Mn^{++} ion.

GEOCHEMICAL PROSPECTING APPLICATIONS: Under favorable circumstances, the Mn content of soils and plants may reflect the presence of Mn ore beneath the cover (Bloss and Steiner, 1960). Mn in drainage sediments may serve as an indicator of Mn ore in the catchment (Ljunggren, 1951; Pavlov et al., 1957).

MERCURY

IGNEOUS ROCKS: Av 0.06; Maf 0.09; Fels 0.04 ppm.
SEDIMENTARY ROCKS: Ls 0.03; Ss 0.03–0.1; Sh 0.4 ppm.
SOILS: Range 0.03–0.3 ppm (Stock and Cucuel, 1934).
FRESH WATER: 0.01–0.1 ppb.
ASSOCIATIONS: Chalcophile; Sb, As, Se, Ag, Zn, Pb in sulfide deposits.
PRIMARY ORE MINERALS: Cinnabar (relatively unstable), native Hg (stable).
SECONDARY MINERAL: Native Hg.
SOIL PHASE: Unknown.
AQUEOUS PHASE: Unknown.
MOBILITY: Probably low in water; apparently very high in vapor phase.
GEOCHEMICAL PROSPECTING APPLICATIONS: As a result of gaseous dispersion of Hg vapor, geochemical prospecting based on the analysis of near-surface soils and rocks for traces of Hg may reveal an aureole adjoining or overlying buried Hg-bearing deposits (Saukov, 1946; Vershovskaya, 1956; Sergeyev, 1957: Fursov, 1958; Ozerova, 1959; Berce, 1960).

MOLYBDENUM

IGNEOUS ROCKS: Av 1.7; Umaf 0.4; Maf 1.4; Fels 1.9 ppm.
SEDIMENTARY ROCKS: Ls 0.1–0.5; Ss 0.1–1; Sh 1; BkSh 10–300 ppm.
SOILS: Av 2; Range 0.2–5 ppm.
PLANT ASH: 13 ppm.
FRESH WATER: 0.05–3 ppb.
ASSOCIATIONS: Siderophile, to a lesser degree chalcophile; W and Sn in contact-metamorphic deposits; Cu and Re in porphyry copper deposits.
ROCK MINERAL: Molybdenite (relatively unstable).
PRIMARY ORE MINERAL: Molybdenite.
SECONDARY MINERALS: Limonite, ferrimolybdite ($Fe_2O_3 \cdot 3MoO_3 \cdot 8H_2O$), jarosite, gypsum, powellite ($Ca(Mo,W)O_4$).
SOIL PHASE: Limonite, clay minerals.
AQUEOUS PHASE: MoO_4^{--} ion; undissociated $MoO_2:SO_4$ (Dolukhanova, 1957).
BIOLOGICAL RESPONSE: Mo is essential for the functioning of nitrogen-fixing bacteria in the root nodules of legumes; Mo in forage is extremely toxic to livestock (Barshad, 1948; LeRiche, 1959).
MOBILITY: Extremely high to moderate, limited (1) by rate of solution of primary MoS_2, (2) by sorption on limonite to form ferrimolybdite at

pH 2.5–7.0 and to a less extent on clay minerals at pH 2–4 (Jones, 1957), and (3) by precipitation in carbonate-rich environments; otherwise, mobility of Mo is independent of pH variations.

GEOCHEMICAL PROSPECTING APPLICATIONS: The Mo content of residual soil has been reported as an effective prospecting tool (Tikhomirov and Miller, 1946; Baranova, 1957; Dolukhanova, 1957; Malyuga, 1958; Mather, 1959). The apparent nonselectivity of vegetation with respect to Mo makes the analysis of deep-rooted plants a possible ore guide (Warren *et al.*, 1953; Baranova, 1957; Malyuga, 1959). The high mobilty of Mo under many conditions makes it possible to use water sampling in reconnaissance prospecting for Mo-rich ores (Belyakova, 1957, 1958). The potentialities of stream-sediment sampling have been demonstrated by Mather (1959) in a tropical environment in Sierra Leone and by Kvashnevskaya (1957) in the U. S. S. R.

NICKEL

IGNEOUS ROCKS: Av 100; Umaf 1200; Maf 160; Fels 8 ppm.
SEDIMENTARY ROCKS: Ls 3–10; Ss 2–10; Sh 20–100; BkSh 20–300 ppm.
SOILS: Av 40; Range 5–500 ppm.
PLANT ASH: 65 ppm.
FRESH WATER: 0.02–10 ppb.
ASSOCIATIONS: Siderophile, to a lesser degree chalcophile; Mg and Co in ultramafic and mafic rocks; Co, Cu, and Pt in sulfide deposits.
ROCK MINERALS: Ferromagnesian minerals (moderately stable).
PRIMARY ORE MINERALS: Ni-Fe sulfides (all unstable).
SECONDARY MINERALS: Hydrated Ni silicates, limonite.
SOIL PHASE: Probably limonite and nickeliferous silicates.
AQUEOUS PHASE: Probably ionic Ni^{++}.
MOBILITY: Moderately high, limited by coprecipitation with limonite, and hydrolysis above pH 6.5 (Crooke, 1956).
GEOCHEMICAL PROSPECTING APPLICATIONS: Experimental work indicates that analysis of residual soil (Malyuga, 1947; Coope, 1958; Yardley, 1958) and vegetation (Rankama, 1940, Warren and Delavault, 1954; Miller, 1959) should be a useful method of finding either primary sulfide Ni or secondary silicate Ni ores in lateritic overburden. Coope (1958) has shown that stream-sediment sampling can be used in reconnaissance prospecting for nickel deposits.

NIOBIUM

IGNEOUS ROCKS: Av 20; Umaf 15; Maf 20; Fels 20 ppm.
SEDIMENTARY ROCKS: Sh 20; BkSh 0.6 ppm.
ASSOCIATIONS: Lithophile; Nb shows almost universal association with Ta; Ti, rare earths, U, Th, P in alkaline igneous rocks; Al in weathering products.

ROCK MINERALS: Pyrochlore (complex niobate) (moderately stable), columbite (FeO·Nb_2O_5) (stable).
PRIMARY ORE MINERALS: Pyrochlore, columbite.
MOBILITY: Probably low.
GEOCHEMICAL PROSPECTING APPLICATIONS: Recent studies in central Africa have demonstrated the applicability of soil and stream sediment sampling in detailed and reconnaissance prospecting for pyrochlore carbonatites (Wambeke, 1960; Watts, 1960). Anomalous concentrations of Nb in residual soil and base-of-slope colluvium have been noted in the vicinity of columbite-bearing pegmatites in Uganda (Webb, 1958a). Experimental work has been done on the Nb content of plants as an ore guide (Tyutina et al., 1959).

RADIUM

ROCKS AND SOILS: Ra in equilibrium with U may be determined by multiplying the U content (q.v.) by 3.5×10^{-7}.
ASSOCIATIONS: Lithophile; a daughter product of U.
SECONDARY MINERALS: Sulfate minerals, particularly barite.
AQUEOUS PHASE: Probably ionic Ra^{++}.
MOBILITY: Apparently fairly low, possibly limited by tendency to be adsorbed on clay minerals.
GEOCHEMICAL PROSPECTING APPLICATIONS: Ra deserves investigation as a pathfinder for U.

RADON

ROCKS AND SOILS: Rn in equilibrium with U may be determined by multiplying the U content (q.v.) by 2.3×10^{-12}.
ASSOCIATIONS: A radioactive daughter product of U.
AQUEOUS PHASE: Dissolved gas.
MOBILITY: Extremely mobile as a dissolved constituent of water; Rn rapidly escapes from natural waters on exposure to air.
GEOCHEMICAL PROSPECTING APPLICATIONS: Rn in soil air has been considered as a method of U prospecting (Gangloff et al., 1958). Similar studies of Rn in natural gas have led to discoveries of U occurrences in sedimentary rocks (Faul et al., 1954; Pierce et al., 1956). Rn cannot form gaseous dispersion halos of great size because of its relatively short half-life, not quite 4 days.

RARE EARTHS (see Lanthanum)

SELENIUM

IGNEOUS ROCKS: Av 0.09 ppm (Rankama and Sahama, 1950, Table 2.3).
SEDIMENTARY ROCKS: Ls 0.1–1; Ss 1; Sh 0.5–1 ppm.

SOILS: Av 0.01; Range 0.1–2 ppm.
ASSOCIATIONS: Chalcophile; As, Sb, Cu, Ag, Au in sulfide deposits.
ROCK MINERAL: Pyrite (unstable).
PRIMARY ORE MINERALS: Almost all sulfides (unstable).
SECONDARY MINERALS: Native Se, ferric selenite ($mFe_2O_3.nSeO_2$).
SOIL PHASE: Limonite, ferric selenite, probably native Se.
AQUEOUS PHASE: Ionic SeO_4^{--}
BIOLOGICAL RESPONSE: The biological cycle of Se is outstanding in that
  certain plants will take up and concentrate extremely large quantities of
  Se from Se-rich soils. Se in plants acts as a severe poison for most grazing
  animals. In addition to the concentrating effect, certain species of "indicator" plants will grow only on soils that are high in Se (Cannon, 1952,
  1957, 1960b).
MOBILITY: Se is highly mobile under oxidizing, alkaline conditions, and
  apparently highly immobile under reducing and neutral to acid conditions; the mobility is limited by the stability fields of the soluble SeO_4^{--}
  ion and of the insoluble native Se and selenites (Lakin and Trites, 1958).
GEOCHEMICAL PROSPECTING APPLICATIONS: Se, because of its association
  with epigenetic sulfides, has been recommended as a pathfinder for base-
  metal deposits. Insoluble Se in residual soils and in plants, for example,
  shows some promise as an indicator of Se-rich sulfide ores (Leutwein and
  Starke, 1957). The Se content has also been reported as a criterion for
  discriminating between gossans derived from sulfides and those derived
  from other primary ferruginous minerals (Sindeyeva, 1955). Indicator
  plants have received a great deal of study because of their usefulness in
  drawing attention to areas of poisoned grazing land. Studies of the distribution of Se indicator plants in the Colorado Plateau area of the western
  United States have led to the discovery of Se-rich U deposits buried
  beneath as much as 50 feet of unmineralized rock (Cannon and Kleinhampl, 1956; Cannon, 1957).

SILVER

IGNEOUS ROCKS: Av 0.2; Umaf 0.3; Maf 0.3; Fels 0.15 ppm.
SEDIMENTARY ROCKS: Ls 0.2; Ss 0.4; BkSh 5–50 ppm.
SOILS: Av 0.1 ppm.
PLANT ASH: <1 ppm.
FRESH WATER: 0.01–0.7 ppb.
ASSOCIATIONS: Chalcophile; Au, Sb, As, Pb, Zn in sulfide deposits.
ROCK MINERALS: Unknown.
PRIMARY ORE MINERALS: Native Ag (stable), galena, argentite (relatively un-
  stable); complex sulfo-salts (unstable).
SECONDARY MINERALS: Cerargyrite (AgCl), Ag-jarosite.
SOIL PHASE: Unknown.
AQUEOUS PHASE: Probably complex ions.
MOBILITY: Possibly fairly low, limited by low solubility of AgCl.

GEOCHEMICAL PROSPECTING APPLICATIONS: By virtue of its common association with Au, Ag should also be applicable as a pathfinder in geochemical soil survey for gold ores. According to Polikarpochkin *et al.* (1958), a high content of Ag in stream sediments is an indication of a sulfide deposit in the immediate vicinity.

SULFUR

IGNEOUS ROCKS: Av 900; Umaf 3000; Maf 2000; Fels 400 ppm.
SEDIMENTARY ROCKS: Ls 8000; Ss 2200; Sh 1100 ppm (Green, 1959).
SOILS: Av 850; Range 100–1500 ppm (Lawton, 1955).
FRESH WATER: Av 5500 ppb.
ASSOCIATIONS: Chalcophile; all elements in sulfide minerals; hydrophile elements in saline deposits.
ROCK MINERALS: Sulfides (unstable).
PRIMARY ORE MINERALS: Sulfides, barite (relatively unstable).
SECONDARY MINERALS: Gypsum, jarosite, saline sulfates.
SOIL PHASE: Ionic SO_4^{--}.
AQUEOUS PHASE: Ionic SO_4^{--}.
BIOLOGICAL RESPONSE: Although sulfur is an essential nutrient for plants and animals, the biological cycle does not materially affect the mobility of sulfate; under some conditions, bacteria can catalyze the oxidation of sulfides to sulfate, and vice versa. Indicator plants for S have been recognized in the Colorado Plateau area (Cannon, 1957).
MOBILITY: As sulfate, extremely high, limited only by the Eh at which sulfate is reduced to sulfide, and the solubility of saline minerals, principally gypsum.
GEOCHEMICAL PROSPECTING APPLICATIONS: Sulfur, as an essential constituent of almost all epigenetic mineral deposits, can be used as a pathfinder by virtue of the outstanding solubility of sulfate in water. Sulfate may be expressed as absolute concentrations, or as ratios of sulfate either to chloride or to total dissolved solids (Kraynov, 1957).

TIN

IGNEOUS ROCKS: Av 32; Maf 6; Fels 45 ppm.
SEDIMENTARY ROCKS: Sh 40 ppm.
SOILS: Av 10 ppm.
PLANT ASH: <5 ppm.
ASSOCIATIONS: W, Mo, Nb, F, and P in alkaline rocks; Be, B, Li, Nb-Ta, and rare earths in pegmatite veins.
ROCK MINERALS: Micas, cassiterite (both stable).
PRIMARY ORE MINERALS: Cassiterite (stable), stannite and many base-metal sulfides (unstable).
SECONDARY MINERALS: Unknown.
SOIL PHASE: Probably cassiterite.
AQUEOUS PHASE: Unknown.

BIOLOGICAL RESPONSE: Sn is not known to be a plant nutrient, although it apparently does enter plants in amounts reflecting the Sn content of the supporting soil.

MOBILITY: Generally low, limited by high stability of primary cassiterite; may be relatively high after liberation of ionic Sn from primary minerals.

GEOCHEMICAL PROSPECTING APPLICATIONS: Spectrographic analysis of the fine fractions either of residual soil or of stream sediments for traces of Sn has been widely used in the Soviet Union (Flerov, 1935, 1938; Ozerov, 1937; Il'in, 1956). The tin content of soil and vegetation in Cornwall, England, have been compared by Millman (1957). Experiments in Malaya, using a rapid field method of analysis, have shown that the tin content of fine stream sediment can be used in regional reconnaissance for distinguishing stanniferous and nonstanniferous granites. (Webb and Tooms, in preparation.)

TITANIUM

IGNEOUS ROCKS: Av 4400; Umaf 3000; Maf 9000; Fels 2300 ppm.

SEDIMENTARY ROCKS: Ls 400; Ss 3000; Sh 4400 ppm (Green, 1959).

SOILS: Av 4600; Range 1000–10,000 ppm.

FRESH WATER: Range 0.2–30 ppb.

ASSOCIATIONS: Lithophile; enriched in alkaline and in mafic igneous rocks.

ROCK MINERALS: Sphene and ilmenite (moderately stable).

PRIMARY ORE MINERALS: Rutile (stable); ilmenite.

SECONDARY MINERALS: Leucoxene.

SOIL PHASE: Ilmenite, secondary oxides.

AQUEOUS PHASE: Unknown.

MOBILITY: Low, limited by stability of both primary and secondary minerals.

GEOCHEMICAL PROSPECTING APPLICATIONS: Inasmuch as ilmenite deposits are magnetic and easily detected by magnetic exploration methods, virtually no work on geochemical prospecting for Ti has been attempted.

TUNGSTEN

IGNEOUS ROCKS: Av 2 ppm

SEDIMENTARY ROCKS: Ss 1.6; Ls 1.8 ppm (Green, 1959).

ASSOCIATIONS: Lithophile; Mo, Sn, and Nb in igneous differentiates.

ROCK MINERALS: Not known.

PRIMARY ORE MINERALS: Scheelite ($CaWO_4$) (moderately stable); wolframite (($Fe, Mn) WO_4$) (stable).

AQUEOUS PHASE: Probably ionic $WO_4{}^{--}$.

MOBILITY: May be moderately high, limited by slow dissolution of primary minerals.

GEOCHEMICAL PROSPECTING APPLICATIONS: In France and in Uganda W anomalies in soil have been found in residual cover overlying W-bearing veins (Holman and Webb, 1957; Granier, 1958). Chemical analysis of stream sediment has shown promise as a reconnaissance method (Theobald and Thompson, 1959). The possibility that the mobility of WO_4 may be high under appropriate conditions (Carpenter and Garrett, 1959) may lead to a reconnaissance method based on the W content of water.

URANIUM

IGNEOUS ROCKS: Av 2.6; Umaf 0.03; Maf 0.8; Fels 3.5 ppm.

SEDIMENTARY ROCKS: Ls 2.5; Ss 0.45; Sh 4.1 ppm (Green, 1959); BkSh 2–300 ppm (Fix, 1958).

SOILS: Av 1 ppm.

PLANT ASH: 0.6 ppm.

FRESH WATER: 0.05–1 ppb (Fix, 1956; Germanov et al., 1958).

ASSOCIATIONS: Lithophile; Co and Ag in some sulfide deposits; V, As, P, Mo, Se, Pb, Cu, etc. in deposits resulting from desert weathering; C in black shales (Bates and Strahl, 1958); P in phosphorite deposits (Altschuler et al., 1958).

RADIOGENIC DAUGHTER PRODUCTS: The natural radioactivity of U makes possible a variety of exploration methods that are not applicable to the stable elements. Each member of the radioactive decay series starting with U and ending with Pb is a different nuclear species, and can be specifically identified and measured by an appropriate combination of chemical and radiometric techniques. The half-life of some of these decay products is long enough that they can form independent dispersion patterns characteristic of their own individual chemical properties. The principal daughter products of U are Th, Ra, Rn, Pb, and He. The gases, Kr and Xe, resulting from natural U fission, have also been suggested as a guide to U ore (Amiel and Winsberg, 1956). Because of their contrasting geochemical properties, the most important of the daughter products are discussed separately under radium, radon, and helium.

ROCK MINERALS: Zircon (stable), apatite (moderately stable), allanite (unstable).

PRIMARY ORE MINERALS: Uraninite (complex U oxide) (unstable).

SECONDARY MINERALS: Complex carbonates, phosphates, and vanadates.

SOIL PHASE: Organic matter.

AQUEOUS PHASE: Ionic UO_2^{++} and $UO_2(CO_3)_3^{4-}$.

BIOLOGICAL RESPONSE: In vegetation, most of the U in the nutrient solution is apparently precipitated in the root tips as autunite, $Ca(UO_2)_2PO_4$. Even so, some U gets through to the upper parts of some plant species where it can be sampled in biogeochemical prospecting (Cannon, 1952, 1957, 1960b; Cannon and Kleinhampl, 1956). Because of the association of Se with U deposits of the Colorado Plateau, Se indicator plants have been successfully used in locating U-rich areas (Cannon, 1957, 1960b; Kleinhampl and Koteff, 1960).

MOBILITY: Extremely mobile under alkaline, oxidizing conditions; limited by Eh of reduction of UO_2^{++} complex, and by tendency to be either precipitated with solid organic matter (Bowes et al., 1959) or by solubility of organic complexes (Manskaya et al., 1956).

Geochemical prospecting applications: The U content of residual soil has been used as an ore guide under many climatic conditions (Coulomb and Goldsztein, 1956; Jones *et al.*, 1956; Gangloff *et al.*, 1958; Illsley *et al.*, 1958). Because of the high mobility of U under desert conditions, the fraction of the U in soil that can be leached with weak reagents may help in exploration (Holland *et al.*, 1957, 1958). Analysis of plants for U has been one of the most successful of the geochemical methods used on the Colorado Plateau (Cannon and Kleinhampl, 1956; Cannon, 1960b; Froelich and Kleinhampl, 1960; Kleinhampl and Koteff, 1960). Under favorable conditions, the U content of vegetation will give an indication of buried ore through thicknesses of as much as 50 feet of barren cover. The U content of fresh water is extremely effective as a method of reconnaissance exploration (Judson and Osmond, 1955; Vinogradov, 1956b; Denson *et al.*, 1956; Fix, 1956; Saukov, 1956; Goldsztein, 1957; Germanov *et al.*, 1958; Illsley *et al.*, 1958; Moyseyenko, 1959; Landis, 1960). U preferentially precipitated in the organic matter of peat bogs may serve as an indicator of U-rich spring water (Armands and Landergren, 1960). Experiments with radiometric methods of analysis of stream sediments have been tried, but have not been outstandingly successful (Chew, 1956). According to Grimbert (personal communication) chemical analysis of sediments has shown considerable promise in France.

VANADIUM

Igneous rocks: Av 90; Umaf 140; Maf 200; Fels 40 ppm.
Sedimentary rocks: Ls 2–20; Ss 10–60; Sh 50–300; BkSh 50–2000 ppm.
Soils: Av 100; Range 20–500 ppm.
Plant ash: 22 ppm.
Associations: Lithophile; strong enrichment in some crude oils, asphaltites, black shales, and phosphorites; Fe, Ti in magnetite; U, P, Pb, Cu, K in secondary U-V minerals; Pb, Zn in some sulfide deposits.
Rock minerals: Magnetite and ilmenite (stable), and to a lesser extent ferromagnesian minerals (moderately stable).
Primary ore mineral: Patronite (VS_4) (unstable).
Secondary ore minerals: Secondary uranyl vanadates; sedimentary Fe ores.
Soil phase: Clay minerals, vanadates.
Aqueous phase: Probably ionic VO_4^{3-}.
Mobility: Probably very low, limited by reaction and precipitation with organic matter.
Geochemical prospecting applications: V may be useful as a pathfinder for V-rich sulfide deposits.

ZINC

Igneous rocks: Av 80; Umaf 50; Maf 130; Fels 60 ppm.
Sedimentary rocks: Ls 4–20; Ss 5–20; Sh 50–300; BkSh 100–1000 ppm.

SOILS: Av 50; Range 10–300 ppm.

PLANT ASH: 1400 ppm.

FRESH WATER: 1–200 ppb.

ASSOCIATIONS: Chalcophile; Cu, Pb, Ag, Au, Sb, As, Se in base-metal and precious-metal deposits; Mg in some silicates.

ROCK MINERALS: Ferromagnesian minerals (moderately stable).

PRIMARY ORE MINERAL: Sphalerite (unstable).

SECONDARY MINERALS: Sulfates, carbonates, hydrated silicates.

SOIL PHASE: Sorbed on limonite and in lattice positions of clay minerals (White, 1957).

AQUEOUS PHASE: Variable partition between floating organisms, soluble organic matter and ionic Zn^{++}.

BIOLOGICAL RESPONSE: Zn is an essential nutrient for almost all plants. For this reason algae growing in streams and lakes can absorb a large part of the Zn dissolved in the water. In addition to the nutritive effect, Zn is also toxic to most forms of plants if it is present in amounts exceeding certain limits. In Silesia, Zn deposits have been indicated by the distribution of a species of violet (Jensch, 1894).

MOBILITY: Moderately high, limited by organic activity and coprecipitation with limonite.

GEOCHEMICAL PROSPECTING APPLICATIONS: As a result of the fixation of Zn in the sesquioxides and clays of residual soils, geochemical prospecting based on analysis of soils for Zn has been a very successful method (Hawkes and Lakin, 1949; Fulton, 1950; Huff, 1952; Hawkes, 1954; Boyle and Cragg, 1957; Miesch and Nolan, 1958; Webb, 1958b). Zn not uncommonly forms epigenetic dispersion patterns in transported overburden (Hawkes 1954; Cox and Hollister, 1955; Byers, 1956) and in peat swamps (Salmi, 1950; Cannon, 1955). A considerable amount of work has been done on the sampling and analysis of trees and plants for Zn as a prospecting method. For most problems in exploration for Zn deposits, soil sampling is preferable to plant sampling because of the greater ease of collecting and analyzing samples and because of the greater homogeneity of the anomalous patterns. Because of its fairly high mobility, Zn forms useful dispersion patterns in ground water (Kennedy, 1956; Sveshnikov, 1957), in stream water (Sergeyev, 1946; Webb and Millman, 1950; Riddell, 1952, 1954; Atkinson, 1957; Boyle et al., 1955, 1958), and in sediments (Hawkes and Bloom, 1956; Boyle et al., 1958; Webb, 1958b).

LITERATURE CITED

Abelson, P. H., ed., 1959, Researches in geochemistry: New York, John Wiley, 511 p.

Agnew, A. F., 1955, Application of geology to the discovery of zinc-lead ore, in the Wisconsin-Illinois-Iowa District: Mining Eng., v. 7, p. 781–795.

Ahmed, M. B., and Twyman, E. S., 1953, The relative toxicity of manganese and cobalt to the tomato plant: Jour. Expt. Botany, v. 4, p. 164–172.

Ahrens, L. H., 1954, Lognormal distribution of the elements: Geochim. et Cosmochim. Acta, v. 5, p. 49–73; v. 6, p. 121–131.

Ahrens, L. H., and Liebenberg, W. R., 1950, Tin and indium in mica, as determined spectrochemically: Am. Mineralogist, v. 35, p. 571–578.

Almond, Hy, 1953a, Determination of traces of cobalt in soils: Anal. Chemistry, v. 25, p. 166–167.

Almond, Hy, 1953b, Field method for determination of traces of arsenic in soils—confined spot procedure using a modified Gutzeit apparatus: Anal. Chemistry, v. 25, p. 1766–1777.

Almond, Hy, 1955, Rapid field and laboratory method for the determination of copper in soils and rocks: U. S. Geol. Survey Bull. 1036A, p. 1–8.

Almond, Hy, Stevens, R. E., and Lakin, H. W., 1953, A confined-spot method for the determination of traces of silver in soils and rocks: U. S. Geol. Survey Bull. 992, p. 71–81.

Altschuler, Z. S., Clarke, R. S., Jr., and Young, E. J., 1958, Geochemistry of uranium in apatite and phosphorite: U. S. Geol. Survey Prof. Paper 314-D, p. 45–90.

American Society of Photogrammetry, 1959, Manual of photographic interpretation.

Amiel, Saadia, and Winsberg, Lester, 1956, Measurements on natural water sources as an aid in prospecting for underground deposits of uranium, in United Nations, 1956: p. 792–793.

Anderson, D. H., and Hawkes, H. E., 1958, Relative mobility of the common elements in weathering of some schist and granite areas: Geochim. et Cosmochim. Acta, v. 14, p. 204–210.

Anthony, L. M., and Mukherjee, N. R., 1956, Hydrogen ion and soluble heavy-metal distribution of soil horizons over the Cleary Hill gold veins, Alaska [abs.]: Geol. Soc. America Bull., v. 67, p. 1805.

Arkhangel'sky, A. D., and Soloviev, N. V., 1938, Experimental investigation of the mechanism of accumulation of copper in sedimentary rocks [in Russian with English abs.]: Bull. Acad. Sci. U. S. S. R., Ser. Geol., 1938, no. 2, p. 279–294.

Armands, Gösta, and Landergren, Sture, 1960, Geochemical prospecting for uranium in northern Sweden. The enrichment of uranium in peat, in Int. Geol. Cong. XXI Session, 1960: p. 51–66.

Atkinson, D. J., 1957, Heavy metal concentration in streams in north Angola: Econ. Geology, v. 52, p. 652–667.

Aubrey, K. V., 1956, Frequency distributions of elements in igneous rocks: Geochim. et Cosmochim. Acta, v. 9, p. 83–89.

Austin, C. F., and Nackowski, M. P., 1958, Geochemical exploration at Darwin Mines, California [abs.]: Geol. Soc. America Bull., v. 69, p. 1531.

Baranova, V. V., 1957, Aureoles of molybdenum dissemination in one section of the Tyrny-Auz mineral district: Geochemistry, 1957, p. 152–158.

Barshad, Isaac, 1948, Molybdenum content of pasture plants in relation to toxicity to cattle: Soil Science, v. 66, p. 187–195.

Bates, T. F., and Strahl, E. O., 1958, Mineralogy and chemistry of uranium-bearing black shales: in United Nations, 1958: p. 407–411.

Bear, F. E., ed., 1955, Chemistry of the soil: New York, Reinhold, 373 p.

Beath, O. A., Gilbert, C. S., and Eppson, H. F., 1939, The use of indicator plants in locating seleniferous areas in western United States: I General: Am. Jour. Botany, v. 26, p. 257–269.

Belyakova, Ye. Ye., 1957, Distribution of molybdenum in subsurface water of certain sulfide deposits in Central Kazakhstan [in Russian]: in Krasnikov, 1957: p. 265–274.

Belyakova, Ye. Ye., 1958, Migration of elements in underground and surface waters of the Upper Kairakty District, Central Kazakhstan: Geochemistry, 1958, p. 176–188.

Berce, Boris, 1960, Method and results of geochemical investigations of mercury: in Int. Geol. Cong. XXI Session, 1960: p. 65–74.

Bethke, P. M., and Barton, P. B., Jr., 1959, Trace-element distribution as an indicator of pressure and temperature of ore deposition [abs.]: Geol. Soc. America Bull., v. 70, p. 1569–1570.

Billings, W. D., 1950, Vegetation and plant growth as affected by chemically altered rock in the western Great Basin: Ecology, v. 31, p. 62–74.

Blackwelder, E., 1927, Fire as an agent in rock weathering: Jour. Geology, v. 35, p. 134–140.

Bloom, Harold, 1955, A field method for the determination of ammonium citrate-soluble heavy metals in soils and alluvium: Econ. Geology, v. 50, p. 533–541.

Bloss, F. D., and Steiner, R. L., 1960, Biogeochemical prospecting for manganese in northeast Tennessee: Geol. Soc. America Bull., v. 71, p. 1053–1066.

Bolgarsky, Michel, 1950, Geology and petrography of the southwestern part of the Ivory Coast [in French]: Gouv't. Général Afrique Occidentale Franç., Bull. Div. Mines No. 9, p. 1–170.

Bowen, N. L., 1922, The reaction principle in petrogenesis: Jour. Geology, v. 30, p. 177–198.

Bowes, W. A., Bales, W. E., and Haselton, G. M., 1959, Geology of the uraniferous bog deposit at Pettit Ranch, Kern County, Calif.: U. S. Atomic Energy Comm. RME-2063, pt. 1, 29 p.

Bowie, S. H. U., Bisby, H., Burke, K. C., and Hale, F. H., 1960, Electronic instruments for detecting and assaying beryllium ores: Inst. Mining Metallurgy Trans., v. 69, pt. 7, p. 345–359.

*Boyle, R. W., and Cragg, C. B., 1957, Soil analysis as a method of geochemical prospecting in Keno Hill-Galena Hill area, Yukon Territory: Canada Geol. Survey Bull. 39, 27 p.

*Boyle, R. W., Illsley, C. T., and Green, R. N., 1955, Geochemical investigation of the heavy metal content of stream and spring waters in the Keno Hill-Galena Hill area, Yukon Territory: Canada Geol. Survey Bull. 32 34 p.

*Boyle, R. W., Koehler, G. F., Moxham, R. L., and Palmer, H. C., 1958, Heavy metal (Zn, Cu, Pb) content of water and sediment in the streams, rivers and lakes of southwestern Nova Scotia: Canada Geol. Survey Paper 58-1.

Britton, H. T. S., 1956, Hydrogen ions: Princeton, Van Nostrand, 4th ed., 2 v., 489 and 476 p.

Broderick, T. M., 1929, Zoning in Michigan copper deposits and its significance: Econ. Geology, v. 24, p. 149–162, 311–326.

Brodsky, A. A., 1956, Hydrochemical method of prospecting for copper [in Russian]: Moscow, Gosgeoltekhizdat, 84 p.

Brown, W. H., 1935, Quantitative study of ore zoning, Austinville mine, Wythe County, Virginia: Econ. Geology, v. 30, p. 425–433.

Brownell, G. M., 1959, A beryllium detector for field exploration: Econ. Geology, v. 54, p. 1103–1114.

Broyer, T. C., 1947, The movement of material into plants. II The nature of solute movement into plants: Botan. Rev., v. 13, p. 125–167.

Brundin, Nils, 1939, Method of locating metals and minerals in the ground: U. S. Patent 2158980, May 16, 1939.

Buck, L. J., 1951, Shrub aids in determining extent of orebody: Garden Jour. [New York Botanical Garden], Jan.–Feb., 1951, p. 22.

Burnham, C. W., 1959, Metallogenic provinces of the southwestern United States and northern Mexico: N. Mex. Bur. Mines and Mineral Res. Bull. 65, p. 1–76.

*Bush, J. B., and Cook, D. R., 1960, The Chief Oxide-Burgin Area discoveries, East Tintic District, Utah; a case history. Pt. II Bear Creek Mining Co. studies and exploration: Econ. Geol., v. 55, p. 1507–1540.

Buyalov, N. I., and Shvyryayeva, A. M., 1955, Geobotanical methods in prospecting for salts of boron [translation from Russian]: Int. Geol. Rev., v. 3, p. 619–625, 1961 [original in Geobotanicheskiye Methody pri Geologicheskikh Issledovaniyakh, Trudy Vsesoyuznogo Aerogeologicheskogo Tresta, vyp. 1, p. 135–146].

Byers, A. R., 1956, Geochemical prospecting in the Flin Flon-Amisk Lake base metal area, northern Saskatchewan [abs.]: in Int. Geol. Cong. XX Session, 1956: p. 359.

Canney, F. C., 1959, Effect of soil contamination on geochemical prospecting in the Coeur d'Alene district, Idaho: Mining Eng., v. 11, p. 205–210.

* Refers to a geochemical prospecting case history.

*Canney, F. C., Hawkes, H. E., Richmond, G. M., and Vhay, J. W., 1953, A preliminary report of geochemical investigations in the Blackbird District: U. S. Geol. Survey Open File Rept., Dec. 21, 1953, 20 p.

Cannon, Helen L., 1952, The effect of uranium-vanadium deposits on the vegetation of the Colorado Plateau: Am. Jour. Sci., v. 250, p. 735–770.

*Cannon, Helen L., 1955, Geochemical relations of zinc-bearing peat to the Lockport Dolomite, Orleans Country, New York, U. S. Geol. Survey Bull. 1000-D, p. 119–185.

Cannon, Helen L., 1957, Description of indicator plants and methods of botanical prospecting for uranium deposits on the Colorado Plateau: U. S. Geol. Survey Bull. 1030-M, p. 399–516.

Cannon, Helen L., 1960a, The development of botanical methods of prospecting for uranium on the Colorado Plateau: U. S. Geol. Survey Bull. 1085-A, p. 1–50.

Cannon, Helen L., 1960b, Botanical prospecting for ore deposits: Science, v. 132, no. 3427, p. 591–598.

Cannon, Helen L., and Kleinhampl, F. J., 1956, Botanical methods of prospecting for uranium: in United Nations, 1956: p. 801–805.

*Cannon, Helen L., and Starrett, W. H., 1956, Botanical prospecting for uranium on La Ventura Mesa, Sandoval County, New Mexico: U. S. Geol. Survey Bull. 1009-M, p. 391–407.

Carpenter, L. G., and Garrett, D. E., 1959, Tungsten in Searles Lake: Mining Eng., v. 11, p. 301–303.

Carroll, Dorothy, 1959, Ion exchange in clays and other minerals: Geol. Soc. America Bull., v. 70, p. 748–780.

Chamberlin, T. C., 1883, Terminal moraine of the second glacial epoch: U. S. Geol. Survey Third Ann. Rept., p. 291–402.

Chapman, R. M., 1958, Geochemical exploration in the Kantishna area, Alaska [abs]: Geol. Soc. America Bull., v. 69, p. 1751–1752.

Chayes, Felix, 1954, The log-normal distribution of the elements (a discussion): Geochim. et Cosmochim. Acta, v. 6, p. 119–120.

Chew, R. T., III, 1956, Study of radioactivity in modern stream gravels as a method of prospecting: U. S. Geol. Survey Bull. 1030-E, p. 153–169.

Chisholm, E. O., 1950, A simple chemical method of tracing mineralization through light non-residual overburden: Canadian Inst. Mining Metallurgy Trans., v. 53, p. 44–48.

*Chisholm, E. O., 1957, Geophysical exploration of a lead-zinc deposit in Yukon Territory: in Sixth Commonwealth Mining and Metallurgy Cong. 1957, p. 269–277.

Chumakov, A. A., and Ginzburg, I. V., 1957, A new rare-metal geochemical province on the Kola Peninsula [in Russian]: Akad. Nauk S. S. S. R., Doklady, v. 114, p. 400–403.

Clarke, G. R., 1938, The study of the soil in the field: Oxford, Clarendon, 2nd ed., 142 p.

*Coope, J. A., 1958, Studies in geochemical prospecting for nickel in Bechuanaland and Tanganyika: D. I. C. Thesis, Imperial College, London.

* Refers to a geochemical prospecting case history.

Cooper, J. R., and Huff, L. C., 1951, Geological investigations and geochemical prospecting experiment at Johnson, Arizona: Econ. Geology, v. 46, p. 731–756.

Coulomb, R., 1958, Statistical study of the geochemical dispersion of uranium in soils [in French]: *in* Int. Geol. Cong. XX Session, 1958: p. 99–112.

Coulomb, R., and Goldsztein, M., 1956, Geochemical prospecting [in French]: Rev. de l'Industrie Minérale, Numéro Special IR, Jan. 1956, p. 140–153.

*Cox, M. W., and Hollister, V. F., 1955, The Chollet project, Stevens County, Washington: Mining Eng., v. 7, p. 937–940.

Craven, C. A. U., 1954, Statistical estimation of the accuracy of assaying: Inst. Mining Metallurgy Trans., v. 63, pt. 12, p. 551–563.

Crooke, W. M., 1956, Effect of soil reaction on the uptake of nickel from a serpentine soil: Soil Sci., v. 81, p. 269–276.

Davidson, C. F., 1951, Distribution of radioactivity: Mining Mag. [London], v. 85, p. 329–340.

*Debnam, A. H., and Webb, J. S., 1960, Some geochemical anomalies in soil and stream sediment related to beryl pegmatites in Rhodesia and Uganda: Inst. Mining Metallurgy Trans., v. 69, pt. 7, p. 329–344, and Discussion, p. 637–660.

De Grys, Antoinette M., 1959, Factors affecting the secondary geochemical dispersion of metals associated with sulfide mineralization: D. I. C. Thesis, Imperial College, London.

*Denson, M. E., Jr., 1956, Geophysical-geochemical prospecting for uranium: *in* United Nations, 1956: p. 772–781.

*Denson, N. M., Zeller, H. D., and Stephens, J. G., 1956, Water sampling as a guide in the search for uranium deposits and its use in evaluating widespread volcanic units as potential source beds for uranium: *in* United Nations, 1956: p. 794–800.

Doe, B. R., 1956, Geothermometry at the Balmat No. 2 Mine, New York: Thesis, University of Missouri, Rolla, Mo.

Dolukhanova, N. I., 1957, The application of hydrochemical surveys to copper and molybdenum deposits in the Armenian S. S. R. [in Russian]: Akad. Nauk Armyanskoy S. S. R. [Yerevan], 90 p. [partial English translation *in* Int. Geol. Rev., v. 2, p. 20–42, 1960].

Dorn, Paul, 1937, Plants as indicators of ore deposits [in German]: Der Biologe [Munich], v. 6, p. 11–13.

Dreimanis, A., 1960, Geochemical prospecting for Cu, Pb and Zn in glaciated areas, eastern Canada: *in* Int. Geol. Cong. XXI Session, 1960: Pt. II, p. 7–19.

Duvigneaud, Paul, 1958, The vegetation of Katanga and of its metalliferous soils [in French]: Bull. Soc. Roy. Botanique de Belgique, v. 90, p. 127–286.

Eckelmann, F. E. and Kulp, J. L., 1959, Lead isotopes and ore deposition in the southeast Missouri lead district [abs.]: Geol. Soc. America Bull., v. 70, p. 1595.

* Refers to a geochemical prospecting case history.

Emmons, W. H., 1917, The enrichment of ore deposits: U. S. Geol. Survey Bull. 625, p. 68–70.

Engel, A. E. J., Clayton, R. N., and Epstein, S., 1958, Variations in the isotopic composition of oxygen in the Leadville limestone (Mississippian) of Colorado, as a guide to the location and origin of its mineral deposits: *in* Int. Geol. Cong. XX Session, 1958: p. 3–20.

Engel, A. E. J., and Engel, C. G., 1956, Distribution of copper, lead and zinc in hydrothermal dolomites associated with sulfide ore in the Leadville limestone [abs.]: Geol. Soc. America Bull., v. 67, p. 1692.

Ermengen, S. V., 1957, Geochemical prospecting in Chibougamau: Canadian Mining Jour., v. 78, no. 4, p. 99–104.

Evans, H. J., Purvis, E. R., and Bear, F. E., 1951, Effect of soil reaction on availability of molybdenum: Soil Sci., v. 71, p. 117–124.

Faul, Henry, *et al.*, 1954, Radium and helium in natural gas: Cong. Geol. Int., Comptes rendus, XIX Session, Algiers, 1952; v. 9, p. 339–348.

Feigl, Fritz, 1958, Spot tests in inorganic analysis [translation by R. E. Oesper]: Amsterdam, London, and Princeton, N. J., Elsevier, 5th ed., 600 p.

Fersman, A. Ye., 1939, Geochemical and mineralogical methods of prospecting, Chap. IV, Special methods of prospecting [in Russian]: Akad. Nauk S. S. R., [Moscow], p. 164–238 [translation by Hartsock, Lydia, and Pierce, A. P., U. S. Geol. Survey Circ. 127, 1952].

Fieldes, M., and Swindale, L. D., 1954, Chemical weathering of silicates in soil formation: New Zealand Jour. Sci. Tech., v. 36B, p. 140–154.

Fitch, F. H., and Webb, J. S., 1958, Contribution on geochemical aspects of the Sandakan Area: *in* F. H. Fitch, Copper deposits of the Sandakan Area: Geological Survey Department, British Territories in Borneo, Memoir 9, p. 125–152.

Fix, Carolyn E., 1958, Selected annotated bibliography of the geology and occurrence of uranium-bearing marine black shales in the United States: U. S. Geol. Survey Bull. 1059-F, p. 263–325.

Fix, P. F., 1956, Hydrogeochemical exploration for uranium: *in* United Nations, 1956: p. 788–791.

Fleischer, Michael, 1954, The abundance and distribution of the chemical elements in the earth's crust: Jour. Chem. Education, v. 31, p. 446–455.

Flerov, B. L., 1935, The application of the stannometric survey for the exploration of primary tin deposits [in Russian]: Redkie Metally, 1935, no. 1, p. 31–39.

Flerov, B. L., 1938, On methods of prospecting primary tin deposits [in Russian]: Sovetskaya Geol., v. 8, no. 10, p. 63–81.

Flint, R. F., 1957, Glacial and Pleistocene geology: New York, Wiley, 553 p.

Forrester, J. D., 1942, A native copper deposit near Jefferson City, Montana: Econ. Geol., v. 37, p. 126–135.

Friese, F. W., 1931, Study of the abrasion of minerals during transport in water [in German]: Mineralog. Petrog. Mitt., v. 41, p. 1–7.

Froelich, A. J., and Kleinhampl, F. J., 1960, Botanical prospecting for uranium in the Deer Flat Area, White Canyon District, San Juan County, Utah: U. S. Geol. Survey Bull. 1085-B, p. 51–84.

*Fulton, R. B., 1950, Prospecting for zinc using semiquantitative analyses of soils: Econ. Geology, v. 45, p. 654–670.

Fulton, R. B., Hoy, R. B., and Kendall, D. L., 1958, Frequency distribution of zinc-lead-copper values in soils of eastern United States: *in* Int. Geol. Cong. XX Session, 1958: p. 81–97.

Fursov, V. Z., 1958, Mercury dispersion halos as prospecting indication at the lead-zinc Achisai deposit: Geochemistry, 1958, p. 338–344.

Gangloff, A. M., Collin, C. R., Grimbert, Arnold, and Sanselme, Henri, 1958, Application of geophysical and geochemical methods to the search for uranium: *in* United Nations, 1958: p. 140–147.

Garrels, R. M., 1960, Mineral equilibria at low temperature and pressure: New York, Harper, 254 p.

Germanov, A. I., Batulin, S. G., Volkov, G. A., Lisitsin, A. K., and Serebrennikov, V. A., 1958, Some regularities of uranium distribution in underground waters: *in* United Nations, 1958: p. 161–177.

Gilbert, R. E., 1951, Geochemical prospecting in the Park City district: Mining Cong. Jour., v. 37, no. 9, p. 58–61.

Gilbert, R. E., 1953, Testing geophysical exploration methods: Mining Eng., v. 5, p. 50–52.

Gill, J. R., and Denson, N. M., 1957, Regional synthesis—eastern Montana and the Dakotas: U. S. Geol. Survey TEI-700, p. 160–171.

Ginzburg, I. I., 1960, Principles of geochemical prospecting [translation from Russian by V. P. Sokoloff]: New York and London, Pergamon, 311 p. [original published by Gosgeoltekhizdat, Moscow, 1957, 298 p.]

Goldich, S. S., 1938, A study in rock weathering: Jour. Geology, v. 46, p. 17–58.

Goldschmidt, V. M., 1937, The principles of distribution of chemical elements in minerals and rocks: Jour. Chem. Soc. [London], p. 655–673.

Goldschmidt, V. M., 1954, Geochemistry: Oxford, Clarendon, 730 p.

Goldsztein, M., 1957, Geobotanical prospecting for uranium in Esterel [in French]: Soc. Française Minéralog. Cristallographie Bull., v. 80, p. 318–324.

Goloubinoff, Vsevolad de, 1937, Differential geochemical prospecting of mineral deposits [in French]: Acad. Sci. [Paris], Comptes rendus, v. 204, p. 1075–1077.

Gorham, Eville, 1955, On the acidity and salinity of rain: Geochim. et Cosmochim. Acta, v. 7, p. 231–239.

Gottschalk, V. H., and Buehler, H. A., 1912, Oxidation of sulphides: Econ. Geology, v. 7, p. 15–34.

*Govett, G. J. S., 1958, Geochemical prospecting for copper in Northern Rhodesia: Ph. D. Thesis, Imperial College, London.

*Govett, G. J. S., 1960, Geochemical prospecting for copper in Northern Rhodesia: *in* Int. Geol. Cong. XXI Session, 1960: p. 44–56.

G.P.R.C., 1961a, Determination of cobalt in soil and sediment samples:

*Refers to a geochemical prospecting case history.

Geochemical Prospecting Res. Centre, Imperial College, London, Tech. Comm. No. 14.

G.P.R.C., 1961b, Determination of molybdenum in soil, sediment and rock samples: Geochemical Prospecting Res. Centre, Imperial College, London, Tech. Comm. No. 15.

G.P.R.C., 1961c, Determination of lead in soil, sediment and rock samples: Geochemical Prospecting Res. Centre, Imperial College, London, Tech. Comm. No. 16.

Graf, D. L., and Kerr, P. F., 1950, Trace-element studies, Santa Rita, New Mexico: Geol. Soc. America Bull., v. 61, p. 1023–1052.

Graham, E. R., 1941, Acid clay, an agent in chemical weathering: Jour. Geology, v. 49, p. 392–401.

Granier, C., 1958, Dispersion of tungsten and arsenic in residual soil [in French]: Soc. Française Minéralog. Cristallographie Bull., v. 81, p. 194–200.

Green, Jack, 1959, Geochemical table of the elements for 1959: Geol. Soc. America Bull., v. 70, p. 1127–1184.

Griffith, S. V., 1960, Alluvial prospecting and mining: New York and London, Pergamon, 2nd ed., 245 p.

Griggs, David, 1936, The factor of fatigue in rock exfoliation: Jour. Geology, v. 44, p. 783–796.

Grim, R. E., 1953, Clay mineralogy: New York, McGraw-Hill, 396 p.

Grimaldi, F. S., May, Irving, Fletcher, M. H., and Titcomb, Jane, 1954, Collected papers on methods of analysis for uranium and thorium: U. S. Geol. Survey Bull. 1006, p. 1–184.

Grimbert, Arnold, 1956, Application of geochemical prospecting techniques to research and to study of uranium deposits in Metropolitan France [abs.]: in Int. Geol. Cong. XX Session, 1956: p. 362.

Grip, Erland, 1953, Tracing of glacial boulders as an aid to ore prospecting in Sweden: Econ. Geology, v. 48, p. 715–725.

Gross, W. H., 1952, Radioactivity as a guide to ore: Econ. Geology, v. 47, p. 722–742.

Hammett, F. S., 1928, Studies in the biology of metals. I The localization of lead by growing roots: Protoplasma, v. 4, p. 183–186.

Harbaugh, J. W., 1953, Geochemical prospecting abstracts through June 1952: U. S. Geol. Survey Bull. 1000-A, p. 1–50.

Hardon, H. J., 1936, Podzol profile in the tropics: Natuurkundig Tijdschr., v. 96, p. 25–41.

*Hawkes, H. E., 1954, Geochemical prospecting investigations in the Nyeba lead-zinc district, Nigeria: U. S. Geol. Survey Bull. 1000-B, p. 51–103.

Hawkes, H. E., 1957, Principles of geochemical prospecting: U. S. Geol. Survey Bull. 1000-F, p. 225–355.

Hawkes, H. E., 1959, Geochemical prospecting: in Abelson, 1959: p. 62–78.

Hawkes, H. E., and Bloom, Harold, 1956, Heavy metals in stream sediment used as exploration guides: Mining Eng., v. 8, p. 1121–1126.

*Hawkes, H. E., Bloom, Harold, and Riddell, J. E., 1957, Stream sediment

* Refers to a geochemical prospecting case history.

analysis discovers two mineral deposits: *in* Sixth Commonwealth Mining Metallurgy Cong., 1957: p. 259–268.

*Hawkes, H. E., Bloom, Harold, Riddell, J. E., and Webb, J. S., 1956, Geochemical reconnaissance in eastern Canada [abs.]: *in* Int. Geol. Cong. XX Session, 1956: p. 358.

Hawkes, H. E., and Lakin, H. W., 1949, Vestigial zinc in surface residuum associated with primary zinc ore in east Tennessee: Econ. Geology, v. 44, p. 286–295.

Hawkes, H. E., and Salmon, M. L., 1960, Trace elements in organic soil as a guide to copper ore: *in* Int. Geol. Cong. XXI Session, 1960: p. 38–43.

Hem, J. D., 1959, Study and interpretation of the chemical characteristics of natural water: U. S. Geol. Survey Water-Supply Paper 1473, p. 269.

Hem, J. D., 1960, Complexes of ferrous iron with tannic acid: U. S. Geol. Survey Water-Supply Paper 1459-D, p. 75–94.

Heydemann, Annerose, 1959, Adsorption from very weak copper solutions on pure clay minerals [in German]: Geochim. et Cosmochim. Acta, v. 15, p. 305–329.

Hoagland, D. R., Chandler, W. H., and Stout, P. R., 1937, Little-leaf or rosette of fruit trees. VI Further experiments bearing on the cause of the disease: Proc. Am. Soc. Hort. Sci., v. 34, p. 210–212.

*Holland, H. D., Curtiss, B. R., McGill, G. B., and Petersen, J. A., 1957, The use of leachable uranium in geochemical prospecting on the Colorado Plateau. I The distribution of leachable uranium in core samples adjacent to the Homestake Ore Body, Big Indian Wash, Utah: Econ. Geology, v. 52, p. 546–569.

Holland, H. D., Witter, G. G., Jr., Head, W. B. III, and Petti, Ruth W., 1958, The use of leachable uranium in geochemical prospecting on the Colorado Plateau. II The distribution of leachable uranium in surface samples in the vicinity of ore bodies: Econ. Geology, v. 53, p. 190–209.

Holman, R. H. C., 1956a, A method for determining readily-soluble copper in soil and alluvium—introducing white spirit as a solvent for dithizone: Inst. Mining Metallurgy Trans., v. 66, pt. 1, p. 7–16.

*Holman, R. H. C., 1956b, Geochemical prospecting studies in the Kilembe Area, Uganda. I Dispersion of copper in the drainage system: Geochemical Prospecting Res. Centre, Imperial College, London, Tech. Comm. No. 9, 136 p.

*Holman, R. H. C., 1959, Lead in stream sediments, northern mainland of Nova Scotia [map]: Canada Geol. Survey Map 26–1959, Sheet 2.

Holman, R. H. C., and Webb, J. S., 1957, Exploratory geochemical soil survey at Ruhiza ferberite mine, Uganda: *in* Sixth Commonwealth Mining Metallurgy Cong., 1957: p. 353–357.

Horizon, 1959, A flower that led to a copper discovery: Horizon [Salisbury, Southern Rhodesia], v. 1, no. 1, p. 35–39.

Huff, L. C., 1948, A sensitive field test for heavy metals in water: Econ. Geology, v. 43, p. 675–684.

* Refers to a geochemical prospecting case history.

Huff, L. C., 1952, Abnormal copper, lead, and zinc content of soil near metalliferous veins: Econ. Geology, v. 47, p. 517–542.

Huff, L. C., 1955, A Paleozoic geochemical anomaly near Jerome, Arizona: U. S. Geol. Survey Bull. 1000-C, p. 105–118.

Huff, L. C., 1956, Comparison of soil analysis with other prospecting methods at a small, high-grade copper lode [abs.]: in Int. Geol. Cong. XX Session, 1956, p. 364.

Hunt, E. C., North, A. A., and Wells, R. A., 1955, Application of paper-chromatographic methods of analysis to geochemical prospecting: The Analyst, v. 80, p. 172–194.

Hunt, E. C., Stanton, R. E., and Wells, R. A., 1960, Field determination of beryllium in soils for geochemical prospecting: Inst. Mining Metallurgy Trans. v. 69, pt. 7, p. 361–369.

Hutchinson, G. E., 1957, A treatise on limnology. Vol. 1, Geography, physics and chemistry: New York, Wiley, 1015 p.

Hyvärinen, Lauri, 1958, Geochemical prospecting for lead ore in Korsnäs: Geol. Tutkimuslaitos, Geotekn. Julkaisuja No. 61, p. 7–22.

Il'in, K. B., 1956, Experiments on comparative application of the shlikh and spectrometallometric methods in prospecting for tin deposits in closed regions [in Russian]: Informatsion Sbornik, Vsesoyuz. Nauch. Issledovat. Geol. Inst. 1956, no. 3, p. 103–107.

*Illsley, C. T., Bills, C. W., and Pollock, J. W., 1958, Geochemical methods of uranium exploration: in United Nations, 1958: p. 126–130.

Int. Geol. Cong., XX Session, 1956, Resumenes de los trabajos presentados: México, D. F., 429 p.

Int. Geol. Cong., XX Session, 1958, Symposium de exploración geoquímica [primer tomo]: México, D. F., 234 p.

Int. Geol. Cong., XXI Session, 1960, Geological results of applied geochemistry and geophysics: Rept. of Twenty-First Session, Norden, Copenhagen, Pt. II, 215 p.

Ivanova, V. F., and Khristianov, V. K., 1956, Neutron logging in prospecting for industrial concentrations of boron: Geochemistry, 1956, p. 192–197.

Jackson, M. L., Hseung, Y., Corey, R. B., Evans, E. J., and Vanden Heuvey, R., 1952, Weathering sequence of clay-size minerals in soils and sediments. II Chemical weathering of layer silicates: Soil Sci. Soc. America Proc., v. 16, p. 3–6.

Jackson, M. L., Tyler, S. A., Willis, A. L., Bourbeau, G. A., and Pennington, R. P., 1948, Weathering sequence of clay-size minerals in soils and sediments: Jour. Phys. Chem., v. 52, p. 1237–1260.

*Jacobson, J. D., 1956, Geochemical prospecting studies in the Kilembe area, Uganda. II Dispersion of copper in the soil: Geochemical Prospecting Res. Centre, Imperial College, London, Tech. Comm. No. 6, 160 p.

James, A. H., 1954, The distribution of the trace ferrides in the magnetites of the Mount Hope mine and the New Jersey Highlands: Ph. D. Thesis, M.I.T. Dept. of Geology.

* Refers to a geochemical prospecting case history.

*James, C. H., 1957a, The geochemical dispersion of arsenic and antimony related to gold mineralization in Southern Rhodesia: Geochemical Prospecting Res. Centre, Imperial College, London, Tech. Comm. No. 12.

James, C. H., 1957b, Geochemical prospecting studies in the Great·Dike chromite district, Southern Rhodesia: Geochemical Prospecting Research Centre, Imperial College, London, Tech. Comm. No. 13.

*Jay, J. R., 1959, Geochemical prospecting studies for cobalt and uranium in Northern Rhodesia: Ph. D. Thesis, Imperial College, London.

Jenny, Hans, 1941, Factors of soil formation: New York, McGraw-Hill, 281 p.

Jenny, Hans, 1950, Origin of soils: in Trask, 1950: p. 41–61.

Jenny, Hans, and Overstreet, R., 1939, Surface migration of ions and contact exchange: Jour. Phys. Chem., v. 43, p. 1185–1196.

Jensch, Edmund, 1894, Zinc flora of Upper Silesia [in German]: Zeitschr. angew. Chemie, p. 14-15.

Jensen, M. L., 1959, Sulfur isotopes and hydrothermal mineral deposits: Econ. Geology, v. 54, p. 374–397.

Joffe, J. S., 1949, Pedology: New Brunswick, N. J., Rutgers Univ. Press, 2nd ed., 662 p.

Jones, L. H. P., 1957, The solubility of molybdenum in simplified systems and aqueous soil suspension: Jour. Soil Sci., v. 8, no. 2, p. 313–327.

Jones, R. W., Frost, I. C., and Rader, L. F., Jr., 1956, A comparison of chemical analyses of plants and soils as aids to prospecting for uranium in the southern Black Hills, South Dakota [abs.]: in Int. Geol. Cong. XX Session, 1956, p. 366.

Jowett, Maurice, and Price, H. I., 1932, Solubilities of the phosphates of lead: Faraday Soc. Trans., v. 28, p. 668–681.

Judson, Sheldon, and Osmond, J. K., 1955, Radioactivity in ground and surface water: Am. Jour. Sci., v. 253, p. 104–116.

*Karayeva, Z. G., and Chesnokov, O. F., 1958, Application of spectrometallometric surveys in exploring rare metal and pegmatite deposits in covered areas [in Russian]: Razvedka i Okhrana Nedr., 1958, no. 6, p. 32–36.

Kartsev, A. A., Tabasaransky, Z. A., Subbota, M. I., and Mogilevsky, G. A., 1959, Geochemical methods of prospecting and exploration for petroleum and natural gas [translation from Russian, edited by P. A. Witherspoon and W. D. Romey]: Berkeley, Univ. of California Press, 349 p. [original published by Gostoptekhizdat, Moscow, 1954, 428 p.].

Kauranne, L. K., 1958, On prospecting for molybdenum on the basis of its dispersion in glacial till: Soc. Géol. Finlande, Comptes rendus, no. 30, p. 31–43.

Kauranne, L. K., 1959, Pedogeochemical prospecting in glaciated terrain: Finland, Comm. Géol., Bull. no. 184, 10 p.

Keith, M. L., and Degens, E. T., 1959, Geochemical indicators of marine and fresh-water sediments: in Abelson, 1959: p. 38–61.

Keller, W. D., 1957, The principles of chemical weathering: Columbia, Mo., Lucas Brothers, rev. ed., 111 p.

* Refers to a geochemical prospecting case history.

Keller, W. D., and Frederickson, A. F., 1952, Role of plants and colloidal acids in the mechanism of weathering: Am. Jour. Sci., v. 250, p. 594–608.

Kelly, W. C., 1958, Topical study of lead-zinc gossans: N. Mex. Bur. Mines and Mineral Res. Bull. 46, p. 1–77.

*Kennedy, V. C., 1956, Geochemical studies in the southwestern Wisconsin lead-zinc district: U. S. Geol. Survey Bull. 1000-E, p. 187–223.

Kimura, Kenjiro, Fujiwara, Shizuo, and Morinaga, Kenichi, 1951, Chemical prospecting in Hosokura Mine districts: Jour. Chem. Soc. Japan, Pure Chem. Section, v. 72, p. 398–402.

Kingman, Owen, 1951, Geochemical techniques and results at Ducktown: Mining Cong. Jour., v. 37, no. 10, p. 62–65.

Kleinhampl, F. J., and Koteff, Carl, 1960, Botanical prospecting for uranium in the Circle Cliffs area, Garfield County, Utah: U. S. Geol. Survey Bull. 1085-C, p. 85–104.

*Kleinkopf, M. D., 1960, Spectrographic determination of trace elements in lake waters of northern Maine: Geol. Soc. America Bull., v. 71, p. 1231–1242.

Klepper, M. R., and Wyant, D. G., 1956, Uranium provinces: U. S. Geol. Survey Prof. Paper 300, p. 17–25.

Klepper, M. R., and Wyant, D. G., 1957, Notes on the geology of uranium: U. S. Geol. Survey Bull. 1046-F, p. 87–148.

Koehler, G. F., Hostetler, P. B., and Holland, H. D., 1954, Geochemical prospecting at Cobalt, Ontario: Econ. Geology, v. 49, p. 378–388.

Krasnikov, V. I., ed., 1957, Geochemical prospecting for ore deposits [in Russian]: Moscow, Gosgeoltekhizdat, 467 p.

Krauskopf, K. B., 1955, Sedimentary deposits of rare metals: Econ. Geology, 50th Ann. Vol., p. 411–463.

Kraynov, S. R., 1957, The feasibility of applying hydrochemical methods to the solution of certain problems in metallogenesis: Geochemistry, 1957, p. 460–469.

Kuenen, P. H., 1959, Experimental abrasion. Fluviatile action on sand: Am. Jour. Sci., v. 257, p. 172–190.

Kullerud, Gunnar, 1959, Sulfide systems as geological thermometers: in Abelson, 1959: p. 301–335.

Kuzin, M. F., 1959, Biogeochemical method for prospecting rare metal deposits [in Russian]: Razvedka i Okhrana Nedr., 1959, no. 11, p. 16–20.

Kvashnevskaya, N. V., 1957, Prospecting for ore deposits by dispersion trains [in Russian]: in Krasnikov, 1957: p. 146–157.

Lakin, H. W., Almond, Hy, and Ward, F. N., 1952, Compilation of field methods used in geochemical prospecting by the U. S. Geological Survey: U. S. Geol. Survey Circ. 161, 34 p.

Lakin, H. W., Stevens, R.E., and Almond, Hy, 1949, Field method for the determination of zinc in soil: Econ. Geology, v. 44, p. 296–306.

Lakin, H. W., and Trites, A. F., Jr., 1958, The behavior of selenium in the zone of oxidation: in Int. Geol. Cong. XX Session, 1958, p. 113–124.

*Landis, E. R., 1960, Uranium content of ground and surface waters in a

* Refers to a geochemical prospecting case history.

part of the central Great Plains: U. S. Geol. Survey Bull. 1087-G, p. 223–258.

Latimer, W. M., 1952, The oxidation states of the elements and their potentials in aqueous solutions: Englewood Cliffs, N. J., Prentice-Hall, 2nd ed., 392 p.

Lawton, Kirk, 1955, Chemical composition of soils: *in* Bear, 1955, p. 53–84.

*Ledward, R. A., 1960, Geochemical prospecting studies for base metals in Tanganyika and Burma: Ph. D. Thesis, Imperial College, London.

LeRiche, H. H., 1959, The distribution of certain trace elements in the Lower Lias of southern England: Geochim. et Cosmochim. Acta, v. 16, p. 101–122.

Leutwein, Friedrich, and Starke, Rainer, 1957, The possibility of geochemical prospecting for selenium, based on the example of the Kupferschiefer and the Tilkeröder Erzbezirk [in German]: Geologie, v. 6, no. 4, p. 349–378.

Lidgey, Ernest, 1897, Some indications of ore deposits: Australasian Inst. Mining Eng. Trans., v. 4, p. 110–122.

Ljunggren, Pontus, 1951, Some investigations of the biogeochemistry of manganese: Geol. Fören. i Stockholm, Förh., v. 73, p. 639–652.

Lotspeich, F. B., 1958, Movement of metallic elements in shallow colluvium: *in* Int. Geol. Cong. XX Session, 1958: p. 125–142.

Lovering, T. S., 1927, Organic precipitation of metallic copper: U. S. Geol. Survey Bull. 795-C, p. 45–52.

Lovering, T. S., 1934, Breckenridge mining district, Colorado: U. S. Geol. Survey Prof. Paper 176, 64 p.

Lovering, T. S., 1952, Mobility of heavy metals in ground water. Part I of Supergene and hydrothermal dispersion of heavy metals in wall rocks near ore bodies, Tintic district, Utah: Econ. Geology, v. 47, p. 685–698.

Lovering, T. S., 1959, Significance of accumulator plants in rock weathering: Geol. Soc. America Bull., v. 70, p. 781–800.

Lovering, T. S., Huff, L. C., and Almond, Hy, 1950, Dispersion of copper from the San Manuel copper deposit, Pinal County, Arizona: Econ. Geology, v. 45, p. 493–514.

Lovering, T. S., Sokoloff, V. P., and Morris, H. T., 1948, Heavy metals in altered rock over blind ore bodies, East Tintic district, Utah: Econ. Geology, v. 43, p. 384–399.

Lueder, D. R., 1959, Aerial photographic interpretation: New York, McGraw-Hill, 462 p.

Lundegårdh, P. H., 1956, Influence of ore bodies on the fine-grained material of glacial drift [in Swedish with English abs.]: Geol. Fören. i Stockholm, Förh., v. 78, p. 97–100.

Lyons, T. L., Buckman, H. O., and Brady, N. C., 1952, The nature and properties of soils: New York, Macmillan, 5th ed., 591 p.

McKinstry, H. E., 1948, Mining geology: Englewood Cliffs, N.J., Prentice-Hall, 680 p.

Malyuga, D. P., 1947, Soils and plants as indicators in prospecting for metals [in Russian]: Priroda, v. 36, no. 6, p. 13–17.

* Refers to a geochemical prospecting case history.

Malyuga, D. P., 1958, An experiment of biogeochemical prospecting for molybdenum in Armenia: Geochemistry, 1958, p. 314–337.

Malyuga, D. P., 1959, The biogeochemical method in prospecting copper-molybdenum ores [in Russian]: Razvedka i Okhrana Nedr., 1959, no. 1, p. 19–22.

Malyuga, D. P., and Makarova, A. I., 1956, An experiment in biogeochemical prospecting of ore deposits in the autonomous territory of Tuva: Geochemistry, 1956, p. 109–116.

Mandl, Ines, Graver, Amelie, and Neuberg, Carl, 1953, Solubilization of insoluble matter in nature. II Part played by salts of organic and inorganic acids occurring in nature: Biochim. et Biophys. Acta, v. 10, p. 540–569.

Manskaya, S. M., Drozdova, T. V., and Emelyanova, M. P., 1956, Binding of uranium by humine acids and by melanoidines: Geochemistry, 1956, p. 339–356.

Marmo, Vladi, 1953, Biogeochemical investigations in Finland: Econ. Geology, v. 48, p. 211–224.

Marshall, T. J., 1959, Relations between water and soil: Commonwealth Bureau Soils, Harpenden, Tech. Comm., no. 50, 91 p.

Martinet, R., 1956, Semiquantitative determination of traces of heavy metals in soils by the "confined spot"; application to the determination of arsenic in geochemical prospecting for gold: in Int. Geol. Cong. XX Session, 1956, p. 369–370.

Mason, Brian, 1958, Principles of geochemistry: New York, Wiley, 2nd ed., 310 p.

Mather, A. L., 1959, Geochemical prospecting studies in Sierra Leone: D. I. C. Thesis, Imperial College, London.

Mehlich, Adolf, and Drake, Mack, 1955, Soil chemistry and plant nutrition: in Bear, 1955: p. 286–327.

Meinzer, O. E., 1923, The occurrence of ground water in the United States with a discussion of principles: U. S. Geol. Survey Water-Supply Paper 489, 321 p. [reprinted 1959].

Meinzer, O. E., 1927, Plants as indicators of ground water: U. S. Geol. Survey Water-Supply Paper 577, 95 p.

Merrill, J. R., Lyden, E. F. X., Honda, M., and Arnold, J. R., 1960, The sedimentary geochemistry of the beryllium isotopes: Geochim. et Cosmochim. Acta, v. 18, p. 108–129.

Mertie, J. B., Jr., 1954, The gold pan: a neglected geological tool: Econ. Geology, v. 49, p. 639–651.

Miesch, A. T., 1954, Statistical analysis of uranium-vanadium orebody as an exploration guide [abs.]: Geol. Soc. America Bull., v. 75, p. 1382.

Miesch, A. T., and Nolan, T. B., 1958, Geochemical prospecting studies in the Bullwhacker Mine area, Eureka district, Nevada: U. S. Geol. Survey Bull. 1000-H, p. 397–408.

Miesch, A. T., Shoemaker, E. M., Newman, W. L., and Finch, W. I., 1960, Chemical composition as a guide to the size of sandstone-type uranium deposits in the Morrison Formation on the Colorado Plateau: U. S. Geol. Survey Bull. 1112-B, p. 17–61.

Millar, C. E., Turk, F. M., and Foth, H. D., 1958, Fundamentals of soil science: New York, Wiley, 3rd ed., 526 p.

Miller, A. D., and Danilov, V. Ya., 1957, Salt dispersion halos of rare-metal pegmatites in the Kola Peninsula: Geochemistry, 1957, p. 620–630.

Miller, C. P., 1959, Geochemical and biogeochemical prospecting for nickel: Ph. D. Thesis, Stanford University, Palo Alto, Calif.

Miller, R. L., and Goldberg, E. D., 1955, The normal distribution in geochemistry: Geochim. et Cosmochim. Acta, v. 8, p. 53–62.

Millman, A. P., 1957, Biogeochemical investigations in areas of copper-tin mineralization in southwest England: Geochim. et Cosmochim. Acta, v. 12, p. 85–93.

Milne, G., 1936, A soil reconnaissance journey in Tanganyika Territory: East African Agr. Res. Stat. Rept., Amani, Tanganyika.

Mitcham, T. W., 1952, Indicator minerals, Coeur d'Alene silver belt: Econ. Geology, v. 47, p. 414–450.

Mitchell, R. L., 1955, Trace elements: in Bear, 1955: p. 253–285.

Mogilevsky, G. A., 1959, The role of bacteria in prospecting for petroleum: V World Petroleum Cong., Gen. Petrol. Geochem. Symp., Preprint Volume, p. 111–115.

Mohr, E. C. J., and Van Baren, F. A., 1954, Tropical soils: The Hague and Bandung, N. V. Viteverij W. van Hoeve, 498 p.

Montgomery, Arthur, 1950, Geochemistry of tantalum in the Harding pegmatite, Taos County, New Mexico: Am. Mineralogist, v. 35, p. 853–866.

Morris, H. T., 1952, Primary dispersion patterns of heavy metals in carbonate and quartz monzonite wall rocks. Part II of Supergene and hydrothermal dispersion of heavy metals in wall rocks near ore bodies, Tintic district, Utah: Econ. Geology, v. 47, p. 698–716.

Moyseyenko, U. I., 1959, Biogeochemical survey in search for uranium deposits in swampy areas [in Russian]: Geokhimiya, 1959, p. 96–99.

Mukanov, K. M., 1957, Investigations of mineralization fields and primary dispersion halos of ore bodies in one of the Kazakhstan polymetallic deposits [in Russian]: in Krasnikov, 1957: p. 185–191.

*Nackowski, M. P., 1952, Geochemical prospecting applied to the Illinois-Kentucky fluorspar area: Ph. D. Thesis, University of Missouri, Columbia, Mo.

Nesvetaylova, N. G., 1955a, Geobotanical investigations for prospecting for ore deposits [translation from Russian]: Int. Geol. Rev., v. 3, p. 609–618, 1961 [original in Geobotanicheskiye Metody pri Geologicheskikh Issledovaniyakh, Trudy Vsesoyuznogo Aerogeologicheskogo Tresta, vyp. 1, p. 118–134].

Nesvetaylova, N. G., 1955b, Geobotanical method of prospecting for copper and polymetallic ores [in Russian]: Razvedka i Okhrana Nedr., 1955, no. 4, p. 17–20.

North, A. A., 1956, Geochemical field methods for the determination of tungsten and molybdenum in soils: The Analyst, v. 81, p. 660–668.

Ozerov, I. M., 1937, "Stannometry" as a prospecting method [in Russian]: Razvedka Nedr., 1937, p. 52–56.

* Refers to a geochemical prospecting case history.

Ozerova, N. A., 1959, On the use of primary dispersion halos of quicksilver in search for lead-zinc deposits [in Russian]: Geokhimiya, 1959, p. 638–645.

Park, C. F., Jr., 1955, The zonal theory of ore deposits: Econ. Geology, 50th ann. vol., p. 226–248.

Park, C. F., Jr., 1957, The problem of vertical zoning: Econ. Geology, v. 52, p. 477–481.

*Pavlov, G. A., Kizyakovsky, I. I., and Undzenkov, B. A., 1957, Results of metallometric operations in the Maly Khingan Territory [in Russian]: in Krasnikov, 1957: p. 211–214.

Pettijohn, F. J., 1957, Sedimentary rocks: New York, Harper, 2nd ed., 718 p.

Pierce, A. P., Mytton, J. W., and Gott, G. B., 1956, Radioactive elements and their daughter products in the Texas Panhandle and other oil and gas fields in the United States: in United Nations, 1956; p. 494–498.

Piper, C. S., 1950, Soil and plant analysis: New York, Interscience, 368 p.

*Pollock, J. P., Schillinger, A. W., and Bur, T., 1960, A geochemical anomaly associated with a glacially transported boulder train, Mt. Bohemia, Keweenaw County, Michigan: in Int. Geol. Cong. XXI Session, 1960, p. 20–27.

*Polikarpochkin, V. V., Kasyanova, V. I., Utgof, A. A., and Cherbyanova, L. F., 1958, Geochemical prospecting for polymetallic ore deposits in the eastern Transbaikal by means of the muds and waters of the drainage system [translation from Russian]: Int. Geol. Rev., v. 2, p. 237–253, 1960 [original in Novoye v Metodike i Tekhniki Geologorazvedochnykh Rabot, Sbornik 1, Leningrad, 1958, p. 46–73].

Polynov, B. B., 1937, The cycle of weathering [translation from Russian by A. Muir]: London, Murby, 220 p.

Prescott, J. A., and Pendleton, R. L., 1952, Laterite and lateritic soils: Commonwealth Bureau of Soil Science, Tech. Comm. no. 47, 51 p.

Raeburn, C., and Milner, H.B., 1927, Alluvial prospecting: London, Murby, 478 p.

Rainwater, F. H., and Thatcher, L. L., 1960, Methods for collection and analysis of water samples: U. S. Geol. Survey Water-Supply Paper 1454, 301 p.

Rankama, Kalervo, 1940, On the use of the trace elements in some problems of practical geology: Finland, Comm. Géol. Bull. 126, 90 p.

Rankama, K. K., and Sahama, T. G., 1950, Geochemistry: Chicago, Univ. of Chicago Press, 912 p.

Ray, R. G., 1960, Aerial photographs in geological interpretation and mapping; U. S. Geological Survey Prof. Paper 373, 230 p.

Reiche, Parry, 1950, A survey of weathering processes and products: Univ. of New Mexico Pub. in Geol. No. 3, 95 p.

Reichen, Laura E., and Lakin, H. W., 1949, Field method for the determination of zinc in plants: U. S. Geol. Survey Circ. 41, 4 p.

Reichen, Laura E., and Ward, F. N., 1951, Field method for the determination of molybdenum in plants: U. S. Geol. Survey Circ. 124, 4 p.

* Refers to a geochemical prospecting case history.

Richardson, P. W., and Hawkes, H. E., 1958, The adsorption of copper on quartz: Geochim. et Cosmochim. Acta, v. 15, p. 6–9.

Riddell, J. E., 1950, A technique for the determination of traces of epigenetic base metals in rocks: Quebec Dept. Mines, Prelim. Rept. No. 239, 23 p.

*Riddell, J. E., 1952, Preliminary report on hydrochemical analyses of streams and rivers in the Gaspé peninsula: Quebec Dept. Mines, Prelim. Rept. No. 268, 11 p.

*Riddell, J. E., 1954, Geochemical soil and water surveys in Lemieux Township, Gaspé-North County: Quebec Dept. Mines, Prelim. Rept. No. 302, 23 p.

Riddell, J. E., 1960, Geochemical prospecting methods employed in Canada's glaciated Precambrian terrains: Mining Eng., v. 12, p. 1170–1172.

Riley, G. A., 1939, Limnological studies in Connecticut: Ecol. Mons., v. 9, p. 53–94.

Roberts, E. E., 1949, Geochemical and geobotanical prospecting for barium and copper: Ph. D. Thesis, Stanford University, Palo Alto, Calif.

Robinson, G. W., 1949, Soils, their origin, constitution and classification: London, Murby, 3rd ed., 573 p.

Robinson, T. W., 1958, Phreatophytes: U. S. Geol. Survey Water-Supply Paper 1423, 84 p.

Robinson, W. O., Bastron, H., and Murata, K. J., 1958, Biogeochemistry of the rare-earth elements with particular reference to hickory trees: Geochim. et Cosmochim. Acta, v. 14, p. 55–67.

Rogers, A. S., 1958, Physical behavior and geologic control of radon in mountain streams: U. S. Geol. Survey Bull. 1052-E, p. 187–211.

Rudolfs, W., and Helbronner, A., 1922, Oxidation of zinc sulfide by micro-organisms: Soil Sci., v. 14, p. 459–464.

Ruxton, B. P., 1958, Weathering and surface erosion in granite: Geol. Mag. [Great Britain], v. 95, p. 353–377.

Safronov, N. I., Polikarpochkin, V. V., and Utgof, A. A., 1958, Spectrometric survey of gold as a method of prospecting for non-placer gold deposits [in Russian]: Metod. i Tekn. Geol. Rab. Sb. 1, p. 100–108.

*Sainsbury, C. L., 1957, A geochemical exploration for antimony in southeastern Alaska: U. S. Geol. Survey Bull. 1024-H, p. 163–178.

Sales, R. H., and Meyer, Charles, 1950, Interpretation of wall rock alteration at Butte, Montana: Colo. School Mines Quart., v. 45, no. 1B, p. 261–274.

Salmi, Martti, 1950, Trace elements in peat: Geol. Tutkimuslaitos, Geotekn. Julkaisuja, v. 51, 20 p.

Salmi, Martti, 1955, Prospecting for bog-covered ore by means of peat investigations: Finland, Comm. Géol., Bull. 169, 34 p.

Salmi, Martti, 1956, Peat and bog plants as indicators of ore minerals in Vihanti ore field in western Finland: Finland, Comm. Géol., Bull. 175, p. 1–22.

Sandell, E. B., 1959, Colorimetric determination of traces of metals: New York, Interscience, 3rd ed., 1032 p.

    * Refers to a geochemical prospecting case history.

Sato, Motoaki, and Mooney, H. M., 1960, The electrochemical mechanism of sulfide self-potentials: Geophysics, v. 25, p. 226–249.

Saukov, A. A., 1946, Geochemistry of mercury [in Russian]: Akad. Nauk S. S. S. R., Inst. Geol. Nauk, Trudy, v. 78, Min. Geol. Ser. No. 17, 129 p.

Saukov, A. A., 1956, Radiohydrogeological method in prospecting for uranium deposits: in United Nations, 1956: p. 756–759, 820–821, 823, 824.

Schmidt, R. C., 1956, Adsorption of copper, lead and zinc on some common rock-forming minerals and its effects on lake sediments: Ph. D. Thesis, McGill University, Montreal.

Schmitt, H. A., 1939, Outcrops of ore shoots: Econ. Geology, v. 34, p. 654–673.

Schmitt, H. A., 1959, The copper province of the southwest: Mining Eng., v. 11, p. 597–600.

Schwartz, G. M., 1949, Oxidation and enrichment in the San Manuel copper deposit, Arizona: Econ. Geology, v. 44, p. 253–277.

Schwartz, G. M., 1955, Hydrothermal alteration as a guide to ore: Econ. Geology, 50th ann. vol., p. 300–323.

Seidell, Atherton, 1940, Solubilities of inorganic and metal organic compounds, vol. 1: New York, Van Nostrand, 3rd ed., 1698 p., with supplement, 1952, 1254 p.

Sergeyev, Ye. A., 1936, Use of spot tests in mineral exploration [in Russian]: Razvedka Nedr., 1936, no. 12, p. 27–29.

Sergeyev, Ye. A., 1941, Geochemical method of prospecting for ore deposits [translation from Russian]: in U. S. Geol. Survey, 1950, p. 15–87 [original in Materialy Vsesoyuznogo Nauchno-Issledovatel'skogo Geologicheskogo Inst., Geofizika, Sb. 9–10, p. 3–55].

Sergeyev, Ye. A., 1946, Water analysis as a means of prospecting for metallic ore deposits [translation from Russian]: in U. S. Geol. Survey, 1950, p. 7–12 [original in Razvedka Nedr., 1946, p. 51–55].

Sergeyev, Ye. A., 1957, Methodology of mercurometric investigations [in Russian]: in Krasnikov, 1957: p. 158–165.

Shapiro, Leonard, and Brannock, W. W., 1956, Rapid analysis of silicate rocks: U. S. Geol. Survey Bull. 1036-C, p. 19–56.

Sharpe, C. F. S., 1938, Landslides and related phenomena: New York, Columbia Univ. Press, 137 p.

Shazly, E. M., Webb, J. S., and Williams, David, 1957, Trace elements in sphalerite, galena and associated minerals from the British Isles: Inst. Mining Metallurgy Trans. v. 66, p. 241–271.

Shvyryayeva, A. M., 1957, The application of the biogeochemical method in prospecting for boron [in Russian]: in Krasnikov, 1957: p. 305–312.

Silman, J. F. B., 1958, The stabilities of some oxidized copper minerals in aqueous solutions at 25° C and 1 atmosphere total pressure: Ph. D. Thesis, Harvard University, Cambridge, Mass.

Simonson, R. W., 1957, What soils are: 1957 Yearbook of Agriculture, U. S. Dept. Agriculture, Washington, D.C., p. 17–31.

Sindeyeva, N. D., 1955, A geochemical indicator of pyrite deposits [in Russian]: Akad. Nauk S. S. S. R., Doklady, v. 104, no. 1, p. 114.

Sixth Commonwealth Mining and Metallurgical Cong., 1957, Methods and case histories in mining geophysics: Montreal, 359 p.

Slawson, W. F., and Nackowski, M. P., 1959, Trace lead in potash feldspar associated with ore deposits: Econ. Geology, v. 54, p. 1543–1555.

Smales, A. A., and Wager, L. R., eds., 1960, Methods in geochemistry: New York, Interscience, 464 p.

Smith, W. C., 1960, Borax and borates: in Industrial minerals and rocks, New York, A.I.M.E., ch. 7, p. 103–122.

Smyth, C. H., Jr., 1913, The relative solubilities of the chemical constituents of rocks: Jour. Geology, v. 21, p. 105–120.

*Sokoloff, V. P., 1950, Sampling and testing of soil and rock for copper, lead and zinc in geochemical reconnaissance: Mines Mag., v. 40, no. 11, p. 15–22.

*Sokoloff, V. P., 1951, Geochemical exploration for copper in the Wallaroo mining district, South Australia: Geochim. et Cosmochim. Acta, v. 1, p. 284–298.

Solovov, A. P., 1959, The theory and practice of metallometric surveys [in Russian]: Akad. Nauk Kazakhskoy S. S. R., Alma Ata.

Solow, Herbert, 1959, Geochemistry: The prospector's new tool: Fortune, February 1959.

Staker, E. V., and Cummings, R. W., 1941, The influence of zinc on the productivity of certain New York peat soils: Soil Sci. Soc. America Proc., v. 6, p. 207.

Stanton, R. E., and Coope, J. A., 1958, Modified field test for the determination of small amounts of nickel in soils and rocks: Inst. Mining Metallurgy Trans. v. 68, pt. 1, p. 9–14.

Stanton, R. E., and McDonald, A. J., 1961a, Field determination of tin in geochemical soil and stream sediment surveys: Inst. Mining Metallurgy Trans., v. 71, p. 27–29.

Stanton, R. E., and McDonald, A. J., 1961b, Determination of antimony in soil and sediment samples: Geochemical Prospecting Res. Centre, Imperial College, London, Tech. Comm. no. 17.

Starke, Rainer, and Rentzsch, Johannes, 1959, Geochemical investigation of the wall rock of some Freiberg vein formations [in German]: Geologie, v. 8, no. 4, p. 395–409.

Stock, Alfred, and Cucuel, Friedrich, 1934, The distribution of quicksilver [in German]: Naturwissenschaften, v. 22, p. 390–393.

Stoll, W. C., 1945, The presence of beryllium and associated chemical elements in the wall rocks of some New England pegmatites: Econ. Geology, v. 40, p. 136–141.

Sveshnikov, G. B., 1957, Hydrochemical investigations in the Irtysh Region of the Rudny Altay [in Russian]: in Krasnikov, 1957: p. 280–285.

Swaine, D. J., 1955, Trace element content of soils: Commonwealth Agricultural Bur., Farnham Royal, Bucks, Tech. Comm. no. 48, 157 p.

Swedish Prospecting Co., 1939, Memo on a geochemical prospecting method [in Swedish]: Malmö, Sweden.

    * Refers to a geochemical prospecting case history.

Taber, S., 1930, The mechanics of frost heaving: Jour. Geology, v. 38, p. 303–317.

Tennant, C. B., and White, M. L., 1959, Study of the distribution of some geochemical data: Econ. Geology, v. 54, p. 1281–1290.

Theobald, P. K., Jr., 1957, The gold pan as a quantitative geological tool: U. S. Geol. Survey Bull. 1071-A, p. 1–54.

Theobald, P. K., Jr., Hawkins, D. B., and Lakin, H. W., 1958, Composition of water and precipitates in the confluence of Deer Creek with Snake River, Summit County, Colorado [abs.]: Geol. Soc. America Bull., v. 69, p. 1651–1652.

*Theobald, P. K., Jr., and Thompson, C. E., 1959, Geochemical prospecting with heavy-mineral concentrates used to locate a tungsten deposit: U. S. Geol. Survey Circ. 411, 13 p.

Thompson, C. E., and Lakin, H. W., 1957, A field chromatographic method for determination of uranium in soils and rocks: U. S. Geol. Survey Bull. 1036-L, p. 209–220.

Thorp, J., 1931, The effects of vegetation and climate upon soil profiles in northern and northwestern Wyoming: Soil Sci., v. 32, p. 283–301.

Tikhomirov, N. I., and Miller, S. D., 1946, On a physico-chemical method of prospecting for molybdenum in the semi-desert climate of the northern Lake Balkhash area [translation from Russian]: in U. S. Geol. Survey, 1950, p. 97–103 [original in Razvedka Nedr., no. 2, p. 34–39].

Tkalich, S. D., 1953, Content of iron in vegetation as a prospecting indication [in Russian]: Priroda, no. 1.

*Tooms, J. S., 1955, Geochemical dispersions related to copper mineralization in Northern Rhodesia: Ph.D. Thesis, Imperial College, London.

Tooms, J. S., and Webb, J. S., 1961, Geochemical prospecting investigations in the Northern Rhodesian Copperbelt: Econ. Geology. v. 56, p. 815–846.

Trask, P. D., ed., 1950, Applied sedimentation: New York, Wiley, 707 p.

Truog, Emil, ed., 1951, Mineral nutrition of plants: Madison, Wis., Univ. of Wisconsin Press, 469 p.

Turneaure, F. S., 1955, Metallogenetic provinces and epochs: Econ. Geology, 50th ann. vol., p. 38–98.

Tyutina, N. A., Aleskovsky, V. B., and Vasil'yev, P. I., 1959, Experiment of biogeochemical prospecting and methods of niobium determination in plants: Geokhimiya, no. 6, p. 550–554.

United Nations, 1956, Geology of uranium and thorium: First Int. Conf. Peaceful Uses Atomic Energy, Geneva, Aug. 8–20, 1955, Proc., v. 6, 825 p.

United Nations, 1958, Survey of raw material resources: Second Int. Conf. Peaceful Uses Atomic Energy, Geneva, Sept. 1–13, 1958, Proc., v. 2, 843 p.

U. S. Geological Survey, 1950, Selected Russian papers on geochemical prospecting for ores: Washington, D. C., 103 p.

U. S. Geological Survey, 1953, Additional field methods used in geochemical prospecting by the U. S. Geological Survey: U. S. Geol. Survey Open-file Rept., Sept. 16, 1953, 42 p.

Vaughn, W. W., Rhoden, V. C., Wilson, E. E., and Faul, Henry, 1959, Scintillation counters for geologic use: U. S. Geol. Survey Bull. 1052-F, p. 213–240.

Vershkovskaya, O. V., 1956, Primary mercury dispersion halos as prospecting indications of mercury-antimony deposits [in Russian]: Razvedka i Okhrana Nedr., v. 22, no. 4, p. 19–24.

Viktorov, S. V., 1955, Applications of the geobotanical method for geological and hydrogeological investigations [in Russian]: Akad. Nauk S. S. S. R., [Moscow], 200 p.

Vinogradov, A. P., 1954, Search for ore deposits by means of plants and soils (in Russian): Akad. Nauk S. S. S. R., Trudy Biogeokhim Lab., v. 10, p. 3–27.

Vinogradov, A. P., 1956a, Regularity of distribution of chemical elements in the earth's crust: Geochemistry, no. 1, p. 1–43.

Vinogradov, A. P., 1956b, Record of session: in United Nations, 1956; p. 820, 821, 824.

Vinogradov, A. P., 1959, The geochemistry of rare and dispersed chemical elements in soils, 2nd ed. [translation from Russian]: New York, Consultant Bureau, 209 p. [original published by Akad. Nauk S. S. S. R., Moscow, 1957, 238 p.].

Vinogradov, A. P., and Malyuga, D. P., 1957, Biogeochemical methods of prospecting for ore deposits [in Russian]: in Krasnikov, 1957: p. 290–300.

Vinogradov, V. I., 1957, On the migration of molybdenum in the zone of hypergenesis: Geokhimiya, no. 2, p. 120–126.

Vistelius, A. B., 1960, The skew frequency distribution and the fundamental law of the geochemical processes: Jour. Geology, v. 68, p. 1–22.

Volobuyev, V. M., 1957, Experimental application of metallometry to exploration of porphyry copper deposits in Central Kazakhstan [in Russian]: Razvedka i Okhrana Nedr., no. 4, p. 31–33.

Wambeke, L. Van, 1960, Geochemical prospecting and appraisal of niobium-bearing carbonatites by X-ray methods: Econ. Geology, v. 55, p. 732–758.

Ward, F. N., 1951a, Determination of molybdenum in soils and rocks: Anal. Chemistry, v. 23, p. 788–791.

Ward, F. N., 1951b, A field method for the determination of tungsten in soils: U. S. Geol. Survey Circ. 119, 4 p.

Ward, F. N., and Bailey, E. H., 1960, Camp and sample-site determination of traces of mercury in soils and rocks: A. I. M. E. Trans., v. 217, p. 343–350.

Ward, F. N., and Lakin, H. W., 1954, Determination of traces of antimony in soils and rocks: Anal. Chemistry, v. 26, p. 1168–1173.

Ward, F. N., and Marranzino, A. P., 1955, Field determination of microgram quantities of niobium in rocks: Anal. Chemistry, v. 27, p. 1325–1328.

Ward, F. N., and Marranzino, A. P., 1957, Field determination of uranium in natural waters: U. S. Geol. Survey Bull. 1036-J, p. 181–192.

Warren, H. V., and Delavault, R. E., 1949, Further studies in biogeochemistry: Geol. Soc. America Bull., v. 60, p. 531–560.

Warren, H. V., and Delavault, R. E., 1954, Variations in the nickel content of some Canadian trees: Royal Soc. Canada Trans., v. 48, sec. IV, p. 71–74.

Warren, H. V., and Delavault, R. E., 1956, Pathfinding elements in geochemical prospecting [abs.]: in Int. Geol. Cong. XX Session, 1956, p. 379.

Warren, H. V., and Delavault, R. E., 1957, Biogeochemical prospecting for cobalt: Royal Soc. Canada Trans., v. 51, pt. IV, p. 33–37.

Warren, H. V., and Delavault, R. E., 1960, Aqua regia extractable copper and zinc in plutonic rocks in relation to ore deposits: Inst. Mining Metallurgy Trans., v. 69, p. 495–504.

Warren, H. V., Delavault, R. E., and Irish, Ruth I., 1952, Biogeochemical investigations in the Pacific Northwest: Geol. Soc. America Bull., v. 63, p. 435–484.

Warren, H. V., Delavault, R. E., and Routley, D. G., 1953, Preliminary studies of the biogeochemistry of molybdenum: Royal Soc. Canada Trans., v. 47, p. 71–75.

Warth, Hugh, 1905, Weathered dolerite of Rowley Regis [South Staffordshire] compared with the laterite of the Western Ghats near Bombay: Geol. Mag. (V), v. 2, p. 21–23.

*Watts, J. T., 1960, The secondary dispersion of niobium from pyrochlore carbonatites in the Feira District, Northern Rhodesia: D. I. C. Thesis, Imperial College, London.

Webb, J. S., 1947, Origin of the tin lodes of Cornwall, England: Ph. D. Thesis, London University.

Webb, J. S., 1953, A review of American progress in geochemical prospecting: Inst. Mining Metallurgy Trans., v. 62, p. 321–348.

Webb, J. S., 1958a, Observations on geochemical exploration in tropical terrains: in Int. Geology Cong. XX Session, 1958, p. 143–173.

Webb, J. S., 1958b, Notes on geochemical prospecting for lead-zinc deposits in the British Isles: Inst. Mining Metallurgy, London, Paper 19, Technical aids to exploration, of Symposium on the Future of Non-Ferrous Mining in Great Britain and Ireland, p. 23–40.

Webb, J. S., and Millman, A. P., 1950, Heavy metals in natural waters as a guide to ore; a preliminary investigation in West Africa: Inst. Mining Metallurgy Trans., v. 59, p. 323–336.

Webb, J. S., and Millman, A. P., 1951, Heavy metals in vegetation as a guide to ore: Inst. Mining Metallurgy Trans., v. 60, p. 473–504.

*Webb, J. S., and Tooms, J. S., 1959, Geochemical drainage reconnaissance for copper in Northern Rhodesia: Inst. Mining Metallurgy Trans., v. 68, p. 125–144.

Wedepohl, K. H., 1956, Investigations on the geochemistry of lead [in German]: Geochim. et Cosmochim. Acta, v. 10, p. 69–148.

* Refers to a geochemical prospecting case history.

White, D. E., and Brannock, W. W., 1950, The sources of heat and water supply of thermal springs with particular references to Steamboat Springs, Nevada: Am. Geophys. Union Trans., v. 31, p. 566–574.

White, M. L., 1957, The occurrence of zinc in soil: Econ. Geology, v. 52, p. 645–651.

White, W. H., and Allen, T. M., 1954, Copper soil anomalies in the Boundary District of British Columbia: Mining Eng., v. 6, p. 49–52.

Williams, David, 1956, Research in applied geochemistry at Imperial College, London [abs.]: in Int. Geol. Cong. XX Session, 1956, p. 380.

Williams, W. R., 1953, Some notes on geochemical correlation with regard to copper in the district of Mpwapwa, Tanganyika: Colonial Geol. Mining Res., v. 3, p. 248.

Winters, E., and Simonson, R. W., 1951, The subsoil: Advances in Agronomy, v. 3, p. 2–92.

Wodzicki, A., 1959, Geochemical prospecting for uranium in the Lower Buller Gorge, New Zealand: New Zealand Jour. Geol. and Geophysics, v. 2, no. 3, p. 602–612.

Wood, G. A., and Stanton, R. E., 1957, A rapid method for the determination of chromium in soils for use in geochemical prospecting: Inst. Mining Metallurgy Trans., v. 66, p. 331–340.

Yardley, D. H., 1958, Significance of geochemical distribution trends in soil: Mining Eng., v. 10, p. 781–786.

Yoe, J. H., and Koch, H. J., Jr., ed., 1957, Trace analysis: New York, Wiley, 672 p.

Zalashkova, N. E., Lizunov, N. V., and Sitnin, A. A., 1958, Experimental metallometric survey for beryllium in areas of beryllium-bearing pegmatites [in Russian]: Razvedka i Okhrana Nedr., 1958, no. 8, p. 9–14.

Zeuner, F. E., 1959, The Pleistocene period: London, Hutchinson, 447 p.

Zhilinsky, G. B., 1956, Heavy-mineral survey maps [in Russian]: Akad. Nauk Kazakhskoy S. S. R., Izv. Ser. Geol., no. 22, p. 66–81.

INDEX OF NAMES

INDEX OF SUBJECTS